Small Steps

Memoirs of a Fighter Pilot

Glossary Edition

Janis,

Thanks for all of your help over the years — you've kept me straight and made my job easier. I'll miss you and M.B. Next year. Enjoy my previous life in the A.F.

Jim Olson
2-20-2015

Cover photo credit: Dale R. Niesen, Shutterpoint Photography (order #74727464, May 25, 2010)

Small Steps

Memoirs of a Fighter Pilot

Jim Olson, Major, USAF, Ret
(1967-1991)

This book is dedicated

to Dad

whose unwavering confidence, constant encouragement and 'gentle prodding' made this book possible

and to Mom

who has always been there for Dad and all of us.

Foreword

My entry into the United States Air Force was more a result of the current circumstances that surrounded me at the end of my college years but was also influenced by two uncles, Uncle Ole who had been in the Air Corp during World War II and Uncle Doug who loved flying and would have been a fighter pilot if his circumstances had been otherwise.

When I joined the Air Force I didn't even consider pilot training because I held pilots to be the absolute best of the best and well above my station in life. Me! A pilot? Get serious. However, as my horizons broadened and my self-confidence increased, pilot training began to be a dream of mine, a dream that came true. As I progressed through pilot training I occasionally felt like pinching myself just to reconfirm that it really wasn't a dream.

My ultimate dream, though, was to become a fighter pilot and the obstacles (a high score on every check ride in pilot training) fell away one by one and soon I was climbing into an F-4 for the very first time.

During all this time my wife, Jean, stood behind me and encouraged me every step of the way. "If you don't apply for pilot training you'll always wonder what might have been." Beginning with pilot training the demands for my time steadily increased until 12 hour days were routine and Saturdays and Sundays were used for catch-up. Jean endured and was the ideal Air Force wife. She was the support and the mainstay for our growing family of Jill and Rebecca and later Amanda. She got them registered in schools, helped them with homework, got them to piano lessons and sat next to them for countless hours as they practiced – and did I mention she almost out ran Hurricane David with the girls in tow?

Jean's list of accomplishments don't appear anywhere in this book but they were many. She held officer positions in the Air Force Wives Club, OWC, and was the OWC president at Homestead AFB during the year I was in Korea. She introduced Janet Reno, President Clinton's Attorney General, at one of their functions. Jean was the area leader for Girl Scouts for the central part of Germany while we were at Hahn AB. She was always an enthusiastic volunteer and with her leadership and organizational abilities straightened out many neglected messes that few others would have tackled. I have told others that if she had been the one in the Air Force she would have achieved colonel below the zone! There never was a more proud husband than myself. Jean was and still is my hero.

Fighter pilots always have daughters is a well-known saying in the Air Force and this fighter pilot had three. Again, I was so blessed. Jill, Becky and Mandy were always a source of extreme pride for both Jean and me. Wherever we went total strangers would pause to tell us how our girls were so well behaved. They were active in Brownies and Girl Scouts and in their numerous schools. And wherever we went Jill and Becky being only a year apart in age had each other as best friends and Mandy had three mothers; lucky Mandy! The girls always had their chores that they did Saturday mornings with a minimum of complaining, they did their homework diligently and were always highly successful in school. I could continue on about the school bus driver in Germany who at the end of his route at the end of the day found Jill in the back of the bus. She had missed her stop because she was reading; or of Becky doing a high speed loop or should I say flop on her bicycle into a German farmer's freshly plowed field; of Mandy being pushed in her stroller around the Linderhof and Neuschwanstein Castles by her Grandfather who lovingly referred to her as 'Konigen,' princess. There are so many family memories but those stories and more will have to await another book.

During my Air Force years I maintained a weekly ritual of writing letters to my mother and father and also to Jean during my Air Force TDYs. My folks saved every letter I ever wrote and filed them in binders. With those letters as memory joggers I was able to reconstruct almost a quarter century of experiences from a young college graduate seeking to avoid the draft to an *Old and Bold pilot* who just 'faded away.'

Jim Olson

Acknowledgments

A special thanks goes to daughter, Rebecca Cosford, for her skillful advice and help. She straightened out the 'typewriting' style I had used in formatting the original document. Over a weeklong visit during the summer, I had expected, with Becky's help, to finish editing the book and get it off to the printers. With her boundless enthusiasm the quick rewrite became a major review of all aspects of the book to include the addition of 75 more pages and 65 photographs. Becky also formatted the book giving it a very professional look. Her encouragement and gentle prodding led me to dig further into my memory, adding 'stories' for chapters Becky thought were lacking; a wee bit thin. In her words, the stories added sparkle and made the book come alive.

I am very indebted to daughter Amanda Kuchta. In the final stages of this project, Mandy showed me the 'world of PDF' and a free on-line PDF program to work with. This allowed me to share the lengthy manuscript with others via e-mail in seeking aid in the final editing.

My wife, Jean, also jumped in with a complete read/edit pointing out many of her husband's errors in writing and memory. "Why, yes Dear, now I remember!"

Last, but definitely not least, is daughter Jill Scherrer who used her amazing editing skills developed from a lifetime of reading. After sending her a copy of the PDF form, Jill submitted daily e-mails, chapter by chapter, of errors that had been missed by a half dozen or more 'reads.' Her proof reading and corrections have given this book a mark of professionalism it otherwise wouldn't have had.

I also want to recognize a very special 6th grade girl, Jasmine, Qronfleh, who chose my book for her Literary Studies project. Jasmine picked up on the theme I built into the chapters on pilot training and titled her project 'Taking Small Steps to Becoming a Pilot' from which I borrowed to title this rewrite.

Table of Contents

Small Steps i
Small Steps iii
Jim Olson, Major, USAF, Ret iii
This book is dedicated iv
Foreword v
Acknowledgments vii
Table of Contents ix
Author's Note 2
Chapter One 3
   In The Beginning – OTS 3
      An Air Force Recruiter 3
      Induction Physical 3
      OTS - Lackland AFB 4
      A First Flight 4
      San Antonio 4
      Life at Medina 5
      Our FTO, Capt Hollis 6
      The First Week 6
      Gigged In 7
      Standby Inspection 7
      The Saturday Parade 8
      Academics 9
      Non-academics 10
      Rank Had Its Privileges 11
      Graduation and Beyond 12
Chapter Two 13
   First Assignment - Bergstrom 13
      Settling In 13
      A Home to Live In 14
      Marking Time 14
      Tyndall AFB 15
      Mexico Beach 15
      Weapons Controller School 16
      Back to Bergstrom 16
      Orders to Korea 16
Chapter Three 18
   The Land of the Morning Calm .. 18
      Off to Korea 18
      A Good Samaritan 18
      Under Way 19
      Divert to Anchorage 19
      The Longest Flight 19
      Korea at Last 20
      A Culture Shock 20
      Assignment Mangil San 20
      Mangil San – the People 22
      A Controller Named Fletch 23
      A Dad Again 24
      Mangil San's Mission 24
      Shift Work 24
      Mid-shift 25
      Swing Shift 26
      Bubble Checks 27
      Day Shift 28
      ROKAF 29
      Choi Do Young 29
      When in Rome… 29
      Four Day Breaks 30
      A Train Ride of Note 30
      Library Officer 31
      The Officer's Lounge 32

Jin Dahl Lea, Herald of Spring 33
FIGMO 33
Curfew! 34

Chapter Four 35
The Air Force's Bone Yard 35
Tucson Arizona 35
A Sunday Trip Up Mount Lemon 35
An Overview 36
Karen Transfers to the U of A 37
The Needle 37
The Bone Yard 38
The Tactical Control Flight 38
An Officer Named Ken 39
The Commander, Jerry Berner 39
Don't Ask, Don't Tell! Billy Thomas 39
The John Smiths 40
The Other Officers 40
Maintenance Section 41
The 83rd Mission 42
Operation Intercept 42
The 84th TCF and 726th TCS .. 42
Training 42
Deployment to Nevada 43
The Sheriff Visits 44
R & R Las Vegas Style 44
Oh, Home On the Mesa 44
Exercise Operations 45
Midair 45
The Collateral Board 46
Pilot Training – Going After a Dream 47

Selected! 48

Chapter Five 49
Pilot Training - Laredo AFB, Texas 49
Moving – Again 49
En-route - Big Bend National Park 49
Laredo AFB 50
Pilot Training Wing 50
UPT Class 73-06 51
Flying Training in a Nutshell.. 51
Academic Training 51
Ancillary Training 52
Altitude Chamber 52
Other Fun Ancillary Activities 53
Parasailing 53
Simulator Training 54
Simulator Instructors 55
Flying Training 55
T-41 Flying Training 56
Mr. Reece 56
A Typical Day 56
First Flight 57

Chapter Six 60
Flying the T-37 60
The Tweet 60
The Attrition Begins 60
T-37 Tipping 60
Getting Ready 61
T-37 IPs 61
Capt. Rodenhauser 61
The Daily Routine 62
The Forms 62

Ground Ops	63
Runways	64
Takeoff	64
Training Areas	65
Airspace Deconfliction	65
More on Capt. Rodenhauser	65
First Flight	66
Contact Flying	66
Solo	67
Formation Flying	67
Solo Emergency	68
Spinning!	69
Contact Check	70
Instrument Check	71
Cross-Country to Biloxi	72
The End of Another Chapter	73
Chapter Seven	74
The T-38 Talon	74
Jimmy H. Doolittle	75
Flying Training - Instruments	75
Vertical S's	75
Steep Bank Turns	76
The Point to Point	76
Unusual Attitude Recovery	76
Supersonic Flight	77
The TACAN Approach	78
The Precision Approach Radar	78
Instrument Landing System (ILS)	79
Contact Flying	79
A Typical Contact Flight	79
T-38 Solo	82
Formation Flying	83
The Key to Formation Flying	84
Four Ship Formation	85
Formation Landings	85
Night Flying	85
Night Round Robin	85
Cross Country	86
Flying at 49,000 Feet	87
T-38 Check Flights	88
Aircraft Assignments	88
Chapter Eight	90
Survival School	90
Water Survival	90
Favorite Water Activities	90
Dragging and Parasailing	91
Basic Survival Training	92
Survival School Academics	93
The POW Camp	93
Evading Is Useless	93
Interrogation	94
The Prison Yard	95
An Ending to Remember	95
The Trek	96
Making Shelter	96
Evading the Enemy Again	96
A Poncho Shelter	97
And It Snowed	97
The Last Night	98
Chapter 9	99
Learning to Fly a Fighter	99
A Fighter at Last	99
The First Tactical Fighter Wing	99

SEA Volunteer 100
First Flight 100
Transition Phase 102
Retraining with Major Charier 103
Fred Wyland 103
Formation Phase................... 104
Tactical Formation 104
Fighting Wing 105
Pod Formation...................... 105
Loose Deuce 105
Air Refueling 106
Typical Refueling Mission... 106
The Boomer 107
First Refueling...................... 108
On the Boom 109
Inverted on the Tanker's Wing 110
Flying a Fighter - BFM 111
A Typical Maneuver Setup .. 111
Fighting a Fighter - ACM 113
Like a Hawk 114
A Typical ACM Engagement 115
Fighting to Win, ACT 116
The Aggressors 116
A Typical Mission 116
Ground Attack...................... 118
The Gunnery Range.............. 119
The Standard Bombing Range 119
The F-4 Bomber 120
Types of Bomb Deliveries ... 120
Dive Bombing...................... 121

Lower Dive Angle Events.... 121
Strafe and Rockets 121
Qualification........................ 121
Range Rules 122
Flying Low Levels 122
A Typical Range Mission..... 123
45 Degree High Altitude Dive Bomb 128
Ground Attack Night............ 128
Hidden Dangers at Night...... 129
Disaster at Night 131
Ground Attack Radar 131
Simulating Nucs 132
Radar Deliveries 132
Qualification........................ 133
Ground Attack Tactical 133
The Curvilinear Approach.... 133
Pop-up Delivery................... 134
Cement Bombs 135
A Typical GAT Mission....... 135
Shooting the DART 137
Dart Tow 138
Good News and Bad News... 138
A Typical Dart Mission........ 139
Finally a Fighter Pilot 140
Chapter Ten 142
Operational Flying In the F-4... 142
Traveling to Germany 142
Finding Hahn AB.................. 143
Arrival at Hahn..................... 144
A New Squadron 144
Hahn Air Base 144

Hahn's Notoriously Bad Weather 145
A 'Below Mins' Accident 146
Tenth Tactical Fighter Squadron 147
Hahn's Other Two Squadrons 147
Flying at Last -- an Instrument Check................................... 148
Zaragosa, Spain and Gunnery Camp 150
Flying at Zaragosa 151
A Practical Joke................... 151
Zaragosa Social Life............ 152
Happy Hour......................... 153
Sitges by the Sea................. 155
A Typical Bomb Range Mission 156
Broken Habit Patterns Are Dangerous 158
One Potato, Two Potato 159
Steve Cole on Flight Discipline 159
Basic Controls of an F-4 161
Switches Galore................... 161
Becoming Operationally Ready - the TAC check..................... 168
An Unsuccessful TAC Check 169
No TAC check, No Leave 170
Another Failed Attempt 170
TAC Check - Yes 171
The Underrated WSO 171
A Night RBS Mission 172
A Night Takeoff 174

Nighttime Fire During Takeoff 174
Night Air Refueling 175
The Night RBS Low Level ... 177
Hahn's Two Missions 180
Air to Air versus the Air to Mudders 180
Exercises 181
'Going Nuc' and Certifying.. 182
The Elephant Walk 182
The Taxiing Tenth or the Gay Blades................................. 182
A Surprise Launch 183
Zulu Alert............................. 183
Beware the 'Queertrons' 184
Victor Alert – Babysitting a Nuc 184
Our Cold War 184
The Dreaded Certification Board 185
Victor Alert - Forced Relaxation 187
Forward Air Controller Experiences 188
The US Army – The Best 189
A Cobra Bite Can Be Deadly 190
Flying in Weather 191
The KC 10 Tankers Saved the Day..................................... 191
A Typical Winter Day.......... 192
Four Ship Weather Trail Departure............................. 193
Low Altitude, On the Wing, Weather............................... 194
Cross Country Flying........... 194
And Then There Was France 195

French Low Levels 195
Emergency Fuel Over France 196
Favorite Cross Country Bases 197
Isle of Man 197
Stonehenge 197
Monster Hunting at Loch Ness 199
A Long Day 200
Test Squadron for Pave Spike 200
A Deadly Accident and a Passive WSO 201
Bombing the Yellow Tank ... 202
In-flight Emergencies 203
A Tiger by the Tail 203
Unintended Landing at Spangdahlem 204
A Convenient Spot to Eject .. 204
Director of Operations Training 205
The 313th Tactical Fighter Squadron 206
A New DO 207

Chapter Eleven 209
An F-4 Instructor Teaching Others 209
Germany to Florida 209
Bayonne Where? 210
Picking Up the Car 210
A Side Trip to DC 211
Arriving at Homestead 211
Homestead's 'Beaches' 212
The Volare! 212

A Trip up North 212
Hello to the 308th 213
Driving to Phoenix 213
IP School and the 310th TFS . 214
Landing From the Back Seat 214
Air to Ground 215
Letter Extract on Ground Attack 215
Rain in the Desert 215
Night Flying 216
Air to Air 216
Problems in ACM 216
The Air to Air Simulator 217
Dissimilar: Flying Against the F-5's 219
The Long Trip Back to Homestead 219
Splitting Up is Hard to Do! .. 220
The Rejoin 220
Learning to be an IP 221
Letter Excerpts 221
Four Different Syllabi 222
Washing Out 222
An Inept Wing Commander . 223
The T Syllabus 226
The C Syllabus 226
The I Syllabus 227
Grade Books - Ugh 227
Continuation Training 228
Area 51, Dreamland 228
Green Flag – Flying Against MiGs 230
Eating an Apple is a Piece of Cake! 231

The Air-to-Ground Battle..... 231
Dangerous Flying 233
Disaster Again!..................... 233
Vertical Jinking 234
Big Time Gambler in Vegas. 234
A Five Hour Flight Home 235
Maple Flag 235
"You're On Fire; Eject" 236
Air Defense Alert 236
Klinker, the Balloon Buster.. 237
Clever Drug-runner.............. 238
Range Control Officer 239
Avon Park Gunnery Range .. 239
The RCO Made It Happen ... 240
Range Safety 240
Bird Strike!.......................... 240
Alligators R Us.................... 241
Orientation Flights............... 241
A Four-Bedroom House....... 242
Filling the Wrong Square..... 242
The 'Comps' 243
And There Were Hurricanes. 243
Saint Elmo's Fire 245
Chapter Twelve............................ 247
Back to Korea 247
The Long Trip West............. 247
Lost Ticket!.......................... 247
A Very Long Day 248
Osan AB............................... 249
The 314th Air Division TACC
.... 249
The Pit 249
More on the SODO.............. 251

Calling the General 252
Passed Over for Lieutenant Colonel................................. 253
Experiences as a SODO 253
Ulchi Focus Lens - Taegu..... 254
Hanil Hotel or Open Bay Barracks 255
Car Electrical Fire................ 256
A Good Deal Trip and Getting Fired...................................... 257
Recalled to Osan 258
To Scramble or Not To Scramble................................ 258
Another Defection?.............. 259
Flight Physical -Diagnosis WPW.................................... 260
An Uneasy Truce 261
Mid-tour Leave 261
Flying Back Home 262
SAM Brooks........................ 262
Cloned at Osan..................... 264
Going Away Party................ 264
General Hefner 265
A New Assignment.............. 265
Jean Goes House Shopping .. 265
The New Boss – Is the Pits... 265
The Day Worker 266
Moving to Panama City........ 267
Chapter Thirteen......................... 268
Fighters As Drones at Tyndall AFB 268
Tyndall – Stability at Last. ... 268
Why Drones at Tyndall?....... 268
The 82nd TATS 269

The 82nd's NCOs, the Best of the Best...... 269

The Air Force's Navy.......... 270

Operations Section 270

The 83rd Weapons Squadron 271

The 84th Test Squadron........ 271

Civilian Drone Contractor.... 271

A Select Group of Officers .. 271

Office Pranks Happened....... 272

Drone Remote Controllers ... 273

Shooting Missiles at Drones. 273

Sub-scale Drone AKA 'Baby Drone'................................. 274

Launching Subscales – Wow! 274

Controlling Subscale Drones 275

Full-Scale Drones................ 275

A Typical Full-Scale Live-Fire Mission 276

'Mike' 276

The Shoot Box 277

Drone Chase......................... 277

Drone Take-off..................... 277

Echo and Romeo 278

The Drone Will Self-Destruct In 280

Live Fire Profiles................. 280

Scoring Without a Kill......... 281

Drone Recovery 281

Good Chute, Good Hook 281

Safety Pilot – Test Pilot 282

Accidents Happened............ 282

A Personal Experience......... 282

Schedule Change or Ejection 283

Controller Proficiency Training 283

Remote Control Touch & Go's 284

New Controller Checkouts... 284

Test Missions....................... 284

Auto-Landing Malfunction... 285

Det 1, Holloman AFB 286

Ferrying F-100s 287

A Viking Funeral 287

Transient Alert..................... 288

A Stone's Throw 288

Ferry Flight Malfunctions 288

A Memorable Flight............. 289

Hot Brakes........................... 290

Accident Investigation 291

F-100 Instructor Pilot........... 293

Back Seat Landings 293

Fred Whitten........................ 294

The Deadly Saber Dance...... 294

Adverse Yaw – What is it?... 294

Max Performing the F-100... 295

Kick the Tires and Light the Fires 296

Tally Ho the Space Shuttle... 296

Wow! That's Loud! 297

The T-33 T-Bird 297

The 95th TFS........................ 298

Flying the T-33.................... 298

Test Pilot Dick Bong............ 298

The Cocked Nose Gear 299

Cross Country to LA............ 300

The Lieutenants 300

Get Home-itis Proves Fatal .. 301

Retirement............................ 301
Champagne Flight 301
Terms and Acronyms Appearing In This Book 303
Glossary 303
Retirement Photo.................. 328
Tasting flight for the last time 329

High Flight

Oh, I have slipped the surly bonds of earth,
And danced the skies on laughter-silvered wings;
Sunward I've climbed, and joined the tumbling mirth
Of sun-split clouds,--and done a hundred things
You have not dreamed of --wheeled and soared and swung
High in the sunlit silence. Hov'ring there
I've chased the shouting wind along, and flung
My eager craft through footless halls of air...
Up, up the long, delirious, burning blue
I've topped the wind-swept heights with easy grace
Where never lark or even eagle flew--
And, while with silent lifting mind I've trod
The high untrespassed sanctity of space,
Put out my hand, and touched the face of God.

John Gillespie Magee Jr., R.C.A.F.

Author's Note

The war in Vietnam affected the direction of my life from becoming a teacher to joining the Air Force. In this book, the underlying theme is when the future is viewed from afar, obstacles to goals in life appear to be like huge, intimidating mountains, but when closer, a pathway can be found between them and intermediate goals achieved. The journey from one goal to the next always begins with small steps.

In writing this book I've tried to be as factual as possible or as memory allows. I've also used the actual names of people who had significant (and sometimes even insignificant) roles. However, in some cases when dealing with embarrassing or controversial situations I've taken the liberty to alter names as appropriate.

Navigation charts use latitude and longitude. A degree of latitude is 60 nautical miles. Hence, ships and planes use knots (nautical miles per hour) as a measure of speed. Throughout the book I usually reference airspeeds as knots. A statute mile is 5280 feet whereas a nautical mile is 6080 feet. This means knots are faster than miles per hour. To get a more accurate feeling for speed, 100 knots is 115 mph. A high performance fighter probably takes off at around 180 knots and lands at 150 knots which would be 207 mph and 172 mph respectively.

After the book's initial release I received feedback concerning the 'Air Forceese' language. There are hundreds of terms that are an integral part of the daily lives of the military that are quite foreign in the civilian world. With that in mind, in this edition I've incorporated a 25 page glossary of most of those terms that I found. If all else fails there is always 'google'.

Chapter One

In The Beginning – OTS

> *The Cessna T-41 is the safest airplane in the Air Force. It can just barely kill you.*

An Air Force Recruiter

As I contemplate where to begin in this story of my flying experiences the thought 'in the beginning' comes to mind and for this story the beginning would have to be in Superior Wisconsin in 1966. I was somewhat of a newlywed and only months away from graduating from college. Upon graduation I would lose my 2S deferment making me eligible for the draft lottery and possible induction into the Army. I hadn't really given much thought to alternatives when I got a post card from the Air Force recruiter. He invited me to come to Duluth and talk about the possibility of Officer Training School, OTS.

The more I thought about it the more the idea excited me since I had resigned myself to either being drafted or joining the ranks of teachers looking for a job. I wasn't too crazy about either prospect. I decided it couldn't hurt to go over and talk with this recruiter.

During the interview an Air Force sergeant very politely asked me numerous questions. I answered them and then asked him some questions of my own. The whole time we were talking he was writing and when the interview was over I still hadn't decided to take the plunge - until he handed me the papers he had been writing on and asked me to sign. They were applications to take the physical examination for the Air Force Officer Qualification Test (AFOQT). For this I would have to go to Minneapolis. Things were just moving way too fast and I declined his offer. Then, the sergeant pointed out that I still wasn't committing myself. Regardless of whether I accepted the OTS offer sooner or later I still would have to take the physical anyway. He was good! I signed on the dotted line.

Induction Physical

In Minneapolis there were a large number of young men like myself being herded from one station to the next as we underwent our physicals. Somewhere in there I also took my AFOQT and then came back home to await the results. The longer I waited the more I wanted a slot at Air Force Officer Training School.

After a couple of months of waiting I was notified by the recruiter that I had indeed passed all of the tests and was qualified to apply for any area in the Air Force including pilot training. Would I still be interested in OTS? *"Yes, yes, a thousand times yes!"* I accepted the Air Force's offer and was given an OTS reporting date for May 29, 1967.

OTS was in San Antonio, Texas at Lackland AFB. I was due to graduate from UWS in January so I took 12 credit hours of graduate night school and substitute taught in Superior for that spring semester.

Although I was qualified to apply for any area I never even considered pilot training. I had never even been in an airplane before and I was convinced that to become a pilot one had to be at least an aeronautical engineer and being able to walk on water wouldn't hurt. Anyway, I selected the field of weapons controller with only the vaguest notion of what one was. While at OTS I again had an opportunity to apply for pilot training but, unfortunately, I still considered being a pilot well beyond my capabilities and stayed with the weapons controller field.

OTS - Lackland AFB

When I departed for San Antonio, Texas and the beginning of OTS I was filled with many conflicting emotions. I was quite nervous because I had never gone off by myself before. I was sad because I knew I was leaving my pretty wife, Jean, for three long months - an eternity to a 22 year old. I was excited because I knew for better or worse my life was changing forever. I was proud because I was going off to become an Air Force officer. I was also fearful of failure; what if I didn't have what it took, 'the right stuff.'

A First Flight

The day I left was very sunny. The ticket I was given was for a departure from the Minneapolis airport so Jean drove me all the way from Superior. After an emotional parting I found myself boarding an airplane for the first time in my life. With brake release the big jetliner began to quickly pick up speed. So did my heart rate. The excitement and thrill of the plane accelerating down the runway and then abruptly rotating upward as it soared off the ground was beyond description. I was fortunate to have a window seat and it must have been obvious that I was a first time flyer because of the way I continued to stare out the window during the climb-out. I will never forget the awe I felt as we passed through a few wispy clouds. I was on my first airplane ride and it was so fitting that it should be on my way to join the Air Force.

San Antonio

The San Antonio airport terminal had signs for recruits to follow. I had very little luggage. We were told to not bring much in the way of personal things because we wouldn't be needing much and storage space was limited. I found a blue Air Force bus and boarded it with my suitcase in hand. When the bus was full it pulled out and began the half hour drive to Lackland AFB.

My memories for the remainder of the day are hazy. I remember things being pretty much as they are depicted in the movies where the long haired recruits are formed up into lines and are given their first marching orders. We must have really looked like a sad lot as we headed off to the in-processing building. I also remember being issued more clothes and equipment than I thought I could carry. At each supply station a young airman would repeat the same instructions over and over in a monotone voice. We were told to strip and then were given our 'issued clothes' in the order we would dress. There wasn't much time at each station and I was sure of one thing at this point - I didn't want to do anything to cause myself to stand out!

Somehow, that long day ended with my being taken to Medina AFB, an annex to Lackland AFB and the home of the officer training school. There, I was assigned to a squadron and a flight and assigned a dorm room with two other young men my age (a flight consisted of 18 officer trainees and a squadron was made up of four or more flights).

Tom Watson, a pudgy fellow from one of the eastern states, was one of my roommates. The other was a tall lanky farm boy from Iowa. I can't remember his name because he washed out of the program soon after it began. When he left, we picked up another roommate, Sherman, whom Tom nicknamed 'means-well.' No matter what Sherman did it was wrong but he 'meant well.' He wasn't quite on the same wave length as the rest of us and he didn't survive the cut either. He washed out due to emotional instability.

Life at Medina

My flight was located halfway down the 2nd floor of a three story barracks building. We all had our rooms on the same side of the hall and on the other side were the rooms of our upper classmen. It was their job to watch over us and 'protect' us from misdeeds that we might otherwise do. They did a good job of it. They had been waiting six weeks for us to come in and during that time they endured their upper classmen.

Now, here we were, moving in across the hall, all in a daze and we still had our long hair. I think that first night stretched on until 1 or 2 am getting settled into our rooms and in so doing listening to the upper classmen's instructions on everything from what order to hang clothes in our closets to the order and position of everything in the dresser drawers and how to make a white collar bed etcetera. Spit shining shoes and boots fit in to the regimen as did frequent pushups whenever a response was considered inadequate. When we finally did get to sleep it seemed like only moments later when we were roused by loud shouting. It was time to get up and begin our first day at OTS. What had I gotten myself into?

Our guardian upperclassmen were telling us to MOVE. "You've got 20 minutes to wash, shave, dress in fatigues, make your bed and get lined up outside on the sidewalk." It wasn't even light outside yet but sleep was the farthest thing from my mind at this point. I stumbled down to the community bathroom, managed to find a sink to share with a couple other bewildered OT's as we now would be called. I shaved in record time and somehow got dressed and out to the sidewalk. Many didn't meet the time constraints and suddenly found themselves lying on the sidewalk doing pushups. I was also aware that there were many other flights that were going through the same shocking experience as they lined up on their respective pieces of sidewalk.

After roll call on the sidewalk, we marched as best we could to the chow hall for our first meal at OTS. As usual we were closely supervised and got our first introduction to eating the 'square meal' and other culinary amenities. Following breakfast we again lined up on the sidewalk and began marching back to our dorm as the sun was beginning to rise above the horizon. The rest of that day consisted of getting shorn of our long locks, getting shots, and attending orientations for academics, meeting our Flight Training Officer (FTO), Capt Hollis, and learning more of the rules and procedures. We were kept busy from that early wakeup until we were told to turn out our lights at midnight. Wow! What a day.

Our FTO, Capt Hollis

Our meeting with our FTO, Capt. Hollis, was very enlightening. Capt. Hollis was a short man standing about 5 feet 7 inches tall but in our eyes he was a giant and one to be feared. He had a very commanding stature and cold blue eyes. His instructions to us were punctuated with periods of silence as his piercing eyes engaged each of ours in turn. Capt. Hollis told us that a third of us wouldn't be here in 12 weeks and a lecture followed on how we had to learn to work together as a group, to help each other. He also explained that the quickest way out of OTS was by slighting academics. If one were to fail an academic test he would be restricted in his little free time. After the second failure, supervised study sessions and more restrictions would follow. After the third failure, the poorly performing OT would pack his things and move over to Lackland AFB to enter the enlisted boot camp.

As time went on and we got to know Capt. Hollis we joyfully discovered a tender person behind the initially fearsome figure. He cared a lot for all of us and felt very badly whenever we lost another OT to attrition. After OTS when stationed just 75 miles to the north at Bergstrom AFB I took Jean back to Lackland to see where I spent three months and we stopped by to visit Capt. Hollis and his wife. It was a very satisfying and joyful visit.

The First Week

The first week at OTS was definitely the worst. Time was always in short supply and when we failed to perform all of our duties punishments resulted. It seemed impossible to accomplish everything in the time given to us.

Punishments frequently were in the form of a gig. We all carried 'gig sheets', little squares of preprinted papers, and when told to we would produce a gig sheet and it was filled out accordingly. Gigs could be earned following the slightest of infractions.

Gigged In

On Saturday morning following the standard marching parade the list of those gigged in was posted. OTs earning above a certain number of gigs during the week were confined to the barracks for the remainder of the weekend while the rest of us visited the OT Club or went to the Base Exchange (store) or did other activities on the small Medina base. Of course it was built into the system that everyone would be gigged in for at least the first two or three weekends.

Discipline and working together were constantly pounded into us. Discipline was measured by our every action and especially by how well we did during the weekly dorm inspection.

Standby Inspection

The typical dorm room inspection occurred each Saturday morning and was called 'standby inspection.' This was without doubt a time of terror for the underclass OT. Even the upper classmen feared Standby. We spent all Friday night preparing. Everything had to be just right. Items in dresser drawers had to be placed using a ruler to make sure everything was exactly in the right position. Coat hangers had to be exactly 1 inch apart. Every surface had to be 100 percent free of lint and dust to pass the white glove inspection. Even the pipes behind the radiator and every reachable surface in the radiator had to be perfectly clean. Our beds were to be made using the 'white collar' method where the top sheet was pulled back over the wool blanket exactly 12 inches leaving a 'white collar' and this along with the rest of the wool blanket had to be pulled tight under the mattress and springs so that a dime would bounce off the collar. I got painful hang nails from tugging that blanket from beneath the mattress to get the required tightness.

Our floors had to be waxed and absolutely glistening. The venetian blinds were to be totally free of dust and set such that if a pencil was placed perpendicular in the blinds it would be level with the floor. Naturally, the last task on Friday night was the floor and once it was shined we would only walk stocking-footed on it.

Each underclassman OT was also assigned an additional duty to clean. Mine was keeping the two clothes dryers clean of lint. The lint trap screen was always one of the first things that was looked at during inspection and when held up to the light, if there was even a speck of lint we failed the inspection. Every Friday night I spent an hour on each dryer. Each discrepancy was a gig given to the flight and subsequently to the squadron. Competition between flights and squadrons was fierce so God help the lowly OT that gained a gig or two for his flight or squadron. I only received personal gigs during my 12 weeks at OTS.

Saturday morning began with our standby inspection right after breakfast. During an hour vulnerability period we had to stay in our room ready to assume the proper position at a moment's notice. When the inspection team hit our building we would know it when the first flight was called loudly to attention - but we never knew where in the building they would strike first. They loved it when they could dash into a room and catch the inhabitants by surprise. When the flight was called to attention the OTs in each room stood rigidly at attention waiting for the fearful moment for the inspectors to arrive.

The team consisted of three upper class OT's who belonged to the wing staff and held the rank of OT lieutenant colonel or OT colonel. When they entered a room the first one in would loudly slap the door with his open hand causing a very dramatic entry. A flinch by an 'inspectee' could result in a gig plus much unwanted attention.

During the inspection, one inspector would walk around the room inspecting, another would be recording and the third would single out one of the OTs. He would put his face right in the OTs and question him on any of the many facts we were expected to have committed to instant memory.

Being chosen for questioning was what I most dreaded about standby. We always addressed other OTs as 'Mister.' An example of the questioning might be, "Mr. Olson, who is the wing commander?" If a response wasn't immediate a gig would result. I think I was fortunate because Mr. Watson was shorter than I, pudgy and just plain looked more vulnerable. He was always asked the questions. What they didn't know was that Mr. Watson was super cool and even enjoyed the attention. He was ready and waiting for them and he never missed a question.

As upperclassmen we had it much easier. The inspectors would still come into our rooms but they wouldn't look hard enough to find anything unless it was really obvious. Since it was upper classman inspecting upper classman we weren't intimidated by them nearly as much.

The Saturday Parade

Following the inspection we had a few minutes to breathe again before going out to the parade ground for the weekly parade practice. Oh how we hated that but not nearly as much as standby. The only good thing about parade practice was that it marked the end of the week. Parade practice lasted for an hour and a half to two hours and much of it was just standing at attention in the hot sun trying to not pay attention to the rivulets of sweat trickling down our backs. However, at some point we would hear, "OTs, atten-hut." "OTs, dismissed." We were free until Monday morning. Hallelujah! Free to get caught up on letter writing, browse in the BX annex, study academics or even go to the OT Club if we could find an upperclassman to escort us.

One of the most amazing things I discovered during OTS was how much value we placed on very simple pleasures that just a couple weeks before we routinely took for granted. For instance that first Saturday night we were all taken over to the OT Club for a couple hours. I didn't much care for beer back then but boy, did it ever taste good on that occasion. After about the third week if you didn't have any gigs and hadn't flunked any tests you could go to the OT Club on a weekend accompanied by another underclassman.

As upperclassmen we could also sign out for San Antonio. However, until graduation we always had to wear our uniforms. To be caught wearing civilian clothes downtown meant immediate dismissal - and occasionally it did happen.

I didn't have any desire to leave Medina for the weekend. I found just being able to walk around outside while not marching, to use the telephone, to go down to the basement for a cold soda or to sit around and talk with the guys was immensely enjoyable. However, I did go downtown one time with a group of OTs from my flight. We rented motel rooms in downtown San Antonio and the first thing we did was jump up and down on the beds with our shoes on - forbidden fruit to us. After that we went out to a fine restaurant and then walked the San Antonio River walkway that was just beautiful at night. In no time at all it was Sunday afternoon and we were back at Medina.

Academics

My discussion of OTS wouldn't be complete without mentioning academics. Our typical day consisted of either morning academics or afternoon academics. The academics building, the largest building at Medina, was located on a hill. There was a long blacktop road leading up the hill and each day we would march by flight up the hill and into 'The Master Bedroom' as the large auditorium was known. It received this name for two reasons; one was due to the boring nature of the subjects we had (leadership, effective writing, awards and decorations, etcetera) and the other was afternoon academics began right after lunch when we all had full stomachs. Both led to a strong inclination of dozing off.

The instructional staff at OTS was truly outstanding. I am sure the assignment was very coveted and the staff carefully chosen. One instructor was especially lively on stage and one of his methods to keep his lectures interesting was he would go through the class roster and pick out an odd name of the day from one of the 500 or so OTs in his audience. In a friendly manner he would then pick on this individual off and on during the whole hour. The unlucky individual would usually join in the laughter - and it kept us awake and entertained. Why, it was even possible at times to forget where we were.

This instructor also carefully picked one OT in each class on the first day and would refer back to this person two or three times each week for the duration. The person picked was always chosen because of an odd name. This person like it or not became the best known OT in the class, even more so than the OT wing commander. In my class his name was Quigley. I never knew what Quigley looked like but I've never forgotten his name.

We usually had about three hours of academics in The Master Bedroom and then would spend an hour or so in our flight room with our FTO, Capt. Hollis. His job was to augment some of the things that were taught en masse as well as work on problems that might pertain specifically to our flight.

One thing that particularly stands out in my mind was researching a report on some aspect of national defense and then presenting it to the rest of the flight. I did mine on the Polaris Submarine; a rather unusual subject you might think for AIR FORCE OTS.

Non-academics

On the half of the day opposite from academics we did physical activities. Every day included physical education. Each squadron had its own color PT uniform; ours were blue. At the scheduled time we would march out to the PT field and join all the other brightly colored groups for an hour of exercises. We had to run a mile every day which was very easy for me but caused a few to wash out. In addition to running we also did the usual exercises.

One not so usual exercise was absolutely diabolical. It hid its torturous nature behind a simple name, the arm roll. You extended your arms straight out to either side and moved them around such that your outstretched hands described small circles. The first time it was described to us we thought, 'heh, this is really going to be easy,' and after a minute it was. After two minutes our confident grins had evaporated. After three minutes our faces were masks of agony and I don't think anyone made it to four minutes.

Oh how we hated the arm rolls, especially after immunizations. Whenever immunizations were given to us (by means of an injection air gun) it was just prior to PT. No explanation was ever given to us but we noticed that even though the first couple minutes of exercising were painful our arms never remained sore for very long from receiving shots.

Another regular outside activity was marching practice. We would each get chances to drill our flight on a concrete marching pad that was the size of two tennis courts. There really weren't that many maneuvers to learn and I loved marching the flight -- it gave me a feeling of power. The commands were forward march, to the rear march, right/left face, about face, column right/left march, by the right/left flank march, and column half right/left march. Of course there was a cadence to which the commands had to be given and the command of execution had to be given on the correct foot. Other than that, I didn't find it difficult. However, we had a few fellows that had minds that turned to mush on the marching pad. When they were drilling us we knew we could expect disaster. A typical sequence would be marching toward the fence that might be 50 feet in front of the column; plenty of time to call out a 'column right' or perhaps a 'right flank' call or even a 'to the rear march.' When one of these guys was in the driver's seat we started grinning as step by step the fence would get closer and closer and closer and the drill OT would just freeze up and march us right into it. And heaven help us if another flight sharing the drill pad with us had one of these guys drilling them at the same time! Capt. Hollis was usually very composed and while his cold blue eyes could strike fear in any of our hearts, there were times when he would absolutely lose it and he'd just shake his head and laugh.

Other activities we had opposite academics were running the obstacle course that we had to do twice; rifle or pistol shooting; and many others including tear gas training.

With the exception of PT and marching practice, the hot, long sleeved fatigue uniform was standard wear. Since we were at OTS during June, July and August, these activities could approach being unbearable. We did wear pith helmets that helped keep us somewhat cool and we also had frequent water breaks but we still had problems with OTs succumbing to the heat.

We had a flag system to indicate the heat conditions. A white flag meant have at it. A blue flag meant it was OK to be outside but use discretion. A red flag meant all outdoor activities were prohibited due to the heat. During July and August, in the afternoons, we saw a few red flags and what a joyful sight they were. Since alternate activities usually weren't scheduled when we got a red flag it meant we went back to our dorm buildings for some unexpected and greatly appreciated time off. A very fond memory of OTS was getting back to my room all hot and sweaty and having an unplanned hour off to put on my PT trunks and head down to the basement for an ice cold soft drink from the vending machine. Now, that was just a little bit of heaven. There was a lounge in the basement and since the barracks weren't air conditioned the basement was by far the coolest place in the building.

Rank Had Its Privileges

Rank at OTS was revered. We seldom saw real Air Force officers other than our instructors or FTOs so our rank structure was mostly based around OT rank. The rank system used on our uniforms was borrowed from the Navy. An underclassman basically had no rank and wore blank shoulder boards. When we became upperclassmen, the majority of us became lieutenants with a thin stripe and a thick stripe on our shoulder boards. Approaching upperclassmen status we could volunteer or request through our FTOs for certain staff or command positions. Then, through an unknown process, the FTOs got together and chose the OTs to fill all of the available positions. Upon graduation of the upperclassmen, these OTs put on the rank of their appointed positions. These included command positions like flight commander, squadron commander, group commander and wing commander, and staff positions such as executive officer for the commanders, vice commanders, and even wing chaplain. Their ranks ranged from OT first lieutenant (two wide stripes on the shoulder boards) to OT colonel (4 wide stripes on the shoulder boards).

During the 12 weeks at OTS the typical OT was extremely rank conscious and was taught to pay the highest regard to it. Failure to render a salute to someone of higher rank was a serious offense worthy of a gig or two. The absence of shoulder boards usually meant an NCO or officer and required a salute.

On the day of our graduation when we were all suddenly 2nd lieutenants, I remember wondering if the OT lieutenant colonels and OT colonels might not consider it a demotion to suddenly find themselves the same rank as even the lowest ranking OT. I happened to see our OT wing commander at the San Antonio airport later that day and someone else gleefully pointed out to me that he was wearing the wrong size 2nd lieutenant insignia on his uniform. As the OT wing commander he was almost considered deity and now he was just a 2nd lieutenant wearing the incorrect size insignia. Years later when I was in pilot training I had two 2nd lieutenants in my class who had held high rank in OTS. They both washed out of pilot training. I think they were anomalies but I wondered at the time if a study was ever done to see if there was a correlation between OT rank and later success or failure in the Air Force. I personally don't think a correlation would have been found.

Graduation and Beyond

The graduation ceremony was part of a military parade that we had practiced each Saturday for a long time. The culmination was almost anticlimactic. At the end of it I was wearing second lieutenant bars and I was an officer. An officer in the united States Air Force! I felt a twinge of envy for my fellow classmates who had parents and wives or girlfriends present. Due to my somewhat unique circumstances I had no one to share this momentous occasion with.

Prior to receiving my commission as 2nd lieutenant I received my assignment to Bergstrom AFB, in Austin, Texas as a weapons controller. I was really excited about the assignment and was anxious to spend more time in this wonderful state. My enthusiasm was dampened slightly, though, when I found that I would only be given travel pay for 60 miles since that was how far Bergstrom AFB was from San Antonio. At 6 cents a mile the Air Force paid me three dollars and 60 cents to fly back to Superior, Wisconsin and then drive all the way back with Jean who, incidentally, was 7 and a half months pregnant with Jill.

Being very cost conscious (a non-flying 2nd lieutenant was paid $302 a month plus benefits - we didn't eat steak very often) I bought a military standby ticket for the trip back to Duluth. At the airport I got in line for the standby fares along with many other newly commissioned 2nd lieutenants. I became particularly worried of getting a seat when I noticed that I was the second person from the end of a long line of new lieutenants. To confirm my fears the person in front of me was the last standby status person to be seated - in the coach section. After a couple minutes a smiling flight attendant asked me if I would like a seat in first class. Boy, would I! With the free benefits that accompany first class I believe I might have been flying a couple thousand feet higher than the airplane.

Jean met me at the airport and when we went home I was greeted with a surprise party by some of our friends. Of course I was filled with stories of my experiences but mostly I felt like I was living in a marvelous bubble that might burst at any moment. I had become so enmeshed in the rigors of OTS that it was just hard to believe that it was over and that now I was a respectable second lieutenant.

For well over a year I occasionally had a recurring dream where a mix-up had occurred and I had been released from OTS too soon. I was back at Medina again as an OT to finish my training! OTS remained in my dreams for years after but, fortunately, on a less and less frequent basis.

Chapter Two

First Assignment - Bergstrom

> *Any landing you can walk away from is a good landing.*

Settling In

Our drive to Austin, Texas was uneventful. We had our few household goods picked up by a moving company and we packed the car with what we would need for perhaps a month. Hopefully, within that time we would have found living quarters in Austin.

Jean might take issue with my brief description in the preceding paragraph. By now she was over 8 months pregnant and her obstetrician, having had an Air Force background, pointed out on a map where we might make emergency stops at military facilities. I was anxious to get to Bergstrom but Jean decided our end of day stops. We still made good time, though, in spite of rather frequent breaks for gas.

We got to Bergstrom and Jean was still pregnant. I signed in at my new squadron, the 727th Tactical Control squadron, known as the 7-duece. With Jean in a motel I did the minimum of in-processing and then was told by my squadron to take time off to get settled. That sounded great to me.

The next day, Jean and I began looking for a house to rent. We had no idea of where to begin so we bought a newspaper in a restaurant and opened it to the rental part of the classified section. With the newspaper opened up on the table next to a map of Austin we were unknowingly asking for help. In no time at all we had a couple Texans telling us where various addresses were. "Oh no, y'all don't want to live over in this here part of town now." They were extremely friendly and very helpful. We picked out one listing for an unbelievably low rent house. Our 'advisors' said it was in a very good part of town so we called and made arrangements to see it.

To fully appreciate the mental state we were in, we were brand new to the Air Force in a strange state, in a strange town, living in a motel room. Jean was ready to deliver at any time, and hurricane Betsy was in the neighborhood giving us torrential rains and spawning tornadoes that reportedly were swirling around the Tower of Texas on the University of Texas campus.

A Home to Live In

We met the realtor at 1003a Lorraine Street and in only a couple minutes said we would rent the house. It was a small single-story run-down house. Inside we found a reasonably sized kitchen, a living room with hardwood floor that hadn't seen wax in years and two bedrooms. The front yard was small and had about a 25 degree slope down to the street. The backyard, however, had a four foot chain-link fence completely surrounding it. The driveway to the house entered from an alley from the back. We were impressed with the obvious good quality of the neighborhood. We also saw that with some work a lot could be done to fix up the house.

In the weeks to come we thoroughly cleaned up the yard and house. Several coats of paste wax on the hardwood floor brought it back to a nice luster. Several gallons of latex paint in pleasant pastel colors brought a nice cheerfulness to the rooms and some creative patchwork on my part allowed me to repair a couple fist sized holes in the wall of the living room. When we noticed evidence of termites we notified the realtor but nothing was done of it during the year we were in the house. Jill was born a couple weeks after we moved in. Talk about great timing.

Marking Time

When I reported for work at the squadron I found that I didn't have a lot to do until I went to weapons controller school at Tyndall AFB in Panama City, Florida. There were several other lieutenants in the same situation as myself; waiting for controller school. We were assigned odd jobs to keep us somewhat busy.

Two of us that said we knew a little about woodworking were given the job of making a huge display/trophy case that would reside just inside the front doors of the squadron. Our plans called for the front of the case to have three sides. The inside would have three tiers, each smaller than the previous giving it a Christmas tree effect. The three sides would be covered with plate glass and the display would also have indirect lighting. Surprisingly, we encountered little difficulty making the case and it actually looked very much like our plans. The squadron commander was quite impressed. The only problem was in cutting the plate glass. We tried cutting it like any other glass. After ruining two huge sheets we had civil engineering cut the rest.

Jean and I learned to play bridge while stationed at Bergstrom. I learned at work and survived not by learning the subtle rules of the game but by learning a few rules of thumb. Three passes to you -- bid three no trump. I had no idea why, though. When leading off in no trump lead the fourth from your longest and strongest suit. Again, I didn't know the reason behind this guidance. Meanwhile Jean and some of the other wives of lieutenants were learning bridge the correct way from the Officers' Wives Club. We had one other couple we played a lot with, Tom and Sue Davenport. Tom and I always played together against Jean and Sue. Oh how we would disgust the girls when we violated the rules of bidding to rely on our rules of thumb – and often 'go set.'

Tyndall AFB

We arrived at Bergstrom during the third week of September. Jill was born on October 18th and we had to pack up the car and move to Panama City during the Christmas holidays for my three month long weapons controller school.

Mexico Beach

We had a good idea of where to stay in Panama City from previous controllers who had attended the school before me. A place called Mexico Beach was what was recommended. Mexico Beach was a small community about 12 miles south of Tyndall AFB, and it consisted almost entirely of beach houses that were inhabited during the summer by their owners and rented out quite inexpensively during the winter. We immediately drove to Mexico Beach, contacted the one realtor in town and found it was a buyers' market. We had our pick of hundreds of duplex houses. We chose one that was not too far from the post office and just a couple hundred feet from the water. We were the only people living on our block. In fact I would guess there weren't more than a hundred people living in this community that boasted a population of thousands in summer.

We had plenty of fond memories of Mexico Beach. Other friends were living there from Bergstrom including our bridge playing couple, the Davenports. They also had an infant close to Jill's age and while Tom and I were at school Jean and Sue had plenty of free time during the day to wander the beautiful white beaches of the Gulf of Mexico.

We all took advantage of the lovely beach when we could. I really enjoyed getting up with the sun and walking the early morning beach to discover what treasures the surf had left behind during the night. The prospects were especially lucrative following a storm when larger waves crashed upon the beach.

The weather was especially nice while we were at Mexico Beach. On one of our old super 8 home movies there is even a blurred scene of me going swimming on New Year's day; blurred because I was moving quite quickly. The water was in the low 60's. But I had the bragging rights to having gone swimming on New Years day!

We spent a lot of time on the beach. When Jean's folks visited us in January, her father and I did a little fishing in the surf. We threw our shrimp baited lines into the surf, planted the poles in the sand with the tips pointed skyward and then relaxed in lawn chairs until a pole was pulled over. We caught a fair amount of fish about 14 or so inches long called 'whiting.' There was another fish that we'd occasionally reel in – we called it a 'toad fish.' This critter looked absolutely ugly, like a fish-toad and it even made a croaking sound. I've since learned they are really quite common. We found that during the spring one could catch a lot of ocean trout (called speckled trout or just 'specks') but we moved back to Austin before they migrated close to shore.

Weapons Controller School

The weapons controller school at Tyndall lasted for three months and consisted of a lot of academic classes on things like intercept geometry and aircraft capabilities to name a couple. In addition we had practical controlling experience on radar scopes. The majority of the work consisted of sitting at the scope controlling a simulated fighter against a simulated target. It was called the T-2 simulator. An instructor sat next to us to help or instruct and airmen technicians sat in another room operating the target generator equipment. They also pretended to be the fighter pilot and would respond on the radio to your directions.

"Fighter 01, turn right 130, climb to angels 13, speed liner." "Roger, turning right to 130 degrees, angels 13. Speed set."

We also were able to participate in mock wars using another product of the computer called the T-4. This not only generated targets but introduced them in a preprogrammed sequence as if a real war was in progress. Fighting the mock war required many players with position names like 'weapons assignment officer', 'fighter duty officer', 'defensive duty officer' and of course 'weapons controller.' We first detected targets, then went through an elaborate process to identify them as friend or foe and finally intercepted them if they were enemy or unidentified.

A third activity we had at our radar scopes was the most stressful of them all, live controlling. This job required us to control two T-33 aircraft and 'bump heads' with them (run intercepts). It was very stressful because we knew we were now talking to real pilots flying real aircraft. It was amazing to watch some of the students who did just great with the simulated targets but just froze up or clanged when it came to live controlling. Most didn't like live controlling but there was a good feeling of satisfaction afterwards.

In every class there were one or two people who couldn't take the pressure and washed out. We were told that they were assigned to missile duty. I never had any trouble with controlling and usually actually enjoyed it.

Back to Bergstrom

When we returned to Bergstrom in March of 1968 we were just about a family of four because Becky was conceived in January. Life at Bergstrom picked up since I now had a job to do. But at that time, new lieutenants were averaging about a year on station before being reassigned, many to Vietnam and Thailand.

Orders to Korea

Since it was the thing to do I volunteered for Vietnam but was instead chosen to go to Korea with a reporting time in September. My assignment was part of an Air Force buildup in Korea following the Pueblo incident where the North Koreans captured an unarmed Navy Intelligence Ship, the Pueblo, in international waters. I would not be home for Becky's birth.

We decided the thing to do would be to move Jean and family back to her home town in Poplar, Wisconsin to be with her folks. That way Jill and Becky would have a 'dad' while I was gone, Jean would be looked after when Becky was due and at the same time she could get her master's degree at Superior. Once again Jean got to make the trip between Texas and Wisconsin while very pregnant

Chapter Three

The Land of the Morning Calm

There are only two basic types of airplanes: fighters and targets.

Off to Korea

It seemed like no time at all and I was on my way to Korea. Jean saw me off in Duluth and it was a difficult good bye knowing I would be gone for 13 months. We decided that we didn't have the thousand dollars it would cost for me to take a mid-tour leave. My flight took me to Minneapolis and then to Seattle. I landed in Seattle at about 10 pm and after collecting my duffel bag I was faced with a problem to solve. I was in the Seattle airport but my flight left from the SeaTac (Seattle/Tacoma) airport and I didn't even know where that was.

Flag of South Korea

A Good Samaritan

Perhaps my face revealed my anxiety because a nice looking man in his 60s asked me where I was going and I told him my dilemma. He introduced himself as a state congressman and offered me a ride to SeaTac a military field used for flights departing for destinations in the Pacific. I was greatly relieved and thankful.

The congressman retrieved his very new and large car from a private lot and we were on our way. During the drive to SeaTac we stopped at his home where his very gracious wife fixed us something to eat. By now it was close to midnight but I wasn't too concerned because I didn't have to be at SeaTac until 5 am. When we resumed our journey it still took half an hour to get to the airport. Mr. Congressman took me directly to my gate and with my heart-felt thanks and a promise to write him, I was off on the last leg of my journey. When I arrived in Korea I promptly fulfilled my promise with a letter.

Under Way

At SeaTac I joined several hundred others, almost all in uniform; a few Sailors, many Army and a few Air Force. After a long wait we were finally allowed to board our 707 aircraft and having been up all night I was asleep instantly. I next awoke a couple hours later to find it was light outside but I knew we were still on the ground. When I asked some people around me I found that we had been sitting on the ground for a couple hours with engines running (for air conditioning) waiting for the morning fog to burn off. Finally it did and after a very long takeoff roll we were airborne and turning to the north. To the north? The Pacific Ocean was west of us, but we were clearly paralleling the coast.

Divert to Anchorage

The puzzle was soon solved when the pilot addressed us. He said that because of the long time waiting for the fog to burn off, we didn't have enough gas to fly directly to Japan. We couldn't refuel without deplaning so the pilot decided to make an enroute stop in Anchorage, Alaska. Many people groaned at the news but to me it was an opportunity to be able to say, "Alaska? Ya, I've been there." After three hours we landed in Anchorage. Keeping with regulations we disembarked for the refueling operation.

The Anchorage Airport was an interesting place to wander around during the hour it took to service the airplane. The aircraft on the tarmac were mostly cargo planes, probably linking up the Asian producers with their American consumers. A striking display in the terminal was of two stuffed bears, one a polar bear and the other a kodiak bear. Both were standing on their hind legs looking very menacing as they stood about 10 feet tall. All too soon we were asked to re-board the airplane to continue our flight.

Our takeoff roll at Anchorage seemed to take forever. I had a window seat and I watched the thousand foot markers pass by, one after another, as we slowly picked up speed. The takeoff roll seemed to be excessive but at what seemed like the last moment we finally rotated and were airborne. At the same time the runway ended. Although it scared me a little I was sure the pilot knew exactly what he was doing. Six months later, I read in the Armed Forces' Stars and Stripes newspaper that the same charter flight ran out of runway on takeoff and crashed killing almost 60 people.

The Longest Flight

We took off from Anchorage during late morning on what was to be the longest day of my life. As we droned on and on heading west towards Japan it gradually occurred to me that the sun was ever so slowly moving east, not west. The obvious answer was we were traveling west slightly faster than the earth was rotating beneath us. A dozen hours later we landed in Japan - but now the time was early morning. We gained a couple hours and although my body was telling me otherwise the day was just beginning. Once again we were told to disembark for refueling but because of customs requirements we were restricted to a very small area of the military terminal.

An hour later we were once again on our way, this time on the short three hour flight to Seoul, Korea. The sky was clear giving a lovely view of the rugged terrain of Korea. The land beneath us was very mountainous with bright green terraced rice paddies filling in the valleys and even stair-stepping up the sides of the mountains.

Korea at Last

When we landed at Kimpo airport in Seoul we were sent through Korean customs and then the Army was instructed to go to the right while the Air Force was sent to the left. I soon discovered that the Army personnel were on their way to get gamma globulin shots as a precaution against cholera. The Air Force had determined the shots to be unnecessary.

While walking across the tarmac to get in line for the two to three hour bus ride to my destination, a lieutenant colonel asked me if I was going to Osan. When I replied that I was, he told me to tag along with him if I wanted an alternative to the bus. We boarded a tail-dragging twin prop airplane. I was soon experiencing my first and only flight on the world's most successful airplane, the DC-3, known to the military as the C-47 Gooney Bird. The Gooney Bird was the hero of the Burma 'hump' and the Berlin Airlift. We landed at Osan probably before the bus left Kimpo. Twice within 24 hours I was the recipient of acts of kindness from strangers.

It was now mid-afternoon and I called my sponsor from base operations. Like me he was a 2nd lieutenant and within minutes he was giving me a quick tour of the base en route to the Visiting Officers' Quarters, VOQ. My temporary room was a quonset hut that was attached to others forming two long parallel rows. The rows were connected by a large community shower with a half dozen shower heads and bathroom.

A Culture Shock

Considering how long my day had been I was told to just take it easy for the rest of the day. Someone would be by in the morning to take me to Headquarters for in-processing. A refreshing shower sounded like a great idea and then I would climb into bed for a nap. I was just about finished with my shower when I heard the sound of a shower on the other side of the room being turned on. I didn't give it much thought. As I was reaching for my towel, however, I was stunned when I discovered my shower mate was one of the elderly cleaning lady mama-sans. She was just enjoying herself to the most and was totally oblivious to my presence. Welcome to a different world I thought.

Assignment Mangil San

The next day I found out that I was being assigned to Mangil San, the chief radar site for the northern half of Korea. Later I learned that of the 8 radar sites in Korea Mangil San was the best assignment. We had the most controlling to do, the most people assigned, and hence the best facilities. By helicopter, we were only 25 minutes from Osan AB. Because Mangil San was located at the northern tip of a long north/south peninsula the trip by land was a grueling five hour trip over primitive roads.

After in-processing I caught the next chopper headed to Mangil San. The chopper was an old veteran from the Korean War. It resembled a giant guppy and was capable of carrying about five or six people and a fair amount of cargo. This was my first helicopter ride and I was very excited as the engine roared and the rotors went faster and faster. In a few seconds I felt the machine begin to rise a bit and then settle back down. It did that a couple more times as if it were straining to break loose from invisible shackles. Finally it struggled into the air. The nose of the chopper dropped a little and our forward speed increased.

When the pilot felt he had enough speed he increased the collective and we began to climb higher and higher. The doors were left open since it was a warm sunny day and I had a great view of the luscious green countryside. By leaning a little to one side I could look straight down at the ground hundreds of feet below. I wasn't complaining at all about how tight my lap-belt was.

We climbed to about 500 feet and turned to a westerly heading. I was enthralled with the sights of the Korean countryside as it passed by - village after village surrounded with verdant green squares that even though I had never seen any before I was quite sure were rice paddies. I could see a sparkling reflection from the fields hinting that beneath the green plants the fields were flooded with standing water. Dirt roads led off in all directions from the villages reminding me of spidery Chinese characters. Smaller paths branched off from the roads and led to even the most remote paddies.

In 20 minutes we were approaching Mangil San. The site was built on a thousand foot tall hill sitting on a point of land that stretched like a pointing finger into the Yellow Sea. I guessed there must be quite a tide at Mangil San because instead of blue water lapping at the edge of the shore, brown mud flats stretched outward for several miles. The top of the hill had been sheared off to make room for three radar antennas and a large operations building. The blasted rubble of rock looked like foam dripping from a frosted glass of beer. Three radar antennas dominated the hilltop and were sheltered from the elements by tubular steel structures. Stretched white coverings made them look like giant golf balls.

As we circled the hill to come in from the far side I could see a very winding gravel road that led to its base where the cantonment, or living area, was located. The helipad was a quarter mile below the cantonment area. A quarter mile below that was the village of Mangil San which consisted mostly of farmers and civilians who worked at the radar site.

The cantonment area was to be my home for the next 13 months and its facilities provided a surprising degree of comfort. There were several buildings of various sizes. One served as the chow hall on one side and housed a small Base Exchange store and post office on the other. Another building was used for vehicle maintenance and civil engineering. A third building was the NCO club annex with a small theater, a library and a barber shop. The largest building was a 2-story concrete block structure, the barracks. The bottom floor housed the enlisted people with up to three to a room. The second floor was for the officers and senior enlisted personnel. All had private rooms. As was frequently the case in the Air Force, rank had its privilege.

About a hundred yards below our compound, the gravel road divided with one branch going off to the right to the Republic of Korea Air Force (ROKAF) compound. Several months later after befriending a Korean lieutenant I occasionally went with him to his quarters. He was embarrassed and apologetic at how crude and lacking in amenities his quarters were. In comparison to the ROKAF officer quarters the rooms of our lower ranking enlisted people were luxurious

Mangil San – the People

When we landed at the helipad two jeeps were on hand to greet us. At first I thought I was the celebrity but in the weeks to come I realized the mail was the celebrity. Mail deliveries were truly cherished events. Mangil San received flights about three times a week and this was usually the only mail delivery. However, whenever people took a truck into Osan they knew better than to come back without first picking up the mail.

Herb, a first lieutenant and the site's executive officer, and the site medical corpsman, Sgt. Douglas, met me at the helicopter. They loaded my personal gear, gave me a nickel tour of the compound and showed me to my room. The rest of the officers were all friendly and put me right at ease. I quickly decided that I was very fortunate to have been assigned to Mangil San. As in all of my Air Force assignments, the people made the difference and Mangil San had some very nice ones that I would get to know closely during the next 13 months.

The site commander was a bachelor, Lieutenant Colonel Stankowski. I liked him although he kept very much to himself. He knew his job very well and also had a quick sense of humor. A big plus was that he reacted well in stressful situations. My most vivid memory of him is when he would sit at the far right side of the bar each evening drinking his beloved Black Label beer. At the time he was the only lieutenant colonel on site and perhaps that was the reason he seemed to keep to himself so much. His operations officer, Major Cottrell, was an old major with a very weathered face and loose jowls even though he was of trim build. I never liked Major Cottrell very much because I didn't feel he could be trusted. He freely talked about others when they weren't there and he didn't have high regard for one's feelings when they were there. I also felt he held a deep resentment that he was subservient to a younger officer.

Next in rank was a first lieutenant, Herb. Herb was not well liked. He lacked in personality and personal hygiene (it was joked that he wore a raincoat in the shower) and didn't seem able to interact with the others. In addition, he was the only Air Force officer who wasn't a weapons controller. Herb was an administrative officer in charge of the 'pencil pushers.' Jim Cardin was a first lieutenant from Tampa. He was quite short (within a couple months of rotating back to the States) when I arrived and was very disdainful of the controller field. I was impressed in a way when he told me he had been in pilot training until he washed out in T-38s when a girlfriend distracted him. I had not known anyone who had flown before but I also recognized the girlfriend thing as a ridiculous excuse for his washing out. I secretly harbored a dream of some day going to pilot training and I pumped Jim for information on what it was like. He almost convinced me it was beyond my abilities.

One of the most likable fellows was Lieutenant Stewart. I'm not sure anyone knew his first name. He was just Stu. Stu was very good controller and he always had a smile on his face. Nothing seemed to rattle him and he could find something to laugh about in just about everything.

We also had three or four Army officers at the site. Their site commander was a first lieutenant. I admired them for their professionalism and military bearing. They headed up an air defense artillery unit and it was their job to use our radar information in assigning targets to their subordinate remote missile or artillery sites to shoot at. Twice a day, they made radio checks with these units and because their communications were so dreadfully awful they could be heard all over the building. I often wondered how they could ever function in wartime with such poor equipment.

A Controller Named Fletch

The person I came to like the most was Fletch (nickname for his last name, Fletcher). Fletch was a 6 foot 7 inch Spaniard from San Diego. His family was very prominent in San Diego and had lived there for generations. Fletch's dad was an attorney and his older brother a B-52 pilot. Fletch had a very out of regulation handlebar mustache, wore a very out of regulation Australian type hat and controlled in a manner that didn't come from the regulations. However, when Fletch was on duty he was a true professional. He was an excellent controller and I learned controlling from him. The pilots loved his controlling style and frequently asked for him to control their missions.

Off duty Fletch was fun to be around - until he got very drunk which fortunately wasn't very often. He was a rather mean drunk and people would avoid him at all cost. Late one Friday night I was coming down the hall from the community bathroom when I saw Fletch reeling down the hall towards me. He had a glass in his right hand and by the look on his face I don't think he even knew I was there. At one point he bumped into the wall particularly hard and with a roar he slammed the glass against the wall shattering it into a thousand pieces. With that he continued on his way to his room. His hand didn't even appear to be cut. Most of the time Fletch was very fun to be around and had story after interesting story to tell. I looked him up a couple years later while on temporary duty (TDY) in San Diego. He was happily working as a deck hand on a wealthy charter fishing boat. He was doing what he loved to do and I have no doubt he now owns his own boat – or fleet of boats.

There were many interesting stories about Fletch and this is one. He had two very expensive virgin wool pullover shirts that he really liked. He tried to keep them hidden from the houseboys because they washed everything in hot water and he knew the shirts would be ruined. First one and then the other succumbed to the houseboys and when he got them back they were hopelessly too small. They fit me perfectly though so Fletch gave them to me and I wore them for years. With a joking type smirk on his face he accused me of bribing the houseboys to shrink his shirts.

A Dad Again

I had been at Mangil San for all of two weeks when early one morning I heard a knock on my door. It was the site commander and our site medic whom we all called 'Doc.' They both had big grins on their faces as the commander handed me a telegram from the Red Cross. I had a pretty good idea what was enclosed and I was right. It was official notification that our daughter, Rebecca, had been born and that Mom and Daughter were both doing fine. Frequently, Red Cross telegrams are a portent of bad news so on this occasion my two visitors were visibly enjoying their task. It felt wonderful knowing I now had two daughters but it seemed an eternity until I received a letter from Jean. The wait was worth it because it had a picture of the most beautiful baby in the world - and every letter for the remainder of my tour in Korea had Polaroid pictures of my daughters. It was hard spending that year away from my family but Jean did a wonderful job of keeping me a part of my daughters' lives as they grew.

Mangil San's Mission

As mentioned earlier, Korea had eight radar sites situated around the country; four were in the northern half and four in the south. One site in the north and one in the south was a Control and Reporting Center (CRC) to which the other Control and Reporting Posts (CRPs) were subordinate. The two CRCs reported directly to the Tactical Air Control Center (TACC) at Osan Air Base.

All radar sites and the TACC were collocated with Republic of Korea Air Force (ROKAF) personnel. Air Force personnel controlled Air Force missions while ROKAF personnel controlled ROKAF missions. When it came to identifying and reacting to unknown or hostile aircraft, we all worked together.

Shift Work

My job at Mangil San was that of a weapons controller. There were usually five controllers assigned and four of us worked shift work. Each shift controller had a weapons technician, a two or three stripe airman that looked over the controller's shoulder assisting where he could. The tech had a multitude of duties; he maintained the log book as a record of all events at our radar scope, he coordinated radar handoffs, he got the home base weather, he activated the fighter scramble alarm when directed and the list went on and on.

I was fortunate in that I had a young, pleasant radar tech; a buck sergeant called Jimmy Ellis. We arrived in the country within two or three weeks of each other so were crewed together for the entire year. I liked Jimmy a lot because we had a lot in common. We were both about the same build, quiet and unassuming and enjoyed each other's company. On many nights, after getting off the hill following a swing shift we sat around the lounge talking until the wee hours.

The shift schedule was on a 12 day cycle and worked like this. I worked three consecutive midnight shifts, after which I got off work at 8 am and reported back at 4 pm to begin three swing shifts. This was called a quick turn. After the third swing, I got off at midnight and did a quick turn to the day Shift starting at 8 am. Following three day shifts I had the next four days off. Then I started all over again.

Mid-shift

The typical mid shift was usually boring. The most common mission was to flight-follow (watch) an EC-130 intelligence gathering airplane. This mission flew 12 hour flights back and forth on an east-west course just south of and parallel to the North Korean border. I would occasionally make a radio check with the pilot and act as a back-up to his navigation equipment to make sure he didn't stray off course (it never happened). During the World Series games, I kept the pilots informed of the scores. We were 14 hours ahead of US time, so a 2 pm game in the States would be 4 am in Korea. The pilots seemed to appreciate the attention. On rare occasions, we might briefly chat about something just to break the monotony, but mostly we maintained radio silence.

I realized just how boring this mission must be to the pilots when one night the pilot I was controlling made a very unusual request. He asked me to do a ground speed check on him. I made a black grease pencil mark on my scope to do the speed check and after three minutes I noted how far he had gone and multiplied the distance by 20 to obtain his groundspeed. In this case, I knew he was on his west bound leg and after three minutes he had moved three miles east. He was backing up in relation to his heading! It was easy to figure out what the bored pilot had done. On that particular evening there was an unusually strong wind out of the west, probably 120 or 130 knots, and the pilot had positioned himself so he was directly facing the wind. Then he lowered his flaps and started slowing until his plane was flying the same speed as the headwind. Playing along with him I asked what his heading was, then in a feigned incredulous voice my report was, *"You're going a negative 60 knots, and I'm glad I'm not paying for your gas. You're getting terrible mileage."* We both enjoyed a good laugh.

Late one night as most of Korea slept, I was monitoring my scope even though I didn't have anything to control when I heard a very faint transmission in English. I turned up the volume and listened more intently and was able to understand a request for anyone to respond. I made two-way radio contact with my late night guest and he explained he was a med-evac Army helicopter en route to a very remote Army post quite close to the North Korean border to pick up a medical emergency. It was a very dark, moonless night and he was hoping to get someone to follow his flight on radar. I asked his position and was dismayed when it turned out to be 160 miles to the east, practically across the country. The pilot was at two thousand feet and I couldn't believe I could even hear him at that altitude and distance. I held out almost no hope of painting him on radar. I expanded my scope and focused in on his reported position and was elated to pick up a small raw radar return every second or third sweep. When I asked the pilot if he was heading 030 degrees he enthusiastically responded that, yes, he was. I asked him to make a right turn for a minute and the raw radar return made a right turn. I responded with *"Radar contact."* When I told him that I was on the other side of the country, it was his turn to be incredulous. I flight-followed him to his destination where he said he'd be on the ground for a few minutes but he'd be back – and he was. I again flight-followed him all the way back to his home base.

As he reported to me, he found it spooky to be flying all alone that close to such a hostile country as North Korea on a dark night and he really enjoyed the company. I later attributed the long range pick-up to a thermal inversion which can allow radar energy to skip along between it and the earth. Under these conditions, line of sight radar can actually follow the curvature of the earth tremendously expanding the radar's range.

I actually looked forward to working my mid-shift on Fridays because that was the night we stripped the floors and re-waxed them. It was an opportunity to do something with my hands and I got to see immediate, tangible results. I got quite good with a heavy duty floor polisher and the Koreans were continually amazed that American officers would do manual labor or that we would be friends with our enlisted people and casually talk as equals with them.

Swing Shift

The swing shift was better than the mid shift because it was typically busier as well as shorter. There was usually an intercept training mission that flew during the early part of that shift. The swing shift also mopped up any flying activity that didn't finish during the day. But, the intercept mission was what I liked. Fletch and I were the only controllers, I think, that really truly enjoyed controlling. The others did it because it was their job, but without enthusiasm. The pilots quickly picked up on those who enjoyed controlling and Fletch or I were sometimes asked for by name to control their intercept missions.

One of the fighter units failed an Operational Readiness Inspection (ORI) because, even though they made their intercepts, they hadn't recorded enough of them with their scope cameras. In the heat of battle they simply forgot to turn them on. Fletch found out about this at the Osan Officer's Club bar from one of the unit's fighter pilots. From that moment on it became a standard call from us at Mangil San. When a pilot called 'Judy' (code word for taking over the intercept) we responded with, *"Roger, scope camera on."* How much aid that was for them, I could only guess but they passed their ORI remake.

Bubble Checks

It was the job of the day shift to take the briefing for the swing shift intercept mission. Often, if it sounded particularly challenging or if I knew the pilots, I stayed around an extra hour or two to run the mission. At the end of the mission if it had gone quite well and if the flight lead seemed quite pleased, I might tell them, *"Vectors to Mangil San are ------,"* when they were ready to go back to base. That was an unofficial invitation for a bubble check, a low altitude fly-by. There were many variations to the fly-by, but frequently it involved flying by in formation to 'visually check out' our radar bubbles. A bubble check was specifically against regulations but a low altitude visual check of the fabric covering our antennas seemed like a reasonable way around the rules. Thus, we were very discreet in our communications and we never voiced the term 'bubble check.'

After providing the implied invitation for a bubble check the pilot would usually reply in a deadpan manner, *"Roger."* Usually, however, this was followed by the flight turning towards our site. When this happened I called down to the folks at the cantonment area to give them a heads up. In a minute or two there would be 50 people outside sitting on the sandbag revetments waiting for the show to begin. Then I flight-followed them on the scope until they were a minute out. At that time I would announce, *"Sparrow (our call sign) will be off scope for a minute,"* and the pilots knew I was going outside to watch.

I saw some really spectacular bubble checks. One time an F-106 flew so low it looked like he actually flew between two of the antennas. He even rolled at the last minute making his wings 'knife-edge' to the antennas so they would fit between. I really suspect, though, that he was a few feet above the antenna. Another flight of F-102's came by in close formation. They had slowed as much as they possibly could and lowered gear and flaps for the fly by. We also had bubble checks by F-4s, F-100s and F-105s.

My favorite bubble checks, though, were given by the F-4's and maybe that influenced me four years later to choose the F-4 over other planes. The F-4 pilots liked to fly a low level route that began in Southern Korea and followed the western coast ending with a mock attack on our radar site. Perhaps this gave their show some legitimacy. If they stayed really low there was only one area, about 15 miles south of our site, where we could pick them up on radar as they climbed slightly to clear a high ridge. Regardless, they usually gave us a one-minute warning call so we could go outside to watch. What I typically saw was a dark green camouflaged F-4 at no more than couple hundred feet streaking towards us from across the valley. Approaching our hill, it would start pulling up and then the rear of the plane would glow orange as the pilot lit his afterburners. Within seconds the quiet would be shattered by a deafening roar as the plane screamed past the top of our hill climbing higher and higher until it was zooming straight up. Upon reaching the vertical, the pilot would do a victory (vertical aileron roll) roll.

I got into a little trouble with Major Cottrell one Saturday morning over a bubble check. I was on day shift but since it was a Saturday morning with nothing much going on, the day crew wasn't at work. I had an early morning intercept mission with two F-4's which finished at about 8:30 or 9 am. I gave the lead pilot vectors to Mangil San and when I observed the radar return begin moving in our direction I added, *"If you approach from 165 degrees you will overfly our compound. There are some sleepy heads down there that need a wake-up call."* They did just that and put on a show that would have made the Thunderbird Aerobatic Team jealous. For 10 minutes they attacked and re-attacked the cantonment area. Everybody just loved it - except Major Cottrell! I think even he secretly enjoyed the show, but felt it was his official duty to chew me out for the illegal demonstration of air power. He didn't call me to complain until AFTER the show. Bubble checks broke up the monotony for us and were a definite morale builder.

Day Shift

The day shift was a totally different story than the other two shifts. During the day shift on week days, the shift controller had company. The site commander, operations officer and the permanent day controller were also on duty. So were a couple more enlisted technicians, one of which was the top ranking master sergeant, the real brains of the entire operation. For most of my stay at Mangil San that man was MSgt Galbraith. On more than one occasion, it was his sage advice that saved the day for the commander. He was the expert on all of the numerous operations plans and exercise plans and, if he didn't know the answer, he knew where to quickly find it.

The Monday through Friday day shift involved virtually all of the war exercises as well as daily training. Whenever this work spilled over into a Saturday the larger crew was on duty then as well. The exercises alone were many -- over 300 a year. Most were small in scale but someone would have to read the plans anyway and be ready to support as required or tasked. Daily training involved flight-following close air support training missions that went to any of the many ranges in Korea, intercept training, flight-following intelligence gathering missions, flight-following when the President of Korea or other dignitaries flew somewhere, air refueling missions and, on occasion, Search And Rescue (SAR) missions. The day shift was a busy time and usually lunch was carried in and eaten at the scope.

I thought it a great opportunity to be able to work side by side with Koreans although I soon discovered that they operated by vastly different rules. This was especially evident when, for an unknown reason, I saw a ROKAF Major kick a ROKAF enlisted man down two flights of stairs. Fortunately, this was not a common occurrence, although a tremendous class structure was maintained between officers and enlisted personnel.

There was also a strict formality between ROKAF Officers of different rank. In the USAF at Mangil San we maintained a comparatively relaxed attitude between officers and enlisted. I don't know if this was due to being confined to the same close-in facilities at a remote location or because we worked very closely together with shift work or perhaps because we just wanted to contrast ourselves to the

ROKAF. Even so, MSgt Ken Galbraith always made sure his techs didn't get overly familiar with their junior officer controllers.

ROKAF

We were given very little guidance in how to deal with the Koreans but some of us learned the do's and don'ts early on. Many never did. There was a guard stationed along the road a quarter mile short of the radar site. He had a guard shack to provide him shelter but what a boring job his must have been. When we drove up the hill for the mid shift which began at midnight, we were slightly annoyed whenever we had to honk the horn to awaken the guard to open the gate. Once, one of those who never did learn how to deal with the Koreans, took the sleeping guard's rifle and opened the gate himself. When he got to the site he presented the rifle to the ROKAF commander causing a severe embarrassment.

We had a meeting early the next morning with our commander who sternly reprimanded the officer who perpetrated the foolish deed. We were told that under no circumstances would we cause the ROKAF to lose face and that the Korean guard as a minimum was probably severely beaten for embarrassing the ROKAF commander.

Choi Do Young

I made many friends in the ROKAF, mostly other lieutenants like myself, and they were all weapons controllers. One with whom I became particularly close was Choi Do Young. He came from a modest family in Seoul and was very extroverted. Do Young (in Korea the first name is the family name) worked straight days so when my breaks occurred on a weekend we would usually do something together. However, Do Young's weekend time wasn't always his to do as he wished. Do Young was not a very handsome person but he didn't know it. He had very high cheek bones and much more pronounced oriental features than most Koreans. When he smiled, though, he smiled with his whole face and the effect was infectious. Do Young loved to perform in front of people and was a talented comedian, an accomplished self-taught magician, and was skilled with a guitar. Because of this, he was in great demand at parties, especially by the ROKAF Officers' Wives Club. Many weekends found him traveling to Osan to perform.

When in Rome...

During one of my weekend breaks that coincided with a Korean holiday, I traveled to Seoul with Do Young. We took a bus for a few miles to the nearest train station and from there traveled by rail. The train stopped at every station along the way and the trip to Seoul took several hours.

We spent two nights and three days in Seoul. The first night, Do Young took me to the YMCA where I got a room not much larger than a walk-in closet. It had a bed and a small writing table in one corner but it had a good view of the downtown area of Seoul. The next morning, Do Young picked me up and we went to his old college campus where I met others of his friends and attended a social organization meeting of young people in the evening. Do Young taught me how to introduce myself in Korean which earned me a round of applause.

The second night I spent at Do Young's family's house. It was a very comfortable place consisting of many rooms, each leading to an outside walkway and a central courtyard. His family was very nice but understandably uneasy with an American house guest.

The next morning we boarded another train and returned to Mangil San. For an entire weekend, I hadn't spoken to a single American. I was truly the minority and it was a unique experience that I have never forgotten.

Four Day Breaks

The four day breaks were very welcome after eight steady days of working. Most of my breaks were spent at Mangil San relaxing, reading, 'bagging rays' in the summer, and hiking in the countryside. Occasionally, though, I would go to Osan AB. Travel was always a problem that usually determined when I would go. On lucky occasions, I caught a helicopter ride into Osan and if really lucky would also be able to return a couple days later by chopper. More often, though, the return would be in the front seat or even the cargo compartment of a 'six-by', a two and a half ton army supply truck (A six by referred to the typical 'army' all-purpose truck. Its cargo area measured six by six feet so the Air Force called it a six by. Its weight capacity was two and a half tons thus the Army called it a deuce and a half). We had several of the 6-by's in our site's motor pool and there were frequent trips made each week. If all else failed, there was always the train but that was the least desirable because the train station was about 15 miles south of Mangil San where one had to catch a bus for the final leg. The buses stopped running by late afternoon and making connections could be tricky.

A Train Ride of Note

During one of my breaks in the winter, I found I could get a ride in on the chopper but there was no planned transportation to get me back. I decided to chance it and hope that a supply run in a day or two would provide me with transportation home. My luck ran out. No trucks came in and, on the last day of my break, I took a cab to the train station outside Osan AB and purchased a ticket. I was fortunate to be able to get a first class ticket, which at times were hard to come by, and always required bribe money. This meant I would be guaranteed a seat and I wouldn't have to share it with chickens or pigs or other farm produce.

When the train arrived, I gratefully climbed aboard, took a seat and showed my ticket to the conductor who punched it. He replied with a smile, *"Mangil San?"* I answered that, yes, I was going to Mangil San and discovered he had already displayed his entire knowledge of English. I settled back in my seat, warm and cozy and prepared for the hour and a half trip to where I would catch my bus. It was mid-afternoon and I could comfortably catch the last bus of the day.

A few minutes later, or so it seemed to me, I felt my arm being shaken and when I opened my eyes I saw the conductor with a horrified look on his face. It took me a few seconds to collect my thoughts and remember where I was, and then I tried to understand what the conductor was so excited about. He kept saying something and pointing towards the rear of the train.

By now I was becoming alarmed because something was obviously wrong. The conductor finally motioned me to stay where I was and off he went. In 5 or 10 minutes we came into a town I didn't recognize and suddenly I became aware of my problem. I had missed the stop where I was supposed to get off. I very quickly began to review my options and I didn't really care for any of them. Before I could reach a full scale panic, my conductor was back. He grabbed my arm and we were off down the aisle. At the end of the car, we exited the train and were immediately met by a conductor from another train pointed in the direction from which we had just come. The two conductors exchanged words and I now found myself in the care of the new conductor. With my new conductor close at my side, we soon were headed back the way we had just come. In 15 minutes, the train stopped at my destination and my new conductor saw me off the train. *"Kom op sum ham nida,"* I said thanking him for his help. He had a pleased look on his face but I suspect he was glad to see the last of the 'ko kun sallam' (Korean slang for Americans and translates to big nose man).

I had missed the last bus! What was I going to do now? The early twilight of winter was settling in and the village lights began winking on. It was much too far to Mangil San to walk, especially in winter. Then, I spotted a taxi. In this small town finding a taxi was a minor miracle! In a minute, I was happy as can be, sitting in the soft seat of his wonderfully warm taxi and the driver was beside himself with his good fortune; a fare all the way to Mangil San with a 'rich' American. I can't remember what the fare was but I know I gladly paid it. After a half hour of bouncing along the rough country road to Mangil San, I gratefully spotted the brightly lit gates in the distance. Never had Mangil San felt so much like home.

I didn't leave Mangil San for all of my breaks. It was nice to just spend four days relaxing. Soon after my arrival, I became aware that the best stereo components in the world were made in Japan and that these components were incredibly cheap to those of us stationed in Korea. I quickly began to educate myself on stereos and designed the stereo system I wanted and could most afford. Within three months, I had purchased an amplifier, a set of speakers and a tape deck. I was in business. My next door neighbor in the dorm was Capt. Al Yashioka from Hawaii. Al's parents owned a music store and he brought with him his entire collection of 200 stereo LP albums. Al always left his door unlocked so we could record his albums to our tape reels and I did just that on many of my breaks. During my stay at Mangil San, I recorded over a hundred hours of music mostly from Al's collection.

Library Officer

An additional duty that I welcomed was library officer. The library was in the NCO Club in a room about the size of a small bedroom. Our library was a branch of Osan

Air Base's library and each month received many boxes of books to put on display. Some were brand new paperbacks that were non-accountable (disposable) and others were on loan for a specified time period. There was also a monthly list of books to send back to Osan. Accountability for books was a major problem and running the library I decided wasn't necessarily done 'by the book.'

On my first break, I traveled back to Osan and stopped by the main library requesting a crash course on running and maintaining our branch. The librarian was thrilled. Someone charged with running a library was asking her for advice on how to do it. Now that I knew the basics, I focused on my second problem, finding someone to run it on a daily basis. I had inherited a young Korean man with the job, but he could speak only rudimentary English. He had to go. The applicants for the new position included a Korean lady, Miss Chong. She was quiet but was fluent in English and was a good reader. She easily got the job. Then, I convinced our finance office at Osan to find the money to send Miss Chong to Osan for a week long school on library management. With civil engineering agreeing to make more book shelves, I obtained approval to move the library to a larger room where we could even move in a reading couch.

Our library was finally in great shape. Miss Chong did a superb job managing it and once a month I scoured the barracks for overdue books to send back during the book rotation. Some months later, someone on the library staff at Osan suggested I have Miss Chong apply for a civil service job. She did, and it was approved giving her a sizeable increase in pay plus benefits and job security should the Mangil San library ever be closed.

The Officer's Lounge

When I first arrived at Mangil San, all officers were honorary members of the only club, the NCO club annex. The annex was nice but the younger enlisted kids were very aware of the officers so we felt we had to be constantly setting the example. Now and then, especially on a Friday night, some of the officers didn't especially feel like doing that.

One Saturday morning as several of us were sitting around, a collective idea emerged that would solve our problem. We would make our own officers' lounge. We investigated the supply building and determined that, with some reorganizing, we could clear out an area large enough for our lounge. With the site commander's concurrence, we consolidated the supply materials into one side of the building, found a source of two by fours and plywood from civil engineering and by day's end had roughed out our lounge. Someone found a counter that fit across the width of the room – a perfect bar. Others located paneling and materials for a false ceiling and one of our Army officers returned from Osan with lounge furniture and a slate billiards table. We pooled our ration cards to buy a stock of liquor and beer, which could be purchased very inexpensively at Osan Air Base.

The lounge was especially nice for shift workers. Many times my technician, Jimmy Ellis, and I would finish the swing shift and get back to the compound at midnight only to find the day workers had all gone to bed. With the lounge, we had somewhere to unwind over a drink or two and play pool. We also now had a facility where we could invite our ROKAF officer friends.

One Friday night, things really got carried away. A bunch of guys got quite drunk and began throwing drinks at each other. This escalated into empty bottles getting smashed on the floor. I was on 'mids' and heard that Major Cottrell, our operations officer and acting commander at that time, had declared the lounge permanently closed. When I got off the hill, I went immediately into the lounge and couldn't believe my eyes. Never had I seen such a mess. Jimmy Ellis and I spent two or three hours cleaning it all up – we even waxed and buffed the floor.

I went over to Major Cottrell's dorm room hoping to bring him to reason. I requested a second chance for the misguided officers but I could see he was still mighty upset and not about to budge. When I mentioned that the lounge was cleaned and gleaming, he began to soften. After an on-the-spot inspection he gave us the lounge back but with a stern warning. Things never got out of hand again. I also felt that Major Cottrell had made a quick rash, emotional decision and was looking for a way out of it. He spent as much time in the lounge as anyone.

Jin Dahl Lea, Herald of Spring

During the spring, I discovered just how beautiful a country Korea really was. Shortly after the last snow melted and before the leaves reemerged on the trees, a low shrub called the jin dahl lea, burst into bloom to herald the coming warm weather. The treeless hill sides around Mangil San from a distance appeared to be bare, but were almost completely covered with the jin dahl lea bushes. When the red azalea-like blossoms burst into being, the countryside turned red practically overnight.

Before the jin dahl lea blossoms faded, the whole world turned different shades of green. The most beautiful green of all, though, was that of the newly sown rice plants. Many times I took walks in the spring enjoying the warm sun and the wonderful sights and sweet smells. In winter, Korea was one of the more forlorn looking places on earth but with the coming of spring there was no place lovelier.

Another pleasure of spring was dahl-ghe; strawberries. For only a few cents in outdoor restaurants or from vendors in the streets one could purchase a big bowl of delicious strawberries frosted white with sugar. Delicious!

FIGMO

FIGMO was an acronym which referred to a milestone in one's Korean tour – when he/she got their orders for their post Korea assignment. The orders usually came with about two months remaining. A Figmo calendar could be found in every dorm room. It was really a line drawing of a pretty lady who had been dissected into 396 numbered pieces. As each day passed the owner could fill in the appropriate numbered space and of course, on the last day of one's tour there would be a single piece remaining to fill in. I only filled my calendar on the first day of each break so I completed 12 spaces at a time. Time seemed to pass more quickly that way.

When I had only three spaces left on my calendar, I packed my bags (my hold baggage with stereo gear had already been crated and sent on) and caught a ride on a six by truck to Osan for final out-processing.

My plane left Kimpo airport in Seoul at 5 am. I checked on transportation from Osan to Kimpo and found that a shuttle bus ran about once each couple hours with the last leaving at 10 pm. My last evening I spent at the officer's club with friends and finally it came time to say good-bye and get to my bus. The trip to Seoul involved a stop at Yong San, the major army post in Korea, on the outskirts of Seoul. There weren't many people on the bus and when it pulled into Yong San everyone got off and the bus driver turned the engine off.

Curfew!

It was then that I discovered that the last bus didn't go on to Kimpo airport. When I explained my predicament to the Korean driver, he was very sympathetic but said he could not go to Kimpo airport because of the 'curfew.' In Seoul there was a curfew from midnight until 6 am. The bus driver suggested that I might be able to bribe a taxi driver to take me in spite of the curfew, so I called one. After a certain amount of haggling, we were, to my great relief, on our way. It was now after midnight and the wide, wide streets of Seoul were totally empty – except for us. Talk about an eerie feeling. We made great time on our way to Kimpo airport and my remaining four hours in the Land of the Morning Calm were boringly uneventful.

Hundreds of 'Retired Warriors', Part of the World's Largest Air Force

Chapter Four

The Air Force's Bone Yard

> *"If we need to eject I'll say 'eject, eject'. If you hear it a third time it's an echo." (F-4 pilot in his crew coordination briefing)*

Tucson Arizona

Traveling to our next assignment was unique. Jean wasn't eight months pregnant this time! We were very excited about the prospects of our new assignment to the 83rd Tactical Air Control flight. I knew almost nothing about the assignment, though. I vaguely knew where Tucson, Arizona was. Just the name filled me with a feeling of mystique thanks to Western TV shows about 'Tucson Territory.' A little research on the base informed me that Davis Monthan AFB was the storage site for retired aircraft, the bone yard. As for the 83rd Tactical Air Control flight, I had no idea what its mission was or even what a 'flight' was. In fact, a year earlier, when I was assigned to the 727th Tactical Air Control Squadron, the 83rd didn't exist.

It was the end of October, 1969, when we arrived on base after a long drive from Poplar, Wisconsin. We checked into the Temporary Living Quarters (TLQ) where we stayed for a few days until we found a nice house to rent. I signed in at my new unit, but was told that the entire organization was deployed out in the desert. I also discovered that the organization consisted of about five officers and about 30 enlisted personnel, the highest ranking being senior master sergeant. I was quite surprised at how small the unit was.

We found Tucson to be an absolutely enchanting place. The city was a very nice size; not too large but enough to offer big city conveniences and amenities. Tucson is built in a valley. To the north, lies the Catalina Mountain range. The highest peak, Mount Lemon, is capped with a white covered radar antenna and is visible from anywhere in Tucson. In the winter it is also capped with a white crown of snow.

A Sunday Trip Up Mount Lemon

During our first Sunday in Tucson, we felt the urge to explore our new homeland so Jean and I decided we would drive up to Mount Lemon. It was a bright, sunny and hot day. We purchased a map from a gas station and were delighted to find a hard surfaced road led up from the back (west) side and another from the front. We decided we would circle around to the west and come up from that direction. From the peak, it would be a short journey down the front side and then back home.

We packed for an afternoon outing and strapped Jill and Becky (two and one years old respectively) into their car seats in our old '63 Ford and off we went. Although it was October, the day was hot. It took about an hour and a half to circle around the base but with the help of our map, we soon found the road leading up the back side of the mountain. The road was steep in places and very winding, but in good shape and we were in high spirits anticipating the welcome coolness of 10,000 foot Mt Lemon. Our trusty Ford was handling the job admirably.

It was then that the pavement stopped! We abruptly found ourselves on a gravel road and not a very wide one at that. We rechecked the map and it clearly depicted a hard surfaced road all the way to the top. Fortified with the thought that the early pioneers wouldn't have quit at such a minor setback, we forged ahead. Soon, however, we noticed that all of the cars we were meeting were high wheel, 4-wheel drives and off-roaders. As they passed, the drivers of these large vehicles gave us prolonged stares. What could that be about? At this point, the car hit a high spot in the road and bottomed out. By the deafening noise, I knew immediately that something had happened to the muffler. I pulled over and a quick peek under the car revealed that it had slipped off the tail pipe. To make matters worse, it was slanted forward making it impossible to just drag it along beneath the car. I backed up until the tires on one side were resting on the ridge of gravel left by the last grader. This allowed me to slip under the side of the car and, with much effort, I was able to slide the muffler back onto the tail pipe. Oh, was I dirty - and more than just a little thirsty. But, we were fixed and moving again. Forward ho and onward towards our destination, Mt Lemon. Adversity be damned.

Half a mile later, the muffler came off again. I repeated the repair but this time I noticed it was easier to slip the muffler back onto the tail pipe. This was bad news. The muffler was bending backwards and soon wouldn't stay on the tail pipe at all. After another half mile, it came off again. By now, Jill and Becky had tired of the loud muffler game and were crying. My temper was getting shorter and shorter and Jean was becoming very silent. I kept on driving. Somewhere on the backside of Mt. Lemon is a '63-Ford muffler and tail pipe assembly.

The remaining trip up the narrow, steep, gravel road was very loud and, as we approached cars, I vaguely remember slouching down a bit hoping they wouldn't get a good look at this foolish gringo. When we got to the top we found some cold water to drink and immediately resumed our journey uneventfully down the front side - a beautiful paved road. Being mostly in idle on the downward journey the car was only rumbling now and when we got back to the TLQ I couldn't wait to turn off the engine and be done with all that noise.

The next week, after getting the muffler replaced, we located a lovely house to rent and soon were all moved in and settled.

An Overview

Many things happened during our almost two and a half year stay in Tucson. Most were good. Our two little girls grew from babies to preschoolers. Somehow, some way, Jean found time to work a half time position with the Head Start program. She had earned her master's degree during my year in Korea and was now putting it to use as a psychometrist. My sister, Karen, came out to visit us and we talked her into transferring to the University of Arizona for her senior year. While there, Karen met and married Mack McCord. One Sunday afternoon, we bought a camper trailer on impulse, which we used a lot for camping in the Chiricahua mountains and at Organ Pipe National Monument. Two or three times we even went into Mexico to camp at Puerto Pinasco on the Gulf of California - primitive but beautiful. Another Sunday afternoon, again on impulse, we bought a four-bedroom house. We had nice visits from family and friends and sadly, Jean's Dad was killed in a tragic car accident back in Wisconsin. I was also selected for pilot training.

Karen Transfers to the U of A

Karen's staying with us in Tucson was a high point of our assignment. She liked the University of Arizona and we vicariously enjoyed her senior year. She was greatly pleased by how many of her credits from the University of Wisconsin - Eau Claire transferred. In fact, I don't think she lost anything. Karen kept things interesting. She became a sister to Jean, and a wonderful aunt to Jill and Becky. She took lessons from a very interesting and gifted guitarist and did a lot of fun outdoors type things with a friend we called Dickie-poo. She met Mack, fell in love and married him in the Base Chapel. I had the supreme honor of giving her away and we had a really nice reception in our back yard.

The Needle

A prominent geographical feature of Tucson's skyline as you looked toward Mt Lemon was a tall stand-alone rock that was silhouetted against the sky. It was well known by climbers and hikers as the needle. Karen and Dick climbed partway to the needle one weekend and, upon Dick's urging, I agreed to go along with him on a journey to the top. We got an early start one Saturday morning, drove the car as far into the foothills as possible and then set off on foot climbing through one ravine after another. We were following a well-defined trail since this was a popular hike, but my ideas of an easy hike were soon proven wrong.

From a distance, what seemed to be small rock boulders that filled the ravines we were climbing up turned out to be chunks of rock the size of small houses. These obstacles took a lot of time and energy to climb around and our trip to the needle took much longer than we anticipated. We did make it... to the base, that is. The needle itself was perhaps another hundred or so feet of sheer vertical rock. Pitons protruding from its vertical surface were evidence that some well-equipped, skilled climbers had gotten all the way to the top but that wasn't for us.

By now it was mid-afternoon so we quickly ate our lunches and finished the last of our canteen water. Our trip back down was mostly in silence. We were both quite thirsty and were thinking of a cold drink that would be our reward upon getting back to the car. Looking back on the adventure, we hadn't planned very well and underestimated the amount of water we would require on a very warm Arizona day.

Had either of us been injured ... well, we hadn't much planned for that either. We met no other climbers on that day.

Many years later, on a commercial flight to San Diego I noticed the Tucson valley coming into view out the left side of the plane. It was a cloudless day with terrific visibility. From my lofty perch, I was able to pick out the back-side road we had driven on so many years before and with delight I noticed I could even pick out the needle, now silhouetted against the purplish haze of the valley.

The Bone Yard

Davis-Monthan AFB is where old and outdated aircraft from all of the Services go to be retired and eventually salvaged. When we got to DM, anyone with a base sticker on their auto could drive up and down the miles of roads that outlined and crisscrossed the storage area. This trip became a routine event for all of our visitors. I never tired of driving past rows and rows of B-52s, B-47's, P-51s, C-54s, C-118s, miles of camouflage painted Army helicopters, orange and white Navy fighters, and countless other types of aircraft. Because of Tucson's year-around low humidity, the aircraft could be stored indefinitely there with minimal deterioration. The openings were all sealed, all liquids were drained, and all glass surfaces were covered with a white plastic type compound.

Decommissioned B-52s in the Desert

Occasionally, some aircraft were taken out of 'mothballs' and given a new lease on life, perhaps with another country's military or even with the Forestry Service. Unfortunately for us unofficial tour guides, the free wanderings among the airplanes came to an end when late one night someone dismantled and stole a tail machine gun from a B-52.

The Tactical Control Flight

Because of the small size of my unit, I found it was a very close-knit one where everyone knew everyone else quite well and first names were used frequently. The unit was so new, it was still being filled in with people and within a year we would have about 9 or 10 officers and about 40 enlisted people. I got to know all of the officers very well and many were very colorful individuals!

An Officer Named Ken

I will remember some of the other people in the 83rd for a long time. We had a really interesting mixture of personalities but we all got along well and worked well together. The only person with whom I maintained contact in later years was Ken Ray.

Ken was a good hearted person of my height and build, but one had to understand Ken to appreciate him. He was an only child and a product of a rural home in the south. To put it bluntly, Ken never learned how to anticipate how a remark or action might affect others and because of this was disliked by many. Ken was very kind hearted, however, and he especially liked my sister, Karen. She respected him but was careful to not do anything that he might misconstrue.

Ken was a hard worker and liked to collect additional duties. His ambitions resulted in such a long list of duties that he really couldn't do justice to any of them. When I arrived at the 83rd, our radar was broken and we weren't expecting to get the needed part for many months. No one seemed interested in assigning me any duties, and with little to do, I finally pried administrative officer and security officer away from Ken. He retained training officer and many other lesser jobs.

The Commander, Jerry Berner

The original commander was Major Jerry Berner. Jerry was a grounded navigator and very experienced in the Air Force. I am sure his job as the first commander of a newly created unit was a difficult one. I liked Jerry very much and greatly respected him because of the wings he wore on his uniform. At that time I knew very little distinction between navigators and pilots. Jerry's wife was also very experienced in the ways of the Air Force. Her name was Verna and she organized and ran the unit's wives club. Because of the small size of our unit, the social structure included all of the wives whether their husbands were officer or enlisted. Also, largely through Verna's efforts, we had a very active bridge group at Tucson.

Don't Ask, Don't Tell! Billy Thomas

When Major Berner was reassigned to Germany, his replacement was a senior captain, Billy Thomas. Billy was also an interesting person. He was effective as a commander and the unit prospered under his leadership. Billy was short but of average build. He had a friendly personality and did not relish disciplining problem airmen.

Billy had feminine mannerisms and we all suspected he was gay because he always had male roommates. From Billy's occasional comments, we were quite sure they didn't help pay the rent. Billy had also been seen coming out of known homosexual bars. One Monday morning, he came to work with a bullet hole through the top of his yellow Barracuda sports car. As Billy explained it, he stopped to pick up a hitch-hiker and, when the guy got in on the passenger side, he immediately pulled a pistol and tried to shoot Billy in the head. Billy said he deflected the gun just as it went off and he vacated the car... on all fours. Our speculation was that perhaps he said something to the hitch-hiker revealing that he was gay and set his 'guest' off. Billy reported the incident to the police and they found his abandoned car the next morning. No arrest was ever made.

I reemphasize that Billy was a good commander and we all respected him. We accepted his probable gay situation as a fact of life that didn't interfere with his job performance. Interestingly, when I was learning to fly the F-4 a year after I left the 83rd, Captain Thomas' name came up again. Two men from the Office of Special Investigation (OSI) asked me several very leading questions but I didn't take the bait. In exasperation, they finally came right out and asked me if I knew if he was homosexual. I replied that, although Capt Thomas had feminine mannerisms, I had no knowledge that he was gay and that he did a very good job as my commander. I later learned that he was prematurely discharged from the Air Force but I don't know on what grounds.

The John Smiths

We had two John Smiths and both were captains. One was tall, lean, slow moving and perpetually pessimistic. In fact he even had a drooping mustache to match his sad demeanor. He was also a bachelor. The other John Smith was the opposite in every respect. He was short (and lean), very active and positive if not hyper. He maintained a very scandalous life style, for that time, in that he lived with his girlfriend for a while before they finally became married. This John also always had a deal of one sort or another going on and I sometimes thought he was skirting trouble with the law. We also suspected that he was into smoking pot.

The Other Officers

We had another bachelor, Gregg, who was the epitome of happy go lucky and living right on the edge of the law. His nemesis was gambling. Every day he would bring in his sports newspapers so he could figure which teams would likely win in coming games. After computing how much he thought they would win or lose by (the point spread), he would call in his bets to his bookie.

David Kalberg was a more normal officer who arrived at the unit after I had been there for about a year. David and his wife, Joanie, were from Montana, and if you were to imagine how an academy graduate who played football might look like, you might conjure up a picture of David. David and Joanie were very sociable and they played bridge.

Terry Speer and his wife also were bridge players. Terry was one of the original officers in the unit and, although a junior lieutenant, he was one of the most capable of the unit's officers. Terry was the mobility officer and the supply officer. Both were time consuming and very important jobs.

Rich Stieg was another married officer who was an especially valuable member of the 83rd. Like Kalberg, he was a younger lieutenant. Rich and his wife, Kathy, were very outgoing. Terry was tall and lean, wore glasses and always had a smile on his face. I believe they were bridge players but my most vivid memory of them was a fabulous party they gave with oil, cheese and chocolate fondues. What a delightful spread.

Hank English was one of the few officers who was senior to me in rank. He became the operations officer after his arrival. Hank and his wife, Ann, were very pleasant people. Hank's biggest problem as operations officer was that he wasn't very stern. He didn't want to make unpopular decisions and this led to trouble for Hank after I left for pilot training.

John Quinn, a late arrival to the unit, but close in rank to me, came from an assignment in Thailand. On his way to Davis Monthan, he traveled to Germany where he purchased a bright red sports car, a Porsche Targe. It was his pride and joy. After his arrival, his Thai wife, Shawalee, joined him. Shawalee was a quiet but very pleasant young lady. By coincidence John and I were to be accepted to pilot training for the same class at Laredo AFB.

Carl was one of the more controversial and colorful officers we had. He talked a great story but bit by bit we were to find out that many of his accounts were made up or greatly exaggerated. I learned that at his previous assignment at Clark AB in the Philippines, he had been caught wearing ribbons and medals on his uniform that he hadn't earned. This was quite typical behavior for Carl. He was married to a Panamanian girl who was very nice but he treated her very poorly. He shocked everyone in the office once when he showed a photo of his wife naked from the waist up. He laughingly explained that he had told her the camera didn't have any film. She deserved much better than Carl.

Last but not least was Lieutenant Dick Farnell, our maintenance officer. He was a tech school trained maintenance officer and the only officer who wasn't a weapons controller. Dick was a Chemistry major in college and was very in touch with nature. He loved camping and hiking - and he dated my sister, Karen, for many months. In fact, we were hoping some 'chemistry' might happen between the two of them, but, alas, it was not meant to be. They were the best of friends and did a lot of fun things together. They were buddies but that was all. We liked Dick (affectionately known as Dickie-poo) and to Jill and Becky he was like an uncle, a very frequent visitor to our home.

Maintenance Section

Our maintenance section, which comprised about three quarters of the personnel in the unit, was run by SMSgt Baldwin, a tall, balding and highly capable NCO whom I'm sure did not want to be in such an odd outfit. My future brother-in-law, SSgt Mack McCord, was a radar technician who worked for Sgt Baldwin. In fact, Sgt Baldwin was very much against Mack dating the sister of an officer. It was too close to 'fraternization' with officers, a constant problem with many of our younger enlisted men and our young officers due to the small size of the 83rd.

Maintenance was comprised of radar maintenance, vehicle maintenance, radio maintenance, power production and crypto. Every piece of our equipment was designed to be transported by two and a half ton trucks (six by's) so we had a fleet of almost 30 vehicles. Everyone had to know how to drive.

The 83rd Mission

The organization was located off on one side of base close to the end of the flight line in an old World War II wooden two- story barracks. The radar equipment and 20 or so vehicles were kept on the far side of the runway and, to run missions, meant a mile drive around the end of the runway. This really was quite convenient. At times we wanted a real-time update on the status of a late flight of fighters. All we had to do was open the door and look out towards the runway. Many times our flight would be lining up for takeoff and a few minutes later would be checking in on the radio ready to 'play' – run intercepts.

Operation Intercept

The 83rd Tactical Control Flight, shortly after its formation, was pressed into service in support of a US Customs drug interdiction mission called 'Operation Intercept.' For six months, the unit's radar and other equipment were deployed at a very remote location between Tucson and the Mexican border. There it could spot drug smugglers as they tried to illegally fly into the US from Mexico. Because these light aircraft can fly at extremely low altitude, 10 or 20 miles of separation from the 83rd radar would sometimes be sufficient to avoid detection.

Although I arrived towards the end of this period and never traveled to the deployed location, I learned that occasionally the 83rd would successfully detect and run an intercept on a drug smuggler. The program was finally considered not worth the expense and was curtailed.

The 84th TCF and 726th TCS

The 83rd had a sister flight, the 84th TCF, located in Phoenix at Luke AFB. Both flights belonged to the 726th Tactical Control Squadron, also at Luke AFB. At Tucson, we enjoyed an autonomy and isolation that the 84th greatly envied. Because of the 200 miles that separated us from our parent squadron, we weren't very often bothered by them and were usually left to our own devices. We relished our independence and learned to make-do and improvise rather than call for help.

Training

Weapons controllers had semi-annual training requirements. These included running a certain number of live intercepts. We also had to run a required number of simulator intercepts. The simulator requirement had been created with the assumption that all units had an intercept simulator. In reality, the squadrons had the simulators but we didn't. At first, we requested waivers to this training requirement since it would be impractical and expensive for all of us to travel to Phoenix to fulfill it. This worked for a while until some officers at our parent squadron headquarters became jealous of the disparity. They found a way to get our waiver revoked and we were no longer able to escape the grueling and highly disliked simulator duties.

One of our more enterprising officers, Karl Schmidt, came up with a brilliant solution to our simulator problems. He went over to the F-4 simulator at our base and talked with the wing's F-4 fighter training squadron about letting us help them train their pilots in F-4 simulators. Their pilots had a requirement to fly intercepts in an F-4 simulator and we had a requirement to run simulator intercepts so an agreement was reached where we could help each other. We loved being able to work in the F-4 simulator since we could avoid the long drive to Phoenix. The wing instructor pilots loved it because we took over a task they disliked doing themselves. Needless to say, this innovative solution to our simulator requirements only incensed certain officers at the 726th TCS.

The 726th was also jealous of us because we had a better radar than they did; it was more reliable and even had longer range. Their ill feelings weren't improved by the excellent relationship we had with our wing or by our having many more intercept missions to work with. One day we were talking among ourselves and someone suggested that we contact the Marines at Yuma Air Station to see if they might have a need for radar control. We did and they did. Now we had even more business, so much that the 726th squadron had to send many of their controllers to us to get intercept training.

Our equipment was very rugged and mobile. We had three vans that were required plus supporting generators. A '53' van housed the communications equipment. Another van called the TSQ-61, housed two radar control scopes and associated equipment. A third van held the radar equipment. All three vans could be transported on the backs of trucks, so they weren't very big. The inside of the control van was a crowded workspace, with two sets of controllers and technicians attending their respective radar scopes. Our equipment, because of our mission, was designed for rapid mobility. Exercises we were involved in required us to tear down the equipment, pack it up and be on the road within a short period of time. Then, we would convoy to our designated location and set up again.

Deployment to Nevada

Our largest deployment was to the top of Mormon Mesa about 50 or so miles to the north of Las Vegas. We were assigned to the 'blue' forces in an exercise and it was our job to help our assigned 'blue' fighters defend our territory. During the deployment to our mesa, everything went without incident. We found our deployed location and began the set-up process. By nightfall, we were on the air with our radar but still had to set up tents and other support structures.

Our campsite was a bustle of activity. I had my 'B-4' bag filled with my personal gear (including a brand new fishing pole) sitting on the ground out of harm's way, or so I thought. When I later went to retrieve the bag, I found that it had been run over by a truck. My pole and many other items were ruined. After the exercise, I submitted a claim and the Air Force paid me for the damage. As it turned out, I never had time to go fishing anyway.

The Sheriff Visits

The next morning, we were visited by the local sheriff. We were in his neck of the woods and he wanted to know what we were all about. The sheriff was given a tour of the compound and equipment by our commander, Capt Thomas, and when he idly commented about how great military C rations were for hunting trips, Capt Thomas very wisely insisted that the sheriff take two cartons (two dozen meals). Before he left, the Sheriff welcomed all of us to his small town of Overton, population 520, which was about three miles away down off the mesa. He said he would make sure the local VFW hall would be open for us every night for as long as we were deployed. He remained true to his word. We were all friends of the Sheriff and on about the third or fourth day of our two-week stay he even took his colored TV out of his living room and insisted that we use it. Of course we set it up in the officers' and senior NCO's tent (our tents were quite large and could comfortably hold 24 cots). We became nightly visitors to the VFW hall and were treated like royalty.

R & R Las Vegas Style

While we were deployed so close to Las Vegas, Capt Thomas really went out on a limb for his troops by saying that everyone would have a chance to go to Vegas on one evening. We set up a schedule and each night, four people would climb into the designated Vegas jeep and off we would go. I had seen pictures of Las Vegas but I just wasn't prepared for what I found. We wandered up and down the strip taking in the sights of the famous casinos. The lights I found were by far the most impressive. To look up and down the strip was a dazzling display of millions of light bulbs and neon lights of every description. I wisely carried only a small amount of money with me that night and sure enough, at the end of the evening it was all gone - slowly attrited by the various schemes of gambling for unrealistic dreams of 'winning'!

Oh, Home On the Mesa

Life on top of the mesa was pleasant except for one thing -- the wind was always blowing so sand was everywhere. It was much like living in a desert. We even found a sidewinder rattlesnake one day and it provided a vivid demonstration of how it got its name. Living amidst the sand was terrible, tough, and relentless. It was impossible to keep tent flaps adequately closed to keep the wind and sand out.

We had portable buildings that consisted of arches over which rolls of canvas were stretched. The ends were made up of wooden sections and the flooring was made from 4 foot by 8 foot by 1-foot thick box halves. The box halves, when mated together, stored all of the pieces of the building. This small-size building was called an S-48 shelter and a large one, measuring 24 feet by 36 feet, was an S-80 shelter.

We hated putting up these structures, but with an experienced team of a dozen men, the task was more unpleasant to think about then to actually do.

Shortly after we got settled in, I had a creative idea to solve the problem of sand blowing into our tent. Knowing that one of the small buildings wasn't being used, I retrieved its end door and door frame structure and lashed it to the end of our tent. After it was tied in place I folded back the tent flaps and we now had a wooden door to keep the sand out. Everyone thought it was a great idea and it made living a whole lot more comfortable.

Exercise Operations

Our controlling work consisted of doing practice intercepts and flight-following prior to the exercise. Once the exercise began, we were on 24-hour shift work doing radar surveillance whenever we didn't have other controlling to do. Once we got into the groove, though, the work was more tedious than hard - until the last day.

Midair

I had just finished my shift about midmorning and, as I was climbing into my sleeping bag, someone came running into the tent to announce there had been a mid-air collision between two fighters. A mid-air collision was the most dreaded nightmare of a controller. We had always been trained that it was our absolute responsibility to keep planes from running into each other. After becoming a pilot, I found out that all responsibility really rests with the person who signed for the plane - the pilot, although a controller could also be punished for not following proper separation of aircraft procedures.

When I arrived at the '61 van' I discovered that Hank English, our operations officer and the guy who relieved me, was controlling an F-106 that was intercepting an 'enemy' F-4. At the final part of the intercept, when the F-106 was strictly visual, he attempted to buzz the F-4 by flying in front of it. He misjudged the set-up and sheared off the nose of the F-4. The F-4 pilot and the Weapons System Officer (WSO) ejected immediately and were unhurt. The F-106 was so badly damaged that the pilot was unable to land and had to eject in the controlled bail-out area at Nellis AFB near Las Vegas.

I must confess my primary thoughts were first, thank goodness I wasn't on scope; and second, poor Hank. Within a couple hours a helicopter arrived at our radar site to transport Hank to Nellis AFB. An interim accident investigation board questioned him extensively and had him submit a lengthy statement. Since that was the last day of the exercise, we began tearing down and packing up for the redeployment.

We had decided that we wouldn't be seeing Hank for a long time and maybe they would even court-marshal him. But, as we were climbing into our vehicles to start redeploying, a jeep came driving up and out climbed Hank with a big grin on his face. He had been completely exonerated from wrongdoing and was released to go back home.

The Collateral Board

A month later, back at DM I was to learn a lesson that I never forgot for the remainder of my Air Force career; do not testify before a collateral accident investigation board.

An accident investigation board is convened immediately after all serious aircraft accidents, especially those that result in a death. The rules are set up in such a manner as to allow the real facts to be freely given without fear of punishment. This is because the Air Force, above all else, wants to understand the true causes of accidents. Any information that is discovered by the accident investigation board is considered non-releasable for any purpose other than accident prevention. The board's goal is to determine what went wrong and what can be done to prevent future accidents. It has no interest in determining fault for the purpose of punishing.

I was to find out later that a collateral board is quite the opposite. This board is usually composed of one full colonel with maybe a helper or two; and its only purpose is to find fault with intentions of punishment. None of the accident board's findings are releasable to the collateral board so the latter must independently conduct its investigation. Because of this, the collateral board has no subpoena power and testifying before it is completely voluntary. In fact, it is common knowledge to career Air Force personnel that the collateral board is out to hang someone. There is no stigma in refusing to testify before it.

The flight received a notice from, I'll call him *Colonel Hyde*, president of the collateral board, asking anyone with knowledge of the accident to contact him. Against the advice of others, and confident that neither I nor any of my fellow controllers was responsible, I stepped forward to see if I could be of service.

I was given an interview time that was right after lunch. I reported 10 minutes early. *Colonel Hyde* was waiting and I found him to be tremendously charming and interested in me. He explained that the court recorder wasn't back from lunch yet and he began to ask me about my personal life in a very friendly manner. How long had I been in the Air Force? Where was I from? How did I end up joining the Air Force etcetera. I even told him that I had an application in for pilot training.

A few minutes later, with me fully at ease and greased for talking, the recorder arrived and, with her face pressed against a mask, she began to verbally record our conversations. Without any warning, my friendly 'Colonel Hyde' turned into 'Colonel Jekyll.' He became accusatory, insulting and very aggressive. He accused me and the other controllers of controlling intercepts forward of an exercise 'no-fly' line. This, and other of his accusations were untrue. I felt like he was trying to break me down. Then I remembered someone back at the flight telling me that testifying was voluntary, so I stood up, excused myself to the colonel, and I walked out. As I left, I heard him shout after me that I was "the poorest excuse he had ever seen for an officer." I will remember those words for the rest of my life. In my mind, I learned more about his nature than he learned of mine, and what I saw wasn't very complimentary. I also decided that the recorder's late arrival had probably been prearranged.

When I returned to the flight, I related what had happened and received a couple, *"I told you so's."* Upon my news, a second controller scheduled to testify later in the afternoon immediately cancelled out. When I got home that afternoon, Jean knew immediately that something awful had happened. It was weeks before I was finally able to put this experience behind me.

Pilot Training – Going After a Dream

An Air Force career became more and more of a goal for me while at Davis Monthan, but I knew that, if I was to spend a career in the Air Force, I needed to be a pilot. Pilots were what the Air Force was all about. The Air Force revolved around its pilots and the pilots made it all happen. With that in mind it was only natural to apply for pilot training.

The time was late fall, 1971 and we were still stationed at Davis Monthan, AFB in Tucson. I had recently celebrated my 28th birthday while the Vietnam war was still being waged although Henry Kissinger was very much involved with the 'Paris peace talks' as America tried to find an honorable way to extricate itself from a very unpopular war.

I had recently seen a request by the Air Force for officers in my rank group to apply for pilot training and I knew that time was quickly running out for me to become a pilot. The age limit for beginning pilot training was 28 and one half. To even have a chance of realizing my impossible dream, I had to act immediately.

I went to the flight surgeon and scheduled the extensive entry physical and picked up the pilot training application paperwork at CBPO (Central Base Personnel Office). Within a couple weeks, I had obtained the required written recommendations and had my application package assembled. Following directions, I sent it by the Air Force courier to the Air Force Military Personnel Center (AFMPC) at Randolph AFB in San Antonio, Texas. There, my application began a lengthy journey through 'the channels of bureaucracy.' Because of several phone calls I had made to find out as much about the application process as I possibly could, I knew the route my application would take. I also knew that there was only one selection board meeting before my age limit expired.

Everything had to click and I made sure that it did. I made daily phone calls as I followed my application's progress. *"Have you seen an application for a Capt. Olson?....Oh, you have.... Good. When do you think your office will have it processed?"* And, *"What is the next office it will go to... and can I have a name over there of who will be processing it?"*

Twice, I discovered my application had been misrouted and was able to have it quickly relocated. Even so, my application just barely made it in time to the selection board. At this point, there was nothing to do but wait. After several days, I received a call from one of the board members asking if I would accept a navigator training slot. I responded that I wanted pilot training or nothing. More days of tense waiting followed. Lurking in my mind during this time, just a millimeter below the surface, was the incident with 'Col. Jekyll' at the collateral board. For the most part I had put the incident behind me but I had told the colonel that I had applied for pilot training. Was it possible that he could affect the outcome of my application? I didn't think so – but still...

Selected!

Finally, I received a call from Davis Monthan's CBPO personnel office. *"Captain Olson, you have been selected for pilot training. Can you come by our office and sign some paperwork? Your pilot training class begins in two months at Laredo AFB and we have a lot of work to do."* I was instantly elated, excited and scared. What was I letting myself in for? Where would this decision lead my life? My predominant feeling, however, was that I had passed a tremendous test and that I was starting a completely new phase of my life. I couldn't wait to tell Jean the news. I felt like I was floating on a cloud. I wanted to stop total strangers in the street and tell them, *"I've just been selected for pilot training."* I didn't of course.

News of my acceptance to pilot training quickly swept through the flight and I received numerous congratulations. A couple days later, another captain, John Quinn, was also selected and was also assigned to Laredo with the same starting date as me. I was selected to be section leader for section I and John was leader for section II. John wasn't a close friend of mine because we didn't share many common interests, but it felt good that I would get to Laredo knowing at least one person.

Chapter Five

Pilot Training - Laredo AFB, Texas

> *The only time you have too much fuel is when you're on fire.*

Moving – Again

The next two months were busy times. Our main concern was selling the house. Shortly after receiving notification of my selection, I was at the Officer's Club and just happened to strike up a conversation with a Lt. Col. F-4 navigator. I mentioned that I was leaving soon for pilot training. Somehow the conversation got around to our need to put our house on the market and he mentioned his wife, Tolva, was a licensed realtor. He asked if she could stop by and talk to us about our house. While I had some reservations about selecting a realtor in this manner, I said yes.

Five minutes after Tolva's arrival, all reservations were dispelled. She was a native Norwegian who met her husband while he was assigned to Norway in an advisory capacity. She spoke excellent English, was a charming person, and Jean and I immediately felt we could fully trust her.

To our relief, Tolva said our house would be very easy to sell because I had made so many nice improvements to it. She was referring to the fenced in yard, slump block fence pillars across the front, fully landscaped lawn and expanded and covered backyard patio. She quickly made arrangements for an open house and did all of the work herself. Our only job was to clean the house and find somewhere else to be on one Sunday afternoon. The house sold for our asking price in just a few days and we walked away with several thousand dollars of profit. While we hated to part with our first ever house, we did not want to face such an uncertain future with uncertain problems that might follow if we had rented it out. We also wanted to clear our VA loan.

My reporting date at Laredo was the end of February, 1972. We planned our departure from Tucson with enough time to take the scenic route. With camper in tow, the four of us set off for Laredo via the Big Bend National Park in southwest Texas.

En-route - Big Bend National Park

My memories of Big Bend are very skimpy. Perhaps the anticipation and excitement of pilot training dominated my thoughts.

I do remember, though, an after dark arrival and the wind blowing fiercely. As I was struggling to raise our pop-up camper, I was worried about damaging it until a kindhearted neighbor camper aided me. The next morning was the beginning of a lovely day, however. The landscape was breathtakingly beautiful and definitely worth the longer route we chose for our trip.

The name of the park, Big Bend, refers to where the border river, the famous Rio Grande, bends from a southerly direction back to the north before it again curves back to the south forming a distinctive feature in the outline of the state. With the river forming the southern boundary, the park includes the Chisos mountains that could be confused as being part of the Rockies except for their volcanic origin. The park, with peaks above 8,000 feet, was rich in dinosaur era fossils and geology.

Laredo AFB

At Laredo we found a very different town. We were in the minority because we didn't speak Spanish. However, the largely Hispanic people were friendly and the town was pretty. Laredo was a poor town with many gravel streets. It was situated right on the Mexican border with Nuevo Laredo (New Laredo) across the Rio Grande River. Many airbase people had live-in maids, young Mexican ladies, who worked for what we might pay our children in weekly allowance. The base was the major employer in the area and I have often wondered how the town survived when the base was later selected to be closed in the interests of saving defense dollars.

Air Training Command Patch

We quite quickly found a very nice 60-foot long mobile home to rent in a very lovely mobile home park on the north side of town. There were many pilots and student pilots living there because it was right off the interstate, an easy commute to work. Jean and the girls were most attracted to the large swimming pool next to the park's community center.

Pilot Training Wing

Laredo AFB had one pilot training wing consisting of four squadrons. One squadron provided training for the T-41 (Cessna 172) beginning trainer, and the remaining three squadrons were orientated to the T-37 primary jet trainer, the T-38 advanced jet trainer and academics. The T-37 and T-38 squadrons were each made up of eight flights, designated A through H. The squadron commander flew periodically with each of his flights. The flight was run by a flight commander usually a senior captain, and 9 or 10 instructor pilots of first lieutenant and captain rank. Attached to each flight for flying purposes were instructors from the academic squadron as well as other 'wing headquarters' pilots, whom we called wing weenies.

PILOT TRAINING – LAREDO AFB

A new pilot training class began with about 55 or 60 students divided into either section I or section II. The highest ranking student in each section was the section leader. Each section was assigned to a particular flight in a squadron, so each squadron of eight flights would really have four classes of students. When we began academics, the most senior class was close to finishing their training in the sleek white T-38. The class ahead of us was well into T-37s and the one in front of them was starting in T-38s. At any given time, a pilot training wing had four classes spread out through three different types of trainer aircraft. The pressure was extraordinary to graduate on-time no matter what, because the next class was coming regardless.

UPT Class 73-06

Pilot training classes were given sequential numbers with the first two digits representing the year. Our class was 73-06. We were the 6th UPT class in the whole Air Force to start training during 1973. An early project for each class was to devise a class patch. Most were very colorful cartoon characters but we chose a very stark black and white patch that simply said, "73-06." Our patch was easily identified, even from quite a distance.

73-06 Class Patch

Flying Training in a Nutshell

Pilot training consisted of three broad categories of training: flying training, simulator training and academic training. Not surprisingly, my training began with three to four weeks of academics before flying training was introduced. With the basics under our belts, flying training started with the T-41 lasting about three weeks. The T-41 was followed by the T-37 and T-38. Simulator training was an integral part of both T-37 and T-38 training. Academics stayed ahead of the flying training syllabus and was a part of our lives until about half way through T-38s.

Academic Training

Academic training was serious business. Each class followed a published schedule with periodic testing on courses including airmanship, aerospace physiology, a systems operations class in each of the three types of aircraft, principles of flight, aural code, flight instruments, navigation, flight planning, weather, applied aerodynamics and aerospace physiology. As in all of my military training, the instructors were highly trained and very professional, making the even most boring subject somewhat interesting. Even so, academic classes were not enthusiastically anticipated. We endured the course-work, studied hard and tried to do our best on the exams. A failed test meant restrictions placed on the individual. With three failures, the student pilot would be eliminated from training.

Ancillary Training

There was other ancillary training that was scheduled heavily at the beginning of pilot training. Much of this was required prior to first flight.

Altitude Chamber

The altitude chamber was a device that was very useful in that it provided direct experience with the initial symptoms of dying from lack of oxygen. Twelve students were seated inside a tank that resembled a submarine. The air was then gradually pumped out to simulate high altitude conditions. We wore our helmets and were breathing 100 percent oxygen. From the ceiling of the chamber hung a limp balloon and as the air pressure dropped to simulate increasing altitude, the balloon became larger and larger. We gradually became aware that trapped air inside our bodies was doing the same. This trapped, expanding gas sought release and usually found it from both ends of our bodies. From the 'north' end it was a burp and from the 'south' end, flatus. Fortunately for us, the gas masks served their purpose and the air we breathed was pure oxygen.

At a simulated altitude of 31,000 feet, we removed our masks to experience the effects of hypoxia, or lack of oxygen to the brain. Possible symptoms were many and varied. We were each given a clip board with a sheet of third grade level math problems to solve. Most of us were unable to do these simple math problems for more than a minute. My mind became very confused. "9 minus 6 is ah, ah, now let me see, 6 from 9 is ah, 3. Ya, that's it, 3."

The primary goal of the training was for each of us to identify our personal symptoms of hypoxia. My first symptom was that my vision became very bright and was followed by a coolness of my skin. Mental confusion followed and, in the altitude chamber, I experienced euphoria. When the instructor told me to put my mask on, I just grinned and didn't make any move to comply until he began to walk toward me. In my mind, I was just fine without oxygen. Because of the serious nature of hypoxia, it was an Air Force requirement for all pilots to go through refresher altitude chamber training every three years.

Almost 20 years later, my training probably saved my life. I was flying an F-100 and during my initial climb-out I noticed my vision getting very bright. I recognized my hypoxia symptoms as I passed through 15,000 feet after takeoff and immediately checked my oxygen gage. It read zero. I declared an emergency and quickly descended to a lower altitude.

A greatly beloved professional golfer, Payne Stewart, was the victim of hypoxia when his Lear Jet depressurized during climb out. There were two pilots plus Payne and two others on board. When ground control lost radio contact military fighters were scrambled. After the intercept they reported the Lear Jet's windows were iced over and it looked like the pilots were slumped over in the cockpit. The plane continued its flight path on autopilot, still being escorted by fighters until it ran out of fuel and crashed in a farmer's field in North Dakota. If Payne's pilots had been properly trained the accident might have been prevented.

We found out first hand that the altitude chamber could also be hazardous. We were warned that on rare occasion someone would get the bends which is caused by nitrogen bubbles coming out of solution in the body, a potentially deadly situation. The evening after we went through the chamber, one of my classmates began having pains in his chest and a shortness of breath. He went to the base hospital and the doctor on duty very quickly determined that one of the student's lungs had collapsed. It was a relatively simple procedure to re-inflate the lung and, after several days of testing, this fellow was told that the chances of his lung collapsing again were extremely slim. However, they also offered him the opportunity to take a medical elimination from pilot training. The rest of us in the section were at first amazed and then amused when he opted for the medical release. He hadn't been a strong *gung ho* type of student, but I believed he could have made it had he tried. We decided he just didn't have the right stuff!

Other Fun Ancillary Activities

Ejection seat training gave us an idea of what it might be like to eject from an airplane. We sat in an ejection seat that was attached to a 20 foot tall rail. Upon pulling the ejection handle, compressed air would blast us about ten feet up the rail. The actual distance depended mostly on body weight and at 145 pounds, I got quite a ride. The barnaby chair demonstrated a severe form of spatial disorientation. The chair had a round rail surrounding it and, once the occupant was seated, he would rest his head sideways on the rail. The chair was then spun to get the fluid in his inner ear's semicircular canals moving to simulate a prolonged turn. When told to do so, the occupant raised his head and immediately his eyes began to shift back and forth uncontrollably. When it was my turn, I discovered that no amount of concentration or will power could prevent my eyes from scrolling. Finally, after a minute had passed, I was able to regain limited control of my vision. What a terrifying experience it would be if this spatial disorientation should occur while piloting a plane. During the next year in F-4 RTU, I flew with a lieutenant colonel instructor pilot who had ejected from an F-4 due to this type of spatial disorientation.

Parasailing

Parasailing was a training exercise that we all anxiously looked forward to. We had many hours of instruction to prepare us for this potentially hazardous activity. We began in the classroom and then moved outside to the Parachute Landing Fall (PLF) trainer. The PLF trainer was a wooden platform that presented two different heights, four feet and six feet, off which we were to jump into soft sand. Upon hitting the sand, we were to practice our PLF, a parachuting maneuver to be performed upon touchdown. It was designed to prevent injury by distributing the landing shock to a wide area of the body. We decided that a PLF satisfactory to our instructors' critical eyes was impossible, but we continued to practice them until we hated the name and our bodies ached from bruises.

From there, we went on to a tower for more hours of training. Now we got to actually hang in a parachute harness and practice procedures that were important immediately after ejecting. Once our PLFs were deemed satisfactory, we were ready for the big event - parasailing.

Parasailing was done on a Saturday. We were bused out to a large field which was devoid of trees for several miles. One by one we parasailed. When it was my turn, I was quite nervous but also very excited. As I strapped on the parachute harness, I was only concentrating on what I had learned and what I had to do in the next few minutes.

A pick-up truck maneuvered into position with a very long rope that was connected to my parachute. With a head nod I indicated that I was ready and the truck began accelerating as I ran behind it. Two helpers held up the parachute to allow it to billow behind me and in seconds I felt my still running feet lift off the ground. I watched absolutely mesmerized as the ground rapidly fell away below me. Up, up and up I zoomed until the tow truck seemed like a little toy below me.

A friend of mine, Skip Boles, had already parasailed and was sitting in the bed of the truck while I was in the air. He had noticed that, before releasing the rope, the truck would stop accelerating. Upon questioning the instructor, Skip learned that, by slowing up, parachute opening shock was greatly reduced. Skip told the instructor that I was the section leader and convinced him to release my rope without slowing. Looking down, I could see the instructor signaling me that I was about to be released. Having watched many go through this, I was relatively relaxed and definitely not ready for what was about to happen. One instant I was enjoying the view of the countryside from 500 feet up and the next instant I felt a tremendous jerk and found myself looking up through my feet at the inside of my parachute. For some inexplicable reason I was upside down. My immediate thought was that my parachute had failed and I was in very serious trouble. Then, a second or two later, my feet swung back down and I could see the countryside again. Everything was back where it belonged, including my feet pointing downward at the ground. Skip howled in delight. What fun! The rest of the ride to the ground was rather anticlimactic for me.

Pilot training was a series of achievements, some were large and others not so large. This was of the latter category but I had parasailed and had passed one more hurdle however small.

Simulator Training

Simulator training was not a fond activity. We understood the importance of the simulator but considered it a poor substitute for real flying. Also, the instructors were usually not pilots but were often civilians who had retired from the military or had some military experience. All were highly experienced in flying their particular simulator, whether it was a T-37 or a T-38, and they liked to impress us with their finesse at doing the very difficult and universally hated 'vertical Ss.' There were four kinds of vertical S's, each more difficult than the previous, and they had the intentional effect of forcing a pilot to speed up his instrument cross check. They are described later.

PILOT TRAINING – LAREDO AFB

The simulator did not fly like its counterpart airplane. The T-37 simulator consisted of a real T-37 cockpit. After climbing in, we put on a headset and closed the cockpit canopy. Procedurally, it was the same as the T-37 on the flight line. The engines started the same way and the familiar high pitched whine could be heard when moving the throttles. The difference was that everything had to be done on instruments - by looking at the gages. Also, when flying the simulator, the control stick didn't feel anything at all like actual flying. The simulator was very sensitive, and even with the greatest of concentration, we looked like ham-fisted neophytes. I came to realize that you had to learn to fly both the simulator and the aircraft. They were distinctly separate skills.

Simulator Instructors

Many, if not most, of the sim instructors were nice. But we felt they were frustrated people who, for one reason or another, couldn't fly and had chosen the next best thing... the simulator. Although we treated them with respect, and sometimes feigned awe following a 'perfect demo of a vertical S,' they weren't really pilots.

No matter how much we disliked the sim, though, it was a necessary evil and a part of the syllabus through which we slowly and methodically moved. Certain sims we learned were even prerequisites for actual aircraft flights, so we took them seriously yet without great enthusiasm.

Flying Training

Flying training was what it was all about. When I got to Laredo AFB, I was convinced that I just didn't have the skills to become an Air Force pilot. Pilot training seemed an impossible dream, an insurmountable mountain to climb, so I decided to treat it as a year of small mountains to overcome... one

T-41 Mescalero

at a time. I established goals. My first was to solo in the T-41. After soloing, my goal became the successful completion of T-41s. After that, it was soloing in the T-

37, and so on. It wasn't until I was well established in the T-38 that I realized I was actually going to finish pilot training and become an Air Force pilot. Of course, my goal from the beginning was to be a fighter pilot.

T-41 Flying Training

T-41 flying training was conducted at Laredo International airport. The Instructor Pilots (IPs) were civilian pilots who were hired by the Air Force. A captain was in charge of the whole operation. There were about 15 civilian IPs with widely varied backgrounds and ages. The youngest were in their late 20's to early 30's. As a rule, the younger IPs were hot heads and could be difficult to fly with.

Mr. Reece

My instructor, Mr. Reece, was about 60 and I considered myself fortunate to have been assigned to him. Mr. Reece was a grandfatherly type. He had a bushy mustache on a long but rounded, fleshy face. His natural expression was one of mild amusement and I never saw him get excited or show a negative expression.

In contrast, one of our two Danish pilot trainees was assigned to one of the young hot heads. About half way through T-41s, when Ole did something incorrectly, his IP yelled and threw his radio mic at him. Ole grabbed the mic, looked his hothead instructor in the eyes, and with a fierce look said in his accented English, *"I'm going to kill you, you son of a bitch."* Ole said the instructor took control of the airplane and returned to the field. Immediately after landing, he went to the captain and requested that Ole be given a new instructor. Ole didn't gloat over this, but he was happy to get a new IP.

T-41 training called for 16 hours of flying which culminated with a contact check. Each flight lasted about an hour and 15 minutes. Some of the 16 hours was solo, but most was dual flying with one's assigned IP. Most of my classmates had come to UPT fresh from the Air Force academy or college ROTC and already had some training in a light aircraft. They had a very easy time of it in T-41s. A handful of us who lacked this prior training had to work considerably harder. I had the distinction of being the only one who had never even been in a light airplane before. However, I noticed that by the time we got to T-37s the advantage those with prior flying had seemed to disappear.

A Typical Day

Our flying day was highly regimented. If we had morning flying, our day began with a flag raising ceremony. If we flew in the afternoon, the day ended with a flag lowering ceremony. Since I was the section leader, I was responsible to see that it was done properly. Following the flag detail, we assembled inside at our respective tables with our IPs. The flying day always started with the hated and dreaded Emergency Procedure (EP) of the day. The standardization and evaluation (stan eval) officer would read through a hypothetical situation leading to an emergency procedure. *"You have just left the east training area, you've leveled at 1500 feet and* you are doing 100 knots. Suddenly you hear a bang and your prop begins to slow. You check your rpm and it is 2900. Your airspeed is bleeding off, now 85 knots. When you check oil pressure you notice it is zero. What do you do?" At this point the stan eval officer begins to shift his gaze around the room. It is deathly silent. The trainees try to become invisible hoping to not be called upon but knowing that at least one will be. "Lt. Larson!" Twenty-five students breathe a sigh of relief as Lt. Larson gets to his feet and recites the bold face emergency procedure for loss of engine in flight and then talks about non-bold face procedures. If the stan eval officer is satisfied with the response, the ordeal is over for the day. If not, Lt. Larson remains standing and someone else will be called upon. It was not unusual for several students to be standing at the end of the EP of the day. With the formalities finished, we would sit with our IPs and they would brief us on our training flight for that day. Incidentally, I would later discover that all flight briefings throughout the fighter force always began with the EP of the day.

First Flight

During my first briefing, I listened with rapt attention to Mr. Reece. I was trying to digest every word he said because in only a few minutes we would be walking out the door to the world of flight. In that world, I would be graded on my every move. I knew the pace moved quickly and catch-up was hard to do. Mr. Reece, talking in his low fatherly voice, quickly described everything we would do, from pre-flighting the airplane to taxiing out to the runway, to takeoff and beyond.

When we got to the little Cessna 172, the Air Force T-41, Mr. Reece demonstrated how to preflight the airplane and explained the reasons for everything we checked. We climbed into the cockpit. I was in the left seat, the pilot's seat, and I felt like I was totally out of place. Looking out of the front windscreen, not a windshield in an airplane, I could see the propeller sticking straight up. In front of me was the yoke, not a steering wheel, and it was only half of a wheel. The gas pedal was replaced with a throttle and there was something strange called carburetor heat. I pulled out my checklist and went through the "before engine start" procedures, one by one; slowly, one by one;... painfully slowly to Mr. Reece... one by one. Finally, it came time to start the engine. Mr. Reece was doing a remarkable job in not showing his impatience.

To make a long story short, I finally got the engine started and all checklist items accomplished up to 'taxi.' I was perspiring and totally maxed out and we hadn't even moved yet. I think Mr. Reece sensed this because he took over; made the radio call to tower for taxi clearance and explained what he did as we went. As I watched I felt like there was no way that I could learn all of that.

We were lined up on the end of the runway and seemingly out of a fog I heard Mr. Reece say, *"you've got it. Let's take off."* Recalling the procedures I'd learned in preparation for this day, I released the brake, advanced the throttle watching the rpm and other gages as the airplane began to move. By now, my excitement level was about as high as it could get. I unsteadily steered the airplane with a combination of turning the yoke (moving the ailerons) and pressing the rudder pedals. I was staying mostly on centerline as the airspeed increased to takeoff speed. The nose became light, began to rise and we were airborne. As I struggled to keep us flying down the runway while simultaneously holding takeoff attitude, I was aware that the ground was falling away below us. What a feeling. I was flying. And then a most embarrassing thing happened. All of the adrenaline that was coursing through my veins helping me to fly this machine decided to take control of my legs. My legs were trembling so much they were bouncing up and down on the rudders. No amount of will power would cause them to be still. I glanced over at Mr. Reece hoping he wasn't noticing. Not only had he noticed, but Mr. Reece was silently laughing - so I laughed with him.

With Mr. Reece's directing, I leveled at 3,500 feet and cruised out to our assigned area, which was one of seven. As we passed visual landmarks on the ground, Mr. Reece pointed out the boundaries outlining each designated area as we passed them by. I tried to ingrain them in my mind knowing that I would be expected to stay within the confines of my assigned area during my check-ride.

When we were established in the area Mr. Reece demonstrated a 45 degree bank steep turn. I was alarmed initially to be leaning that much and fought a desire to lean away from the turn. Then it was my turn and, following directions, I turned the yoke to begin banking. Approaching 45 degrees of bank, I turned it the opposite direction to steady the wings at 45 degrees. Upon Mr. Reece's advice, I advanced the throttle to maintain airspeed and, using 110 percent of concentration, I maintained the turn for 360 degrees. The 60 degree bank turn I found more to my liking. I was becoming accustomed to looking out the side window at the ground. In fact I was enjoying it! With the wings set in this steep bank, the propellers seemed to be biting into the air to pull us through. It took considerably more power to maintain airspeed but I was actually getting the hang of it.

Then came the stall series; the wonderful stall series where you tell the airplane, which is half a mile high, to stop flying. With the wings level, I began a climb until the nose was a ridiculous 30 degrees high. There was no way the airplane could continue doing this. Then I was told to pull back the throttle. I watched the airspeed drop lower and lower until the whole airplane seemed to be about to shake apart. Then it happened. At the stall, the nose abruptly dropped from 30 degrees high to 30 degrees low. With the addition of power, we were flying again but what a sensation when the nose dropped. Wow!

Without warning Mr. Reece pulled the throttle to idle and said, *"You just lost your engine. What are you going to do?"* Of course he meant that we were going to practice doing a forced landing and, with the skillful hands of a master, he glided down towards the ground as he decided upon a suitable small plot of somewhat level ground. While monitoring his altitude, Mr. Reece set up on a crosswind approach to his selected landing site and then turned to line up with it. At about 100 feet, he advanced the throttle to climb back out. I was impressed but convinced that I would never be able to do that in only 10 or 11 more flights - but of course I did.

The remainder of the flight was spent in the traffic pattern practicing landings. I thought this was decidedly the most difficult part of flying and surely there was no way I'd ever be able to solo. By the end of the flight, I was consistently landing the airplane and feeling quite proud. In subsequent flights, however, I discovered that the learning curve tended to flatten out. I also learned that the pace never slackened from the first flight to the last and graduation from T-41s.

My first solo flight was momentous. The indescribable feeling of *'now you've done it!'* as the airplane left the runway will be with me forever. I was assigned one of the farthest away areas and I actually found it. I practiced my assigned maneuvers and came back to the traffic pattern. Since my no-flap landings were my best, Mr. Reece had me only fly no-flaps and I was back on the ground. I'd flown an aircraft all by myself. I'd done it. Maybe I really would make it into T-37s after all.

During T-41s our goals were to get to T-37s. We realized we were the new guys on the block and looked up to the students wearing the T-37 patches. We almost worshipped the students wearing the T-38 patches. We were on a path that, for about two thirds of us, would lead to the 'silver wings' of a pilot. We yearned for the future but kept our concentration on the immediate goals of the present. The road began with the lowly but awsome T-41.

Chapter Six

Flying the T-37

The three most useless things to a pilot: runway behind you, altitude above you and air in your fuel tanks.

The Tweet

We had been at Laredo AFB for five or six weeks and, after graduating from the T-41, I was assigned to B flight for T-37 training. My major accomplishment to date was my T-41 transition check flight. I had been given a reasonable check pilot and I'd done quite well. I had really made it to T-37s.

T-37 Tweet

The Attrition Begins

My class had started with 60 students but by the beginning of T-37 training we had already lost a dozen due to lack of flying proficiency or through Self-Initiated Elimination (SIE). Those who were eliminated were reassigned to administrative duties at Laredo until an assignment could be found for them to another base and school for missiles or weapons controlling.

T-37 Tipping

The T-37 had two nicknames. The official one was the 'Tweet.' Another one was the 'Dog Whistle,' a direct reference to the high pitched noise made by its engines.

Flying the T-37

Like the T-41, the T-37 was made by Cessna but it was only made for the Air Force. The T-37 is very small for a twin engine jet so, when sitting in the cockpit, the pilot is about the same distance off the ground as in a car. While on a cross country flight, I learned a trick to get the absolute maximum amount of fuel into the plane. You tip it. After the plane has been fueled, two people push down on the tail raising the nose completely off the ground. When the plane has been tipped, a few more gallons of fuel can be added to the tanks.

Getting Ready

As is the case when learning to fly any new airplane, an extensive amount of ground training preceded T-37 flying training. Even before finishing in the T-41, we began learning all about the varied systems in the T-37. We had to learn about the flight instruments, the engines, flight controls and how they worked, flying characteristics such as how it enters a spin (and more importantly, how it recovers from a spin), the electrical system to include what is battery powered and what is engine driven generator powered, and a whole lot more. There were sophisticated mock-ups of many of these systems to demonstrate the particular item in use and there were movies to augment our learning. One particular movie that impressed us all was on spinning, a maneuver that I had a particular aversion to. In this movie, footage was shown of the T-37 entering spins, spinning, and recovering from them. They even showed T-37s that didn't recover from spins. Some of the film was photographed from the cockpit of the spinning aircraft and some from other airplanes. None of the film decreased my anxiety about SPINNING.

T-37 IPs

Our T-37 flight had about a dozen IPs with another half dozen IPs who were attached to the flight for flying purposes but worked elsewhere in the wing. Each full time IP had two students and the attached IPs usually had one. We only flew during one half of the day so the IPs' workload wasn't all that bad. They would fly twice a day, once with each student, and while we were in academics, they would work on their additional duties.

Capt. Rodenhauser

My assigned IP was Capt. Karl Rodenhauser. Karl was about my age and close to my date of rank. I was very fortunate to get Karl as an IP. He always carried a smile and I liked him a lot. Karl had an extensive knowledge of flight aerodynamics and was filled with interesting stories. For instance, he told us about when they once flew an experimental airplane that was designed to fly really high. Well they got it up there only to find they couldn't bring it back down. Karl would pause and smile at moments like this, waiting for us to ask him to go on. He loved telling stories. In this case, the pilots had found themselves in an aerodynamic corner. They were right at Q (maximum airspeed for the airframe) so if they pushed the nose over to descend they would exceed that structurally limiting airspeed. But, they were at such a high altitude that they were also just above the stall speed and couldn't slow without stalling out. With that, he began to tell us what we were going to do on our flights that day. When we protested, asking him what happened to that airplane, he got a twinkle in his eyes and said he'd tell us another time.

Another time, as we were leaving our working area at about 15,000 feet Karl said, *"I'll bet I can fly this plane all the way to Barfly* (our practice runway which was about 50 miles away) *and not have to touch the throttles until after we touchdown on the runway."* This was too much for me to believe and I told him he was on. To my amazement he did it. More about Karl later on

The Daily Routine

Our day began much like in T-41s except we didn't have the flag ceremony. We were to be at our IP's table in the flight room at the prescribed time and were to stand until our IPs arrived. Following that was the 'Stump the Dummy' emergency procedure situation. After the EP, the flight commander would make announcements and we received a weather briefing.

On bad weather days, we really groaned because we had unbelievably boring pubs checks. The IP whose additional duty was flight publications would take us page by page through each of our publications making sure all of the pertinent page changes were in place and all of the 'pen and ink' changes were made. This process could easily take up to two hours.

Fortunately, most days we had suitable weather for flying and we avoided pubs checks. Our IP would brief both of us (his two assigned students) at the same time. This saved time on the instructor's part and was easily done if he could keep both students on the same syllabus sortie. About 20 or 25 minutes before our scheduled takeoff time, he would select one of us and we would step lively to the Personal Equipment (PE) room where we grabbed our helmets, harness and parachute. Since our planes were all parked near our squadron building, it was usually only a short walk to our assigned aircraft. The ritual at the plane was usually to look at the forms first.

The Forms

The forms are standard to all Air Force aircraft and are held in a flexible plastic loose leaf folder. The forms are known as the 781s and contain several sections, 781a, 781k, etc., each for its own purpose. Only three sections held our interest. The very front page, the 781a, was for the current aircraft status. If the status was a red X, the plane was not to be flown until a proper maintenance authority signed off. Reasons for a red X were many; the plane wasn't refueled yet, there was a safety-of-flight maintenance problem, or the forms simply hadn't been reviewed by the maintenance supervisor yet that day. This form also showed how many times the plane had flown that day.

Another form of interest was the delayed maintenance form or 781k. A quick review of this form could reveal that a wingtip light was burned out or other minor non-safety-of-flight discrepancies. It was embarrassing to write up a minor malfunction after flight only to have the maintenance supervisor dryly point out it was already in the K section.

A third section to check was the current discrepancy section. In this section you might find maintenance write-ups from previous flights that day or write-ups that hadn't been fixed or transferred to the K section.

Ground Ops

First, we checked over the forms and signed acceptance of the plane in the A section. Then came the preflight. Each plane had its unique preflight checklist and I discovered that every IP had his own additional 'pet' checks. Most items we checked were pretty obvious. Tire condition; is there enough tire tread left and can you see any gouges or punctures in the tires. Were the gas tanks filled and the gas caps tightened securely? Were there any missing or loose rivets in the sheet metal skin? Were the engine intakes clear of foreign objects that might otherwise be sucked into the engine?

Fluid leaks were very important to notice, especially gas or hydraulic fluid. Pooled fuel or oil in the tailpipe of the engine was also an ominous sign. Access panels should all be tightly fastened so they didn't fall off during flight. The list went on. The preflight inspection usually took anywhere from five to ten minutes depending on how much time was available. Frequently, if running late, the IP would say to just jump in and he would do the preflight – in two minutes flat. He would literally run around the airplane with his checklist in hand. An unbreakable rule in flying is to always have the checklist available – don't rely on memory for anything.

Finally, we were ready to strap in, an easy task in the T-37. Each cockpit had a canopy that was hinged in its center. When the canopy's motor was activated, it rose up from the side rails to resemble gull wings. Once raised, it was a simple matter to climb in over the side railing. The canopies were always in the raised position when arriving at the aircraft. After placing our parachutes on the seats, we rested our helmets on the canopy rail and completed the preflight inspection.

A humorous note: During the wives' day orientation, one of the IPs who wasn't very well liked because he was too cocky and aloof was showing how the canopies closed, "*just by pushing this button here.*" His smile turned to anguish and horror when he heard the crunching sound the closing canopy made as it crushed his new, custom-made, form-fit, one hundred and fifty dollar helmet he had left resting on the far-side canopy rail of the airplane.

Putting on a parachute and helmet took only a minute or so. Going through the 'before-start' checklist was another minute or two and the actual engine start just a little more. Part of this initial procedure called for us to adjust our seat height and then bounce up and down to make sure the gears under the seat meshed with the seat ejection rail. We were told the seat could fall to the floor, all the way to the down position, if the gears weren't meshed properly. Early in T-37s I would find out in a personal way why this was in the checklist.

A call to ground control got permission to taxi to the inside runway where we got in line for takeoff. Then there was a 'before taxi' checklist and a 'taxiing' checklist to accomplish. Another radio call, this time to tower to notify them of our readiness to takeoff. When it was our turn and tower gave clearance, we pulled out onto the runway to line up on the centerline.

Runways

All pilot training bases had three runways. The outside runway was a nice concrete one that was usually reserved for the T-38s. The middle runway, also concrete, was for anyone doing instrument approaches. The inside runway, mainly for T-37s, was blacktop and shorter than the other two. In addition to these runways, there was an auxiliary field about 40 miles from the base used for T-37 touch and go landing practice. The aux field consisted of a small tower control unit and a fire truck to respond in case of a crash. It greatly relieved congestion from the main base. Before taking off, a quick call to the squadron Supervisor Of Flying (SOF) resulted in a work area assignment. Now, a quick run through the' before takeoff' checklist and we were finally ready to takeoff.

Takeoff

Takeoff, in many respects, was the most exciting part of a mission. The transition from resting on the ground to flying was rapid and potentially dangerous. At engine run-up, the engine instruments were checked to make sure both engines were still operating OK. At brake release, acceleration seemed meager but quickly built up. Groundspeed was checked at a prescribed distance down the runway and, if not at least at a pre-computed value, the takeoff was aborted because something was wrong. The engines weren't developing sufficient thrust.

At this point instruments were checked again. At a pre-computed speed, called max abort speed, we were committed to taking off because the remaining runway was no longer enough to stop on. At another pre-computed speed, nose wheel liftoff speed, the nose became light and rotated up. Takeoff attitude was established with the control stick and, shortly after the main wheels bounced once or twice, the plane was airborne. Once definitely airborne, gear was raised followed by flaps.

This was a busy time. We flew a prescribed ground track depending on the area that we had been assigned. We maintained a ten degree climb until reaching a prescribed airspeed and then adjusted pitch to maintain the climb airspeed. The climb airspeed didn't remain entirely constant, though. As altitude increased, climb airspeed decreased and a somewhat simple formula was used to re-compute it. Maintaining a precise climb airspeed was especially important when assigned to the nearest working area. Failure to do so would result in not being at the area's minimum altitude when reaching it. Having to call the SOF to announce making a 360 degree turn prior to entering the assigned airspace was embarrassing; all because the pilot hadn't followed the climb schedule.

From takeoff until established in our assigned airspace was incredibly busy. There were so many things to think about and do that I always felt greatly relieved upon entering the assigned area when we could start practicing the syllabus maneuvers for that flight.

Training Areas

UPT Air Force Base locations were chosen for availability of nearby uncongested airspace. To the north of Laredo was the T-37 airspace. It was a rectangle that probably measured 60 miles by 40 miles and was divided into six smaller portions. The boundaries could be determined by landmarks on the ground, as well as navigational aids should the ground not be visible. In addition to lateral limits, there was a minimum and a maximum altitude that permitted other air traffic to fly beneath or above the airspace.

The T-38 airspace was east of Laredo, with Mexico as its southern border. This airspace was larger because the T-38 flew considerably faster than the T-37. It too was subdivided into smaller parcels. Both the T-37 and T-38 areas had corridors for entering and exiting. The entry corridor had the same ground track as the exit corridor but was above it.

Airspace Deconfliction

The squadron SOF was usually a senior captain or major and an experienced IP. He sat in a small room surrounded with charts and it was his job to assign airspace to the squadron's aircraft. In addition to calling for airspace assignment before takeoff, we were required to call when entering our area. Another call was necessary to obtain permission to leave. The highest threat for a midair collision between trainer jets was in the entry and exit corridor.

Since the SOF did not have radar to see where we were, he would attempt to deconflict his airplanes by time. This didn't always work. While I was at Laredo, a descending T-37 hit another T-37 from above, killing a student and an IP. As a result of that accident, we performed a weaving maneuver while descending through the corridor in order to visually clear the flight path in front of and below our craft.

Flying training in the T-37 began with the 'contact' phase which was basic aircraft flying. In the contact phase we learned how to take off and land as well as aerobatics, stalls, spins, slow flight and confidence maneuvers. Part way through this phase, we also began the instrument phase. The first major test was the contact check ride and shortly after that was the instrument check. Most of the people who were eliminated in pilot training were lost by the end of the T-37 instrument check. Following instruments was formation flying and low level navigation.

More on Capt. Rodenhauser

As mentioned earlier, Karl was one of those people who can pass through your life and you never forget him. Capt. Rodenhauser took a very strong interest in me as a student and I felt privileged to have had him as an IP. He had an exceptional knowledge of the principles of flight and took the time to explain the 'why' of flying to me. He was also a very gifted pilot. Karl had a subtle sense of humor and sometimes my Manx gullibility kept me guessing at when Karl was joking and when he wasn't.

One feature I liked about Karl was his patient and calm demeanor in the air. Some IPs were notorious for being 'screamers' but not Karl. He did occasionally lose his temper, though. When he did, he would suddenly bang his right hand on the instrument panel covering in the front of the cockpit. At such times I would try just a little harder. One time, however, he seemed to be especially patient. Then, in a blur, he banged his left hand on the panel covering. After about 15 seconds he calmly asked, "*Do you know why I didn't bang the panel covering with my right hand?*" When I responded that I didn't, he continued, "*Because I was sitting on it so I wouldn't bang the instrument panel covering.*"

During the contact phase, Karl sensed apprehension in me about doing stalls and spinning. He greatly relieved that anxiety when he told me that I had already experienced the most sensational maneuver in an airplane. It was, he said, the straight ahead stall in the T-41. As I thought about that, it made sense to me. The straight ahead stall was performed by pulling the plane's nose up into a 30 degree or more climb with the airspeed rapidly bleeding off. As the stall speed was reached, the wind over the wings and lift was abruptly interrupted causing the nose to suddenly plunge downward until flying airspeed was again attained. I would later learn that Karl had greatly misled me and had set me up for a stark experience.

First Flight

My first flight in the T-37 was a real confidence builder. I expected it to be a very difficult plane to fly but it wasn't. It was more complicated and there were a dreadful number of procedures to memorize but it flew smoothly and responded instantly to control inputs. For the most part, it was a very forgiving airplane. As Karl demonstrated to me on that first flight, if you let go of the controls, the airplane would right itself to a somewhat wings level condition and fly the airspeed it was last trimmed to.

When we got back to the traffic pattern to practice landings, I felt I had a natural ability to land it. The procedure for landing was to fly the plane into ground effect, pull the throttle back to 85 percent power and hold the plane a foot or two off the runway until it stalled out. A good landing would touch down at about 65 knots.

Contact Flying

The first contact flights consisted of flying out to our assigned area, practicing slow flight, stalls and three aerobatic maneuvers. Then we would exit the area and fly the 40 or 50 miles to our auxiliary field, practice touch and go landings there, and finally fly back to Laredo for one or two more landings until we were low on fuel.

Solo

The primary goal at that time was to become proficient enough to fly solo, a requirement for us to continue in UPT. I was quite worried about this and was absolutely convinced that I would never make it to solo. I would be eliminated. I was sure. On my fifth T-37 flight, we completed the area maneuvers and I didn't feel I had done all that well. The learning curve was flattening out. We went back to the aux field for touch and go practice and, after my third not so sterling landing, Karl told me to full stop on the next one. Now I was totally dejected. I had done so badly Karl was going to fly home.

T-37 'Tweet' Solo Patch

When I full stopped, he told me to shut down the right engine. I did as he instructed. He opened his canopy and climbed out. When he turned around, he had a big grin on his face and told me I was cleared solo. I was incredulous. I asked him if he was sure. Karl told me that if he had the slightest doubt, he wouldn't be letting me go solo. I think I would have been quite scared if I had been given time to think about it, but I immediately taxied to the end of the runway, turned around, applied power and in seconds was airborne in my now, quite light airplane. I was absolutely ecstatic. I had made it. I was soloing in the T-37. All by myself! Oh what a feeling. And then my thoughts embraced the fact that it was totally up to me to land now that I was airborne by myself. In the initial solo, we were supposed to do three landings but Karl, who was monitoring from the control unit, told me to full stop on my second one. I guess he didn't want to push our luck.

When we were debriefing after the first flight, I asked Karl what gave him the confidence to clear me solo, especially on a somewhat lackluster flight. He then told me he hadn't been at all confident. It was an act to give me the confidence he felt I needed. I never forgot Karl for that, and years later as an F-4 IP, I used the same technique with my students who were having problems of their own.

Formation Flying

Our first introduction to formation flying was in the T-37 and it was only that, an introduction. The

T-37 four-ship formation

majority of our formation training came in the T-38. Most of T-37 formation flying was two- ship but there were one or two four-ship flights for orientation. Formation work consisted of pitch-out and rejoins, fingertip maneuvering and route formation which is all explained in the next chapter.

Solo Emergency

Two or three sorties later I was sent off solo to a flying area. Now, I would be by myself for an entire mission. I was surprised at how calm I felt about this. The mission description called for me to fly to the area, practice a minimum of three aerobatic maneuvers, and then recover at Laredo for touch and go landings. Everything had gone too smoothly. I was in the area and feeling on top of the world. I did some mild clearing maneuvers called wifferdils and then went into the aerobatics. I first did an aileron roll, a very mild maneuver. That went well, so I did a barrel roll which also progressed smoothly. With soaring confidence, I decided to do a loop, one of the more demanding aerobatic maneuvers. I dived down to the bottom of the airspace to get the required entry airspeed and then pulled up into a 4 G pull. At 4 G's my 140 pounds of body weight multiplied to 560 pounds as I was pushed downward into the seat.

As the nose of the T-37 reached 45 degrees of pitch, I suddenly felt a violent shudder in the cockpit and then felt like I was falling. My heart leaped into my throat. I'm being ejected! A moment later, I noticed I couldn't see over the side rails anymore. My seat had fallen to the floor of the cockpit. I had forgotten to 'jiggle' the seat before engine start. Now I was in a real fix because the seat couldn't be raised in flight. This was an emergency that we had never discussed during our morning EP sessions.

My first thought, of course, was that the aircraft was still climbing at 45 degrees attitude and running out of airspeed. I pushed forward on the stick and arced over to level flight. I noticed that if I raised my chin as high as possible I could see over the canopy rail. I wasn't scared anymore because I was flying the airplane OK. I decided I wouldn't worry about being unable to see the runway during landing until the time came. I called the SOF to report leaving the area for base and headed for home. When I got in the landing pattern, I called for an immediate full stop not thinking that, perhaps, I should have told someone on the ground of my problem. I pitched out doing a 180 degree turn to downwind, flew a fine base turn making the required radio calls and, with my chin sticking almost straight up and with straining eyeballs, peered out over the front with cross checks out the side for height reference. When I felt close to the runway, I pulled power and started slowing above the runway. I almost immediately touched; a hot landing and a mobile right up I thought, but I was down safe and sound.

Later, I was told that I had really startled the runway controller who sits in his control unit adjacent to the landing zone. When I flew by on short final, he couldn't see anyone in the cockpit! When I explained my problem, I was given a slap on the back for a job well done but told to not keep it a secret next time.

Spinning!

My greatest flying fear in pilot training was spinning, a required maneuver in the T-37. Ironically, the T-37 was the only Air Force jet where spinning was an allowable maneuver. The reason for this was because the T-37 was an extremely stable airplane. The airplane would recover itself from a spin if you just took your hands off of the controls.

I had heard others talk about spins. I had seen movies of it. I was afraid of it. However, I treated spinning like I would treat a dreaded visit to the dentist. It was something that initially only mildly worried me, but as the day got closer, I worried more and more. Finally, that fateful day arrived. It must have been about the 10th or 12th flight in contact. Karl thoroughly briefed me on the procedure and with his unique pudgy faced grin he said, *"Heh, don't worry about it. It isn't as bad as a T-41 stall."* The procedure was long and difficult for me to remember but Karl had a solution to that also. His simplified procedure was, *"First you stall it, then you yaw it. To recover you un-yaw it then you un-stall it."* Simple to the max.

By the time we got out to our working area, I was really in a frazzle. Karl said, *"Well, let's get right into it and get it over with."* He announced he would demonstrate a spin first, then I would do one. As with the procedure, he stalled the airplane by pulling the nose up and pulling back on the power. Continuing on, he yawed the now stalled T-37 by smoothly applying rudder and we gracefully entered a spin. I was amazed. It wasn't bad at all. In fact it was almost fun. For the recovery he un-yawed by applying opposite rudder. When the rotation stopped he un-stalled by smoothly pushing forward on the stick. Then it was my turn. I climbed back up in altitude since we had to be above 18,000 feet to begin a spin with recovery by 10,000 feet. Following Karl's directions, I stalled, then yawed and we were spinning. I hastily un-yawed and un-stalled and presto, we were flying again. Boy oh boy, was I ever proud of myself. Piece of cake this spinning was.

For the next several rides we went through the spin procedure without any trouble at all. I really had the hang of it -- or so I thought! One beautiful day, Karl wasn't available for our training flight. I was assigned to fly with Capt. Frey instead. Unlike Karl who had flown his entire career in Air Training Command, Capt. Frey was a seasoned, combat experienced fighter pilot. He had flown the F-100 in Vietnam.

T-37 'Tweet'

Capt. Frey was a likable guy who didn't seem to take the pilot training 'Mickey Mouse' stuff too seriously. He did take his IP duties seriously though.

On our flight, everything had gone quite well and then it came time to spin. I climbed up to 18,000 feet and confidently pulled the nose up and pulled power. As the T-37 entered the stall, I applied rudder as I had so often done with Karl. Things were different. Instead of smoothly entering a graceful spin, the airplane snapped abruptly downward and entered a very uncomfortable spin. It seemed like we were pointed straight at the ground. I quickly pushed the opposite rudder pedal to un-yaw and I was thrown sideways in the cockpit. To un-stall I pushed forward on the stick like I had always done and, yipes! Now we were pointed straight down and I was hanging in the cockpit by my harness. Heaven forbid! We began spinning in the opposite direction!

I didn't like hanging from the straps, so I pulled back on the stick and again applied opposite rudder to stop the rotation. Then I again pushed forward on the stick and again was thrown forward as we once again began spinning. Now I was terrified. We were probably passing 14,000 feet by now and at 10,000 if there were no signs of recovery we would have to eject. I glanced over at Capt. Frey desperately seeking help. He had his arms folded and was laughing. He finally took the controls and in seconds had the T-37 fully recovered. With that we climbed back up to 18,000 feet and on that day, I learned how to recover from a spin.

As we climbed back up after my first ill-fated attempt at a spin, I was confused. What had gone so wrong? Then it occurred to me. Karl also was afraid of spinning. I imagine he had a harrowing experience or two with student pilots and found it much more comfortable to be on the controls with his students when they went through their spins. With Karl, I really had never done a spin recovery. He had been there doing it for me. He knew just how much rudder to apply and just how much stick to use. He was good at flying the airplane but he sure hadn't done me any favors. Capt. Frey really taught me how to spin.

Contact Check

My first check ride was scheduled for the following week. Like all of my classmates, I was scared of this because so much depended on doing well on it. Airplane assignments at the end of training were made in order of the pilot's graduation in the class. A block of aircraft assignments would be available to our class, including one A-7, three F-4s, one F-106, several OV-10s and many 'heavies' (B-52, C-141, KC-135, C-130 etc.). The top ranked person in the class would get first choice of the list, then the second ranked and so on. One bad check ride and there was no chance of being near the top and getting a choice assignment.

I had finished my last contact syllabus ride and knew my check would be the next day. My stomach was all butterflies until the next day wondering who I would get for my check pilot from wing stan eval. Most of the check pilots were very fair but there were two or three that were much harder. One of the harder ones was a first lieutenant named 'Mayday Marty' who was notorious for failing students on their checks. Everyone feared and disliked Marty. Maybe he was this way because he was short and not very good looking. He also wasn't a particularly good pilot. His nickname, 'Mayday' came from his propensity for calling in emergencies on situations that would cause most IPs to simply return to the field and land – but not Mayday Marty.

When I arrived at the squadron the next morning I immediately went to the scheduling board to see who my check pilot would be. It was Marty! I walked over to wing stan eval for the briefing, which ended with a 'stump the dummy' question and an answer period. I found his desk and went over to it. Marty didn't smile or do anything to put me at ease. In fact, he had a talley sign in plain view on his desk showing how many students he had passed so far that year and how many he had failed. He had failed many more than he had passed.

The briefing went fine and I even did reasonably well on the question answer period. Then we got suited up and went out to the airplane where I began to preflight the craft. During engine start, something on the plane broke and there wasn't a spare aircraft ready so we aborted the mission. I was so relieved. I would have to go through the same thing the next day, but chances were that I would get a different check pilot. As we walked back in, Marty informed me that, had we flown, I would have already flunked the check. I thought he was joking. Then Marty went on to point out a terrible thing I had done. He said, "*Remember when you looked at the pitot static port hole?*" Of course I remembered. I checked it every flight. It was a small sixteenth inch wide hole on the side of the airplane. It had a white circle painted around it to make it easier to find and it provided barometric pressure for many of the flight instruments such as the altimeter and airspeed indicator. Marty went on, "*You touched inside the painted circle with your finger. That circle was painted there so you don't touch inside it.*" I knew you weren't supposed to touch the hole because grease or dirt from your glove might block it, but what Marty was saying was ridiculous. A glance at his face revealed that he was dead serious. Prudence advised that I not respond and I didn't.

On the following day I got a different check pilot, a very fair one, and I did quite well. I also gave out the alarm to the other students in my class about Marty.and the pitot static port.

Instrument Check

Throughout the T-37 phase of pilot training, I had problems clearing my sinuses. We were taught in the altitude chamber that any trapped gasses in our bodies (for example in our sinuses, inner ears, stomach, intestines, and even small air pockets in tooth fillings) would expand as pressure decreased. Usually this isn't a problem and the body is able to equalize the pressure. However, it can be much harder, sometimes impossible to equalize the pressure when congested with a cold and the effect is severe pain. Sinuses are usually the most difficult to equalize but the process can be aided by the valsalva procedure, which involves pinching the nose and blowing with a closed mouth. The action causes pressure to build up until the trapped air is expelled.

I was quickly approaching my instrument check when I came down with a cold and the flight Surgeon put me on DNIF (Duty Not Including Flying) status. It was hard watching the rest of my classmates finish their instrument checks ahead of me but there was nothing I could do. I finally received permission to fly although my sinuses were still quite bad but I needed to get on with flying.

Since I was the only one left who hadn't had an instrument check, it was scheduled for the very next day. As it turned out, this was the day for our flight's wives orientation day. While the wives were being entertained, I would be sweating out my instrument check. I felt a bit uneasy about the timing because I didn't know how I would react if per chance I busted my check. But, my luck seemed to be holding. I didn't get Marty for a check pilot. In fact, my check pilot seemed quite reasonable. During the briefing I explained to him about my sinus problems and then we went flying.

The first part of the flight was performed at high altitude and went quite well. Then, I had to do a VOR penetration, a very busy and complicated procedure requiring the computation of descent rates, timing the outbound leg, precisely flying VOR courses and terminating with a touch and go on the middle runway. When I pulled power and lowered the nose to begin the VOR penetration, I immediately felt the stabs of pain behind my eyes - my sinuses. Without saying a word, I dropped my mask and pinched my nostrils, starting valsalvas to keep the pressure equalized. I found that the pain would return if I stopped even for a few seconds. I completed the entire procedure one handed because one hand was needed to valsalva. The penetration and approach weren't flawless, but on a scale of 1 to 10 I would have graded myself about a 7.

I felt pretty good after landing, mainly because it was over. I had flown better instrument flights but I knew I had passed and it was behind me. Now I would just debrief, perhaps a few minutes of 'stump the dummy' and I'd be able to join Jean with the other wives. During the debrief, my check pilot seemed very happy. He said he had never seen a more impressive penetration - one done with only one hand - and he completely dispensed with our 'stump the dummy.' I scored an excellent on the check with a percentage score in the low 90's. It was the best instrument check score in my class. After that ride, I realized that I was going to get through pilot training and my score on the instrument check kept me in the running for a fighter upon graduation. What a glorious day. What a glorious life.

Cross-Country to Biloxi

The weekend cross-country mission marked the end of T-37s. It was a carrot to keep us on track through the flying syllabus. Some students had special destinations they wanted to go to for their cross-country; frequently an air base near their home if it was within range of the T-37. Then, they had to find another student and two IPs who also would agree to go there.

Richard Hewlett, a student from the Air Force Reserve wanted to go to Keesler Air Base in Biloxi because it was near his home. He asked me if I would go along and, since I had no place in particular to go, I agreed. The way Richard built it up about how his Dad would put us up for the weekend, our IPs also signed on.

Flight planning before we started out turned into a two hour marathon for Richard and me as we followed the procedures we'd learned in an academics class on flight planning. We needed to plan the entire flight, computing fuel used and the time and distance for each segment, beginning with starting the engine. We got into one chart and, using that data, went into a second chart and so on until we finally had our forms all filled out. Our IPs arrived a half hour before scheduled take-off and checked our figures deciding they were close enough. I couldn't imagine how we were going to do that at every stop-over on our cross-country. I need not have worried. Our IPs did the remainder of the flight planning and what took us two hours took them about five minutes. They used rules of thumb instead of charts from the flight manual.

We three hopped (three sorties or flights) to Biloxi and Richard's Dad was waiting for us when we landed. We had a great time enjoying his southern hospitality.

The most exciting event during an otherwise routine cross-country was our landing back at Laredo. A storm was blowing and we had 35 knot cross-winds. This was right at the very edge of the aircraft's limits. Karl said he would do the landing and I thought it a great idea. We did a straight-in approach and on final, we had such a crab into the wind to stay on runway centerline, we were looking out the side of the cockpit at the runway. I could tell by Karl's quietness that he had his hands full and he seemed cheerfully proud upon successfully landing.

The End of Another Chapter

We were already into T-38 academics and gazing more and more wistfully at the sleek white airplanes as they passed us by on Initial in the traffic pattern. There were just a handful of odd sorties remaining in this phase of our training and we couldn't wait to get on to the next and final phase. Something could still happen to any one of us but we were picking up the confidence of successful student pilots; students who would graduate.

Chapter Seven

The T-38 Talon

How are pilots and air traffic controllers similar? If the pilot screws up the pilot dies. If the controller screws up the pilot dies.

The T-38 was the golden fleece of pilot training. The UPT students who wore the white T-38 patch on their sleeves were really special. They had met the greatest challenges of the training program and they had succeeded. They were flying the supersonic jet trainer, a jet that was unforgiving of trainee mistakes.

T-38 Talon

Of those who soloed in T-38's, very few washed out. And that is why this phase was such a milestone to us.

With my practice of setting intermediate goals, I had set my sights on soloing in that amazing machine when I was just halfway through training on the T-37. The difference upon walking into the T-38 building was palpable. The instructors seemed more professional in their treatment of students. We were still second class students in a way, with segregated toilet facilities but more was expected of us. We had proven we had 'what it takes' and they assumed we would all graduate. It was their job to teach us the high performance aspects of flying.

Before even finishing my last check ride in the T-37, I already had been given extensive academics on the basic T-38 systems and its flying procedures. I had even flown the simulator several times. I was ready to go.

That first morning we met our assigned flight instructors. Each had two students, and gave them flight publications and indoctrination briefings. Just as I knew it would be, I was overwhelmed thinking that it would be impossible to remember everything that was required of me. Also following previous patterns, it took just a week before it was all old hat and I was beginning my steady march across the 'sorties flown' tracking board.

Jimmy H. Doolittle

My assigned instructor pilot was Jimmy H. Doolittle III, the grandson of the famed aviator and Medal of Honor recipient who commanded the Doolittle raid on Tokyo during World War II. His grandfather, who was still alive, was without doubt a legend in his own time. Whenever the founders of the US Air Force are mentioned, Jimmy Doolittle is there. So, I felt very honored to have his grandson as my IP. Capt. Doolittle's other student was Peter Hammer, one of our two Danish students and someone who would become a lifelong friend. We had Capt. Doolittle as our instructor until just about the end of training when he achieved a career changing goal, an assignment to test pilot school.

Flying Training - Instruments

Flying training for the T-38 began with five instrument sorties flown 'under the bag.' The bag refers to a canvas type material that is pulled from behind the ejection seat along bungee cords until vision outside the front cockpit is totally obscured. Shortly after takeoff, the IP in the rear cockpit says, *"I've got it,"* and with a feeling of mild dread, the student pulls the bag forward, shutting out the outside world. I always found myself pausing a moment or two, almost like I might do before diving into cold water, and after taking a couple deep breaths responding, *"I'm ready. I've got it."* The remainder of the ride, an hour and a half, would be flying by instruments, completely under the hood.

This was some of the most demanding flying I've ever done, much worse than actually flying in weather. A typical sortie would involve flying an instrument procedure ground track out to a designated working area.

Vertical S's

In the area, we practiced flying precision instrument maneuvers known as vertical S's, which had been first introduced in the simulator. A vertical S-a was the most basic. While flying a constant airspeed of 300 knots, the pilot would slowly raise the nose while adding just a smidgen of power to establish a 1,000 feet per minute rate of climb. Approaching a thousand feet of climb, power had to be reduced while the nose was lowered until the jet was at a constant airspeed (300 knot) descent of 1,000 feet per minute. The procedure was then repeated. A Vertical S-b was executed in the same way, except in a 30 degree bank turn. A Vertical S-c had the addition of reversing the turn after each climb or descent. Vertical S maneuvers taught me that mental energy can cause sweat; profuse sweat. The concentration required for vertical S's was enormous.

Steep Bank Turns

Another maneuver demanding great concentration was the steep bank turn because it was executed at constant altitude and airspeed. From wings level the bank was slowly increased to 60 degrees while adding sufficient power to prevent the airspeed from changing. This required continual references to the airspeed indicator, the altimeter to maintain altitude, the attitude indicator to make necessary corrections and the rpm gages to make minute power changes affecting airspeed. In addition to the above instruments, the heading indicator was occasionally checked to roll out on the directed heading. If a pilot had a poor instrument cross check, the steep turn maneuver would reveal it.

Now, to really appreciate the difficulty of this maneuver you need to know about precession of the attitude indicator. Whenever the jet is in a prolonged turn, the attitude indicator, which is really a calibrated gyroscope, tries to resist the unlevel situation and return to level. To maintain level flight during a turn, the pilot must constantly make minute adjustments on the attitude indicator. The first hint of precession will be seen on either the VVI (Vertical Velocity Indicator) or the altimeter. As you can see, a steep turn requires a continual cross check of virtually all instruments in the cockpit. The simple steep bank turn required two pages of explanation in the instrument procedures manual. I don't think anyone ever busted an instrument check because of a steep bank turn, but I'm sure it denied many from getting an 'excellent' rating.

The Point to Point

The most dreaded procedure of all in instrument flying was the 'point-to-point.' The pilot might be on the 075 degree radial at 35 miles and the IP would say, *"OK, take me to the 150 degree radial for 20 miles."* By looking at the heading situation indicator, or HSI, we were required to quickly determine a rough guess of a ball park heading and while executing it, refine the point-to-point heading to come within a couple miles of the point.

Perhaps the most common mistake was to get 180 degrees out and, instead of going to the 150 degree for 20, going to the 330 degree for 20. That mistake could result in a busted check ride.

Unusual Attitude Recovery

The Unusual Attitude Recovery was set up by the IP saying, *"OK, close your eyes and no peeking."* Since the IP sat behind the pilot, it was impossible for him to confirm compliance, but during my flying career, I never once peeked. It would have spoiled the fun, and they were fun. The IP would take control of the aircraft and fly it in climbs and descents, rolls and turns, enough to eradicate the 'seat of the pants' feeling of knowing the attitude of the aircraft. Then he'd say, *"Recover."* At that moment, the student would open his eyes, quickly check attitude indicator, airspeed indicator and altimeter and recover the aircraft to safe level flight.

The favorite of many IPs was a very nose low attitude but with low airspeed. The first gage that is checked is the attitude indicator and the natural reaction is to pull back on the stick really hard without confirming that there is enough airspeed to do so. Such an action would result in stalling the aircraft and another five minutes in the debrief.

In all of our minds, the mark of a really good IP was the one who, before beginning the instrument return to base, would say, "*OK, I've got it. Pull back your bag, sit back and relax for a few minutes.*" Translation: I'm bored silly back here and not having any fun. Let me fly the plane for a few minutes. Capt. Doolittle was always a good IP.

Supersonic Flight

On my first instrument ride, he took the plane and announced that I was going to be the first in my class to fly supersonic - faster than the speed of sound. He climbed up to about 35,000 feet, and using the afterburner, pushed the nose over into a shallow dive. Following his commentary, I watched the altimeter and airspeed indicator as we passed through the sound barrier. The needles on both indicators jumped back and forth a couple times. Jimmy announced, "*That's it. We are now supersonic.*" The airspeed needle seemed to struggle from .95 to 1.0 but, once I saw the needle jump, acceleration was fast and smooth.

As the needle approached 1.6, which is 1.6 times the speed of sound, Capt. Doolittle asked, "*Do you realize we are traveling at 14 miles a minute?*" The only way to know when passing into supersonic flight is by watching for the jump in the needles as the jet passes through its own shock wave. It is heard on the ground as a sonic boom. In a way, I was disappointed that it wasn't more dramatic. Chuck Yeager, the first human to fly supersonic, almost lost his life in the process because of the extreme turbulence he encountered. Then again, the X-1 wasn't designed to fly supersonic and the T-38 was.

Capt. Doolittle was a very gifted pilot and, as we said in the business, 'he had good hands.' During one ride, my map case cover opened as I did a loop, hurtling my maps behind my seat. Not wanting them to continue flying around the cockpit for the rest of the mission, I was attempting to reach for them when Capt. Doolittle said from the back seat, "*don't worry, I'll get them back for you. Just hold out your hands.*" Gently nosing the aircraft over until we were at zero G, he floated the maps to the top of the canopy. He then pulled the throttles back slightly, slowing the aircraft so that the maps slid forward along the top of the canopy until they were above me. Slowly pulling back on the stick, he ever so gently placed them in my hands.

Inevitably, the fun break would end, the bag would go back into place and instrument flying would recommence for the return to base. This return would require flying a point-to-point to a holding fix, and then a turn or two in the holding pattern while waiting for our turn to shoot the TACAN penetration and approach.

The TACAN Approach

The TACAN is a radio beacon situated close to the runway which, along with the HSI, allows the pilot to determine the airplane's relative position. Every base has two or more TACAN approach procedures published in an 'approach plate' book that all Air Force aircraft carry. These procedures require only a working TACAN receiver in an aircraft to be flown to a 'non-precision' landing which means that the procedure will bring one close to the end of the runway but not exactly lined up with it. However, since only a TACAN is needed, it is a means of landing in bad weather even without a radio.

The procedure usually begins from the Initial Approach Fix (IAF), which is about 30 miles from the runway at 18,000 feet. A typical approach begins with a fast descent while flying toward the station on a specific radial. There will be altitude restrictions along the way, for example, a requirement to be at or below 5,000 feet by 16 miles. It might also include arcing at a certain distance from the runway to a different radial. Arcing is usually required when the initial heading during descent isn't aligned with the runway. These approaches were considered especially challenging.

To arc, the pilot had to compute a lead point to begin the turn to the arc and then use corrections to stay within it. A lead point was computed for turning back inbound to intercept the new radial. Failure to monitor the HSI was a very bad mistake and would result in blowing the entire TACAN approach.

Sometimes the procedure would begin on one TACAN station and, partway through, would switch to a different station to finish the approach. Regardless, the last portion always had a straight-in course to fly from at least 10 miles out. By the Final Approach Fix (FAF), usually five miles from the runway, the plane needed to be slowed to final approach speed with gear and flaps down. At the FAF, a descent was made to the minimum descent altitude, MDA, and the landing was continued visually once the runway came into view.

The procedure sounds complicated and it could be. To get behind on a TACAN penetration during an instrument check was a horrible experience and just about guaranteed a busted check.

The Precision Approach Radar

Another approach that we frequently practiced was the precision approach radar or PAR. On this approach, a radar controller directed the pattern and the pilot followed his every direction. "*Stud 10, turn right to 010.*" I turned right to 010 degrees. "*Stud 10, turn right to 090.*" I turned right to 090. "*Stud 10, this is your final controller, how do you hear?*" I responded that I heard him loud and clear. To save another transmission, I also reported my gear down and locked, and my intentions such as low approach or full stop. From that moment on, the controller used a very precise radar scope to direct even one-degree heading changes to keep the jet on course. At the proper point, he announced the initiation of final descent.

Just like the Vertical S-a maneuver, Final Descent required power to be reduced a couple percent and the nose lowered three- degrees on the attitude indicator. The pilot responded to both glide path and course directions at this point, and frequently the Controller would also report the distance from touchdown and the jet's altitude. Finally, at 'Decision Height' or DH, he would instruct the pilot to go around if the runway wasn't in sight.

It was possible to land using PAR in almost zero visibility, but even after achieving the highest instrument rating, pilots were limited to 300 feet. If the runway was not in sight at that point, he added power to begin climb-out and go around.

Instrument Landing System (ILS)

A third commonly flown instrument approach and the most reliable and precise was the Instrument Landing System (ILS). Similar to the TACAN, it relied on information from a beacon on the ground, but was much more precise. The ILS instrument in the cockpit gave exact directions for glide path and course until touchdown. To fly an ILS approach, a radar controller would usually give directions until established on final approach, at which time the pilot transitioned to ILS equipment. A vertical bar represented runway alignment. When the bar was to the right of center the plane was directed to the right until the bar moved back to center. Using a little lead, the heading correction was taken out to keep the bar centered. A horizontal bar represented the glide path. When above glide path, the bar was below center on the instrument. Of course, when on glide path the bar was also centered. A skilled pilot could fly the entire ILS approach with both bars constantly centered.

Contact Flying

After five flights under the bag learning instrument flying, we began to learn to fly the airplane as well. Most of the initial emphasis was placed on the takeoff and landing My first takeoff was unbelievable. The T-38 accelerated very rapidly compared to the far slower T-37. Mentally, I was so far behind the aircraft that I felt like I was just barely hanging on to the tail.

I did a lot of 'armchair flying' before my next flight where I sat in a straight back chair with closed eyes and my checklist on my lap, mentally going through the takeoff procedure. My second takeoff was much better.

Why don't you come along on a typical contact flight. We'll begin after the 30 minute flight briefing with the IP when we go to the chute room.

A Typical Contact Flight

We are in the chute room now. The first item to put on is the anti-g suit. This is quite an invention. It resembles a corset except it is worn from the waist down. Air bladders are located on each calf, each thigh and over the lower abdomen. In the aircraft when the suit's air hose is hooked up to the G sensing system the bladders automatically inflate when excessive G's are pulled and the more G's there are the more the bladders inflate. By inflating, the bladders press against your body to prevent blood from pooling below the waist allowing more for the brain. This prevents graying or blacking out. Now I throw a parachute on my back, a flight helmet on my head and earplugs to protect my ears from the damaging noise of jet engines being started up on the flight line.

There is our aircraft over there. You can tell by the tail numbers. Ours is 392. The T-38 is all white, about 50 feet long with a long, slender black nose. It has short stubby swept back wings, the black nozzles from two jet engines protrude outward from the back part of the fuselage and the two pilots sit one behind the other, in tandem, each with his own controls and instruments. The plane was designed to be an advanced jet trainer but a variant, the F-5, was made that would carry heat seeking missiles. It has been sold mostly to third world countries for an air defense role.

The exterior inspection will take about 5 minutes. I start in front of the left wing and while following my checklist work my way completely around the plane checking the landing gear for hydraulic leaks, and 30 or so more items just to be sure everything is where it is supposed to be.

Now, we climb into the plane, the

T-38 Talon

crew chief takes the steps away and we strap in. That is quite a job in itself. First, there are the shoulder straps, then the lap belt, G suit connection, two parachute connections, two oxygen hoses and the radio cord. We get out the check list again and go through about 30 or so more items and are finally ready to start engines.

I signal the crew chief to hook up the starting unit to the right engine. The unit is really a huge fan that causes the compressor blades in our engine to rotate. At 10 percent rotation, the throttle is advanced providing fuel and ignition and the engine starts. A minute later we are starting the left engine and in a couple minutes we are ready to taxi. After calling the tower for taxi instructions we are rolling.

We have about a half mile or so to taxi to 'last chance' where a ground crew does one 'last chance' inspection of the aircraft and then we are next to the center runway. "Arc 61, this is Laredo Tower, you are cleared unto 21 center for takeoff; squawk 0400, contact departure control on channel 4 when airborne."

Now the pace picks up. We taxi out and line up on the runway which is 150 feet wide and 8,000 feet long, stop straight ahead, pump up the pressure on the brakes, do a couple more checks, run the engines up to 100% power, check engine instruments, release brakes and we are off and rolling. After 20 feet or so I advance the throttles to afterburner and the increased thrust presses us back into our seats. At 1,000 feet I check the speed to confirm that the engine is giving acceptable power. If it isn't I'll pull the throttles to idle and abort the takeoff. Our critical engine failure speed today is 126 mph. I computed it before leaving the squadron and it is the speed at which you can lose one engine and still have enough runway to continue the takeoff.

At 130 mph I pull back on the stick to lift the nose wheel about 4 feet off the runway and at 155 mph the plane leaves the ground. When safely airborne gear is raised followed by the flaps and then a radio call to departure control tells them we are airborne. I released the brakes about 12 seconds ago. In another 15 seconds I've pulled the throttles out of afterburner.

Capt Olson preparing for a T-38 flight

Afterburner is only used when absolutely necessary because it is a very wasteful way to get power and uses gas 4 times faster than 100 percent non afterburner (called military or mil power). Now I'll maintain a steady 300 knot climb. We've been assigned a standard instrument departure so at eight miles I start a left turn to pick up the 125 degree radial back to the base, level at 13,000 feet until beyond the base, intercept the 310 degree radial on the other side of Laredo and begin a climb to 17,000 feet. Beyond 20 miles we can continue to climb to our assigned altitude.

As you can see a lot happens in a very short time and if you aren't mentally prepared at brake release you will get hopelessly behind and might even be a hazard to yourself and others.

Departure Control just told us to contact Houston Center (FAA) on channel nine so we check in with Houston and are given a working area. Since we will be flying a visual contact mission we'll work low, between 10,000 and 22,000 feet. If we were on an instrument mission we'd work anywhere from 25,000 to 45,000 feet. By using our own navigation we determine we are next to our area so we turn right to enter it. However, we are cruising at 23,000 feet so actually we are above our area and still need to descend down into it.

The easiest and most fun way is to relax pressure on the stick, roll inverted and pull down into a split S maneuver. In only a few seconds we are now at 14,000 feet and ready to go to work. Area work consists of loops, cuban 8's, chandelles, immelmans and other aerobatic maneuvers. Airspeeds will vary from 250 to 500 knots. Then we quickly do some stalls and after a half hour we are ready to go back to the pattern to practice landings.

Houston Center tells us we are cleared to go back home and assigns us an altitude and heading. While we are doing this, we do our required cockpit checks. Houston hands us off to Laredo arrival control and after a few miles, they hand us off to approach control and at 10 miles with the field in sight we go to tower freq. and are visual for the rest of the mission.

After doing a couple pitchouts to overhead touch and go's, we practice a simulated single engine and a no flap and then a closed pattern for a full stop. We are almost out of fuel. We taxi back to the ramp, park the aircraft, shut down the engines, do a few more checklist items and the mission is over except for the debriefing.

T-38 Solo

Flying solo in the T-38 was perhaps the biggest milestone in UPT, more so than flying solo in the T-41 or T-37. A very unnerving observation for our class was that five students in the class ahead of us washed out of pilot training because they couldn't complete this task. As such, it was a great relief when everyone in my class successfully soloed.

The solo ride in the T-38 was a pattern only mission and lasted for just about 45 minutes. It consisted of taking off on tower frequency and flying the entire mission in the traffic pattern. The biggest trouble in flying the T-38, however, was in landing. It took much more finesse than the T-37.

T-38 'Talon' Solo Patch

When I initially had trouble with my landings, Capt. Doolittle told me to imagine a big hoop at the very end of the runway. I just had to fly the jet through that hoop. It was a relatively simple procedure to transition to a landing attitude and hold the airplane off the runway until slowing to touchdown speed. After landing, one had to hold the landing attitude until the plane slowed a bit more and then move back the stick. This caused the nose to rise from about 3 degrees up to 10 degrees and that attitude was held until slowing to about 70 knots. This procedure was called aerobraking and greatly reduced the landing roll. It was also really neat to watch from afar. Like a white horse rearing up.

The solo ride of substance was the Area Solo ride which lasted an hour and a half and involved doing everything that we would do on a normal contact ride except stalls. During my first area solo, I recalled the unfortunate seat failure that I experienced on my first T-37 solo. I felt assured that lightning surely couldn't strike twice and my seat would likely remain perched securely in its position. This solo would be just a routine mission; until I turned into my assigned area that is.

As I began doing my aerobatic maneuvers, I suddenly became aware that the radios were unusually silent. I keyed my mic for a radio check and discovered by the sound that I wasn't transmitting. I quickly thought back to the many stump the dummy sessions in the squadron ready room. Many of these emergency procedure situations involved losing radios, so I was confident that I knew what to do. I changed my transponder squawk to 7700 for a minute to indicate an emergency. This causes bells and whistles to go off in air traffic control to alert them. According to procedure, I now had their attention. I changed the code to 7600 indicating radio out. Within seconds, I heard on my emergency receiver (known as 'guard channel'), *"Stud 11, if you are NORDO (no radio) squawk flash."* I flipped a switch on my transponder to send out a flash signal. *"Stud 11, if you have any other emergencies squawk flash."* I was aware of no other problems, so I stayed silent. *"Stud 11, understand you do not have any other emergencies. For RTB (Return To Base) fly 250 degrees, descend and maintain ....."* I followed the controller's instructions until I was level at 1500 feet with the runway in sight in front of me.

Using standard NORDO signals, I rocked my wings on initial to indicate my radio was not working and pitched out to downwind. I lowered gear and flaps and began my final turn. A glance at the control tower showed a green, flashing light, a signal that I had clearance to land. As I pulled off the runway, another glance at tower showed another green light clearing me to taxi back to parking. My area solo in the T-38 was over. Back at the squadron I was secretly pleased when several instructors patted me on the back saying I had done well. Of course, I also knew I had done as I had been expected to do and that is what flying is about.

Formation Flying

Throughout our stay at UPT, formations of the sleek, white T-38s were a very common sight. We marveled at how steady they looked as they flew overhead. Four sleek, white jets locked together as one. We also listened to upperclassmen at the officers' club talk about students who had just washed out. After eight months, their flying training ended because they couldn't fly in formation. So, it was not without apprehension that my class began the formation phase.

We started out in two-ship formation. We briefed together, two students and two IPs. We started engines at the same time, taxied together and took 10 seconds spacing on the takeoff, joining to close formation after we were in the air. As a two-ship formation, we flew to the area where we practiced various maneuvers. First one student would lead and the other would fly on the wing. Half way through the allotted area time, our roles would change.

Upon entering the area, the leader would usually start out by making gentle turns with the wingman flying close formation. This was a precise position that allowed about three feet of wingtip clearance. If the wingman seemed to be managing OK, the maneuvering would increase in intensity until we reached pitch attitudes of plus or minus 70 degrees and bank angles of 90 degrees. The secret to flying wing was in the leader. He had to be smooth and plan well ahead.

To get practice on both wings, "cross-unders" would be given to direct the wingman to move from one wing to the other. Pitchout and rejoins were practiced extensively. The lead would give a circular hand signal and then very rapidly snap into a 60 degree bank turn away for 180 degrees. After 10 seconds the wingman would follow. This would place the two aircraft about two miles apart. The lead signaled the rejoin by rocking his wings. He then went into a 30 degree bank turn, allowing the wingman to get cutoff to rejoin back to close formation.

We also practiced route formation and echelon formation but my most favorite formation flying maneuver was close trail and extended trail. In close trail, the wingman flew a position behind and below the lead, not to exceed about 50 feet. When he called 'in,' the lead was free to do any kind of maneuvering, including mild aerobatics. Extended trail was even better. It was quite similar to close trail but was flown up to a half mile back.

The Key to Formation Flying

I mentioned that the secret to formation flying was in the leader but it was more than that. There were many techniques passed out by different IPs but the universal advice was to stay relaxed. When a student started to bob on the wing, which was frequently, the words he would most likely hear from his IP would be "relax, you've got a death grip on the stick." I found that if I made myself move my fingers up and down on the stick it helped me to relax. I also stirred the stick constantly and would make a correction the second I noticed a deviation from the ideal position. In other words, flying fingertip formation meant always applying corrections. If you started bobbing too much, the answer was to move out a few feet, settle back down and then move back in. All of the other maneuvers in formation were nice but the breaker was close or fingertip formation.

Perhaps due to Capt. Doolittle's influence, I was the first to be cleared solo formation in my class and when I had completed my first solo I finally felt quite confident that I would not only finish pilot training but even get a fighter assignment. Many of the formation sorties were flown solo and we had about 15 two ship formation sorties followed by a check ride. It was considered a serious phase of pilot training and there were a few students that ended their flying career in this phase. I took my two ship check ride with Peter Hammer, the Dane, flying the other airplane. We both had our check rides on the same sortie and we both did quite well. The high score I got on this check just about assured me that I would be able to choose a fighter when the aircraft assignments came in just prior to graduation time.

Four Ship Formation

Four ship formation was also introduced to us. I say introduced because there were only three or four sorties devoted to it. The techniques and skills for formation flying were the same but there were different procedures to follow for numbers three and four in the formation. A rejoin procedure for a four ship was a good example. The definition for standard formation had number two on leads right wing, three on his left wing and four flying on three's left wing. During a rejoin, for instance, even if number two was slow in rejoining, three had to wait for him to get on board before he could rejoin on the opposite wing.

Cross-unders also demanded extra consideration as did echelon formation. But, the most exhilarating part of four ship flying to me was being in the number four position during extended trail formation. I vividly remember watching as lead, a mile and a half in front of me pulled up to start a loop, followed by two, then three. By the time it was my turn to begin my pull up I could see three planes in front of me all in a column appearing to be flying straight up and the sight became more and more impressive as the loop progressed until we were all back to level flight. Aerobatics was a blast in four ship extended trail.

Formation Landings

We did two ship formation takeoffs routinely after the first or second ride but only those who were going on to fly a fighter got to do a formation landing and that was usually on the last ride of pilot training. Because of this policy I was excited and a little nervous about the prospects of landing only a few feet away from another airplane but when it became my turn to do a formation landing I loved it and throughout my flying career continued to love formation landings. In fact, I enjoyed the formation phase of pilot training more than any other.

Night Flying

Like formation flying, night flying was also only done in the T-38. It was flown towards the end of the program and it was a short phase. We flew the entire phase in one week. My first flight was on Monday night and it went so well my instructor pilot cleared me solo and sent me out for a second solo sortie that same evening. No sooner had I gotten airborne then my heading indicator and navigation instruments all quit. I notified the ground of my situation but since it was a very clear night and we stayed within 25 miles of Laredo AFB (the field was always in sight) they didn't get too concerned but did tell me to land 15 minutes early when my fuel weight was at a reasonable point.

Night Round Robin

On Tuesday night the entire squadron flew a round robin sortie where we flight planned and then flew at high altitude from point A to point B, then C, D, E and finally back to Laredo. It was a long sortie but I was mesmerized at the sight of Texas at night. Off in the distance I could simultaneously see the lights of most of the major cities; Dallas, Fort Worth, San Antonio, Austin and Houston. They appeared like softly glowing galaxies embedded in the blackness of space.

On Wednesday night we flew solo round-robins to Del Rio AFB, about 150 miles up the Rio Grande river from Laredo. That sortie was mostly uneventful as I listened to the planes in front of me and behind me make the same check-in calls in sequence to Houston Center. We all had 3 minute spacing and there were about 20 airplanes. An interesting and to this day unexplained phenomenon occurred during my return from Del Rio. While in level cruise I suddenly had a feeling of rocking side to side like sitting out in the lake in a canoe that was broadside to the waves. I immediately checked my engine instruments - they were normal. Then I thought it might be a form of vertigo that I had never heard about before so I checked the turn and slip indicator. It has a small black ball resting in a slightly curved glass tube and acts basically like a carpenter's level. In level smooth flight it should be centered. The ball was slowly rocking back and forth with me so it definitely wasn't my imagination. I finally decided it must be just a wind phenomenon. Now, as I look back on it with much more experience I think it was an aircraft problem with the stability system.

On Thursday night I had a solo out and back to Amarillo, Texas only it turned out to be a solo out. The back didn't happen until the next day because during my preflight check on Amarillo's ramp I discovered a hydraulic leak in one gear well. The leak couldn't be fixed in time for me to rejoin the flow. The squadron contacted Jean to let her know I wouldn't be home that night and I got a room at the BOQ.

The next morning my jet was fixed and I cruised back to Laredo at 39,000 feet. There wasn't a cloud in the sky and visibility was virtually unlimited. It was a completely different world. The only sounds were a slight comforting drone from the engines and occasionally Houston Center would talk to someone on the radio. At one point after turning toward Del Rio I thought to look for the reservoir that borders Del Rio. Although it was 75 miles away I felt like I could reach out and touch it; it was right there. Fortunately, even though I was completing my night out and back during the day it did count so I didn't have to repeat the sortie.

Cross Country

Our cross-country missions were flown late in the pilot training program so we viewed them not as an evaluation but as a reward. I really wanted to go to Denver partly to see the Rocky Mountains from the air and also to see brother-in-law Jack and his wife, Dorothy. You can tentatively plan on going somewhere but not until you show up the morning of the cross-country and check the weather will you know where you are going. In my case I found someone else who also wanted to go to Denver so we planned to go as a two-ship formation.

Flight planning for the cross country was extensive and took perhaps 45 minutes of poring through charts, figuring climb speeds and distances and a myriad of other

The T-38 Talon

figures. We had to do this planning knowing that our IPs could do the same planning in 10 minutes using rule of thumb figures rather than having to work through graphs and charts. The flight to Denver took two sorties because we didn't have enough fuel to make it non-stop. The prevailing wind was always from the West. When we got to Peterson Field in Denver I called Jack and he and Dorothy drove out to pick me up for the evening. Of course I proudly gave them a tour of my T-38 and then we had an enjoyable evening at their home.

The next morning I had to be back early because we had to return to Texas. I brought along a 30-06 rifle that Jack was holding for me - it had belonged to my father-in-law and was given to me following his death. My IP wasn't too crazy about doing it but I managed to fit the rifle in under the front seat and there it stayed for the trip home. Later, when I was flying fighters in TAC, I discovered that what I had done was very much against safety rules. If I had run the ejection seat down too far it could have become damaged and perhaps even malfunctioned if needed. In the F-4 objects under the seat had even caused unintended ejections.

Flying at 49,000 Feet

Capt. Olson prior to a training flight

It was a bright and cloudless November day for our return and when we checked the weather the fuel figures showed we could come tantalizing close to Laredo with one flight. With that motivation to get home a bit sooner, our IPs got into the act and they figured that if we returned at 49,000 feet we could one hop back - and that is what we did. It took forever to climb to that altitude. Airliners seldom fly above 39,000 feet. This was almost a mile and a half higher. The air is so thin at that altitude that the Air Force requires pressurized space suits for flight at 50,000 feet or above. I think only a T-38 could fly at that altitude because it is so sleek and devoid of drag inducing devices that most other airplanes have. Years later I had a mission requiring me to fly an F-100 at 42,000 feet and I could only stay there with the use of afterburner and when I had to make a 30 degree bank turn I literally fell out of the sky to a lower altitude.

When we leveled off at 49,000 feet I was forever impressed when I observed the other T-38 I was flying with. It was about 100 feet to the side and leaving spectacular white contrails in its wake but what was so striking was its attitude. All airplanes in level flight will have a nose high attitude and the higher the altitude the more nose high it will be. In an airliner it is much easier to walk towards the rear of the plane than to the front because the latter is 'uphill.' At 49,000 feet, our aircraft's attitude was considerably more nose high than I had ever seen before. At that altitude we were burning very little fuel and with a nice strong winter wind from the west the geography literally swept by beneath us. In a little more than 2 hours the familiar sight of the winding Rio Grande came into view while still at a colossal distance and as we got closer, we recognized other familiar landmarks. It was almost with regret that we received directions from Houston Center to descend and we had to leave our lofty perch.

T-38 Check Flights

The T-38 phase took up more than half of pilot training and it consisted of many dreaded check rides. Each was a small mile-stone in our paths to our silver pilot's wings. The first was the contact check that occurred shortly after initial solo and demonstrated that the student was proficient at flying the aircraft. Next and half way through the phase was the midcourse check. I imagine the purpose of this check was to insure that adequate progress was being made. Then towards the end of the T-38 phase came the two-ship formation check, an instrument check and a final all around check called the navigation check. The specter of a check ride was never far. As we entered each round of check rides the scheduling officer/IP wrote a score card on the scheduling board to keep track of the progress. On one side read 'Christians' and the other read 'Lions'! You can guess who the Christians were. Many years later as an F-4 IP and in charge of scheduling I revived this score card and my students loved it.

Aircraft Assignments

Throughout the year at UPT a commonly talked about subject was that of aircraft assignments, especially when classes in front of ours received their list of aircraft to choose from. Assignments came down as a block of aircraft and associated bases and they represented just about every type of aircraft the Air Force flew, from small O-2 and OV-10 forward air control propeller driven planes to supersonic fighters like the F-4, F-106 and A-7 to the heavies; C-130 and C-141 cargo planes, KC-135 refueling tankers and B-52 bombers. If a class had 40 students left in it towards the end of training, a list of 40 assignments would arrive. Who got what aircraft was decided by the merit system. The top student in the class got to choose first, then number two, then three and so forth. Out of 40 students I was ranked six and I was worried because there were only five fighter assignments, one F-106, one A-7 and three F-4s. More than anything I wanted one of the F-4's.

Throughout the year everyone talked about taking a fighter and I was just positive that I would not get one. I need not have worried as it turned out. At the mass meeting of all students where we did our selections number one in the class chose a KC-135. I was shocked. Number two took a C-141. Number three, a friend of mine, Skip Boles, took an F-4 to MacDill AFB. Number four choose a C-130 and number five, Dan Larson, initially wanted an F-4 but during the year I really talked up the A-7 airplane and it paid off. He took the A-7. I very happily chose the 2nd F-4, also to MacDill.

T-38 Pilot Training Class 73-06, Sect II (Capt Olson 2nd row on right)

I was in seventh heaven. For me, a dream had come true due to a very supporting family and countless hours spent late at night and during weekends studying academics, mentally armchair flying upcoming missions, memorizing power settings and airspeeds and altitudes and never allowing myself to become distracted – or overly confident. Now, all that stood between me and an F-4 at MacDill AFB in Tampa, Florida were a few 'routine' sorties and Undergraduate Pilot Training would be history but forever in my memories.

Chapter Eight

Survival School

> *Though I fly through the valley of death I shall fear no evil for I'm the meanest SOB in the valley.*

Graduation from pilot training was anticlimactic for me. We had a formal dinner and, in addition to presenting wings to the graduates, a few awards were given out. I received one that was called the leadership trophy. I talked for a couple minutes on behalf of my section and we were all ready to get on to bigger things. It was also an emotional time because most of us probably wouldn't see each other again, except perhaps by chance.

Water Survival

On the way to MacDill AFB and F-4 RTU (Replacement Training Unit) I was sent to the Air Force Water Survival School, a four-day course at Homestead AFB, south of Miami.

Water survival began with two days of academics and two days in the water practicing emergency situations that might be encountered in a survival situation. The school might have been fun in warm weather, but while I was there the temperature never exceeded 60 degrees with a steady, cold wind out of the north. Since the water temperature was about 70, it was a temptation to huddle in the comparatively warm water to keep warm.

Favorite Water Activities

The first water activity simulated the consequences that follow an over-water ejection. We practiced entering the water and releasing from the shoulder harness. To do this, we climbed a 60 foot tower and, after putting on a parachute harness, we were attached by parachute risers to a 1,000 foot long cable that slanted down into the water. It was a fun ride until we entered the water. On the way down, there were things that had to be done; simulating the disposal of the oxygen mask, simulating a check for a good parachute canopy, and inflating our 'Mae West' life preservers. As the instructors loved to say with a grin, *"when you feel your boots filling with water, pull on your harness releases."* This would separate us from our parachutes.

Now the task was to swim back to shore - through some obstacles. First was the parachute canopy that was laying on the water. We were taught how to swim out from under a canopy; roll over on your back, find a parachute seam near your face and follow it to an edge by pulling it downward toward your feet. This should quickly remove the parachute from on top of you - hopefully before the parachute sinks. My problem during this that almost put me in a panic was my life preserver began to deflate while I was under the canopy. Fortunately, I found the oral inflation tube before going under and was able to re-inflate it. After the canopy exercise we practiced climbing into and out of 12 man life rafts, smaller three or four man rafts and the small one man raft - each requiring specific techniques not to mention a good deal of strength. I noticed, however, that the more technique one used the less strength one needed.

We received advanced training from the deck of the water survival school's 100-foot ship. A very great danger when parachuting into water when it is windy is being dragged by an un-collapsed chute. With a lot of strain on the parachute risers it can be very difficult to release them from your harness especially if you are on your stomach.

Dragging and Parasailing

We were all totally soaked and huddled in the cold, drafty, metal hull of the boat. It was an overcast day and the air temperature was in the high 50's. We were not entirely enthusiastic to climb up on the windswept deck to be dunked in the water again. But, we did. I put on a parachute harness and then got in line on the back deck. When the guy in front of me was dispensed with it was my turn and I stood on a step under a metal boom that extended out over the back of the ship. Survival school guys attached my harness to parachute risers that in turn were attached to a rope. This whole assembly was suspended from the rail and when I stepped off the step I was slid out over the water.

The ship was moving at about 15 knots so the water was speeding by quite quickly under my feet. As I dangled there I was facing the boat looking at the deck crew. One of them had his hand on a lever that when moved just a little would release my parachute assembly from the rail. I thought that this must be what a condemned man must feel waiting for the gallows trap door to drop open. The 'executioner' loved his work. He was talking to me reviewing one more time what I was suppo - in mid-sentence he let me go. I plunged into the water and in three seconds I reached the end of the 50 foot drag rope and the ride began. I was on my stomach and taking a tremendous amount of water directly in my face. As I was instructed to do, I managed to roll onto my back and by spreading my legs I became somewhat stabilized. Then, it was a simple matter to reach the connectors on my harness and release myself from parachute/tow rope. We were warned that it was very important to release the connectors together. I did and instantly found myself bobbing in the water, the executioner's ship quickly receding in the distance. A smaller boat was closing in to pick me up so I wouldn't miss the next fun filled event. I decided that being dragged was pretty low on my list of fun things to do.

A more fun activity except for the cold was parasailing. We again found ourselves huddled in the cold, drafty, dank hold while we waited. When it was my turn I came topside and put on a parachute harness and that in turn was attached to an opened but deflated parachute. A smaller motor boat was paralleling our larger ship and a line was attached from that boat to my harness. At a signal from the motor boat the deck crew held up my canopy so it would catch the wind and inflate. As soon as it did, I felt myself being rapidly lifted into the air and the motor boat roared off. I quickly sailed upward. I excitedly watched in delight as the world dropped away beneath me. The large vessel I had been standing on only moments earlier became smaller and smaller as I ascended to about 500 feet.

At a signal from the boat I released myself from the tow rope and began a gentle descent back to the water. During the descent I went through the previously practiced tasks of getting rid of oxygen mask, inflating my life preserver, checking my risers and canopy and prepared to enter the water. The tow boat was on hand to retrieve my parachute canopy. When the tow boat moved off to connect with the next student I found myself floating in the water. Bobbing in the water within a quarter mile of me were several other students who were waiting for the next fun event – the helicopter pick up.

I waited my turn until a helicopter reached me for my water pickup. After a half hour wait I saw with relief that the chopper was heading for my position. As it centered over me the term rotor wash gained new meaning. The rotors sucked up a tremendous amount of spray into the air. Through squinting eyes I could just barely see what I was doing. When the retrieval device was lowered to me I waited for it to ground out in the water so it could discharge its static electricity and then I folded down a narrow seat. The device had some buoyancy and partially floated but on its side. I found myself struggling to keep my head above water while trying to hold the device upright and then straddle the seat. Finally I was properly positioned with my arms wrapped around it.

I prayed the para rescue jumpers (PJs) would take note and start pulling me up without delay because I was once again in danger of going back under. My prayers were answered and I was quickly hoisted out of the water. As previously instructed I let the PJs pull me in through the chopper door and for me the day was finally over. A hot shower and cold beer suddenly seemed really great.

Basic Survival Training

My school date for basic survival training was, like water survival, less than ideal. I attended the school during the last two weeks of November of 1972 after graduating from F-4 RTU and on my way to Germany. The survival school was located at Fairchild AFB in Washington State. It was cold, the days were short, and the snows were just around the corner. We had about several hundred men and women in my class - the school was required for all aircrew members, male and female, officer and enlisted, colonels and airman third class. Failure to successfully complete the school meant separation from the Air Force. It was considered that important.

Survival School Academics

The school had three parts. It began with several days of academics and then our class was divided into two groups. One group went immediately out into the national forests of Washington State for 'The Trek' as it was called. The other group went to the POW camp. After completing the trek or the camp the groups switched activities. Some people much preferred the POW camp to the trek and others favored the trek. Since I've always enjoyed being in the woods the trek was much more to my liking, but neither came anywhere close to being fun.

Academics lasted for several days and we had classes on all aspects of surviving in the wild following a bailout. We learned all about making shelters, finding food, making a fire, first aid, and survival crafts. Some of it was practical work and in one class I made a survival belt from a parachute riser. We also learned a variety of uses for nylon riser cord. We learned skills we would later practice when out on the trek. A good deal of time was also spent on the POW camp situation.

The POW Camp

I was in the group that went to the POW camp first. In academics we were taught what was expected of us if we were ever captured. We learned that during the Korean War many captured American soldiers behaved very badly because first of all, they had no prior training in how to react in a POW situation and secondly, they were unrealistically expected to only reveal their name, rank, branch of service and service number. Due to the lessons of Korea we were taught differently. We were told that we should put up mild resistance but not to the point of inviting torture and that we should invent stories to give our captors but to give those stories reluctantly and in bits and pieces. Stall as much as possible and make them work for any information they might get. In addition we were taught different means of resisting during interrogation as well as different methods of interrogation.

What was taught during academics was demonstrated to us very vividly in the POW camp and we got to practice methods of resistance including trying to escape. The camp lasted for only two days but seemed like two weeks. What I learned during those two days will be etched into my memory forever.

Evading Is Useless

The ordeal began when we were bussed after dark to a 'drop off' point. We were dressed as we would be during a combat mission, flight suit devoid (sanitized) of all insignias except rank and nametag. We represented a cross section of people who flew in the Air Force; pilots and navigators of course, but also flight surgeons and flight nurses, enlisted load crewmen, flight engineers, refueling boom operators, para rescue people (PJ's), weapons controllers from the relatively new AWACS airplanes and many more. Our ranks were from one stripe airmen to silver oak leaf lieutenant colonels - and I'm sure at times even higher ranking officers had gone through the school.

On this particular evening it was very dark and upon being unloaded we were instructed to use whatever evasive maneuvers we could think of but that we had to cross an area of land and reach the safety of the other side. What we didn't know was that no one ever reached the other side. We all would be captured and interred in the prisoner of war camp.

When I was only halfway across I think I began to realize the futility of evading capture. First, to one side I heard the sharply uttered command, "halt, do not move" followed by other harsh orders. The words were English but with a very strong Asian accent. As the minutes passed other evaders to my left and right were captured and briskly led off into the darkness to meet their fate - and then I heard movement through the brush coming towards me. I flattened myself on the ground, closed my eyes and remained motionless hoping to avoid detection. "Get to your feet, imperial dog. You are a prisoner of the People's Republic," I heard from a threatening voice very nearby. I remained motionless thinking perhaps it was someone else the owner of the voice had spotted. This notion was dispelled when I felt a boot roughly nudge my side. I got to my feet and felt my hands being tied behind my back. I was a prisoner of war with only one thought of reassurance - whatever was in store for me would be over in a couple days.

I can't reveal some details of the POW camp because they are classified but during the next day and a half we got a thorough introduction to what it must be like to be a POW. The realism was so complete that in a very short while after capture we felt like and acted as if we were really in a POW camp and these interrogators really were the enemy.

Interrogation

Short of actual physical torture we were manipulated and coerced until we were confused, frustrated and scared. One by one we were unexpectedly led off at unpredictable times to be interrogated. Different techniques were used in the process and we were expected to develop effective resistance techniques. If we did something wrong that would have resulted in extra harsh treatment or even punishment or torture, the interrogation would pause and the interrogator would say, 'academic situation. Now, you just responded this way and....' For a minute or two he was an instructor, not the feared enemy interrogator. We wanted to prolong this respite for as long as possible. That was not to be, however, and just as soon as the interrogation had stopped it would start again. I think I learned my lessons well because I never had very long sessions, maybe a half hour at a time, but some of the POWs were absent for quite a while longer.

One of the most feared techniques of torture allowed for the school was the infamous box into which a POW would be crammed and left for a long period of time. There were stories of some people coming unglued in 'the box.' When it was my turn I quickly adjusted to the setting and found it comforting knowing that this dark wooden container afforded me a great deal of privacy. Being thin and wiry I actually had enough room that I could sit down in a hunched manner and I fell sound asleep.

One POW who must have been double jointed was able to turn completely around in the box but the joke backfired on him when his guard became enraged and stuffed him into a smaller box that there would be no turning around in. We were reminded that there was nothing to be gained by taunting your guards.

The interrogations lasted for all of the first night and into the next day. When not being interrogated we were kept in jail cells. We were guarded of course and punishment would swiftly follow if anyone was found to be sitting down or sleeping.

The Prison Yard

Finally, our POW group was released into a prison yard and that was a welcome relief. In the yard we gained some security by being together in a large group. We were assigned specific tasks and performed manual labor but if careful we could speak to other POWs without being caught. By our military rules our leader was the SRO, senior ranking officer, even though the enemy would try to pick out a weaker person of lesser rank and try to make him the leader. Their goal was to sow dissension within our ranks.

It was our goal to maintain our military discipline to include following a proper chain of command. Our SRO appointed a POW structure of command under him like any other military unit. At one point, our SRO was marched away and 'executed.' Others during that day and following evening met similar fates. Sometimes their disappearance would be followed by a gunshot - but they were never seen by us again in the camp. We later found out that they had really lucked out. They were pulled out and the exercise was over for them.

An Ending to Remember

The second night was cold, the air was cold, the ground was cold, we were hungry and spirits were lagging. But we were kept busy. Finally the long cold second night was over and the sky in the east began to brighten but our ordeal seemed far from over. We expected to see some sign that the POW camp was over but there was none. In fact, at one point we were once again, for the umpteenth time lined up for yet another propaganda talk. The enemy commander got in front of us and launched into another diatribe about how our country was wallowing in moral decay. On and on he lectured us. And then, with a slight smile on his face he called us all to attention and called for an about face. As we executed this maneuver, we were anticipating yet more harassment. What befell our eyes, however, took our breaths away and brought tears to our eyes. All feelings of fatigue and despondency were erased. Before us the sun was rising above the horizon and the Stars and Stripes was being raised on the flagpole. And then the Star Spangled Banner began playing. We smartly saluted the flag and we cried. To this day that remains one of the most emotional moments of my life. I will remember it always.

The Trek

Early the next day we boarded busses for the long ride into the national forests of Washington State. The Survival School had an area especially designated for their use – and it was in a very remote area. We never thought of it at the time but this was part of the area where Big Foot or Sasquatch supposedly roamed the woods. When we arrived we broke up into large groups of 25 or 30 people and the trek began.

Our large group was broken up into smaller groups and we had 'forced marches' of several miles to reach our particular campsites for the first night. It didn't take long to find who was physically fit and who wasn't. Our group leader was a major who appeared fit. He was a transport pilot. Within two hours our line had strung out and he was at the end of it struggling to keep up. I don't know if he succeeded in the trek portion of survival school or not. To my surprise, at the head of the line was a hefty flight nurse. I believe she could have carried the major on her back if she so chose. Also near the front was a black female airman who didn't know the meaning of the word quit.

When we reached our destination we broke up into even smaller groups, squads, and our first task was setting up camp; making our 1 person shelters for the night. After making shelters we would then have the luxury of preparing supper.

Making Shelter

The first night we were directed to make our shelters from parachute panels. We were supervised as we tried to recall what we had learned in academics. Several instructors were with us and they were expert woodsmen. The shelter was a two sided lean-to that used a straight pole for the apex of the shelter. We were taught how a small stone could be easily tied with parachute cord into an edge of parachute allowing the material to be pulled very taut. When the structure was complete I cut pine boughs and laid down a 2 foot layer. My sleeping bag went on this layer and barely allowed room for me to fit in – but by morning the boughs had flattened so much I was almost on the cold ground.

We each had been provided with the newly invented freeze dried food packs and by simply adding water and heating we had very adequate meals. They were called MRE's (Meals Ready to Eat) and replaced the historic C rations and K rations of yesteryear. We were very fortunate in our squad because we had a very creative lieutenant who combined all of our foodstuffs and added vegetables he found somewhere and we dined on delicious stew.

Evading the Enemy Again

The next day we continued the trek but in a more serious manner. We were now broken up into 3 person squads. We had maps and our mission was to travel to another destination using map reading skills. To make matters more interesting the enemy was between our destination and us and we were warned to avoid capture. We began from a gravel road and our destination was several miles through the woods and across another road. When released, 20 or so groups charged into the woods. It was late November and we had quite limited daylight and little time to waste if we were to reach our destination in time to make another camp.

I took charge of my group of three since I seemed to have much more woods experience then they did and I probably outranked them as well. I held my group back and led them off down the road. I reasoned that the enemy would be waiting straight out in those woods. We would be more successful if we walked down the road a couple miles before heading into the woods. We would 'flank' the enemy.

Before long the muffled sounds of the others was left behind and by counting our steps we knew how far to the left we had deviated. All we had to do was travel a straight line to the next road and come back the same distance and we'd be there. The trek that day was very peaceful. We never saw anyone until we were approaching our destination. Many of the squads straggled in for quite some time afterwards because they had been detained by enemy patrols.

A Poncho Shelter

That night we were instructed to construct shelters using our vinyl ponchos and parachute cord. These were two-man shelters because they required two poncho halves to construct them. Once again when we had our shelter made we filled it with pine boughs.

We had a bit more time that evening and our instructor demonstrated how to make a fire with flint and steel. He carried a small piece of 'lighter wood' with him that he had gotten from an old pine tree that had been felled by a lightning strike. The pitch had accumulated in the base of the tree and the wood had a very high percentage of pitch. He scraped off some of this pitch that he then added to very dry moss and after just a few strokes of his flint had a flame. By carefully adding progressively larger bits of tinder he quickly had our campfire going. Many of us were so impressed we tried to make our own fires but even with borrowing his 'lighter wood' we were unsuccessful.

The weather up until now had been dry and cold with the nighttime temperatures dropping into the low teens. We had warm sleeping bags, the kind that were more of a tube without a designated top or bottom. The first night one of the instructors told us that it was best to sleep in the nude and we would stay warmer that way. Also, he said to keep your clothes and especially your boots in the bag with you. I did as he suggested and I was never cold. I also discovered the pleasure afforded by warm boots and clothes when dressing in the morning.

And It Snowed

The next morning it was snowing and I mean snowing. When we awoke we already had a couple inches on the ground. It was the first snow of the season and it was accumulating rapidly. This was the last day of our trek but our destination was a considerable hike and it required traversing a burn area that required climbing over countless fallen tree trunks – a hard way to hike and a hard way to measure distance.

We were taught to measure distance by counting our steps – a certain number was roughly a mile. Once again a piece of parachute cord came in handy. With each hundred steps you tied a knot in the cord.

Because of the heavy snowfall visibility was limited so we really had to rely on dead reckoning – using direction and distance. Also, because of the snow, it wasn't as cold and I actually enjoyed the hike. Our food kits each day contained cocoa packets and many people who didn't want to bother boiling water discarded their packets of powder. I collected each one I could and during the next day's hike would eat the sweet powder for an energy boost. I think I actually gained weight during my three days in the woods.

That afternoon my squad was one of the first to reach our destination and we were absolutely delighted to find it consisted of log cabins with heaters. Our last night was spent in relative luxury. The Trek was all but over. We were told the buses would be picking us up by eight the next morning for the ride back to Fairchild AFB and graduation.

The Last Night

Back at Fairchild before leaving for the Trek I had planned for this occasion. When packing my backpack I had included an extra flight suit that I would put on the last morning for the trip back. After 3 days of grubbing through the woods wearing the same clothes it was a real pleasure to take a hot shower and put on clean clothes. I had even packed shoe polish and shined my boots for the occasion.

The ride back was one of delirious happiness – we were finished with basic survival school. Well, most of us were finished. A few individuals had fallen out on the trek due to illness or injury or just being physically unfit. They would be given rest and treatment back at Fairchild and then pick up with the trek again with the next class. The 'can-do' black female airman injured her leg on the second day and against her will was medically evacuated. I really felt sorry for her but with that spirit I'm sure she did OK with the next class. That afternoon we had a graduation exercise and the next day I was on an airplane heading back to Poplar, Wisconsin to join my family before we started out for Germany and yet another experience.

Chapter 9

Learning to Fly a Fighter

In reference to a student after a less than satisfactory performance in air to air, "his situational awareness jumped into the map case."

A Fighter at Last

F4 RTU! I was finally here. It seemed like a dream to finally be at a fighter base and about to learn to fly a fighter. I was on the verge of achieving my loftiest goal.

The Vietnam war was still going on in March of 1973 but the end appeared to be in sight when I arrived at MacDill for F-4 RTU. The initials RTU stood for replacement training unit. The F-4 RTU was there to train pilots to fly the F-4 so they could replace other pilots in Thailand or South Vietnam, collectively known as South East Asia or SEA.

First TFW Wing Patch

The First Tactical Fighter Wing

MacDill AFB was home for the first TFW which was charged with training replacement pilots for the F-4. There were four squadrons; the 27th TFS, the 71st TFS, the 94th TFS and the 4501 (45 O First) TFRS. They each had very

F-4D from Udorn Air Base, Thailand, taking off

colorful squadron patches but the 94th was the most famous. It was of a patriotic top hat lying in the middle of a ring and the squadron was known as the 'hat in the ring' squadron. The 94th was originated during WWI by the famous fighter ace Eddy Rickenbacker. Rickenbacker spent a lifetime in aviation and founded the nation's first major airlines, Eastern Air Lines.

SEA Volunteer

When I in-processed at MacDill I was asked if I was a volunteer for South East Asia (SEA) and since I had already spent 13 months away from my family I replied that no, I wasn't. When I got to my assigned squadron, the 71st Tactical Fighter Squadron, I was called into the operations officer's office and asked quite pointedly why I wasn't a SEA volunteer. I explained that I had already volunteered and had been sent to Korea for 13 months and now I would like to have an assignment with my family. But then sensing that perhaps I had underestimated the significance of the volunteer statement in my records I asked about it and was told that to not have one was a bit of a stigma. I immediately went back to the personnel office and changed my status to volunteer. That made my squadron happy also.

As with any new airplane, our first endeavor was F-4 aircraft general academics, a very fast moving course where we learned how an F-4 flew. We studied all about the airplane's hydraulic systems, there were three, the pneumatic system, fuel system, electrical system (very complicated), life support system to include the ejection system, the flight control system and various lesser systems. We also learned about the emergency procedures associated with various system failures. This academic class led to the simulator training. Our first of perhaps 30 simulator sorties was to practice ground operations and basic flying with a very generous supply of emergency procedures. I vividly recall a feeling of extreme frustration at all that could go wrong and did on this first simulator mission.

First Flight

The first two weeks were a very busy time but we soon found ourselves appearing on the squadron's scheduling board for I-1, the first flight. The flight was in the back seat and was to introduce and teach basic instruments. I was shown a quick preflight inspection by my IP, Capt. Ray Rider, and then he helped me get strapped in. I was basically a passenger until we got airborne but I was very excited when we pulled out onto the runway. We lowered the canopies, did some last minute checks and an engine run up, and then Ray released brakes and plugged in the afterburner. I was impressed. When the burners lit, I was pressed back into my seat and by the time my eyes found the

71st TFS 'Lead Sled'

airspeed indicator we were already at 100 knots. At 170 knots we rotated and were airborne. Gear and flaps were retracted and then I heard Ray say, "are you ready for it?" I gingerly grasped the stick with my right hand and placed my left on the throttles, took a quick glance at all of the instruments hoping it would all suddenly make sense - it didn't - and I replied, "roger, I've got it."

When Ray released control to me it was very obvious because the rock steady attitude of the plane immediately changed. I determined that the F-4 was very pitch sensitive as well as roll sensitive compared to the T-38. During that first ride, if you will excuse a fighter pilot expression, I was '---holes and elbows' trying to keep up with what was happening. I was so busy that I completely tuned out the radios that Ray graciously took over responsibility for. I still couldn't keep up but by the end of the ride I was starting to feel somewhat less of a klutz.

I got a satisfactory on that ride but I could tell by the debrief that Ray wasn't really satisfied with my performance. In fact as the weeks went by I got the distinct feeling that he just didn't like me very much. He seemed to grade me harder than he did others but since I didn't know how well others flew I didn't know for sure.

At the beginning of each week before we could fly we had to fill out a 'bold face procedures' test where we were given a sheet of paper with the 12 or 13 procedures listed on it and under each one we were to write the proper steps of the bold face procedure. These were procedures that were considered so important and time critical that a pilot had to know them instantly by heart. Out of control recovery for instance was **Stick forward. Ailerons and rudder neutral. If not recovered, maintain full forward stick and deploy drag chute.** I will have that memorized until the day I die. However, during the weekly test, if anything was different, even punctuation, it was

27th TFS Patch

considered a failure and you were grounded until you successfully retook the test. On one such test I accidentally wrote the 3rd procedure second and rather than erase it I wrote the 2nd procedure third and then used a double headed arrow to show they should be reversed. Ray counted it wrong and I suffered the consequences.

An excerpt from a letter from 15 April, 1972 reveals some of my feelings about the F-4 from that time.

> *I have flown the F-4. I don't know how to describe flying 25 tons of airplane with 38,000 pounds of thrust coming out of the tailpipes. We take off with 9 tons of fuel (3,000 gallons) and burn most of it in an hour and a half.*

The plane is a lot trickier than the T-38 and infinitely more complex. It will truly be a challenge. The nice thing about the F-4 is I should be able to plan on flying it for several years and actually get quite familiar with it before being moved on to something else. At Laredo I was just getting to the point of knowing what I was doing in the T-37 when they moved me on to the T-38. Likewise, when I was starting to get comfortable in the T-38 I graduated. However, as one goes along it becomes easier and easier to learn a new plane.

I have had four flights so far and next week will get three more and then a check ride on what I've learned which is flying aerobatics, somewhat tricky confidence maneuvers, high speed maneuvering and of course landing the plane normally, no flap and single engine. On Friday I should get my first of five instrument flights and the following week four more culminating in an instrument check. After that we get into night flying, formation flying, air to air (dog fighting and intercepts), and finally bombing, rockets and guns on the air-ground gunnery range.

Transition Phase

The second ride began the 'transition' phase where we learned how to basically fly the airplane to include performing aerobatic maneuvers and the various types of traffic pattern landings. The phase consisted of seven sorties, the last being a transition check ride.

F-4 D retracting gear on take-off

My basic airmanship went quite well, especially the aerobatics which I've always loved, but I had trouble with the landings. I consistently landed hard - but according to Ray, within limits. After each sortie we would do five or more overhead patterns and touch and go landings but I never seemed to get any better. Naturally, I blamed myself. I also felt badly because I wasn't cleared crew solo; meaning my crewed Weapon System Operator (WSO) who was also a student and I couldn't fly together. I had to fly with an IP - because of my landing problems. However, I struggled through the phase and failed my transition check ride because of my landings.

LEARNING TO FLY THE F-4

Retraining with Major Charier

I was given two additional rides with a different IP and a recheck. It was on the next ride with the different IP, Major Ron Charier, when after a typical hard touch and go landing he told me to stay on the stick with him and he would demonstrate one for me. Just before the wheels touched the runway, he smoothly came back on the stick until it was against the stops and the wheels lightly touched down. I was amazed and exclaimed with wonder, 'so that is how it is done!' I tried the next one and for the first time did a light touchdown. From that moment on I prided myself in being able to finesse a 'grease job' landing. I also passed my recheck without a hitch -- but with great stress. Looking back on it I can't help but think Maj. Charier must have really wondered about Ray Rider as an instructor. It must have been obvious to him that I'd never been taught or demonstrated how to land softly.

I knew that if I had flunked that check I would have been eliminated from the school and probably sent to a B-52 or some other big plane (we called heavies) where new pilots act as co-pilots for three or four years before becoming pilots. During that time period I had felt absolutely numb. Capt. Rider twice asked me if I wouldn't rather fly something like a C-130 and he even sent me to the hospital to have a thorough eye examination for depth perception. Years later, when I was myself an RTU IP I realized that the 'counseling' and eye exam were steps in the elimination process. Capt. Rider had tried to eliminate me. Looking back at it now, I wonder if it could have had anything to do with my initially not submitting a SEA volunteer statement. I'll never know.

A week later I also had my instrument check and passed that one easily. I was now finally cleared crew solo and my troubles were over or so I thought. Ray Rider had different ideas.

Fred Wyland

I was crewed with Fred Wyland, a highly experienced C-141 navigator who had thousands of hours of flying time. Fred deservedly made major while in RTU. He was of my height and weight with light brown hair cut in a flat head style. He possessed a very easy-going attitude but was a truly professional airman. Fred did well in academics and learned his WSO duties very well. He was always there and very supportive when I needed him and I really liked flying with him. He must also have had nerves of steel because I never heard Fred sound alarmed or worried while we were flying together. Certain sorties in the syllabus were designated to be flown crew solo and we always looked forward to those rides.

94th TFS 'Hat in the Ring'

Formation Phase

The formation phase was enjoyable. We did some four-ship fingertip flying but formation in a fighter meant flying tactical formation, an entirely new concept for us. The basic tactical flown at the time was an unwieldy one called fluid 4 and consisted of lead and number three, the element lead flying 6,000 feet line abreast with the wingmen flying on the outside of their respective leaders.

Tactical Formation

Fluid 4 was difficult to fly and maintain proper position. It required a great deal of attention to maintaining position and making turns for the formation was even more difficult. I think that this formation is why almost all of the fighters shot down in SEA were numbers two or four. They had to spend most of their time flying formation and not looking around for enemy fighters.

Fluid 4, however, was beneficial; it taught me energy management. I frequently found myself trading altitude for airspeed or vice versa to maintain or regain position. As two or four, if the flight turned into me I slowly began climbing straight ahead while keeping the flight in sight. At exactly the right moment I dropped my wing and begin my turn inside of the flight. Because I was now so slow from trading airspeed for altitude I could make the turn faster than one and three and then lower my nose to trade that altitude back for airspeed. If done correctly I'd be right back in position.

A turn away was harder I thought. Here, I would just go into a steep banked, high G, nose low turn of 90 degrees finishing well ahead of the flight but with much less airspeed due to the high G turn. Once again it was of the utmost importance to maintain sight (or regain sight). It is a very bad feeling (not to mention dangerous) to know three other flight members are within a couple miles of you but not knowing where. It was also very humbling to have to punch the mic button and say, "uh, lead, this is four. Where are you?" Now, I'd have to play altitude in an attempt to gain back my airspeed before the rest of the flight completed their turn or I'd be left behind which would inevitably result in an irritated call from lead, "come on, four, get back

4501st TFRS Patch

into position." For the remainder of my flying career I used the fluid maneuvering lessons I'd learned and it made me a much better pilot. This energy/airspeed/altitude management lesson was lost to later pilots when fluid 4 formation was recognized as being tactically unsound and dropped from the syllabus.

Fighting Wing

We also flew a fighting wing formation that was flown by two aircraft. The wingman flew in a 60 degree cone behind his leader. The purpose was to be able to stay with and protect a leader who was in turn attacking someone else. Hopefully, it was decided, the wingman could give some form of protection to his leader while the leader was engaged. In actuality, the only protection the wingman was giving was to soak up any missiles that might otherwise hit his leader. Fighting Wing was a lot of fun to fly, though, because you really got to max perform the airplane.

Pod Formation

A third formation that we flew was called a pod formation and was used during a bomb drop where the leader would establish the dive that hopefully would result in bombs hitting the target. The wingmen dropped their bombs at the same time as the leader. It could have been called formation bombing and was a bit unnerving diving at the ground while flying formation off of another plane. With jamming pods on it was thought all of the fighters would have greater survivability. This formation was practiced a couple times during the air to ground phase but no one really took it very seriously. The syllabus said we would do it so we did.

Loose Deuce

One other formation was simply called 'loose deuce' and was developed by the Navy in Vietnam. It was a brilliant formation because you flew a simple 6,000 feet line abreast of your leader; it was easy to fly and very flexible and provided good lookout coverage all around the two airplanes. This formation became the most commonly used formation after Vietnam and was simply called 'tactical.'

Tactical formation also taught me to be able to tell distances in the air between myself and another flight member. Initially, when the IP got me into a 6,000 foot line abreast position with lead I would stare at lead trying to figure out, 'OK, what makes this picture 6,000 feet.' About that time my IP would say we're drifting away. We're now 8,000 feet. It still looked the same to me. Finally at 9 or 10 thousand feet I'd be able to discern that, yes, lead was indeed getting smaller so I'd put in a healthy correction and wait and wait for lead to start getting bigger. My IP would be uncomfortably silent. Suddenly, yikes! Lead's aircraft is getting bigger like gang busters. Holy smoke! And, with that I would put in a healthy away correction. I finally learned to monitor a heading and to make smaller corrections sooner. After a couple flights I started to notice that my 'mind's eye' was really learning to see very minor changes in apparent distance - and not only to other F-4's but to other types of aircraft as well. We practiced this skill every time we flew until it was second nature to swiftly drop into the prescribed formation and then aggressively stay there while constantly, vigilantly, checking '6' for bandits.

Air Refueling

During the formation phase we also began the air refueling phase. Air refueling wasn't a separate sortie. It was tacked on to other syllabus sorties. Our tanker we refueled from was the KC-135, a modified Boeing 707. Trailing behind the aircraft was an extendible boom that in the stowed position hugged under the tail but when deployed it hung down and just a little aft of the tail. The end of the boom had two little wings and the 'boomer' who operated the boom actually flew the boom during a refueling by using hydraulically activated controls.

When the pilot of the receiver airplane was in position, the boomer fine tuned the position of the boom so it was just in front of the refueling receptacle located behind the rear cockpit on the back of the F-4. At the correct moment he 'stabbed' the boom into the

'F-4D Hanging on the Boom'

receptacle and if both the tanker and receiver showed a good contact, the boomer started the gas flowing. On a training mission we usually took on about 2,000 pounds (300 gallons) each during a period of 2 or 3 minutes. During that period, the receiver pilot had to keep his airplane within a 6 or 8 foot cube of space. Without any doubt, air refueling was the most intense demanding activity I ever had to do in the F-4.

Typical Refueling Mission

During a typical mission, after takeoff we flew directly to the IP or initial point. Approaching the IP we contacted the controlling agency and were told where the tanker was along the hundred mile long refueling track. Armed with that information, the WSOs in each aircraft would get really busy on their radar scopes trying to be the first to call out the contact that would be the tanker. Following the WSO's directions the lead pilot flew an offset and

Phantom II Patch

parallel course resulting in a head on intercept with the tanker. At 21 miles separation and 11 degrees angle off, the tanker was told to begin a 180 degree turn and if done correctly, half way through the turn someone in the flight would call a 'tally' on the tanker and the tanker would roll out about 3 miles directly in front of the fighters.

From here to the pre-contact position, the four ship flight lead carefully controlled overtake so he could close quickly on the tanker but not too much that might result in an embarrassing overshoot. I was greatly impressed every time during the rejoin at how quickly the tanker got big in the windscreen. We just weren't accustomed to flying formation off of such a large aircraft.

Approaching a 200 foot aft position the flight lead would clear two to the tanker's right wing and three and four to the left wing where they would wait their turns. When given clearance lead smoothly closed to the pre-contact position. When stabilized there the boomer cleared him to the contact position where contact was made and refueling began.

When he was through, lead would fly to the outside of number 2 and would clear number 3 down for his turn. Then it was number 2 and finally 4. A 4-ship could get the standard 2,000 pound training offload in about 15 minutes.

The Boomer

When in the contact position, an experienced boomer was a great help. I've had boomers that just about required me to hook myself up to the boom and I've had boomers that would skillfully 'stab' me the moment my refueling receptacle was within reach of the boom.

The tanker had two aids for the fighters to use for positioning themselves. One was the director lights which were located way up under the front end of the tanker. They were lights that laid flush to the bottom of the tanker and consisted of symbols to show where you were in relation to the boom. The farthest

IR door open and ready for gas

aft lights were two inverted Vs and if thought of as an arrow would direct you to move forward . The next symbol was a single upside down V which meant you're getting closer. Next was a circle that meant you were in the proper fore/aft position. In front of that was a right side up V and finally a VV. The only problem with these lights was that in the F-4 at normal sitting height, they were hidden behind the canopy bow. You had your choice of driving your seat way up and trying to see them over the bow or driving your seat down to see the lights beneath. Either choice was uncomfortable and unnatural to me.

The second aid was on the boom itself. The same symbols were painted on the part of the boom that slid in and out of the outer boom casing. The Vs were painted in red and the circle was green. When in perfect position fore and aft you were said to be 'on the apple.'

Both of these indicators were only for fore and aft position. For up and down position, the pilot had to pick out references on the tanker such as moving up or down until the tanker's outside engines appeared to be resting on the canopy bow. It soon became a sight picture you just recognized. A comparison can be made to driving a car. A new driver frequently references the centerline and road edge but with driving experience this is no longer necessary – you just have the picture.

Refueling altitude was usually 26,000 feet. The air is quite thin at that altitude making refueling all the more difficult because of the F-4's pitch sensitivity in thin air. Another thing that added to the difficulty of air refueling was since we went immediately to the tanker, we were always heavy and sometimes would completely fill up before getting the full 2,000 pounds of gas. This caused us to be thrust limited. It wasn't unusual to find the two throttles all the way forward and

Unofficial Phantom II patch

you would still be sliding back resulting in a disconnect from the boomer. When this happened you would back away a little and put one engine in min afterburner and modulate the other one resulting in a greater overall thrust.

First Refueling

My first time on the boom was very exciting. First of all, it was a totally new experience as we closed in to the distance of a football field to something so large as a KC-135. Then, what an experience it was to fly up to the wing of the tanker. My IP kept telling me to move in closer, closer, and when we came to the end of the refueling track and the KC-135 began a 180 degree turn I realized why I was supposed to stay tucked in; it was too easy to start falling back and if that happened you were out of formation. In addition, if you weren't close on the tanker's wing you also weren't in position to drop down into the pre-contact position when your turn came. That was a no no because other flight members then had to unnecessarily wait on you and they were all burning gas while doing that.

The common currency in the air was gas and it was always considered sinful to waste it and of course when the person lowest on gas reached 'bingo' fuel, usually the mission was over for everyone. If the same person always bingoed out first, he would get a reputation for not being a 'good stick.'

On the Boom

When it was my turn to go to the boom, the boomer said, "number two, cleared to the pre-contact position." I pulled back on the throttle to move back and down and before sliding back 20 feet I felt my IP push the throttles right back and then some. I didn't understand but I knew that he had his reason to do that. Then, I noticed that my pulling the throttles back had slowed us 10 miles per hour, more than enough to slide back the couple hundred feet needed for the pre-contact position. I had to match my speed with the tanker or I'd fall back too far resulting in a tail chase - COSTING EVERYONE GAS.

That is exactly what happened to the next student after me. Where it took me one or two minutes to get to the boom, it took him 5 minutes. At two ship lengths behind the boom I was co-airspeed with the tanker and I called, "stabilized in the pre-contact." The boomer came right back with "cleared to the contact position." I gingerly moved forward and up and watched as the deployed boom with its miniature wings passed within a foot or two of my canopy and then disappeared behind me. My IP directed me verbally so I didn't even notice the director lights that were operated manually by the boomer until contact was made.

"Up two, forward two. Forward two. Forward one. Steady." My concentration was so completely intense that the rest of the world ceased to exist. There was the tanker with its boom and there was me and we had to stay together. I felt a firm nudge as the boom entered the refueling receptacle. I vaguely noticed a small green light on my canopy bow light up indicating a good contact. The boomer also called out a contact that I was supposed to acknowledge. I had such a death grip on the stick and throttles I didn't want to chance moving a finger to activate the mic button. My IP made the acknowledgment. I was bound and determined to not fall off the boom but the plane was moving up and down and sideways left and right, and sliding back and then forward as I frantically fought to make the appropriate corrections.

Finally, my IP said, "heh, Jim, relax. Move your fingers and toes around." As soon as I did that, the plane settled down and I found myself back in complete control. It seemed like an eternity until the boomer announced, "I show you've taken on 2,000 pounds. Disconnect on my mark. One, two, mark." It was almost like I had overdrawn my will power bank. When I heard the "one, two...." I began to porpoise up and down, a maneuver that usually only gets more severe as it progresses but the boomer got the boom unplugged and pulled away. He was probably as happy as I was.

The IP who gave us our phase brief prior to the air refueling phase made a statement that I will never forget. He said, you don't get better with refueling. You get more relaxed. That was true with me and I never ever fell off of a boom throughout my flying career.

We had four day air refuelings and two night refuelings. The refuelings were always in conjunction with another type sortie; formation, air intercepts, night ground attack. The weather varied also making a demanding task even more so.

Inverted on the Tanker's Wing

I remember one refueling mission very vividly. It was a crew solo ride. The tanker was flying in thin cirrus clouds. Visibility in the clouds was at least 5 miles but there was no horizon; no down or up. While waiting on the tanker's wing tip, we reached the end of the refueling track and had to turn back. The tanker went into a 180 degree turn using 15 degrees of bank. When he rolled out of the turn I was on the up-wing and my semicircular canals that told my brain what my attitude was never sensed going wings level. My senses were telling me that we were continuing to roll inverted. I suspected we were probably wings level but I asked Fred anyway what our attitude was. He confirmed wings level but my brain was telling me something different. In my head we continued to roll. Now I was becoming scared. If I broke off from the wing what would I do. My cognitive brain was saying we were wings level but my senses were saying we were inverted.

I knew a KC-135 couldn't fly inverted even if he wanted to. I told Fred that I was getting screwed up in the head and to keep telling me our attitude until I told him I was OK. Boy, did he talk to me. Finally, my reasoning brain won out and I was able to persuade my senses that we were wings level. That never happened to me while on the boom; perhaps because it took so much concentration flying on the boom there was nothing left to conjure up false attitude perceptions.

Night refueling, according to the IPs, was a piece of cake. "It's just like day refueling except you can't see anything" they loved to say. In fact I heard the same comments about night transition and night ground attack. For the most part I felt night refueling was if anything more easy because the director lights were so much easier to see. There was only one time I had trouble on the boom at night and it happened on a solo mission with Fred. We had taken off at twilight and I had my instrument and cockpit lights up quite high. Normally, as it gets darker you continually turn your lights down until they are at the lowest level possible where you can still see them. In this case I had gotten so caught up with the refueling rendezvous that I overlooked doing that. When I got on the boom I felt very uncomfortable. It was so hard to see anything and my aircraft control wasn't really great. Then I noticed that my outside visibility was greatly diminished due to a red glowing reflection on my canopy from my cockpit lights. I called for a disconnect, backed out to the pre-contact position, adjusted my lights and then moved back in for the rest of my off-load. I learned a valuable lesson about night flying that night.

Flying a Fighter - BFM

We began real fighter training with the air-to-air phase. It began with BFM, Basic Fighter Maneuvers. This consisted of two student pilots with IPs in their back seats going up and practicing maneuvers that were first developed during WWI but are still applicable when two planes are dog fighting. They even continue to carry names from that era; luftberry, immelman, chandelle. One plane was the target and the other practiced a BFM maneuver and then they exchanged roles.

BFM required maneuvering in 3 dimensions varying airspeed, altitude and aircraft attitude to move from a far off distance of 3 or 4 miles to a close in position at the bandit's 'six' o'clock where he could be shot down. This required an ability to not only visualize 3 dimensionally but also to predict where the target would be at the completion of the maneuver. Sometimes, several sequential maneuvers were required but it was all 3 dimensional requiring continuously assessing the dynamics of the attack and modifying your maneuvers accordingly.

To better understand the air to air phases a brief explanation of terminology is in order. Much of the terms originated from the birth of military flying, world war I. An identified hostile aircraft was called a 'bandit'; if unidentified it was a 'bogey.' In training the words target, bandit or bogey were commonly used interchangeably. If you could see the bandit it was 'tally ho' or you had a 'tally.' If you were referring to a friendly aircraft you said visual. If you were coming to the aid of your wingman who was under attack you might say 'I have a tally and visual.' There were many other terms, too many to explain without lapsing into boredom.

Effective BFM was a skill that was partially learned but also an aptitude as well as an attitude. If a student didn't have this aptitude it showed itself very quickly and resulted in washing out of the program. This and the follow on Air Combat Maneuvers (ACM) phase was usually where pilot washouts occurred.

Some of the BFM maneuvers were the low speed yo-yo, the high speed yo-yo, lag roll, barrel roll attack, immelman attack, quarter plane and zoom, the scissors and the more exciting vertical rolling scissors. Most of these maneuvers were offensive but there was also a defensive aspect to BFM - so called last ditch maneuvers designed to prevent you from being shot down.

A Typical Maneuver Setup

An example of a typical setup began with the target or bandit aircraft 3 miles out in front of the fighter and in a 3 to 4 G turn simulating that it was dog-fighting another airplane. I could use an immelman or a chandelle attack. For an immelman attack my first task was to get as much airspeed as I could, supersonic if possible, and close the range. To do that I had to make a quick judgment on where the target would be about a minute from now, point my nose in that direction while lighting the afterburners and push forward on the stick to almost zero G.

At a quarter G it felt like I was floating out of my seat but this is where you got the fastest acceleration due to greatly reduced drag and at the same time it got the jet pointed downhill greatly helping in picking up airspeed. This maneuver also got me out of the bandit's level to avoid detection and gave me vertical turning space so I could pull up into his six o'clock.

The most common mistake was not getting far enough below the bandit. Then when pulling up into the vertical for the final attack a vertical overshoot resulted. I checked my altimeter knowing I needed at least 10,000 feet to successfully complete the attack. As a visual reference, when I could see him well above my canopy bow, I was in position to begin my pull.

A glance at airspeed showed I was just slipping through the mach. Another check on the bandit and I could see a small dark silhouette of an airplane and enough of the wings to determine what relative heading he was passing through. I pulled the throttles out of afterburner, calculated he would complete another 180 degrees of turn during my pull and pointed the nose there. Finally, I came back on the stick into a 4 to 5 G pull. My G suit fully inflated helping to keep my blood from being pulled from my head which could result in a brown-out, momentarily losing vision. Even with the G suit I've got to really tighten my stomach muscles as well and forcibly grunt to keep full vision.

The plane started to resonate with a low frequency vibration caused by air separating from the wing, the first indication of stalling. I knew that my drag would go way up so I backed off the stick just a little. I wanted to just 'pull to the burble' as we called it. During the pull I readjusted my lead point thinking I would end up too close to the bandit. I also checked airspeed and plugged the afterburner back in. Airspeed/energy management was critical and could determine the winner in air to air fighting.

I completed the half loop or immelman inverted and in pretty good position, about a mile behind the bandit. A glance at airspeed confirmed that I had too much overtake so I pulled the throttles out of AB and back to idle and contemplated putting out the speed brake. I decided that wouldn't be necessary. With overtake under control I again advanced the throttles.

With my left hand I activated a multi position switch on the right throttle selecting 'heat' for heat seeker missiles and got the sight reticle on the bandit. A growling sound in my headset meant the guidance head of the training missile was tracking the target. I switched into self track mode for a better PK (Probability of Kill). I was still getting a good growl and confirmed that it wasn't from another source such as the sun or a white background cloud and pulled the trigger and radioed fox II.

The target hadn't changed his maneuvering at all and I still had good controllable overtake so I selected guns on the throttle switch. The sight immediately sank downward toward the nose of my airplane forcing me to point way out in front of the target for the necessary lead for a firing solution. At 2,500 feet, I called 'tracking, tracking', kill, knock-it-off' and rolled out wings level (knock-it-off meant to terminate the engagement).

The canned engagement was over. I did quite well and I sat back and relaxed just a little knowing that now it was our time to be target and I was eager to watch the other pilot and evaluate his attack. My IP would critique his progressing attack as well but first of all we needed to get pointed back to the center of our working airspace and climb back to 20,000 feet. All fights went downhill because an F-4 couldn't maintain a level 4 G turn at that altitude.

My IP reminded me to call for a fuel check. When maneuvering in full afterburner the F-4 burned up four times as much fuel as in full power without afterburner. You could actually see the gas needle fall and not infrequently planes returned to base with emergency fuel or less. Some even diverted to another closer base because they didn't pay close enough attention to fuel.

We carried external tanks which gave us enough fuel for two engagements each. Then we joined up 6,000 feet line abreast for the trip back home. Home plate was 65 miles on the nose and the rule of thumb for getting back using the least fuel was to climb in mil power at 300 knots until your altitude was half the distance to the runway. At that point, you selected a throttle position that corresponded with half closed nozzles (almost idle power) and began a 250 knot descent. As we reached 20,000 feet we were 40 miles out and started down for a straight in approach to initial. Over the numbers we took 5 second spacing in the pitch for a full stop landing.

In spite of air conditioning my flight suit, gloves and G suit were soaked from perspiration. Air to air combat is fun but also very hard work.

After landing, we went to maintenance debrief, then to the personal equipment room to turn in our helmets for cleaning and inspection and hang up G-suits and parachute harness and then grabbed a coke on the way to debrief the mission.

The lead IP was in charge of the debrief and this was where a skilled IP showed his stuff. He carried a tape recorder that recorded all radio calls as well as any sounds that came through the intercom of his airplane; talk with his student, the heat growl sound from the missile, an audible sound from the angle of attack system; it was all there. My IP also added his own comments such as airspeed and altitude, heading passing from time to time. During the debrief his commentary also helps him as he reconstructs each engagement on the chalk board. The debrief was where you solidified what you learned; where you learned from what you did right as well as what you did wrong.

Another hour and some change and the sortie was finally over. I checked my watch and saw that I had 45 minutes for a quick lunch and then get to a simulator mission and academics after that. It was a typical 12 hour day at RTU. At the moment, the life of an IP seemed luxurious. Years later I would find out differently.

Fighting a Fighter - ACM

The ACM (Aerial Combat Maneuvering) phase was a follow-on to the BFM phase. In ACM we used the skills learned in BFM and applied them in coordination with a wingman in what was still a canned setup but a much more realistic wartime scenario. There were two parts of the phase, defensive and offensive.

Very simply, in defensive, the two students flew a 2 ship formation 6,000 feet line abreast (standard tactical by now) and were attacked by a 3rd F-4 flown by an IP. The students would have to react properly and negate his attack. It was frosting on the cake if they could also get to an offensive position.

Offensive ACM was much more fun. The students were now the attackers and as a 2 ship formation got to attack the lone IP in what was called sequential attack. First, one airplane engaged the IP, who limited his maneuvering to something the students could cope with. The second student pulled up

Test F-4 with telemetry package on centerline

into the vertical to 'hawk' the fight from a couple miles above to be in a position to take over offensively and also be a lookout for his wingman to warn of other bandits.

Dog fights always went in a circle and they almost always went downhill because you never had enough energy to do otherwise. If three or four airplanes were in the circle each trying to shoot the one in front of them it was called a 'luftberry', a German term from WWI. As a rule of thumb if a kill couldn't be made within one or two 360's it wouldn't happen and the wingman would maneuver into position and call his leader off. If the leader didn't come off, the wingman would have to go back into the vertical and reposition for another entry. You might think of it as two foxes taking turns chasing a rabbit.

Like a Hawk

By far the most difficult part of offensive ACM was getting down from a mile or so above the fight and ending up in a position from where you could shoot the bandit. It required excellent spatial visualization and aircraft control. A frequent happening was for the lead to engage the bandit and after 10 circles and 3 or more attempts the wingman was still not able to enter the fight resulting in a 'knock-it-off' and a pinked (failed) ride.

A Typical ACM Engagement

"Lead has a bandit, 1:00 high, I'm engaged." The fight is on. I notice lead immediately roll into bank and his nose abruptly comes up. The typical dirty smoke trail of the F-4 disappears indicating he has lit the afterburners. I respond in required protocol, "two's free" which tells lead that I did hear his call and will cover him. In the past both wingmen have made the engaged call at the same time blocking each other out. With two engaged on the same target a very dangerous situation is sure to develop with a possibility of a mid-air between the two wingmen occurring.

I now need to maneuver away from lead so I can reenter the fight from a position of advantage. There are different ways to do that. I can do a 'counter-flow' where I turn in the opposite direction and get what is called an outside entry or I can go high and hawk the fight for a turn or two. Knowing the dangers of the counter-flow are not being able to regain sight of the fight, I elect to go high. I slam the throttles into full AB and pull my nose up into an almost straight up climb.

My attention is mostly on keeping sight of lead and the bandit but cross checking my own instruments so I don't run out of airspeed. When I'm a mile above the fight I roll over unto my back and start to anticipate where I can reenter and call off my leader. It takes a tremendous amount of lead to do this so I float over the circle they are flying and visualize a reentry about where the fight is now but one turn later.

As I pull the nose down into a dive I'm reminded of my low airspeed by the buffet I feel on the stick - not far from a stall, but at this slow airspeed a plane has a much smaller turn radius. Now, with my nose approaching straight down I can feel airspeed building very quickly and I pull the throttles back to idle to prevent my airspeed from getting too high. The consequence of too high airspeed would be a vertical overshoot ending up under the fight. By just rolling a little this way or that I can fine tune where I'll end up in relation to the bandit. The circle of the fight has loosened a little so I lag roll away just a little and then come back in with steadily increasing G's, switch to heat on the throttle switch, key the mic button and call lead off.

"Lead, come off right, I'm engaged." This is really a request and if lead thinks he is about ready to take a shot he could deny my request in which case I'd have to pull away and reposition for another try. But, lead is ready to swap roles and even before hearing him respond I see him roll away. "Roger, you're engaged, one is free."

The geometry of my attack is working really nicely and I'm coming in from the outside of the bandit - he can't see me. I get a heat tone in my headset and just as I call out a fox two meaning a heat missile shot, the bandit has noticed one breaking away and has guessed what is happening. He reverses his turn and suddenly, instead of seeing his belly, a high PK shot, I'm now looking at the back of his plane and angles are building. He has effectively negated my heat shot. I quickly toggle to guns on the throttle switch, yank in a bunch of lead so my sight is out in front of the bandit and then relax on the back pressure to allow him to fly through my gun sight.

Before he gets to my sight I squeeze the trigger to simulate a long burst of 20 mm bullets. It is a low probability of kill shot but it also builds angles quickly allowing a graceful exit without becoming the new target. The bandit is starting to get big quickly in my windscreen so I ease off more back stick pressure and as soon as my sight passes through him I rapidly roll 180 degrees away from him, relight the AB and disengage.

Since this is a partially canned setup and the learning objectives are accomplished, my IP calls "knock it off," and all three planes in turn repeat the call. A couple directive calls are made to get all three planes heading back together and we all begin 300 knot climbs to get back to altitude without wasting time.

"Lead has 5200 over 2500, 5.5 G's." The other two aircraft respond with their fuel and G readings. Good, we've got just enough gas left for one more quick setup but we might have to go sparingly on use of the afterburner. On to the next setup.

Fighting to Win, ACT

Air Combat Training was the culmination of the air to air phase, the graduate school if you will. If you were able to learn your lessons in BFM and ACM you did fine in ACT. The importance in this final phase was in developing tactics to be used as a team against another team of fighters - nothing was canned. Realism was added by having the aggressor team from Nellis AFB, Nevada flying the smaller, highly maneuverable F-5 deploy to MacDill.

The Aggressors

The F-5 was a good simulator of a MiG 21 Fishbed fighter, the primary Soviet air-to-air fighter in the early 70's. Even the markings on the F-5s were made to resemble the MiG. The Aggressor pilots were highly trained in Soviet tactics and they conducted the briefings telling us what we could expect.

A Typical Mission

A typical mission will be a 2V2, meaning two F-5s versus two F-4s. Rules of engagement are reviewed, rules that will ensure flying safety and fairness. Each team will have GCI (Ground Control Intercept) support so they will know approximately where the 'bad guys' are. The engagement will begin under a preplanned scenario. The F-4s are protecting their country defined by the limits of our operating area airspace. We know the F-5s will come from the direction of MacDill. We will have altitudes that begin with the numbers three or seven and the Aggressors will have one, five and nine. All aircraft will be at an assigned altitude by 10 miles separation and stay there until a tally (visual contact) is made with the enemy. And, there are several other rules that are reviewed. An unobserved Fox 2 is a kill, or a combination of two other shots will be a kill. Kill removal is to fly straight ahead for 10 miles and then return to base. Paramount, though, are the rules that will reduce the likelihood of a midair collision.

The F-4 is limited to 5.5 Gs when its external tanks are empty. In a real war situation, the external tanks would be jettisoned allowing up to seven Gs. We will fly clean, with no external tanks, allowing us to pull the extra Gs. An added advantage is a clean F-4 accelerates noticeably faster without the extra drag from the tanks; it really flies like a different airplane.

We do formation takeoffs and I'm amazed at how we are airborne in only 2,000 feet. The plane seems to spring off the ground. Flying the clean F-4 is delightful. We normally climb out at 10 degrees pitch but today it is much steeper and any movement on the stick commands instant response.

On the way to the area we take turns doing weapons checks making sure our weapons systems to include captive heat missiles and F-4 radars are working properly. Soon, we are inside our 'country' and on CAP (Combat Air Patrol).

We don't have to wait long. GCI informs us of two bogeys, unidentified aircraft, approaching our airspace and we are given snap vectors to intercept. Our IPs in the back seats acting as WSOs are busy on their radar acquiring contacts on the bogeys and soon we are approaching the bandits at over a thousand knots of closure. Our rules of engagement require a visual ID before we can attack. Oh, this is happening fast.

GCI calls 10 miles separation and we make sure we are at our altitude. At 5 miles we really start straining to see who gets the first 'tally' for an ID. An F-4 is usually visible at this range but not so for the small F-5. Finally at 2.5 miles I spot an F-5 and call him out as a bandit. My wingman soon calls the other one out and we both proclaim we're engaged. From that moment, the afterburner is lit and mostly stays lit because the bigger F-4 is going to always be needing just a little more energy. We are burning jet fuel at a fantastic rate. We coordinate occasionally between each other but mostly we are each on our own.

I'm trying to work a vertical fight because in our academics we were told the F-4 has more thrust and to slow down with an F-5 is to die. I pull up with max G into a steep climb looking over my left shoulder at my F-5 as he points his nose at me but I can tell I'm quickly leaving him behind. His relative movements are slow showing he doesn't have much airspeed. When I think I have enough separation to turn back on him I stomp on left rudder slicing the nose down to the left. At the same time the F-5's nose also falls and we reverse roles. Now I'm closing fast on him and try to find his heat source in my gun sight. Just when I think I've got him I can't believe what I see. The F-5 has done an amazing turn and is now almost pointed back at me. We meet head to head and since I'm going down-hill, I unload G and zoom for separation and more airspeed.

I strain to look over my right shoulder now to maintain a tally. An old axiom comes to mind, loose sight, lose fight. Once again I've got separation distance and I yank the throttles back to idle and momentarily drop the speed brakes to slow some for a faster turn and with a max G turn I'm now pointed back at the F-5.

My back-seater says, 'go radar', and I select radar on the throttle switch. He has the F-5 locked up on radar, calls out one thousand one, one thousand two, one thousand three for the required settling time of the computer to compute a track for the simulated missile and calls to me, 'cleared to fire.' I eagerly call out, 'Fox one on the F-5 headed south passing 15,000 feet.'

I call for a fuel check with my wingman. We are both rapidly approaching bingo fuel and need to disengage our respective bandits. My Fox one is not a high probability of kill shot but at least I got something off. I'm also in a good position to disengage as I meet the F-5 head to head again. My backseater IP calls out two contacts at 2:00 and I look off in that direction. I immediately see one black speck and soon make it out to be an F-4, my wingman. I call out my position to him and try to determine if he will need some help in disengaging. He does. I ask my IP where our bandit is and he says he is out of the fight, not a factor, so I make a hard turn toward my wingman and soon see a much smaller speck behind him, the other F-5. I call out the position to my backseater who goes to work locking him up on radar but the F-5's warning equipment or perhaps his GCI must have warned him because I see his nose come off my wingman and he disengages, turning to meet me head on. There is insufficient time to get the lock and I call to my wingman to 'bug out north', meaning to disengage together and lets go home.

A final fuel check shows we are both at about 1500 pounds of gas. We've each burned over 8,000 pounds or 1,200 gallons of jet fuel in not much more than 10 minutes. Using what is now standard procedure, we rejoin to 6,000 feet line abreast tactical formation, put home plate on the nose and begin a 300 knot climb until reaching the twice your altitude distance out. Then, with half nozzles we start a 250 knot descent. At that throttle setting, you almost can't even hear the engines and fuel consumption is extremely low. I notice that at level out on initial approach I still have 1,200 pounds left. I waggle my wings to signal my wingman to move in to close formation, call him over to tower freq and announce our presence to tower. "Tower, Lion flight, five mile initial for two full stops." As I touch down on the runway, I marvel at how lightly the clean F-4 flies. A glance at the clock shows we've been airborne for 35 minutes. Incredible; but I command my attention to the now common tasks of rolling out, dropping the parachute, taxi back - the mission isn't over until engine shut down. As I un-strap I'm thinking about the mission. I somehow feel that we did OK. We didn't kill anything but we survived to fight another day - not bad for a first fight against the Aggressors.

Ground Attack

Ground attack I very quickly decided was what I liked the most. Dropping bombs was fun. Shooting rockets was even better. Strafing was absolutely the greatest. Dog fighting was hard work and results weren't always clear with some battles being won in the debriefing. Not so with ground attack. Seconds after dropping a practice bomb we would hear our score read back to us by the Range Control Officer, RCO. Ground attack was also more dangerous we would soon come to find out in a very horrific manner.

The Gunnery Range

The bombs we dropped in ground attack were about two feet long, made of steel and had stabilizing fins on the tail end. A spotting charge was inserted into a hollow tube in the bomb's tail. At impact with the ground a very noticeable white puff of smoke allowed remotely operated scoring cameras on flank towers to triangulate the bomb's impact point providing a score. The score was called by telephone to the range control officer in the main tower and he relayed it to the aircrew.

We did all of our range work at Avon Park gunnery range, a large tract of land located about a hundred miles from MacDill AFB in central Florida. The range layout was standard throughout the air force. A description of a standard range follows:

The Standard Bombing Range

In the picture below of Avon Park the tactical range with its 8,000 foot runway complete with SAM and AAA sites is on the left. Mirror image conventional ranges are on the right side. The large 'nuc' circle is at the far right – each ring is 500 feet apart.

There are two side by side ranges that from the air look like huge dart boards lying on the ground. They are mirror images of each other but never are both ranges used at the same time. The bulls eye for each is a white bread van type truck body and each has concentric bulldozed circles at 100 feet, 200 feet and 300 feet intervals. These circles that are etched with white sand for contrast, allow fairly precise air scoring and understandably some grumbling from pilots who

Avon Park Bombing Range from high altitude

think a bomb might be closer than the score they received from the RCO. The two bomb circles fit inside a huge triangle made of range service roads. At the left and right points of the triangle are located the flank towers which are used for scoring. Another very long road runs from each bomb circle's bulls eye perpendicular to the base road. This is called the run-in line and when making a bomb delivery, pilots try to fly somewhat parallel if not over this run-in line. Failure to do so will result in a 3/9 o'clock error.

The range control tower where the RCO stays is located exactly on the center point of the base road. The two ranges are on either side of him giving him a good view of each bulls eye.

There are two other fixtures on each range and they are both resting on the base line and extend away from it. The first is the skip box, a 100 by 200 foot rectangle of plowed up earth and is used for scoring a simulated napalm type level bomb delivery. Because napalm isn't used anymore the skip boxes have been removed from Avon Park ranges. The second is another longer rectangle that is inside of the bulls eye. At the end of this rectangle are two side by side strafe pits that have targets that are parachutes with black bulls eyes stretched out between vertical poles. Each target has its own run-in line. Range maintenance crews disk the ground behind the parachutes every week to keep the ground soft. This reduces the risk of ricochets from the 20 mm strafe bullets. Also behind the parachutes are acoustic scoring devices that are protected from bullets by raised mounds of dirt. When the bullets pass over the scoring devices they are traveling supersonic and their shock waves are easily detected and scored providing very accurate scoring.

Dropping Mk 82 five hundred pound bombs

The F-4 Bomber

The F-4 carried an external bomb and rocket carrying dispenser called a SUU 20. It was carried on an inboard pylon and was about 8 feet long and a foot wide. It had two tubes opening to the front for carrying 2.2 inch Folding Fin Aerial Rockets, FFAR, and under this device hung 6 BDU 33 practice bombs. We flew the F-4E that, unlike the C or D models, had an internal nose mounted 6 barreled 20 mm cannon that fired at a rate of 100 rounds per second. A full load on the gun for training missions was only two or three hundred bullets but we usually set the rounds limiter to 150 bullets for gunnery practice. The gun was most effective when firing short bursts.

Types of Bomb Deliveries

We practiced many different kinds of weapons deliveries but we were only projected to qualify in 6 of them. The most difficult to me were the very high angle dive bomb deliveries.

Dive Bombing

The highest and steepest delivery was the 45 degree high altitude dive bomb where the roll in altitude was 21,000 feet with a pickle (bomb release) at 14,000 feet and a minimum pull out altitude of 6,000 feet. It was designed to be used in an area where small caliber AAA was a major threat. Although not a very accurately delivery bombs could be dropped with the fighter never getting close to the threatening AAA. The lower altitude 45 degree dive bomb was easier to do even though it was still a difficult delivery. The 30 degree dive bomb improved accuracy considerably because it was easier to establish an accurate 30 degree dive and then track the target with the sight. Roll in altitude for 30 degree was 8,000 feet with a pickle altitude of 3700 feet and a min pull out altitude of 1500 feet.

Lower Dive Angle Events

The 20 degree low altitude low drag was a difficult delivery for most pilots although it was one of my favorites. The 10 degree high drag delivery was really fun because the bomb release was so low to the ground it was easier to finesse a good score. Some got so good at this delivery that they could get one bulls eye after another. Roll in altitude was 3,000 feet with a pickle altitude of 500 feet and a min pull out altitude of 300 feet.

The last bomb delivery was my all time favorite, the level skip delivery. Run-in altitude to the skip boxes that were located right next to the range tower was 75 feet. Minimum altitude was 50 feet. Flying that low almost made my toes tickle and I loved the thrill of it.

Strafe and Rockets

Strafe was almost the identical pattern to 10 degree high drag. The only difference being the pattern was altered so the aiming target was the strafe panel instead of the bulls eye. The panel or parachute was located exactly 1500 feet beyond the base road that the range tower was on and the 1500 foot line was used for a minimum fire position or foul line. If the range officer observed white gun smoke coming from your airplane after it passed the 1500 foot line you were fouled. I'll talk more about that eventuality later. The last event that also was a really fun one was rockets. To me it was a cross between 10 degree bombing and strafe. This was another delivery many pilots had trouble with that I just loved. I think I felt more comfortable close to the ground and perhaps was able to concentrate more in that environment and found weapons delivery there easier to do. Both skip and rockets, my two most fun events, were discontinued after I finished RTU.

Qualification

We were expected to qualify in 30 degree dive bomb, 20 degree low angle low drag, 10 degree high drag, rockets, skip, and strafe. Certain accuracies were required on deliveries before they could be counted for qualification. For 30 degree, the bomb had to hit within 145 feet of the bulls eye to count for qualification and for 10 degree the max miss distance was 110 feet. To qualify in an event, for any string of six bombs dropped, at least three had to be within qualification distance. Failure to qualify in one or more events was listed in a student's grade book but didn't affect his completion of RTU. He could complete qualification at his next assignment.

Range Rules

The rules for a controlled flight on the range were very rigid. Each flight had exactly a half hour during which each of its four planes had to drop six bombs, strafe three times and make three rocket passes. That usually left enough time to repeat two additional patterns if requested by an IP. The math figures out to each plane making a delivery pass every two minutes. The only way to do this was for every flight member to be in position and we were harangued unmercifully if we started lagging behind. Airspeeds were always between 300 and 450 and all turns were high G.

The bombing pattern was always a rectangular flight path. One side was the run in for weapons delivery. The second side was the pull off of target which was really a climbing 180 degree turn. The 3rd was called downwind and the 4th was the base leg from where you rolled in again for the next weapons delivery. Each of the 4 jets was expected to be within seconds of their respective corners at certain times and a cadence was set up that kept everything running smoothly. Lead calls "one is in," and the RCO responds with "cleared one, three your score was 60 at 6 (the scores lagged by 2 airplane deliveries). Immediately after lead's clearance, two begins his turn to base leg and calls, "two is base." At that time three should be just rolling out on downwind and four is pulling off from the target.

If anyone is lagging they should be aware of it quickly and pull in their base leg closer to the target to get the spacing back. Failure to do so might result in the following call made by the flight leader, "two, take it through high and dry and get the spacing back." One time I even heard a "two, safe it up and take it home" call. Yikes! That meant a pinked ride.

Flying Low Levels

A natural extension to air to ground was flying low level routes to the range. Whenever possible it was considered sound tactics to approach a target from as low as possible to retain the advantage of surprise and the way to do this was by flying a preplanned low level route to the target. Low levels in RTU were more of an orientation and proficiency was not required.

They were fun to do and we got to fly them many times as a way to get to the range. The alternative, of course, was to climb to 18,000 feet, and approaching the range to let down to whatever would be the first event's pattern altitude. There were two low levels, one approaching the range from the north and one from the south and compared to low levels I would fly in Europe they were very easy to follow.

F-4 D's moving into echelon formation for range entry

A Typical Range Mission

Our 4-ship has just completed our turn to the run-in heading approaching Avon Park range. We are in close or fingertip formation at 18,000 feet. The INS says the range complex is 25 miles on the nose. There are a lot of puffy clouds in the area and my occasional glances down at the ground as we approach the range reveal patches of nondescript Florida terrain between the clouds. I'm wondering about how much pressure lead must feel to find the range visually - not thinking he has been here so many times both in the air like today and as range control officer that he could probably find it in his sleep.

The flight leader calls us over to the range control frequency and checks us in. The RCO greets us with clearance to enter the range and reports the previous flight is still on range but in the process of leaving. He also reads the weather to us and the winds from surface to 8,000 feet in thousand foot increments. They are the same as we were given before leaving the squadron so our wind corrections won't have to be changed. Lead acknowledges and calls out our line-up, squadron assigned pilot numbers for bomb score record keeping and list of events we'll be doing. The RCO responds back with the range we'll be working on. Today it is right range, left traffic. Each flight member parrots it back in turn; right range, left traffic.

This is a busy time compressed portion of the flight. We are approaching the range at six miles a minute and there is a lot to do. The INS now shows the range only four miles ahead as we level at 8,000 feet. Lead calmly orders the flight into a right echelon formation for the pitch out that will give us pattern spacing. I'm already on the right side so I stay put but I see three and four slide back and begin crossing over to join on my side of lead. No sooner are they in place then I see lead's wings flash and simultaneously hear on the radio, "one is up" as he snaps into about 80 degrees of bank and vanishes in his turn to downwind. I start counting to five and do the same, "two is up." Three and four follow suit.

The first event is 30 degree dive bomb. I had previously set in the correct mil setting adjusted for winds on my bombing sight for 30 degree. When I select A/G on the weapons delivery mode switch I'm relieved to see the sight depress indicating that so far my switches are set correctly. I have a green light on the left inboard station and when I select master arm on I also get amber. I now have confirmation that all of my switches are set correctly and the first bomb is just waiting for my right thumb to depress the pickle button on the stick grip.

Everything is happening too quickly and I'm really scrambling trying to stay caught up. At not much more than two minutes per pattern, the longest I'll be wings level at any time will be for only a few seconds before it will be time to start another turn. I hear lead call "in" which is my cue to begin my base call. I jam the throttles forward and wrap in 90 degrees of bank and pull on the stick to make a quick 90 degree turn to base and call, "two's base." I yank the throttles back to maintain 350 knots.

"Cleared one," I hear the RCO say and I hear my IP caution me to wait for one's clearance from the RCO before calling base. The radio sequence is critical so we don't start stepping on each other on the radios. Seconds later I am fast approaching the run-in line and I can see the target approaching my left wing. The concentric bomb circles don't look very big from way up here. With the proper lead I again ram the throttles forward and rapidly roll into about 120 degrees of bank, begin a four G pull to bring the nose down and pointed just below the target and call, "two's in." I hear "cleared two." When the nose is pointed where I want I relax back pressure on the stick and do an unloaded roll out to wings level. The sight is offset too much to the right of the target. I've got enough time to make only one correction. I feel my throttles snap back. Thanks IP, I think. I forgot about my speed and he set my throttles for me. In a 30 degree dive, the throttles need to be almost back to idle to prevent going too fast. Forgetting to pull the throttles back could result in so much airspeed it could be difficult to pull out without hitting the ground. By bomb release *the airspeed should have accelerated to 450 knots. I hear the IPs voice begin to give a countdown on the altimeter so I can get a feel for how the sight is tracking the target and can anticipate bomb release. I make a quick unloaded roll of 50 degrees left bank, pull for one second, and unload again to roll wings level. That was my correction. The sight now is closer to the run in line. It will have to do. "6.7, 5.7," I hear in my headset; 2,000 feet more to release altitude. "4.7, ready, pickle." I push the pickle button and immediately begin a four G wings level pull out making sure I maintain the pull until the nose is well above the horizon. My IP asks where my sight was at pickle and I tell him it was well short of the target. "I thought so," he replies. "Use more aim off distance on your next roll-in." During my pull out I glance left to pick up lead so I don't cut him off in my turn. I see him so I continue my climbing turn to downwind and 8,000 feet. My airspeed has bled off to 350 knots and I maintain that in the climb.*

"Two, your score, 180 feet at six, cleared four." Yuck, what a lousy score I think. We bet quarters between pilots on each bomb. That won't win anything. That isn't qualifying either. For each event we do three patterns to drop two bombs so if I don't like what I see on the next pass I decide I'll go through dry. With my IP's prodding, I place my aim off distance farther beyond the target and when I roll wings level my IP tells me to check dive angle. A quick glance shows we are close to 30 degrees. The biggest errors come from being shallow on dive angle. This is looking a lot better and at the pickle call, my pipper (center of the sight) is very close to the bull. I pickle off the bomb and begin my recovery pull. The score comes back 75 at three. My IP comments approvingly on the improvement.

Next pass will be dry so I use the time to get ready for 20 degree. All I have to do is change the mil setting on my sight. A quick review of my flight line-up card where I recorded my mil settings and wind corrections shows that at this lower altitude I'll need to be offset 75 feet to the left of the target at bomb release. I don't think I really thought much about cross wind correction on the 30 degree. Maybe that's why I missed the target to the right. The pace of the pattern remains fierce but everyone is keeping good discipline and position. That is a direct reflection on the flight leader. Ours is really good.

On my first 20 degree I don't like what I see. The sight got to the target before pickle altitude and I go through dry. The second and third passes work out well. One of the two is a qualifier and the other just misses at 3:00, a cross-wind error. Darn!

I change mils again for the last bombing event, skip. Skip is a level delivery with a run-in altitude of 75 feet. Skip bombing is simulating dropping napalm and since the canisters don't explode, you don't have to worry about fragging yourself hence you can get really low. Also, for the same reason, accuracy is extremely important. A 50 foot miss is a total miss. I dial in the mils and the sight sinks almost to the nose of the F-4. The skip box is located right next to the range tower and we have to extend base leg out to provide enough run-in room to be able to descend to 75 feet. As I call in, I only roll into about 100 degrees of bank since we are now flying the downwind pattern at only 3,000 feet and when I roll out I find that at this low altitude it is easy to track straight towards the skip box. To qualify all I have to do is to have the bomb hit somewhere within the 50 by 200 foot box. I roll wings level and push over to get down to altitude. My IP is silent. It is up to me to watch my own altimeter when this low.

My airspeed is set at 375 knots and I continue pushing over and we continue to descend until approaching 100 feet. I level out and decide to just let us sink the remaining little bit and if I don't get there, this is close enough. The wild palmetto bushes are flashing by and I feel an almost indescribable excitement, a tingling at the experience. Flying this low is fun but also very dangerous. The biggest danger is hitting a bird, especially a 10 pound turkey vulture. It could really ruin your day. I'm almost afraid to move the stick but we are tracking the target nicely and it is just a matter of waiting for the sight to reach the skip box and then pickle the bomb, but it is all rushing by so quickly. I'm not aware of it but my sight is passing along the ground at 700 feet per second. It will run the length of the skip box in less than a third of a second. The sight hits the box, I pickle and begin an immediate pull. The RCO responds, "long, two." The next one I'm better prepared for and I get it in; one for two.

I pull back on the stick and it is up for rockets, another favorite event of mine. We are back to a 3,000 foot pattern and as I'm soaring back up to downwind, I reach down, deselect master arm, deselect bombs and select rockets and dispensers. With rockets, since they fire forward, I don't turn the master arm on until pointed at the target. Following lead, I roll into a bunch of bank, cob the power to it and pull the nose around and down to the target. This is very similar to a 10 degree bomb delivery, only easier - for me anyway. Some students really are having trouble with this event although I don't understand why. The sight is depressed only a little more than for strafing and is easy to place just a little short of the target. Approaching the maximum range for shooting the rocket, I slowly pull the nose up until my sight is right on the target and now the important thing for rockets - controlling G. I very easily allow the stick to move smoothly forward as I track the target and then squeeze the trigger to shoot a rocket. I can't hear anything but the sight is unforgettable as the rocket swooshes way out ahead of the airplane leaving a long thin white trail of exhaust smoke. It looks like it is going to be long and just at the end it seems to push over right onto the target. That is exactly how it is supposed to look. I'm anticipating a good score. "Shack, two," says the RCO. All right! A bulls eye. Rockets will be the first event I qualify in with an average miss distance of only 30 feet.

Two more passes of rockets to shoot one and we are up for strafe – absolutely my most favorite of favorites. The 20 mm bullet is about the size of a long cigar except half again as wide and costs two dollars each. The bullets come in several types but all we shoot is TP or training ammo with a solid metal bullet tip. The pattern is very much like rockets except shooting is much closer in. To score well, you have to begin shooting at about 2,000 feet slant range and stop by 1500 feet or you will be fouled.

As I pull up after the last rockets pass I put the master arm back to safe, change my mils to 38 for strafe, deselect left inboard station and select nose station. Then I select guns and when safely pointed away from everything on downwind, I put the master arm to arm. An amber light under the nose station shows the gun is ready to fire. Lead has already rolled in on his first strafe pass, called a sighter burst. I'm a bit behind. I quickly roll left, pull and call base. I roll out for all of three seconds and it is time to begin my roll in on the strafe target. Since the sight is depressed so little I can pull the nose directly to the target this time and I do. I want to roll out with the sight about a hundred feet short of the 'rag' and just keep it there while I fly down the chute getting my speed adjusted and getting a feel for the winds. Strafing psyches out more pilots than any other event. Approaching 400 knots I pull the throttles to idle and the whole plane seems to suddenly stabilize. I have the stick trimmed a little heavy and as I see the foul line approaching my feet I smoothly raise the sight just to the bulls eye of the rag, push slightly forward to keep it tracking there and momentarily squeeze the trigger. I'm back off of it before I hear a response and a split second later I hear the sound of the gun, a low frequency sound like a blender might make. A lazy recovery at this point can result in a foul from the RCO or even being struck by one of my own ricochets so I very smartly pull back on the stick and the F-4 almost swaps ends and begins to climb away from the danger zone. Just before the rising nose blocks my view I see dust rise up from the vicinity of the rag and I'm confident I'll get some hits. The bullets seemed to hit just a wee bit to the right of my sight but the gun seemed quite accurate. Many pilots get a name for themselves because they are always writing up the 'bore-sight' on their guns blaming the aircraft maintenance people for their poor performance at shooting.

The RCO gets a direct readout from the acoustic scorer and I get my score with no delay. "18 hits two, cleared three." I'm really pleased with 18 hits on a sighter burst. Qualifying in strafe is 25 percent. We normally don't shoot more than 100 bullets so I'm almost there. On my next roll in I'm really confident and I coolly wait for the foul line to march up. The rule of thumb is when the foul line seems like it is under your feet, fire. Just as I put the pipper on the target and hold it I hit some turbulence and catch myself just in time from wasting some bullets. The turbulence was enough to knock my aiming off target. I pull back on the stick and call off dry. One more try. On the last pass I detect just a hint of right cross wind and drop my right wing just a little until the plane stops drifting. The foul line is approaching, speed is set, dive angle good, the air is smooth, ready, ready, and I squeeze the trigger long and hard as I track the target. I'm elated. The rag seemed to erupt in dust. That might be my best pass yet. I snatch back on the stick. The radio comes alive. "76 hits, two, nice shooting." Fantastic, I think. A range mission is a lot of work requiring much preplanning and it's dangerous to the unsuspecting or unprepared but it is also just plain fun.

I hear one ahead of me call up for rejoin, 300 knots and I put everything behind me to concentrate on the next task at hand. Lead climbs to 8,000 feet and goes into a 30 degree bank turn over the range as he observes three and four on their last strafe passes and then they are up for rejoin also. Just as four is raising a wing up to kill his overtake as he comes aboard I hear the next flight checking in. They are probably 20 miles out on their run-in and will be overhead in two or three minutes. For us it is RTB and it should be a good debrief.

Thanks to a good flight lead, everything went as planned and like clockwork and that never happens by chance. What a beautiful day.

45 Degree High Altitude Dive Bomb

A delivery that I didn't cover in the preceding story was 45 degree high altitude dive bomb. Fortunately, we didn't have to qualify in 45 degree because it was a difficult delivery. Roll in was started from over 4 miles up and from that altitude, just being able to see a target is difficult. The roll in had to begin at 300 knots with immediately pulling the throttles to idle even before roll out because at that dive angle, airspeed builds at a very fast rate. If you forgot to come to idle you would become supersonic very quickly and there wouldn't be enough altitude to pull out. At 45 degrees of dive, you can't see a horizon. The whole view out the front is of 'dirt' so it is hard to establish a wings level attack, thus, it is also hard to track the target with your sight. Finally, when in a 45 degree dive you are at about seven tenths of a G, meaning you feel like you are floating out of your seat which is uncomfortable when pointing at the ground. I thought the delivery was very exciting, especially the 2 miles of altitude that was required to pull out following bomb release. Not many people pressed the pickle altitude. Like I've said before, I much preferred staying down in the weeds with the lower dive angle deliveries.

Ground Attack Night

Ground attack night was a short phase. We had four rides, two of which were combined with night air refueling. It was a short phase but a very exciting one as well. We weren't required or expected to qualify at night, just be able to be safe and have our bombs hit the earth! Like all night flying, cockpit lighting was extremely important and as we flew the 25 minute ride to the range we were encouraged to continuously readjust cockpit lighting until it was as dim as possible but still allowed us to be able to accurately read the instruments that really counted like the altimeter and the attitude indicator.

Obviously, the target had to be illuminated some way to be able to drop a bomb on it. We had two ways. One consisted of 'the logs' that were devices on the ground that held oil pots. There were five pots. One was located on the bulls eye. The other four were set up around the target at 3, 6, 9 and 12:00. This gave a good picture of where the target circles were and also provided clues to aid in determining dive angle. A second way of illuminating the target was with flares that were dropped by another F-4. We all liked the logs much better than the flares.

A night ground attack mission using the logs was pretty much like a day mission as far as flight conduct only easier because we only did the two events, 20 degree low angle low drag and 30 degree dive bomb. Other deliveries were unsuitable or even dangerous at night. So, it was onto the range, drop six bombs in eight or 10 passes and leave. However, when we used flares it was quite different. There were some inherent dangers associated with bombing under flares that we were thoroughly briefed on before each flight.

> *"Two is off," "three is in." "Cleared, three."* We had an additional call at night calling off target so the range officer could more easily keep track of us in the dark. I was on my first ground attack night mission and I was just mesmerized by this different world. The flare ship had already dropped a flare and now the whole range area was illuminated by a harsh bright light. I pulled back on the stick and after the nose was well above the horizon on my attitude indicator I rolled into bank.

Hidden Dangers at Night

We were warned repeatedly of many dangers at night. Most were about optical illusions and the one I was reacting to right now was not doing a complete recovery pull and turning to downwind while still descending, a potentially fatal mistake. Do everything with reference to your instruments we were told. Half way through my turn I remembered another phenomenon, the Moth Effect, and I relaxed back stick pressure to widen my turn. The moth effect is the tendency for a bombing pattern to get tighter and tighter because of the reluctance to get too far away from the 'light' of the flares, hence, the name.

> *I leveled at 5,000 feet in preparation for another low angle low drag when my score came in. "Two, unscorable at 6." A common tendency at night, I recalled, was to dish out on roll in and get shallow which would explain a short bomb. I resolved to hold my nose up longer during the next roll in. "One is in." "Cleared one." "Two is base." I called. I rolled into bank and automatically cobbed the power in and pulled. Looking out the left side and down at a 20 degree angle I could see the night range of Avon Park under the glare of a single point of light that slowly descended from the black sky above us. "One is off." I smoothly rolled into 90 degrees of bank and used*

some bottom rudder to get the nose down to begin my pull towards the target. "Two is in," "cleared two."

I was again thinking of how everything is to be more methodical at night. Slower roll ins, cross check everything on instruments. When I rolled out my IP was already calling out the first altitude. "4.1." My sight was much closer to the target. Good. I set power with the throttles. "3.1." It was tracking just a bit to the right. Gee! What was that? Out of my peripheral vision I'd seen a large dark object race by me and then, immediately, I knew what it was; a phenomenon called phantom wingman. I'd seen my own shadow from the flare race by me on the ground below; distracting, even startling, but not dangerous. "Ready," I hear from the back seat. My sight is just about to the bulls-eye. "Pickle." I depressed the pickle button and felt a slight thud as the ejector cartridge in the SUU 20 fired ejecting the little practice bomb away from the airplane. At first I could never detect the bomb release but now with experience I usually could. I came right in with four Gs in two seconds and immediately got on the gages to monitor my pull on the attitude indicator. I was aware of a momentary small flash of light coming from somewhere beneath me. That would be the light from my bomb's spotting charge. Good, I hit the earth again, I thought with a slight smile. I just know that is a bulls eye. "Two's off." "One your score..." I continue my climbing turn to downwind. I soon hear my score; 130 at 6. How in the world? Maybe I have the wrong mils set in I think to myself.

I tell my IP that I thought the last bomb would have been a bull and he says I was still shallow. He reminds me that we are up for 30 degree dive bomb and I reach up to the sight and crank in the new mil setting while cross checking instruments. Suddenly, the whole world goes black. The flare burned out. I hear the RCO tell everyone to hold high and dry and he gives clearance for the flare ship to come in to drop a couple more flares. We carry it straight through for one pattern and soon the lights come back on.

"Two's in," I call. I'm concentrating on 30 degree dive bomb now. This night bombing isn't nearly as bad as I was told. In fact it is kind of fun. I've got good aim off distance. I set the throttles to control my speed, roll out and begin tracking the target. I hear from the back seat, "7.7, 6.7" as my IP begins calling out the altitude. I'm supposed to pickle at 3,700 feet, 3.7. Then I hear, "why are we still in 45 degrees of bank?" I quickly glance at the attitude indicator. I'm in 45 degrees of left bank. I'm shocked. I thought I was wings level. I roll to wings level and call through dry beginning a gentle pull out. Wow, what a lesson that was. They told us to cross check instruments and I hadn't. I know that if I had tried to complete a 4 G pull out while in 45 degrees of bank I probably wouldn't have had enough altitude to prevent hitting the ground. I think to myself I'm glad that happened with an experienced IP in my back seat and not when I was crew solo with Fred. Yes, flying at night is dangerous and so is complacency.

Disaster at Night

Two months earlier, a crew solo from another class and another squadron at MacDill was flying a mission just like I was. Everything went well on the flight. During the rejoin afterwards a crew solo was taking longer than usual to join up. When queried on the radio there was no answer. Then, the flight lead spotted a fire on the ground several miles away. The solo flight never did show up and in the morning they found the wreckage.

An accident investigation team was assembled to investigate and my IP, Ray Rider, was assigned as the pilot member. They found that at the time of the crash the airplane was operating normally. The pilot flew it into the ground with no attempt to recover. They also noticed that there was a small tower on the ground within a couple miles of the crash. The small tower had a single flashing red light on it. The likely explanation for the tragedy was that during the rejoin the pilot was trying to fly the plane visually while his student WSO was trying to find lead on his radar scope. No one was cross checking instruments. The pilot thought the flashing red light was from lead's plane and tried to rejoin on it. Yes, flying at night is dangerous.

Ground Attack Radar

The Ground Attack Radar, GAR, was a phase mainly for the WSOs. They really only had two phases where they led the way, air intercepts and now GAR. During all other times, the WSO eagerly took his rides whenever or wherever he could. In knowledge they were expected to know all about the front-seater's job as well as their own. But, they only received a third of the flying that the pilots got and even less recognition. Following a crew solo flight, the pilot's grade sheet would be filled on both sides with comments. The WSO's grade sheet would be adorned with the comments, "Flown crew solo. Good job helping out his pilot." In contrast, the pilot was just vaguely aware of the 'how to' of things that happened in the rear cockpit.

In operational units after RTU I knew many WSOs that were more capable than some pilots but the fact remained, even if the pilot was a second lieutenant and the WSO was a colonel, the pilot was the one in command and anything that happened to the plane was his responsibility. For that reason alone, WSOs were relegated to a second-class existence. So, I was truly happy for them to begin a phase where they got to be the stars and where our student WSOs flew more than the pilots. I was also quite eager to slow up the pace and pressure that had become a way of life during the last several months.

A radar delivered bomb rarely was as accurate as a visually delivered one so why do it? There were two situations where you would. First, if you couldn't see the target because of darkness or weather you had to rely on radar. The second was if the bomb was so powerful that a quarter mile miss wouldn't make much difference - a nuclear weapon. The training bomb we used was the Mk 106, a light weight, high drag bomb that was similar in size to the Mk 33 practice bomb and had the flight characteristics of a bomb with a parachute attached; nuclear bombs had parachutes attached.

Simulating Nucs

The two delivery modes were designed with nuclear weapons in mind. The first was a lay-down delivery that would give a dirty ground burst. We flew in level at 1,000 feet and 500 knots and released the bomb in level flight. When released the bomb had so much drag that it would all but stop its forward motion in the wind-stream and fall almost perpendicular to earth.

The second was a much more fun delivery, the Low Altitude Drogue Delivery or LADD. This delivery was designed to give an air burst for a nuclear bomb. At a predetermined point before the target, the pilot got pitch and course steering bars on his attitude indicator. They were centered and at the activation point a high pitched tone was heard in the headset and the pitch bar started rising on the ADI. The pilot began pulling into a climb to keep the pitch bar centered. The computer that commanded this commanded a three and a half G pull up in one and a half seconds until reaching 45 degrees of climb. The pilot held the 45 degree climb attitude until the tone stopped and the steering bars deflected out of view. At that point the bomb was released and the pilot rolled inverted to pull the nose back down to below the horizon and begin an escape maneuver. The maneuver provided the pilot 80 seconds 'to get out of Dodge' and, with a real nuc, avoid being cremated in the nuclear explosion.

A really neat aspect of the LADD delivery was we could watch the bomb hit. We could observe a small white puff of smoke about the time we rolled out on downwind after completing the climb recovery.

The unconventional (nuclear) range was at the same location as the conventional range and used the same scoring cameras. The bomb circle was different though. The bulls-eye was a 20 foot tall white pillar which was located beyond the two conventional circles and there were 4 concentric rings surrounding it each at 500 foot intervals. These circles were also etched in white sand and easily seen from the air.

Radar Deliveries

There were several different ways of determining the bomb release point. The most simple was using the 5 mile bomb strobe. The radar in air to ground mode swept back and forth and had a visible cursor at the 5 mile point. The WSO had computed wind corrections and based on flying at 500 knots, he knew how many seconds from the 5 mile point the bomb should be released. He put this time into the bomb release timers and when the 5 mile cursor strobe reached the bulls eye, a visible radar return, he pickled activating the timers. At expiration of the timers, the bomb was released.

A more complicated method was required for targets that didn't present a radar signal. In this case the WSO had to compute an 'offset aim point' prior to the mission. In his target study and mission planning he located a nearby object that would show up on radar. This was called an Offset Aim Point, OAP. He then computed how many feet north or south and how many feet east or west the target was from the OAP. These values were entered into the offset windows of the bombing computer.

During the run in, the WSO had to identify the OAP on radar and placed his cross hairs on it. When he selected 'insert' on the computer, the cross hairs would jump from the OAP to the target. Now, assuming he did his measuring correctly and found the OAP and had a very accurate cross hair positioning, the computer knew exactly where the target was. The WSO already programmed the computer with the bomb's bomb range adjusted for winds. When the computer determined it was that distance from the target it automatically released the bomb.

At the range, there were two OAPs available. Radar reflectors had been set up 10,000 feet short of the target and also at 2,000 feet long of it. Either could be used for an offset bomb delivery. For a LADD type maneuver, instead of a bomb release signal, the computer initiated the pitch and steering bars.

Qualification

The WSOs were expected to qualify in radar lay-down and radar LADD. 500 feet was the maximum miss distance for lay-down qualification and 2,000 feet was the maximum for a LADD. In addition to all of his duties of finding the OAP and numerous switches and settings to enter, the WSO was expected to make sure that the front seater had his switches set correctly. For instance, if the master arm wasn't on, a bomb wouldn't be released. If a bomb wasn't released because of a switch error the WSO bought it regardless of whose fault it was. Sometimes a simple switch error meant the difference between a WSO getting qualified in an event or not. A radar pattern meant driving 30 miles out on downwind, a short base leg and then driving another 30 miles back in to the target. On a typical GAR mission, a WSO would have a chance to do two radar lay-downs and two radar LADDs. A switch error was very costly to a WSO.

We also had visual lay-down and LADD maneuvers that the pilots were expected to qualify in. After the rigors of the conventional events; strafe, dive bomb, rockets etcetera, this was quite easy and the student pilots quickly qualified.

Ground Attack Tactical

Air combat tactics was the graduation exercise for air to air and ground attack tactical was the graduation exercise for the air to ground. We had been taught the basic skills of finding where over a target we had to fly the aircraft for bombs to hit it. Now, we were told that someone might try to prevent us from dropping our bombs by shooting at us. It was our job to learn how to drop bombs where the risk to us would be minimized to an acceptable level - but still get the job done. With the Vietnam war still smoldering we benefited from the latest techniques tested under actual combat conditions.

The Curvilinear Approach

There were two basic methods to reduce risk while dropping bombs on the target. The first was called the curvilinear approach. This method was for a low threat area where there were enemy gunners but they just weren't very good shots I guess.

Under standard bombing that we had been doing, everyone in the flight rolled in from a base leg and flew down the same 'chute' releasing their bombs at about the same point. To a gunner on the ground we were very predictable and in time he could zero in on the range and lead required. In curvilinear we made this more difficult by varying where we would roll in from. The most common curvilinear pattern was from a wheel shaped pattern above the target. With the flight circling from above the altitude that the enemy's AAA could reach, one after another would call "in" with the direction coming in from and then slowly roll into a descending turn that would result in finding a 'chute' to the target from where you could drop a bomb. Our rule of thumb was to have no more than five seconds of wings level time. Airspeed, altitude and heading should always be changing until a brief roll out for the bomb release.

Pop-up Delivery

The second method for a tactical delivery used the element of surprise. It was called the pop up attack and the name pretty much described the maneuver. We entered the attack from a low level route and at a preplanned point while flying at 300 feet or even lower while heading in a precise direction we began a four G pull up to usually 20 or 30 degrees. This provided four or five seconds while in your zoom climb to find your target off to one side of your heading. At the preplanned pull down altitude we rolled over partially inverted and pulled the nose of the aircraft over to the target. When the proper dive angle was established we rolled wings level for two or three seconds of tracking time until reaching pickle altitude. The no more than five seconds of wings level on final rule also applied to pop up attacks. After the bomb release it was imperative to get back 'into the weeds' again quickly. The pop-up was a dangerous tactic where the Air Force lost many planes and pilots because they ran into the ground for one reason or another. The most common, and frequently fatal, mistake was popping too close in to the target resulting in too steep of a dive angle and not enough altitude to pull out.

A variation of the pop-up was the straight-ahead pop. It required exacting precision in mission planning because the target was always directly ahead on the nose during the run-in. After doing the pull-up the pull-down was done by rolling completely inverted until established in the dive. After rolling back upright, if everything worked correctly the target should be still on the nose. This wasn't a very popular maneuver because of the difficulty of acquiring the target in time to drop precise bombs.

During GAT we didn't use the practice bomb dispenser, the SUU 20. Instead we used the real equipment for actual bombs, a TER mounted on each inboard pylon. TER stood for Triple Ejector Rack and was a device that almost all conventional bombs could be 'bolted' to. As the name implied, three bombs could be attached to each TER. When a release signal was sent to the TER, an explosive cartridge fired causing an ejector foot to spring outward pushing the bomb away and down. Our little practice bomb, the BDU 33, also fit on the TER. On a typical GAT mission we had a TER on each inboard pylon.

Cement Bombs

On one of the last missions of GAT we carried 'cement bombs' which were actual 500 pound bomb casings filled with cement instead of explosives. Everything was real except there was no bang.

Another change in GAT was the range itself. We didn't use bomb circles anymore. This was the real world. Our targets were spread out over the tactical part of the range. There were about 10 different targets to attack; two different SAM sites, a AAA site, an airfield, a truck convoy and a tank farm are the ones that come to mind. The targets were actual size and adorned with real salvaged trucks and airplanes. The SAM sites modeled the Soviet SA 2 and SA 3, the main threat in Vietnam. The missiles were plywood but from the air everything looked very real. Pallets of wooden crates positioned by the airfield provided even more realism. There were even stacks of new wings for a B-58 -- which left the Air Force inventory several years earlier.

Another unofficial F-4 patch

An acoustic scorer near a stack of engine nacelles allowed scoring for tactical high angle strafe. Other targets that were within sight of the flank towers could also be scored with prior arrangement. All other targets had to be air scored which wasn't very accurate but notoriously kind to a pilot's ego.

A Typical GAT Mission

We've entered the range by flying a low level route with one minute spacing between airplanes. At the 420 knots we are flying, lead is seven miles ahead of me. The terrain is passing by at a rate of seven miles every minute, a mile every eight and a half seconds. My altitude is 300 feet and the scrub pines of central Florida are just a blur beneath me. Occasionally during the route I've spotted lead's smoke trail but now that we are on the range my mind concentrates on the critical tasks at hand. The first is switches. We never arm up until over the extensive range complex because every now and then due to switch errors or a system malfunction, a bomb is unintentionally released.

Tactical Air Command Patch

I activate all of the switches now and get the reassuring amber light on the left inboard. I have 'bombs triple' selected for the first time ever. At pickle, 3 bombs will be released at .2 second intervals. A cross-check of my airspeed shows I'm within 5 knots of 420. I make a correction. My timing is right on.

I can see the Initial Point (IP is the last check point prior to the target) rapidly approaching. It is a distinctive bend in a small river that meanders through the range. When I hit the river I re-hack my clock and turn 17 degrees right to the final run in heading. We are maintaining radio silence for the entire attack. The first call will be an up call at which time we can expect to be cleared by the RCO. From the IP to the pop up point is one minute and 40 seconds. I should be hearing lead's call any time now. The radios have been eerily silent. I've been tempted to key the mic just to see if they are working. Just then the radio briefly comes to life. "One is up." Silence. "Cleared one." More silence. I look ahead for lead and just then see the small dark plan form silhouette of an F-4 as it zooms skyward.

Forty seconds on my clock is the accelerate point. I push the throttles forward and accelerate to 500 knots. At this increased speed the plane's wings seem to be vibrating in the thick air. I can feel the speed in my control stick. I adjust the throttles and unconsciously trim the stick forces to neutral. At one minute and 40 seconds I pull into a 4 G pull and key my mic. "Two is up." A pause. "Cleared two," responds the monotone voice of the RCO.

As the Florida landscape falls away beneath me I look over my left shoulder searching for my target, a SAM site. I have only seconds to acquire it or abort my pass. Careful target study of recce photos before the mission will pay off now. The rule is to go from big to small. I chose to start with the airfield. There it is at left 10:00. Now, using the 8,000 foot runway as a measure, I move my gaze half of that distance to the south of the southern end of the runway and then a little to the east and... Tally ho on the SAM site. It is harder to see than the photos showed. It is much more overgrown with brush. I'm in a good position and just about to my pull down altitude. I smartly roll to the left and glance at my altimeter. The picture doesn't look quite right. I see that I have a thousand feet to go yet to my apex altitude. I relax on the stick and although I'm now inverted, facing my target, the F-4 is still climbing upward. I play my back pressure and stop the altimeter at the apex altitude and bring the nose down to my target. I'm in no hurry now as I finesse my dive angle thinking of the five second rule of thumb. I'm light in the seat but everything is under control and working out. Boy, this is fun. I can visualize my 30 degree wire and I'm just about on it. I do an unloaded roll to wings level and start tracking my target. For the winds my wind correction aim point is a quarter diameter of the SAM circle to the east. I make one quick wind correcting jink, pickle and pull to break my descent rate. In a ten degree glide I sail back to 300 feet and start my evasive turn to egress the target area. "Three is up." I was too busy to look for the smoke of my practice bombs but my IP says I did a nice job. We'll talk about it later.

After four comes off target we climb to 8,000 feet and set up a curvilinear wheel for our last three bomb drops. After the pop up pattern, this is slow paced but still fun to watch the other planes in turn roll out of the wheel and enter into a dive onto the target. During the recovery, a small pinpoint of white smoke that quickly blossoms into a cotton ball testifies about our accuracy.

It doesn't take very long for us to each drop our remaining three bombs and lead calls up for high angle strafe. I quickly safe up the inboard stations and set up my switches for the gun. The target is the stack of silver engine nacelles. This is my one and only opportunity to do this event. In the

Dart being recovered in Luke AFB desert recovery area

briefing we were told to not expect to get any hits. It is familiarization only. In regular strafe, wind correction is basically not applicable but for high angle strafe it is ten feet per knot and that is significant. The event is very much like dive bomb except I will point my nose right at the target. I estimate I'll need about 150 feet of wind correction to the east and when it is my turn I roll in. With my sight upwind of the nacelles I roll wings level and pull the throttles back. I figure the stack of nacelles must be about 50 feet across so I place my sight 3 of those to the east. Boy, does this seem strange, shooting so far away from what I want to hit. I track for a second and then squeeze one long burst. At 100 rounds a second, the gun fires out in a second and a half. It is by far the longest burst I've ever fired. The sound reminded me of an egg beater. I pause momentarily waiting to see my bullets hit and then remember that is a no-no. I start my recovery pull. The RCO tells me I got 35 hits and I'm absolutely elated. I listen intently as the other flight members roll in. I'm the only one to get any hits. I do love strafing. Lead makes a final fuel check and calls for a rejoin. It's time to go home.

Shooting the DART

Shooting the dart was an event that really belonged in air to air but it could be fit in just about anywhere in the latter part of RTU. The dart was an aerial target that was towed on a 1500 foot steel cable by another F-4. It was called a dart because it looked like one - or, I guess it might also stand for 'dragged aerial retrievable target.' It was made by cutting two identical tall isosceles triangles with 12 foot long sides and a three foot wide base from one inch thick plywood. After slotting the triangles lengthwise along their middles the triangles were slipped together to form a symmetrical 'dart.' When viewed from the tail, it was a symmetrical X. The dart was covered with aluminum foil so it would reflect radar energy and a corner reflector was fitted into the tail to make it even more visible to radar.

Dart Tow

The F-4 carried a special dart tow rig in place of one external fuel tank. With a dart attached this device was very unwieldy and to the unprepared could have been an emergency just waiting to happen. On takeoff the F-4 had a very heavy wing and because of very little clearance between the dart and the runway, a very shallow rotation was required. Until the dart was unreeled on its cable, the maximum speed was about 220 knots. Thus, on dart missions, the tow ship had to take off a half hour early and the shooters still delayed their takeoff until they heard back from the tow saying the dart was successfully deployed. Frequently, when deploying the dart, it would detach from its cable and be lost. And, after all of that, if the first shooter destroyed the dart on his first pass, well, it was considered an expensive mission to orchestrate and fly.

The actual dart firing was controlled by the chase pilot - you might say he was the range control officer. A typical dart mission, besides the dart tow, involved three shooters and a chase. When the chase pilot cleared someone to be the next shooter, he would descend from a position several thousand feet above the previous shooter and dart tow. As always, time was gas, so it was always a matter of pride to be able to get into the shooter position quickly.

When ready, the dart tow began a 60 degree two G turn and the shooter was cleared in to fire. The shooter began from about a mile behind the dart but closing on the dart occurred quickly by cutting to the inside of the turn. The trick was to control the closure so you would have time to get a tracking solution on the dart at about 2,000 feet, shoot and break off by 1500 feet. Penetrating inside of 1500 feet of the dart resulted in a foul and you were through shooting for the day. After each pass the chase closed on the dart and visually checked it over for bullet holes. A single hole was good enough for a hit. Hits on 2 out of 3 consecutive missions resulted in qualification.

Good News and Bad News

On my first dart mission I got a hit. On my second mission I again got a hit and was the first in my class to be dart qualified. On my third mission flown crew solo I shot well inside of 1500 feet, missed and was fouled which also meant a failed ride. My makeup ride was with my IP, Ray Rider. I just needed to fly one more dart mission where I fired at the dart. Ray made it quite clear to me that if I did my firing beyond 2,000 feet, meaning I was playing it super safe, he would fail me again. He said I had to show that I could close in to normal firing range, shoot and pull off before the minimum 1500 feet. I had no intention of playing it safe. There was a target out there and by golly I meant to hit it.

What Ray didn't tell me was that if I fouled again I would once again be up on an elimination ride. I fouled again on that ride based on Ray's range estimation. To me it was a very questionable estimate on his part because we didn't have a radar lock so lacked radar ranging. I was scheduled to fly with the Operations Officer and suddenly the implications of my situation hit me. This could be my last ride in RTU if I again failed. I suspected Ray was hoping I would fail.

Before the flight the Ops Officer told me to relax and just fly the plane the way I'd shown I could. Then he asked me if I was aware that I was the only student in my class to be qualified in all weapons events. I was shocked to hear this. We had some really 'good sticks' in my class with lots of flying experience. I think he was trying to tell me that he had no intentions of failing me at this stage of the game. He also restored my confidence in myself and I flew a really good flight. I even felt like I had hit the dart but upon close examination - by Ray Rider who was the chase - there weren't any holes in it.

A Typical Dart Mission

I've been cleared to shoot. I push the throttles up to go from 350 to 370 knots. The dart is at 350. I don't want too much airspeed or I'll overshoot and that is very uncomfortable to say the least. Also, though, I've been known to stagnate at 2500 feet and not be able to close enough to be able to shoot. I cut to the inside of the dart's path - to get cut-off. That will really generate closure. My IP tells me we're locked up with the radar. This isn't necessary but it is a great help. With a radar lock, my gun-sight is being fed range information and inside of 2500 feet it will tell me where to aim to be able to hit the target (Without a lock you can 'stiffen' the sight so it is computing for a 1500 foot target). Also, I get a range bar on the sight reticle so I can accurately tell the range to the target. The only gotcha with a radar lock-on, though, is the radar can transfer lock along the metal tow cable to the dart tow. A good back seater will recognize that and break lock but if it is unrecognized, the sight will give very erroneous distance information.

The dart is easily visible now, trailing way behind and outside of the tow's flight path. My range is 2500 feet and closing too rapidly so I do a high yo-yo maneuver that slows me. Now, I find the dart is 3,000 feet and pulling away again. This is frustrating and I'm getting tense. I pull back to the inside for cutoff and closure, check my airspeed and, darn, I'm at 340 knots. I jam the throttles forward and stroke the AB momentarily. The airspeed jumps almost immediately to 370. I pull the throttles back again and concentrate only on my cutoff overtake. The range bar is shrinking, 2500 feet, 2300, 2100. I do a slight yo-yo again, just enough to slow my closure slightly. Now, things look more under control. I've never done anything before that required such intense concentration. My IP isn't offering any help. He's only doing the role of a WSO. 2,000 feet and the bar is still slowly shrinking. I pull my sight very gradually up to the dart. When I relax back pressure to hold it there the sight responds to the change in G and jumps out in front of the dart. 1900 feet. I push forward slightly to move the sight back to the dart and it moves right through it again. I feel like I'm trying to push a limp length of spaghetti. Then I remember the sight stiffening switch and when I engage it, half of the 'limpness' goes away. 1,800 feet. Now, I'm able to manage the sight better. I gently pull it up to the dart. 1,700 feet. I should have fired by now. I release the stiffening switch. The sight stays on the dart. I squeeze a small burst and immediately pull up and roll away. We've been warned that a good solid hit can cause the dart to disintegrate and if you wait to see if you hit it, the wreckage might end up in your engines.

My IP murmurs, "gutsy. That was min range." I tell him I was aware of my range. I reposition three to four thousand feet behind the dart again. If I didn't get a hit I get one more try and then it is someone else's turn. The chase is right next to the dart now. I wait. "No hits on the dart." I know, I can do better. "Call ready two." "Two is ready." This time I will get a hit!

Finally a Fighter Pilot

The end of RTU was almost anti-climactic. It had lasted only seven months but in looking back on it, seemed to last a whole year. I had reached not just a goal but a dream that I'd had for a long time – of becoming a fighter pilot. More importantly, I'd learned an important lesson in life. If you don't try you can't succeed. I'd also gained a lot in self-confidence – in spite of Ray Rider or maybe because of Ray Rider.

Our graduation was a formal 'dining out' where we all wore our mess dress uniforms and unlike dining ins our wives were welcome.

During the last couple months of RTU the war in Vietnam had ended and our POWs had returned home. In fact, our guest of honor was a former POW. He gave us a wonderful motivational talk briefly touching on his experiences as a POW and as he was finishing up we were waiting for his last profound words that would be the frosting on the cake. His words were to stay with me for a long, long time. They were, "**DEAD BUG!**"

The wives who were present must have thought we had all gone mad because in an instant every officer present to include the wing commander dove for the floor; chairs went flying, drinks spilled, and a hundred fighter pilots were lying on the floor – because ...

According to fighter pilot tradition that goes back who knows how long, when 'dead bug' is called out, the last person to hit the floor has to buy the bar. As I lay on the floor I thought, 'fighter pilots are sure different.' I couldn't imagine a crowded room of school teachers responding this way!

When the assignments came through, two of us had orders to the 50th TFW at Hahn AB Germany. I'd never heard of it but after a little research I discovered it was one of four F-4 bases located in central Germany quite near the Mosel Valley.

It was late October of 1973 and after a stop-over at basic survival school at Fairchild AFB and a week of deer hunting in Poplar Wisconsin our family of four would be starting another chapter – in Deutschland. We couldn't wait.

F-4 RTU Class 73BRM (Capt Olson is 9th in back row)

Chapter Ten

Operational Flying In the F-4

The most common bombing technique used by F-4 pilots that predated computers — TLAR or 'That Looks About Right.'

Traveling to Germany

The last week in November of 1973 marked the beginning of great change in our family and my Air Force career. My nightly dreams were vivid of experiences from recently completed basic survival school. Deer hunting was underway in Wisconsin and I got a little fork horn buck by stalk hunting on a rainy afternoon. It was time to pack our belongings for the long trek to Germany. Before leaving Tampa we had divided our belongings into three groups; storage, surface transport to Germany, and a couple hundred pounds of interim necessities to be air transported.

50th TFW Patch

Our routing to Germany was from Duluth to Minneapolis to Atlanta and then to Charleston where we went from civilian transport to military transport. At Charleston we got on a chartered Boeing 707 that was nicknamed 'the cattle car' because of the way the seats were placed very close together and all seats were always filled. The cattle car was a crowded airplane.

Our takeoff was at midnight. Our flight followed the coastline north passing about 50 miles offshore from Newark and New York City and then on to Gander, Newfoundland where we stopped to refuel. As we passed by the New York City metropolitan area we received a stunning view off in the distance of the city's lights due to an unusually clear sky. Our next and final leg took us across the North Atlantic, which was hidden in darkness. By four am eastern time I could see the promise of dawn as the sky gradually lightened. Our flight continued along its great circle route across a snow covered England, then the channel and the Netherlands. We were over a snow covered, forested Germany when we began our let-down to our destination of Wiesbaden Air Base in Frankfurt. It was three pm in Frankfurt and nine am back in Charleston. Our trip across the Atlantic had taken nine hours.

While I was collecting our bags and keeping an eye on Jill and Becky, Jean had found a phone and by prearrangement, a representative of Volkswagen soon arrived and took us downtown to pick up our brand new Alaskan Blue Volkswagen 412 station wagon. Within minutes we were on the streets of Frankfurt and totally on our own. I marveled at the feeling of freedom and independence I felt. We were foreigners in a strange country, a country that spoke a different language and had different customs and money but this was our car and we were in it and had the ability to go wherever we wanted. No matter what else happened, we had the car as a sanctuary, a safe haven.

Finding Hahn AB

When we got back to the hotel, we ate a quick meal in the hotel's cafeteria and were relaxing in our room marveling among ourselves that it sure didn't feel like eight pm. Why, it seemed more like early afternoon which of course it was back in Wisconsin where our biological clocks were still residing!

At that point there was a knock on our door and my somewhat embarrassed sponsor, Lt. Dan Dick, had finally caught up with us. He was told our flight would be arriving that evening. He was absolutely incredulous when he learned we already had a car, had mapped out the route to Hahn and were planning on driving there the following day. I later found out that it was customary to meet incoming families, transport them back to Hahn, reserve a room for them on base and even find someone's extra car for them to drive until they got one of their own.

Dan told us that when he and his wife arrived a year and a half ago they had waited in the airport lobby six hours for their sponsor to show up after which the sponsor got lost trying to drive back out to Hahn. Needless to say, he was quite impressed at how independent we were.

Dan was a very likable fellow with a boyish grin his predominant feature. He was very apologetic about not being there to meet us. After writing out instructions for driving to Hahn he departed and we tried going to sleep. However, it was 10 pm and our bodies knew it really was only four pm back home and sleep came with great difficulty. I was the first to awaken the next day - at noon.

It was snowing and we had many things to do before departing on the two hour drive to Hahn. Frankfurt's latitude of 50 degrees north is the same as Winnipeg, and at the end of November, it started getting dark early as we struck off on our adventure. Showing more courage than we felt we departed for Hahn. It was nearly dark and snowing. We had an almost empty tank of gas (gas stations closed at six). We were in a strange country not knowing exactly where we were going. We were unable to speak the language and totally ignorant of the international road signs and driving laws. We also soon found our departure time on a Friday afternoon was the busiest traffic time during the whole week. We managed to get some gas for the car just before the stations closed and then got on the autobahn. The maximum speed we achieved was 35 mph with one two-mile stretch taking a half-hour to traverse. Finally, the traffic thinned as we headed out into the countryside in the direction of Hahn. About the time we began breathing easier we discovered we had made a wrong turn and were down in the Rhine River valley. We shouldn't be. We should be way up there somewhere beyond the river banks!

That mistake cost us 15 miles and twice Jean did an emergency recall of her high school German to ask directions and did marvelously. I was so proud of her not to mention relieved. I knew she had German in high school but it is a big leap to go from that to speaking the language to natives you stop along the highway. She really saved the day. Without further incident, not including maneuvering around snowplows, we arrived at Hahn at 8:30 pm.

Arrival at Hahn

I found our way to the Visiting Officers Quarters (VOQ) and as soon as I walked in the gal on duty said in an almost frantic voice, "are you Captain Olson?" A friend from pilot training and RTU, Bill Gracy, was also stationed at Hahn and he had been calling all week long to see if I had arrived yet. Then, that evening, Dan Dick had called several times expecting each time to find us there. He finally called Rhine-Main AB thinking we were delaying because of the snow. When he found that we had checked out that afternoon he really became concerned. He was sure we were either stuck in a snow bank somewhere or hopelessly lost.

A New Squadron

My new unit, the 10th Tactical Fighter Squadron, was having a going away party that night at the officers' club. Upon Dan's invitation, we located a baby sitter at the VOQ and Jean and I dragged ourselves over to the club to meet the squadron. I was very glad we did because any apprehensions we may have had were quickly dispelled by a bunch of very friendly and sympathetic people. In the 10th squadron we found a family that cared for each other and looked out for each other. We never again encountered a squadron that we felt that close to.

Hahn Air Base

Hahn Air Base, we quickly discovered, was a delightful base located in a very picturesque part of Germany. To easily find it on a map, I would find Luxembourg and move due east into Germany until I came to the Mosel river. Then I'd find the twin towns of Traben-Trarbach which straddled the Mosel river. The Traben-Trarbach road climbed out of the valley to the east and passed by Hahn AB. The town of Hahn was too small to be seen on most maps. The nearest city that might be seen on a map was Sohren, about five km to the northeast. The first town we lived in was Wahlenau. After living there for two years, the house we were renting, was sold so we moved to Lötzbueren, another neighboring town that was much closer to Hahn AB.

The countryside was a mixture of rich farmlands separated by forested hills. In the European fashion, barns and farmhouses were located in small farm villages and the farmer drove his tractor out to his fields. This custom was a natural result of intermarriage and inheritance laws causing a farmer's fields to be frequently separated. A farmer seldom had several fields adjacent to each other.

Farming villages had asphalt roads connecting them to all other surrounding villages providing easy access for a farmer to his widely separated fields. Tractors were very common sights on these roads. So, each village had four and even five roads connecting it to its neighbors and the large number of roads could make it confusing to say the least for navigating in your car. From the air it was even more confusing because most villages looked very similar. During night flying the roads were outlined by street lights causing the villages to resemble brightly lit Chinese characters floating in a black void.

The first owners of Hahn were the French who chose the location and built the base because at the end of the Second World War when Germany was partitioned that part of Germany came under French jurisdiction. However, prior to the Korean War we acquired the base from France and the 50th Tactical Fighter Wing moved from a location in France to Hahn. At that time they flew the F-86 Saber Jets.

Hahn's Notoriously Bad Weather

In the four years I was at Hahn a very common question people asked was why was the base built here? I never received a satisfactory answer. The most common answer was "oh, the French built it," as if that was reason in itself. The question was asked because Hahn had the worst weather of all US Air Bases. The bad weather was a direct result of Hahn's high elevation, 1,649 feet above sea level. The base was made by bulldozing off the top of a hill providing enough level ground to make the air base without taking any farmland. Not considered at the time was that hilltops suffered from a meteorological phenomenon called 'upslope fog.' In the winter and especially at night, if a slight breeze occurred from either of two very common directions the cold moist air moved uphill where it became colder and supersaturated. The moisture then condensed to form 'upslope fog.' Another hindrance to flying at Hahn was at 1,649 feet we were the highest base by 250 feet in Germany. Bitburg and Spangdahlem air bases were only 35 miles distant and had field elevations of 1,400 feet. When they had 500-foot ceilings, Hahn would have a ceiling of 250 feet which was below minimums for flying.

Another detriment to Hahn's location was that five miles to the east of Hahn's runway was a 1,500-foot high ridge that lay parallel to the runway. It was right beneath the IFR downwind when Hahn was on runway 22. Because of this ridge, the downwind for that runway was 1,000 feet higher than what you would normally expect. I heard one of our squadron's pilots one day telling how radar approach control forgot to have him climb the additional thousand feet so he flew the entire pattern in the clouds - and a thousand feet low. He didn't catch the mistake until

RAPCON told him to descend out of ... and he had never been there. On the next clear day I purposely flew the ground track of that pattern 1,000 feet low and was alarmed at how close I came to the hilltops, at times with no more than a hundred feet of clearance. That was the scenario of an accident that had happened in the past but fortunately not while I was there.

I believe Hahn was the only base that used cloud seeding in an effort to tame nature. A tower had been constructed at one end of the runway and when the weather conditions were right crystals were blown into the air to cause the fog to condense into ice particles. On occasion it made a difference and that end of the runway might be above minimums but it really wasn't reliable enough to be worth the expense or effort.

A few years before I arrived at Hahn the base received several inches of wet snow and before it could be removed a very big high pressure area known as a Siberian high moved down over Central Germany causing temperatures to plummet and the wet snow to freeze solid. With the high pressure came crystal clear skies and for over two weeks the high pressure stayed. For over two weeks Hahn couldn't turn a wheel during some of the best winter flying weather the base had seen in years.

A 'Below Mins' Accident

We did have one accident where weather was a direct cause. The crew involved was highly experienced and had been on a late afternoon practice mission for a high visibility bombing competition. While they were on their mission the weather closed in and by the time they got back to base it was almost dark. The pilot saw the runway too late on his first attempt and had to go around. Now, at this point the Supervisor Of Flying (SOF) should have told them to divert to their weather alternate base, but, considering the high experience of the crew he made what turned out to be a very bad decision. He told the crew to try again if they had enough gas. On the next attempt the same thing happened and the SOF, this time with the director of operations' concurrence, told the pilot to try it one more time. On the third attempt, the pilot got slightly off course and when he looked up and saw the runway lights offset to the left, he immediately banked left to correct to course. What he didn't notice was that when he banked left he increased his descent rate and the next thing either crew member remembered was the F-4s radome (nose) disintegrating as they began to hit the tops of pine trees. Both crewmembers immediately ejected, got about one chute swing each and were on the ground uninjured.

The SOF and the DO were both fired for not following written directives. Fran and Jack, the two crewmembers, were both given flight competency checks the next morning and both received excellent ratings. The accident didn't hurt their flying careers. The pilot had made an innocent flying mistake.

Weather was always a factor at Hahn. I once saw a chart in the Air Force Association magazine, which compared the average weather at all of the Air Force's bases. There wasn't another base that even came close to having such bad weather -

in all categories. Hahn was in a league of its own. I learned instrument flying at Hahn.

Tenth Tactical Fighter Squadron

The primary job of the 10th Tactical Fighter Squadron was nuclear strike. If World War III began our aircraft sitting 15 minute alert were required to be airborne in that length of time and on their way to their preplanned target in East Germany or in one of the other Warsaw Pact countries. We were pawns in a deadly serious game. We were each a number representing a nuclear weapon. For many of our targets we would be the third delivery vehicle to drop on it in the space of a couple hours. We were also expendable and although we didn't talk about it, we were well aware.

Hahn's Other Two Squadrons

Upon our arrival at Hahn, there was only one other squadron, the 496th TFS, the Fighting Falcons. Their role was air defense and if war had broken out they would have taken to the skies armed with air to air missiles. As I explain later, we often envied their mission which involved flying during exercises. The other squadron was the 313th TFS, the Lucky Puppies. The 313th was formed midway through my Hahn assignment and they picked up the same role as the 10th, 'air to mud.'

After arriving at Hahn, my security clearance was confirmed and I was given access to the top secret walk-in vault. I was also invited to start spending some time there every day to learn all of the various war plans that I would have to know to carry out my job.

10th TFS (Singing Sword)

A more immediate goal, however, was to get a local area checkout and an instrument check. Since it was so close to Christmas and we had to get completely moved into our house in Wahlenau I didn't think it would be realistic to expect to get the instrument check before the end of January. There were two things I was quite ignorant about; hence, I hadn't factored them in. One was Hahn's notoriously bad winter weather and the other was aircraft maintenance.

These were President Carter's draw down years when he drastically cut military spending in the field. To us it meant not having enough spare parts on hand to fix airplanes quickly. On an average day we usually flew only half of the schedule. The other half would be coded MND-S for Maintenance Non-Delivery - Supply.

Flying at Last -- an Instrument Check

My first flight in Germany occurred on January 25th. It had been my first flight in four months. I was rusty! I was slow. I was constantly behind the aircraft mentally. During the takeoff you always came out of afterburner at 300 knots. It was procedure. At 350 my IP whispered "AB." Even though I was slow it all started coming back to me and I really felt good to be flying once again. I was very confident I would have my instrument check completed in a couple more weeks and then look out world because here I come.

The next week I was scheduled to fly twice and three times the week following. During that next week I had a maintenance cancel and a weather cancel. The week after that saw all three sorties canceled because of weather. Each day started out with a promise for flying and then it would begin raining lightly - still OK for flying. Then the temperature might drop a little and the rain would turn to snow.

Another way to see a weather cancel for flying is the upslope fog that I previously mentioned. A slight shift in the wind could close the base in less than five minutes. A friend was telling me of his four-ship that pulled out onto the runway for takeoff. The first three planes took off using standard Instrument Flight Rules (IFR) but before he could release brakes fog began rolling across the runway dropping visibility to almost zero. He taxied back and his flight weather diverted to Ramstein AB and then took the 'blue goose' (Air Force bus) back to Hahn.

496th TFS (Fighting Falcons)

Finally, during the third week of February flying began to pick up. Looking back on it I think the wing commander or director of operations may have directed that I start getting some scheduling priority if they ever wanted to get me checked out. During that third week I flew four times, two of which were at night. I was actually getting a feel back for the aircraft. When I was told that for the next week I would get three more flights including my instrument check I knew I was on a roll. Or so I thought.

I got two of those flights in and my instrument check was scheduled for Friday - I was anticipating a glorious weekend. Then the fog rolled in and we didn't turn a wheel all day long. The check was rescheduled for Monday morning but early Monday we had a base-wide recall for a local four-day exercise. The week after that, the first week of March, was dedicated to an exercise supporting the Army so again I didn't appear on the flying schedule.

With the squadron soon deploying to Zaragosa, Spain for semiannual gunnery camp it was becoming even more important to get that instrument check so I could get on down to Spain and qualify dropping bombs. Gunnery qualification was a requirement for becoming Operationally Ready (OR). Now, with a couple week layoff, the squadron powers to be decided I should at least go cross-country on the weekend following the Army exercise. I was elated. Yes, yes, yes. I did have one reservation, though. I had a head cold that wasn't completely over and with a history of sinus problems high altitude flying such as on a cross-country could be risky.

But, I chose to ignore my cold, made sure I had plenty of Afrin nasal spray and on Friday afternoon we took off; destination RAF Alconbury. We gassed up and flew back to Bitburg AB where we stayed overnight. On Saturday we flew back to England where, after gassing up, we again departed for Germany, this time Ramstein AB. Our plans called for more of the same on Sunday but by now my sinuses were squealing and whistling to me with every climb-out and I couldn't ignore the warning or pain any longer. I called off the remainder of the cross-country and checked in with the flight surgeon who promptly assigned me to 'duty not including flying' (DNIF) status. The new plan now called for me to get two additional flights during the last week of March with the second being an instrument check. Then, if that all happened as planned I would be able to join the rest of my squadron at Zaragosa.

A sequel to the cross-country story: My IP and I were scheduled to fly a certain tail number aircraft but at the last minute for some long forgotten reason, our aircraft were swapped. On Friday afternoon, while crossing the channel, our wingman in what was originally our aircraft lost all radios and then half of his electrical systems. They declared an In-Flight Emergency (IFE), landed on our wing at Alconbury and sat there until Tuesday waiting for their plane to get fixed.

My squadron deployed to Zaragosa and a week later I got the upper hand on my cold, got off DNIF status, finally got my instrument check and prepared to follow them. A letter I wrote on 9 April 1974 quite accurately conveyed the problems I had with maintenance and weather.

313th TFS Patch (Lucky Puppies)

> *"I finally had my instrument check and it went well. I feel 20 pounds lighter and five years younger. I was scheduled for it on the Thursday before I left for Zaragosa. I was at the squadron at four am, put on a pot of coffee and at 5:45 my check pilot came in. As the briefing progressed the fog began to roll in and by the time we were ready to go out to our plane we were completely socked in. However, by 9:30 the weather was lifting so we headed out to fly. During the preflight I discovered a fuel leak and turned the plane down. My long awaited flight was canceled. Then, about noon maintenance called and said the plane was fixed. Fortunately, another check pilot, Tom Roth, was found so I re-filed a flight plan, got another weather brief, briefed the mission and we hurried out to the plane. By now*

the sun was shining and so was I. Everything went smoothly. Tom was the kind of check pilot who went out of his way to make you feel relaxed. He was also an excellent pilot and I liked him a lot. I passed the instrument check just fine but we didn't get overhead patterns in so we were still incomplete.

I spent the day on Friday trying to get airborne to go to Zaragosa. The plan was for Tom to fly in my back seat and we could complete the overhead patterns and the check at Zaragosa. Then, Tom would return with someone else in the jet leaving me at Zaragosa. Twice we got on the runway and twice had to abort for minor maintenance problems. After the second abort it was too late for that day so we made plans to try again the following morning, Saturday. By 10:30 Saturday morning the fog had burned through and we were on our way to Spain. The weather in Zaragosa was lovely and it was the beginning of a grand day. On climb out we entered cirrus clouds at 20,000 feet but broke out by southern France. Our route took us south of Luxembourg, southeast across France to Bordeaux, south along the coast to Bayonne, then to San Sebastian, across the Pyrenees mountains, over Pamplona's famous bull rings and finally to Zaragosa. We flew at 38,000 feet and the visibility was unlimited. Crossing the Pyrenees we could see halfway across Spain towards the Mediterranean and perhaps a hundred miles or more of coastline along the Atlantic.

We did a VFR letdown at Zaragosa and since it was Saturday afternoon, we were the only ones flying. We had plenty of gas left so Tom suggested we alternate overheads and he would do the first. We beat up the overhead traffic pattern for 30 minutes. Tom was not at all a conservative pilot and his first pattern was a tight one so I made mine a little tighter than his. Then he flew one tighter than I did and so it went until we reached bingo fuel and had to land. After landing I discovered that most of the squadron was on the golf course and we had put on quite a show for them."

Zaragosa, Spain and Gunnery Camp

We all loved going to Zaragosa although we might not let our wives and families know that. "Oh, gosh darn, we've got to go back to Zaragosa again next month." The weather was always nicer than at Hahn even though it got cold enough in the winter to require jackets. Zaragosa had a lot of sunshine and clear skies and that is why Ramstein, Bitburg, Spangdahlem and Hahn deployed from Germany every six months to fill their semiannual bomb dropping requirements.

Germany, France, Belgium and Holland all had bombing ranges we occasionally went to but a combination of bombing restrictions, distance and typically poor weather usually added up to non-effective missions. We relied almost totally on Zaragosa. When we finished with our bombing it usually meant a slow ride home on the very next C-130 support flight and back to Victor Alert. Yes, everyone liked going to Zaragosa where we worked hard and played hard.

Another reason we liked Zaragosa was we didn't have to pull alert in Zaragosa. That was the good news. The bad news was for those who weren't at Zaragosa. They got to pull the entire alert. When the squadron deployed to Zaragosa they would take 12 of the best planes. Of the remaining planes, about five supported the nuclear alert commitment, a couple might be down for a hard break or waiting on a spare part and a couple would be getting prepped to be swapped out with planes at Zaragosa. In other words, there weren't any planes left at home for local flying - just sitting alert.

Flying at Zaragosa

The flying at Zaragosa was just plain fun. You got to fly eight to ten times each week and always with your crewed back seater and the missions were fun - going to the range to drop practice bombs and strafe. We bet a quarter on each bomb and a dollar on strafe. The last thing to be done at the end of the debrief was to figure out who owed money to whom.

F-4D with two 370 gal tanks & eight missiles

The down side of flying was the early brief times. Two squadrons were usually deployed to Zaragosa and each would on alternating weeks have the early brief times. Because Spain did not recognize daylight savings time, during the summer months the first takeoff was at 5:30. The first brief time was at 3:30. We used to joke that it only hurt for a couple hours. Actually, with half of the day's work finished we really felt pretty good walking back into our shared squadron building at 7 am meeting other aircrews that were just starting their day. By noon we would each have two sorties and the afternoon free for golfing.

A Practical Joke

An amusing anecdote comes to mind. In Zaragosa's deployed operations building, the two deployed squadrons shared many facilities such as the operations counter with its backlit scheduling board, personal equipment room and main briefing room. There was also one large room that had two eight foot room dividers separating two identical operations areas where each squadron's people could hang out, make phone calls, do mission planning, etcetera.

On one Monday morning after the o'dark thirty brief and long before the other squadron's people were due to come in, Lieutenant Eric Wilson, a pilot with an extraordinarily devious mind, came up with a wicked idea. "Heh, I wonder how long it will take those turkeys from Bitburg to figure it out if we slide the room dividers over one foot each morning." Immediately, eight guys were united in a common endeavor; to trick the 'turkeys' from Bitburg. Each squadron's designated area was about eight feet deep by sixteen feet wide. By Friday we had our desks spread apart luxuriating in our 22-foot wide area. Bitburg could barely fit their furniture inside their ten-foot enclosure. They never gave any sign that they noticed. The squadron rotated out that weekend and we moved everything back for the newcomers.

Zaragosa Social Life

The primary reason for liking Zaragosa was because of the camaraderie. For two weeks at a time we concentrated solely on flying the best we could during the week and on weekends we just relaxed. I got to know many people in the squadron in a way that would not have been possible under different circumstances.

F-4 ready to air refuel (note the open IR door behind the cockpit)

During the week everyone was usually subdued, especially when on early briefs. We usually gathered at the club for happy hour followed by dinner in the main dining room. After dinner a few might drop by the bar again to watch the television but most retired to their rooms to write letters or watch TV and to bed by nine. This sedate existence continued through the week until Friday. During the mid-afternoon on Friday the C-130 arrived from Hahn bringing in a dozen replacement aircrews and an equal number would climb on board for the noisy four and a half hour ride back to Hahn.

Happy Hour

At 4:30 happy hour began at Zaragosa and we celebrated the new arrivals and we celebrated the week that just ended. Happy hour typically started out with a couple of pitchers of red sangria, a mixture of wine and fruit juice. One pilot would pull out a dollar bill and announce, "I've got a number between zero and 99 - we start out to my left." With that each participant (everyone present) would guess a number when his turn came. The number had to be between the last two numbers guessed and the game's leader would respond after each guess with "high" or "low" or the dreaded "we've got a winner." With each guess the range narrowed and the chance of hitting the number increased. The so called winner got to buy the round - and had the honor of starting the next game. That was called the dollar bill game.

Another way of deciding the winner for a round was a dice game called 'trips out to horses.' I much preferred this game although it took longer. One person began the game usually by pounding the bar top with the dice cup and yelling at the top of his lungs, "heh, who feels lucky?" Of course, just like in the dollar bill game, everyone was feeling lucky. With that he would begin by slamming the dice cup upside down on the counter and at the last moment raise the cup before the five dice inside could stack up. Under some rules, stacked dice bought a round. To avoid being the winner at this game you had to roll trips - three or more of one number. If there were a dozen people in the game, two or three would usually be eliminated during the first round. The last player then brought them back for the second round, which ended up back at the beginning of the line. This continued, round after round until just about everyone was out. One final round of horses or sometimes just high dice out chose the new winner to buy the next round.

After a couple hours of such raucous behavior we usually retired to the dining room and dinner over which plans were made for the evening. There was almost always a 'downtown Zaragosa foray' to be led by an 'experienced Zaragosa-ite.' The downtown expedition began at the bus stop around eight pm where we would board a Spanish bus for the half-hour ride to downtown Zaragosa. Our flying always took us away from the city so I had no idea of what to expect on my first visit. When I found myself looking up at the tall modern buildings from the tree-lined sidewalks of this beautiful city I was greatly surprised and impressed.

We got off the bus at an area known for its stand-up exotic food bars. I quickly discovered the Spanish words for mushrooms, snails and squid and there were many things I just pointed to and didn't really care to know what they were. They were all good though. From here I just tagged along as we went from nightspot to nightspot where we each ordered our 'cubra libre's' which was really Cuban rum and American coke. The nightclubs had no cover charge and were crowded with an elite younger than 40 Spanish clientele. The entertainment was very loud recorded music. I found my first trip to downtown Zaragosa to be enlightening but by the end of the evening I was more than ready to get back to base. I only went back at night one more time during the next three years. The activities in the BOQ were frequently much more interesting.

Another Friday night activity usually had a benign beginning over an after dinner drink at the bar. It began with someone fooling around with the dice cup and then someone else pulling out a dollar bill and three others announcing that they each would cover a quarter. The name of the game was 4, 5, 6 and it was a wicked game that once started easily continued until sunrise. If you were winning it was considered poor manners to pull out of the game and if you were losing you wanted a chance to win your money back. Usually hundreds of dollars changed hands and I heard stories of Vietnam origin of homes being lost during these games. I never participated in 4, 5, 6 or any other gambling game because I knew I would feel badly either if I lost my own money or if I won someone else's. For me it was a lose – lose situation.

Saturdays were usually more sedate with many people not showing their faces until noon or later. There was one notable exception. On this occasion only a few people drifted off to their rooms during the wee hours of the morning. The majority closed the bar and then began drifting from room to room always in search of more beer. When absences in the ranks were noted a concerted search effort was undertaken until the recalcitrant partygoers were found - usually in their beds. After the beer ran out, someone noticed that the sun was up and that the O' Club dining room was probably open for breakfast. It was.

We surprised the kitchen staff by the sudden appearance of 20 or so unshaven and still slightly raucous pilots. After filling up on steak and eggs we felt quite revitalized so when another fellow observed that it sure was a nice day for golf, we soon found ourselves opening the golf course. A quick head count showed that the previous night's lesson had been learned well. We hadn't lost anyone. So, we had an impromptu tournament. By noon, however, the non-stop pace began taking its toll and I don't think we had more than eight or so people left when we continued on to the bowling alley for the afternoon's activities. Ah, the energy of youth.

Practical jokes were another common fare at Zaragosa and some probably live on to this day in their retelling by fighter pilots on Friday nights at Zaragosa. Perhaps the best I heard and of which I fully believe because I knew the victim as an 'old head' when I arrived at Hahn went like this.

Saturday nights were usually much calmer than Friday nights but not always. On one Zaragosa Saturday night after a serious evening of drinking, Joe Dunaway was discovered to be missing. He was found sleeping in his bed and couldn't be roused. Joe it seems had more than his share of the beer that evening. Someone came up with an idea. It could have been Eric! Joe was tenderly removed from his metal frame bed. The mattresses were removed and the bed was disassembled. Within minutes, the bed was reassembled in the parking lot outside of the BOQ. The parking lot was shared by the O' Club, BOQ and Chapel. The bed was remade with sheets and blanket and finally, Joe was put back to bed - naked as a jay bird. As the story goes, when Joe awakened later that morning he was greeted by a bright warm sun and the curious stares of church goers as they walked by on their way to the morning church service.

Sitges by the Sea

I regretfully only went on one weekend trip during all of my visits to Zaragosa. It was to Sitges (we pronounced it Seeches). I had heard many grand stories from the 'old heads' about this resort town on the Mediterranean so when I discovered a group was planning on going it didn't take much to convince me to tag along. We had a three-day weekend and four of us rented a car for the 150 mile five hour journey. This was the Spain of the infamous dictator Franco and we had been warned numerous times to avoid trouble when off base. Franco's power was enforced by the notoriously brutal LaGuardia Seville. We had all heard horrible stories of this machine gun carrying national police force. On our journey to Sitges we prayed we wouldn't encounter the LaGuardia. We didn't. But, our plan if we had was simple. Yes Sir. No Sir. Three bags full, Sir. Humbleness counts for a lot.

Our trip to Sitges was very interesting in a boring sort of way. Although we didn't encounter danger, we got to see the real Spanish countryside and it was far different than what we had seen at 500 feet and 420 knots. In many ways I was reminded of the desolate beauty of Texas until we entered the small towns. The modern elegance of downtown Zaragosa contrasted sharply with the dusty dirt streets and tin roofs we encountered. Spain we found really was a third world country outside of the big cities and you had to use Spanish to communicate – English was rarely spoken.

The highways we took to Sitges were all two lane and full of sharp curves and hills. We didn't make very good time but we had no intentions of speeding or in any other way highlighting ourselves. We took our time and enjoyed the experience. The highway took us almost due east and then we began climbing through rising terrain that millions of years ago might have been small mountains. As we passed over the summit we were greeted by a view of the blue Mediterranean 15 miles ahead. The highway continued on to the coast where we turned north on a smaller road that followed the coast. In another half-hour we were entering Sitges.

Sitges was a small tourist town that huddled tightly along the beaches of the Mediterranean. Only 15 or 20 miles to the north lay Spain's second largest city, Barcelona. Sitges was several miles long and everything was centered on its only visible industry, tourism. The weather was warm and sunny and from the car window we drank in the sights the beaches had to offer. We soon found a nice looking two-story hotel and got a room at a reasonable rate. We quickly discovered the water that came from the pipes was brackish, undrinkable. We assumed the whole town shared the same problem and for the remainder of the weekend relied on bottled water for washing hair and brushing teeth and beer for drinking.

For the next two days we roamed the town taking in the nightspots and the sights. We played in the Mediterranean and sunned on the golden beaches and marveled at the lack of modesty of the European women. Everyone wore bikinis including many older women who were 50 pounds or more past their prime.

Sitges was a European vacation spot for the more economy minded. It was several hundred miles south of Marseille, Nice, Cannes and Monaco so a longer drive for most European vacationers. Sitges at night was a delightful surprise. We wandered from nightclub to nightclub and there was something for everyone; every nationality seemed represented especially America. When we walked into the Texas Club I knew I was home. It wasn't a very big place but a small band was playing one American ballad after another. I soon found myself joining in song with the other patrons. I was amazed that they knew what I thought were exclusively American songs and then I realized they were being sung in many languages - all at the same time and no one seemed to notice. What an experience.

Sitges was a fun place to spend a weekend and it was easy on the wallet. San Miguel beer cost 35 cents and street side stands abounded selling golden fried poi-jo – roasted chicken, that was 'finger licking' good. The weekend ended way too soon and we were back in the briefing room preparing for another flight to Bardenas Reales Range. We carried back with us many fond memories and stories.

A Typical Bomb Range Mission

> The time is 11:00 and I'm listening to the debriefing of our gunnery range flight. I have an immensely contented feeling that always follows a good flight and I let my mind drift back over the preceding five hours.
>
> Although few non-flying people know it, a flight begins not when they hear that deafening roar of the jets taking off but two and a half hours before. This morning it began for me at 6 o'clock as I prepared for a 6:30 briefing. First, there was a flight plan to be filed following a weather briefing, computing takeoff and landing data and a quick mind refresher on gunnery range procedures.
>
> 6:30 found four sleepy eyed pilots and their equally sleepy eyed Weapons Systems Officers (WSOs) sipping hot coffee as the flight briefing began. The flight leader for my flight was Capt. Bill Lax and I was confident it would be a good flight. The weather was good and Bill is one of the better flight leaders in the squadron. At times he is a bit cocky but it is a cockiness born of natural abilities and he doesn't shirk the responsibilities of a flight leader. Most importantly he is aware of his wingmens' limitations and experience. Bill also displays a quick grin that makes everyone try just a little harder.
>
> The hour-long briefing began with the usual items; time hacking our watches, an abbreviated mission description, weather brief and a quick discussion of the emergency procedure of the day. Then the flight leader covered the standard items such as starting engines, check in, taxi and runway lineup procedures. Finally, we got to the heart of the briefing;

range procedures and techniques for dropping good bombs on the range. Everyone develops his own techniques and as can be expected this part of the briefing turns into an active discussion. Each pilot listened intently hoping to perhaps pick up on something new that he hadn't tried before, something that might just give him an edge in winning the quarters that day. Then, Bill gave the lineup of events. First we would do a radar low altitude drogue delivery simulating a parachuted nuclear bomb. Following that would be a visual low altitude drogue delivery, two 45-degree dive bombs, two 30 degree dive bombs, three 10 degree low altitude passes and five runs on the strafe target.

Following the brief we took the usual leisurely five minutes to get a drink of water, don anti-G suits, collect parachute harnesses, helmets and checklists and make sure the jet was released by maintenance. Then, to add a bit of spice to the mission we placed the customary standard bets. Everyone pays a quarter to the person with the best bomb in each event as well as a quarter for the best average distance in each event.

Because of the 'leisurely' five minutes we were already five minutes late leaving the squadron building and so the race was on. Before climbing into the cockpit, I did a rapid exterior preflight looking for obvious faults with the plane such as hydraulic fluid leaks, oil and fuel leaks, proper tire inflation, drag chute installed OK and a number of other items which could make the plane unsafe to fly. Then came the strap-in, a very routine but important task for every flight. Two leg restraint straps on each leg are fastened. In case of ejection they will pull my legs in towards the seat preventing the possibility of leaving my kneecaps on the canopy rail. A clip on each side of the seat fastens the survival kit to my harness. The kit is actually a fiberglass case that lies right under my seat cushion. It contains a life raft, cans of fresh water, flares, an emergency radio, signaling mirror, medicines and a myriad of other valuable survival items. Two shoulder harness straps connect me to my parachute. Finally, a lap belt similar to an automobile seat belt is fastened and tightened until it hurts. If the lap belt wasn't fastened or tightened enough and I encountered negative Gs I would suddenly find myself floating around the cockpit or possibly bouncing off the top of the canopy. It's not the recommended way to fly.

At the pre-briefed start engine time I've completed the interior cockpit checks and have all of the switches set. It was a matter of fighter pilot pride to start engines on time and be ready to go at check-in time. If a problem should occur we were expected to get word to the flight leader. I give a signal to the ground crew and then start first number two (the right) and then number one (the left) engines.

When starting engines the first thing heard is the rushing of air from the starting unit that causes the engine blades to start turning. At 10 percent rpm I advance the throttle and depress the ignition button. This provides fuel and 'fire' and the engine continues winding up until reaching idle, 65 percent rpm. After starting both engines I quickly run through the remaining checks confirming the flight controls work as advertised, the instruments are functioning correctly and all remaining switches are in their proper position. We are number four in a four ship flight and all we have to do for the present is wait for the flight Lead to check us in on the radio.

While waiting my mind reviews what we have just done making sure nothing has been forgotten.

Broken Habit Patterns Are Dangerous

The checklist is designed to prevent you from forgetting to do certain tasks or from doing things out of order. But a break in a habit pattern at a critical moment has caused pilots to miss doing very important things that they otherwise wouldn't have forgotten in a million years. An example of this is being on downwind in the traffic pattern and just as you're ready to put the gear down getting a master caution light caused by a fuel level low condition. Your normal habit pattern has been interrupted and in dealing with the fuel low light it is now very possible to forget to put the gear down, a task that usually is automatic and sequential.

At Hahn I was at a low enough experience level that I wasn't as susceptible to that happening but I was trained to know that eyes will see what they are expecting to see and ears will hear what they expect to hear. Thus, when my WSO (also affectionately known as GIB for Guy In Back) calls out the checklist item 'flaps', I should respond 'set to half' and he should visually check the flap position indicator to see that they are at half.

Many years later at Hahn AB after they had switched from the F-4 to the F-15, a classic accident occurred due to this principle. During the pre-takeoff flight control system checks, the pilot moved the stick left and told his crew chief he was doing so. For a thousand times each had done this after engine start and the response was always 'left aileron up, right aileron down' and the crew chief reported it this way again. However, the airplane had just been worked on by maintenance and the flight controls had been hooked up in reverse. What the crew chief had really seen was left aileron down, right aileron up. The pilot then moved the stick to the right and again both heard and saw what they expected to hear. On the runway prior to releasing brakes, the pilot should have 'stirred' the stick one more time and visually checked the flight control surfaces. He didn't. On takeoff, the F-15 began drifting to the right and he countered with left stick that caused the plane to drift more so he gave it more stick. The pilot probably never did figure out what was wrong with his airplane. Seconds after getting airborne, he rolled inverted and crashed.

"Lion flight check." My thoughts are instantly back to the present. "2," "3.", "4."

"Lion flight, go channel 10."

"2," "3," "4."

"Lion flight check."

"2," "3," "4."

"Ground control, Lion flight, taxi with four."

Ground control gives taxi instructions and in numerical order we taxi out to the end of the runway maintaining 300 feet spacing between aircraft. As of this moment we are no longer four airplanes. We are each a quarter of a larger entity - a four ship.

To do the best job we can we will always strive to look and sound that way. It begins on the radio. At check-in, two is the first to respond to lead's "Lion flight check" but three sets the cadence. If he delays a second in responding after hearing "two" then four should delay the same amount and we all sound alike. Something that has been drilled into us is wingman discipline.

During taxi out, if lead should taxi with his right main gear in the taxi line, then two will put his left main on it and three will have his right gear on the line and so forth. It might be 20 degrees outside with a terribly cold wind blowing and you might be just getting over a cold, but if lead should taxi with both front and rear canopies open so does everyone else. If the lead GIB closes his canopy, then all of the GIBs will close their canopies. Among fighter pilots this 'follow the leader' routine indicates an attitude of discipline and pride, both of which are absolutely essential for four planes to fly in close proximity and do the job assigned to them.

One Potato, Two Potato

Sometimes a bit of humor might be injected into the situation but flight discipline is inviolate. On a cross country once I was waiting to taxi out at Kelly AFB, in San Antonio when a flight of arriving Air National Guard F4s checked in with ground control after clearing the runway. Potato was their computer assigned call sign for that day. I heard lead check in his flight. "One Potato," followed crisply by "Two Potato,", "Three Potato," "Four." The ground controller couldn't suppress a laugh as he gave taxi instructions.

Steve Cole on Flight Discipline

I learned my best lesson in flight Discipline from a captain in RTU. His name was Steve Cole and he was an excellent pilot and flight leader. He also had the rare distinction of having shot down not one but two MiGs in Vietnam. I was in one air-to-ground flight where Steve was a back seat IP; he wasn't the lead. The flight lead had a wing administrative job and was attached to the squadron for flying. He also had a reputation of not being very demanding or even of being a very good pilot. It was early in the ground attack phase and the flight just didn't click very well. I didn't know why. I had not dropped very good bombs, nor had anyone else.

During the debrief, Steve was very quiet, not saying a thing. He merely listened and responded to the flight lead. At the end of the debrief, Steve said he wanted the students to stay a few more minutes. He had something to say to us. As soon as the last instructor had left the room Steve began HIS debrief. He had written down notes on everything from initial check-in until engine shut down and now we relived the flight as seen by Steve Cole. He began with asking someone why they weren't ready at flight check-in. At the beginning of a feeble excuse he roared, "not acceptable." "You will be up on the radio two minutes prior to check-in or you will get word to lead through maintenance. Is that understood!" He wasn't asking a question. On taxi out we hadn't mirrored lead. Holding short of the runway, our aircraft weren't lined up in a perfect line and so it went for perhaps an hour. Not once did he allude to a weak flight lead. That would have been unprofessional and lacking in discipline. I suspect he followed our talk by talking with his superiors about the flight lead's poor conduct of the flight but his message to us was that it was our job to be there and to cope no matter what.

During that debrief by Steve Cole I learned what it was to be a good flight lead and more importantly a good wingman. You couldn't be a good lead without first knowing how to be a good wingman. That was one of the most valuable flying lessons I ever received.

> *Short of the runway Lion flight lines up and the 'quick check' maintenance crew goes over each plane one last time making sure there are no maintenance problems. An arming crew goes right behind them pulling the safety pins on the guns and bombs. As each plane is checked he turns on his rotating beacon signifying he is ready.*
>
> *"Lion flight, channel 11."*
>
> *"2," "3," "4."*
>
> *"Lion flight check."*
>
> *"2," "3," "4."*
>
> *"Tower, Lion flight is ready for takeoff."*
>
> *"Roger, Lion flight. Winds are 130 degrees at 12 knots. contact departure control. You are cleared for takeoff."*
>
> *Four planes close their canopies as one when the leader signals and four planes pull out on the runway together and stop at their proper positions. Leader is on the left of the runway centerline. Two is to the right with 10 feet separating their wing tips. Three is to the left of lead and four is on the outside and to the left of three. In effect they are at this moment two two-ships and will perform formation takeoffs. When four pulls into position lead signals by making a circular motion with his hand to run up engines and do final before takeoff checks.*

After applying full brake pressure I run up one engine and then the other to one hundred percent power. As each engine in turn stabilizes at 100 percent I check its instruments. Each engine must be done separately because if done together the tremendous thrust would push the plane down the runway on skidding tires. Engine instruments check OK and I give an exaggerated head nod to 'three' indicating I'm ready to go. When lead sees everyone is ready he calls us to departure control.

"Lion flight, channel 12,"

"2," "3," "4."

Basic Controls of an F-4

Before going on let's review how an F-4 is controlled. First of all, the power from the engines is not controlled by the right foot on a gas pedal but by the left hand on two throttles, one for each engine. They slide forward for increased power and of course back for less. Full back is 65% power or idle power. As you reach full forward you approach 100% power which is also known as military power or just plain 'mil.' At times maximum available power is required so you have to move the throttles an inch or so to the left to move them around a mechanical stop and now you can continue to slide them forward in the afterburner range. The afterburner works very simply by spraying fuel into the jet engine's exhaust noticeably increasing thrust. The afterburner has four stages from minimum to maximum afterburner and although the engine's thrust almost doubles the amount of fuel used quadruples. It is a very inefficient use of fuel and to be used sparingly.

Switches Galore

The left hand is almost always kept on the throttles. The throttles have various switches located on them such as the engine ignition, speed brake, microphone, and numerous weapons selecting switches. The left hand might momentarily leave its position on the throttles to reposition other switches such as the landing light, gear handle, drag-chute and flaps switch but then it goes right back to the throttles.

The right hand has a more difficult job. It operates the control stick which is exactly that - a stick that comes out of the floor of the aircraft with a handle or stick grip on the end. Moving the stick this way and that causes mechanical linkages and cables to move back and forth. These in turn are connected to hydraulic actuators which then move the appropriate control surfaces; the ailerons and spoilers for roll and stabilator for pitch.

The stick grip also has many switches on it. One switch is actually a button, the pickle button. With the proper switch settings in another part of the cockpit each time your thumb depresses the pickle button one or more bombs are released or missiles might be fired. Another switch is a trigger that fires the gun. A button that is operated by the 4th finger engages the nose wheel steering while on the ground or operates the air refueling disengage feature when in the air. Finally, a trim button is a large round switch that is operated by the thumb and controls the aircraft trim. This switch can be moved up and down or left and right and is used to 'trim out' flight control forces on the control stick. This is easily the most often used switch and a skilled pilot will usually have all stick forces trimmed out -- 'hands off.'

The stick operates in a similar fashion to the control half wheel in a light aircraft or airliner. A Fighter aircraft just doesn't have the room in the cockpit for a wheel and also a stick is easier to use with one hand. Back and forward controls pitch and left and right controls roll. To climb at 10 degrees you would move the stick back until the nose was ten degrees up, then you would center the stick. If you wanted to roll into a 45 degree right bank, you would move the stick to the right until the plane began rolling right. Approaching 45 degrees of bank you would again center the stick to maintain the bank.

The feet have a fairly easy job to do. In the air they operate the rudders and on the ground they operate the brakes or control the nose gear steering. The rudder, located on the tail, operates essentially like the rudder of a boat causing the tail to fishtail in the direction the rudder is moved. The F-4 was one of the last fighters that required the pilot to use the rudder for coordinated turns. Failure to use the rudder during a hard turn could easily result in a phenomenon called 'adverse yaw' and loss of aircraft control. The F-4 was still a 'stick and rudder' aircraft. In all newer fighters 'the computer' is essential in positioning the flight control surfaces to produce the optimum performance of the aircraft relieving the pilot of that skill. I explain this in much greater detail in the last chapter when describing the F-100 flight characteristics.

"Lion flight check."

"2," "3," "4."

We are making formation takeoffs so one and two will take off first followed in ten seconds by three and four. I can see lead's cockpit by looking through my element leader. By the roar I can tell both one and two have run up their engines. Then they begin moving together and after what seems like a couple seconds I hear the loud roar explode as their afterburners simultaneously light generating 30 thousand pounds of thrust. Within seconds they are thundering down the runway and I notice the run-up signal from three. I run my engines up to 85% and stabilize. Engine instruments all check out. three looks back to me and I give an exaggerated head nod. He pats the front of his helmet signaling his head will nod forward momentarily for brake release. As his helmet dips my feet come off the brakes and I jam the throttles into full afterburner trying to beat him. It is much easier to drag the brakes a little if I get the jump on him than trying to catch back up which is the other alternative. When my burners light I'm pressed back into my seat. I'm beginning to move too far forward so I pull the throttles back just a little and slide back into position. In eight seconds we are already up to 100 knots. I disengage nose gear steering because at this speed the rudder is now effective for steering. In another seven seconds we are at 150. I have the stick pulled back and I feel the nose getting light As three's nose raises off the runway so does mine and I adjust back stick pressure to match his attitude. Now we are at 175 knots and simultaneously we lift off the runway.

I see three look over at me to confirm I'm still with him and with an almost imperceptible upward nod of his head he raises his gear handle. This is the most demanding part of a formation takeoff. The common tendency is to sink below the stacked level position - it looks terrible to anyone watching from the ground. I keep stirring the control stick fighting to maintain perfect position. I momentarily take my left hand off the throttle, find the gear handle and slap the handle up. Back to the throttles for a needed adjustment - in that brief moment I started moving too far forward. A couple seconds later I see three's head nod up a second time signaling raising the flaps. The flap handle is much more difficult to find than the gear handle. I find it on the first try and raise the flaps to the up position. Approaching 350 knots three signals back and forth with a closed fist to come out of afterburner and then slightly fishtails his aircraft, a signal to slide out from close or fingertip formation to route, which is two to four ship widths. We quickly rejoin on one and two becoming a four ship again for the trip to the range.

"Lion flight, channel 14."

"2," "3," "4."

We are on range control frequency and we are in luck. No one is on the range and the weather is good. We all copy the range winds in thousand foot increments and are cleared on. We are a hundred miles from Zaragosa AB at 18,000 feet. We push over beginning a descent to 4,000 feet and push up our airspeed to 420 knots. Looking through the flight I can see the range approaching. Our first event will be a visually delivered low altitude drogue delivery or VLADD.

We over-fly the range tower on our downwind run as we head away from the target circle. Lead makes a call to echelon right. I feel three pulling his power slightly to drop back and then he begins to cross below and behind one and two. I follow and cross behind three so we are now in a right Echelon formation. At 10 miles from the range lead signals with his right hand and in a flash he has rolled into 60 degrees of bank and is gone. Now we are a three ship. I hear lead on the radio calling he is on base. 15 seconds later two rolls into 60 degrees of bank and is gone, then three and finally myself.

I begin a turn to final based on time and start a descent to 1,000 feet on the radar altimeter. The range target should be about 35 miles or so on the nose when I roll out. I can see the smoke trails ahead of the other three flight members. We have about seven miles separation from each other.

My GIB has the radar reflectors of the target on his radar and he gives me some steering guidance. I continue my descent now to 200 feet. The rocky sandy terrain flashes by outside. The terrain isn't too unlike Arizona's desert at this time of year. Up ahead I hear the progress of my other flight members as they deliver their VLADDs or RLADDs. There is a final call with clearance from the range officer. A steady tone is suddenly heard over the radio and I can see the climbing smoke trail of an F-4 20 miles in front of me as it pulls up into a 45-degree climb. The tone disappears indicating the bomb has been released and the smoke trail reverses into a turning descent. As two begins his pull it is time for me to push it up to 500 knots. At eight miles a minute we quickly approach the range.

I pick up the run-in line and offset slightly to allow for a predetermined crosswind correction. As we pass a landmark on the ground that is exactly 10,000 feet from the target I depress the pickle button and hold it. On my attitude indicator two bars jump into view, one horizontal and one vertical. The two bars will give me course and climb guidance for the bomb delivery. All I have to do is fly the airplane to keep the two bars forming a cross. In four seconds the steady tone on the radio comes on and the horizontal bar begins rising telling me to pull back on the stick to start a 45-degree climb. The computer is programmed to command a steady increase in G until reaching four Gs. In moments I'm in a 45 degree climb and the rusty desert colored terrain that had been rushing past my cockpit seconds before is now falling away beneath me as I sail effortlessly skyward. The steady tone in my headset stops and the pitch and course steering bars disappear from view. The small practice bomb has been released. Aware that my airspeed is decreasing as fast as my altitude is increasing I move the stick to the left and roll inverted. With smoothly increasing back-stick pressure I pull the nose down to below the horizon and with a controlled descent I continue my pull down into a left turn to go back outbound. The next event will be the same except my GIB will get to do it with radar.

Half way through my turn I glance over my shoulder at the big bombing circle and am rewarded by seeing a white puff of smoke - which is my bomb hitting. It looks well within scoring range. I pick up number one and then two on final and soon hear three calling base turn and then I am following. My back seater, Lee, is very experienced having been at Hahn for two years already and I am comfortable flying with him. He has the target on radar halfway through the turn to final and very efficiently confirms all of my switch settings and ensures I am accurately following his headings. We work well together and our RLADD is a good one, definitely in competition for the dollar bet.

Instead of rolling inverted after the RLADD is released I let the plane soar up to 14,000 feet and start setting up switches for 45-degree dive bomb. My primary responsibility right now, though, is fitting back into the flight. We are transitioning from a long strung out radar pattern to a tight overhead pattern. I quickly pick up the other three in the flight and use cutoff to get myself into position. Delaying the flight now will result in a remark later during the debrief.

We have quickly adjusted spacing so one plane is in each corner of the box pattern above the bombing circle. In sequence one, two and three roll in on the target. When it is my turn I roll into 135 degrees of bank (half inverted) and begin my roll in. As my nose approaches the target I roll wings level and check my dive angle. I'm actually aimed about 2,000 feet beyond the target which is close to what I wanted but my dive angle is 27 degrees - shallow meaning my bomb will be short. Also, my sight isn't tracking towards the target the way I want it to. I roll back into a bunch of bank and pull on the stick to make one tracking correction - it is all I will have time to do. When I roll back wings level my sight is tracking better now. Lee has been counting down on the altimeter for me so I can judge when to pickle the bomb off - we're descending 1,000 feet a second. I hear him suddenly say in a higher pitched voice, "power." Heck. I had forgotten to pull my throttles back after rolling in. I yanked them back to idle and checked my airspeed. Instead of 450 I already have 500 knots. I know the higher airspeed means I'll need more altitude to pull out. Do I go through dry? No, I decide. Being fast will compensate for being three degrees shallow. It just might work. I hear Lee's voice, "readyyyy - pickle." I touch the pickle button on the control stick at the 'ready' call and by the time I hear 'pickle' I've already come in with a four-G recovery pull. Our G-suits inflate in protest to the sudden increase in G. It is a welcome sight to trade the brown earth view through my canopy with the beautiful blue of the sky. With the nose well above the horizon I roll into left bank and start searching for number three.

It is absolutely incredible how fast things happen in the gunnery pattern. When the weather is like it is today and we have a good flight Lead and when everyone obeyed crew rest the night before and is mentally and physically up for the mission and we don't have any aircraft malfunctions and nothing unexpected happens such as a bird strike with a turkey vulture or a light aircraft bumbling through our restricted airspace, this is a fun, even a routine mission.

But let one thing happen and it no longer is routine. Let two things happen and it can become a spectacular never to be forgotten and sometimes tragic sortie. The gunnery range is a dangerous place - so dangerous that a rescue helicopter is always sitting alert nearby to respond if and when needed. Most gunnery ranges experience accidents during each year and usually they are fatal. The way to counter accidents is through awareness. Our flight briefings and debriefings stress safety and learning from the mistakes of others. We also have monthly flight safety meetings and wide dissemination of all accident reports - and still they occur.

We had what was classified as an accident on the range during this deployment. Fortunately, it did not result in a tragedy. I was airborne at the time of the accident but it didn't occur in my flight, but it could have. After coming off after the last RLADD pass, Randy, the pilot, was climbing up to his downwind altitude, 5,000 feet on this occasion, and he was trying to do too many things at once. There are at least six switches to set or reposition when going from a LADD type pass to regular conventional bombing. Randy had thought he had rolled wings level at 5,000 feet and was looking on the right side of his cockpit trying to confirm the position of one of his switches when the airplane slowly rolled into left bank. The back seater, Frank, watched as they rolled left but didn't say anything thinking that Randy was just starting his turn to base a little early. Frank focused his attention back inside the cockpit to do something and now both were looking inside. The aircraft continued its left roll until it was inverted. Now the nose was quickly dropping as well. Moments later Frank glanced outside and to his horror saw only the earth where there should have been sky. He yelled, "Randy, what's going on?" At that point Randy looked outside and quickly realized what had happened. Instead of reassuring Frank that he could recover he just concentrated on applying aileron to roll wings level and back stick pressure to pull out of their dive. Meanwhile, as far as Frank was concerned, something terrible must have happened to his front seater and death was imminent. Frank pulled his ejection handle about the same time that Randy began his roll back to upright flight. The F-4 came within a thousand feet of impacting the ground. During the accident investigation it was determined that Frank's ejection seat left the aircraft while the plane was still in 90 degrees of bank. Frank got about one swing in his chute and he was on the ground. The entire Air Force learned from Frank's and Randy's mistakes.

> *I am amazed. My errors did at least partially cancel out and my bomb score was 120 feet at three. Just about all of my error was due to cross winds and not flying the aircraft across the target. The hardest part of bombing for most of us was doing just that. I found it took an incredible amount of finesse to be able to roll in so that when you went wings level your ground track was where it should be. The greater the dive angle the more difficult this was to judge. Even if you had the finesse, if the crosswinds were other than what you were expecting you could end up with the same situation. Finally, upon rolling wings level and recognizing a correction in flight path was needed you had enough time for one correction or maybe two if you were really quick - then you were in a take it or leave it situation. The extremely aggressive yanking and banking flying that was required to make corrections seemed like a very unnatural thing to be doing while hurtling at the ground at almost supersonic speeds.*
>
> *After another 45-degree pass we were up for two 30-degree dive bomb passes. In comparison this would be simple. Instead of 14,000 feet we level*

off at 8,000 feet and the pattern becomes tighter and faster. At roll in a 30 degree dive is established and bomb release is at 3,100 feet. With a good four-G pull we bottom out at 1,500 feet and once again soar back up to 8,000 feet for a second pass.

Following the second 30-degree dive it is up to 4,000 feet for ten degree low angle bombing. The roll-in is much more gentle using only 100 degrees of bank – just slightly inverted. After rolling out with the nose pointed just beyond the target I check to see that I have ten degrees in my dive although following the higher angle events this seems like nothing – but, I'm reminded that the shallow angle events are the most dangerous because you are closer to the ground, thus, have less room, or time, for error. There is also room for complacency because it isn't as scary. I adjust my throttles to hold 450 knots and have time enough to make a couple course corrections before bomb release at 600 feet. A prompt recovery pull has our F-4 pointing back up again by 200 feet.

After two ten degree passes lead calls up for strafe. We follow in order. There are several switch changes required in very little time. The bombing dispenser has to be deselected, the inboard station has to be deselected, master arm to safe, the center station then has to be selected along with guns and when the nose is pointed in a safe direction, the master arm is switched back to on. With the master arm I am gratified and relieved to see both a green and an amber light. That is a positive indication that the SUU-21 gun pod that is hanging on the centerline station (the F-4D, unlike the E model, didn't have a built in gun) will fire when the trigger is squeezed.

The target is a parachute stretched out between two 20-foot tall poles. There is a black two foot diameter circle on the center of the chute and just like in RTU, scoring is by acoustical scorer and virtually any bullets passing through the chute will score. My roll in is just about the same as for ten degree bombing except there is no aim-off distance to point at. I point the nose right at the target and do an unloaded roll to wings level. Instantly, I'm aware that something isn't as it should be. My sight is well short of the target. Resisting the immediate impulse to raise it to the target I try to analyze what is wrong and then the answer comes to me. I forgot to change the number of sight depression mills. The sight is depressed by 115 mills and it should be only 38 mills. Now is not the time to be changing the mills and I call off dry. On the next pass, though, I am ready. When I roll wings level the sight is just below the target. I pause a couple seconds setting speed and waiting for the range to close. At approximately 3,000 feet I raise the sight smoothly to the target, track momentarily and at what seems to be about 1800 feet squeeze off a brief sighter burst to see where the gun actually is shooting. The six rotating barrels of the 20 mm Gatling

Gun shoot at a rate of 6,000 rounds a minute or a hundred each second so even a short sighter burst fires a dozen bullets. I squeeze and pull. We are constantly warned to not wait to see your bullets hit or you will fly through the ricochet pattern. Just before the nose of my F-4 blocks out the target I see the dirt kick up from my bullets. They hit just a little to the right of where I was aiming. I will adjust my aim accordingly on the succeeding three passes.

Our last pass is designed to be dry to give us an opportunity to safe up all switches over the range as well as join up the flight so we can inspect each other. Every now and then someone will have ricochet damage or a hung bomb or two that might need to be jettisoned over the range. Everyone is clean. It is time to go home and I hear Tiger flight checking in behind us.

The return flight is uneventful as we fly a loose route formation to the visual entry point at Zaragosa. Bill aligns the flight in an echelon formation as we make our turn to initial and we perform a four-ship pitchout. During the return we've been very silent in the aircraft but that is the way it has to be. Extraneous talking is seldom done. Even straight and level flight requires total vigilance by everyone in the flight to include both front and back-seaters. 'Shooting the breeze' is saved until after the chocks are in place and the engines are shut down.

"Uh, what was that, Bill? I was sort of day dreaming I guess. Oh, yes, who do I owe quarters to?"

Becoming Operationally Ready - the TAC check

The instrument check cleared me for flying the F-4 in instrument conditions. Combined with the instrument check was a qual check that qualified me for flying the F-4 in visual conditions. The last and most difficult obstacle was the TAC check. For the 496th it consisted of an intercept mission or perhaps an ACT mission. For my squadron it required flying a low-level route terminating in an air-to-ground weapon delivery. As with the instrument check, weather and maintenance were constant hindrances.

A prerequisite for the mission qual check was weapons qualification in all events. During the spring of 1974 I spent almost five weeks in Zaragosa getting my weapons qualification. When the squadron returned to Hahn I only needed the check to become fully OR (Operationally Ready) and qualified to begin sitting Victor Alert. On the 26th of May I wrote, "I wish I could say I was flying a lot but it isn't the case. For various reasons I won't go into it is very hard to get a plane to fly even when you are scheduled to do so. Consequently I'm still waiting on a TAC check which is all I need to become fully OR."

On the 9th of June I reported that flying was picking up a little. *"I flew three times this week -- almost unprecedented for me at Hahn."* Then I went on to explain that the first flight was spent entirely in the GCA pattern because the gear wouldn't retract. This was the third time in a row it happened to this plane. I'm sure the wing commander had some choice words for the director of maintenance at his 'stand-up' meeting that day. The second sortie was a thrilling low level flown across Germany. The third was flown on a Saturday during a local exercise and was an intercept mission. Only the low level would have been preparation for my check.

An Unsuccessful TAC Check

A week later on the 16th of June: "flying has been picking up a little. I got five flights in last week but still no TAC check and that is the reason I can only take one week of leave. The TAC check consists mainly of flying a low level and although I had five flights only two were low level and both had to be broken off half way through because of weather."

On the 29th of June I wrote that the weather in Germany had been terrible for flying low levels. The predominant weather was "low scud type clouds, dirty and raggedy, sweeping across the skies dropping rain when they saw fit and more dangerously concealing thunderstorms as well." I described an attempted TAC check.

> *"I attempted to fly my TAC check last Thursday. We took off below a low overcast and the check pilot was flying in another aircraft in close pursuit. The beginning of our low level start route point is 45 miles south of Hahn where the Luxembourg, French and German borders meet and the low level takes us clear across France just south of the Belgium border. Shortly after takeoff we encountered some of that scud I already described and had to climb up a little between layers of clouds. We navigated on instruments to the start route point and occasionally I could see the ground through holes in the lower deck. Close to the start route point I found one hole a little larger than the others so I did a half roll, pulled down through it and leveled off at a thousand feet just skimming the bottoms of the clouds. I should explain that we were on a Visual Flight Rule clearance (VFR) which makes it is absolutely verboten to fly in clouds. I wasn't a flight lead so the check pilot had briefed me to fly like I was a single ship and he would do whatever was required to keep me in sight. It was impossible for him to follow my inverted pull down so I imagine he just gritted his teeth and pushed over and popped through the thin layer of clouds. That is what I would have done if I didn't have a check pilot watching me. We began maneuvering once again toward the start route point but the clouds just got worse and worse so I told the check pilot I was calling it off and began hunting for a hole to get back up between layers. For the next ten minutes I was flying up one valley and then another. When I saw a bright area I would maneuver towards it only to find a hole too small to zoom up through. Finally I found a hole that looked large enough, zoomed up through and gave the lead back to Tom, the check pilot. In a mocking distasteful voice he said, "gee, thanks a lot."*

No TAC check, No Leave

Two weeks later, on 16 July:

> "You probably already found out about the delightful time Jean, her mother and the girls had camping in Bavaria - while Jim was at Hahn still trying to get a TAC check complete." I had put in for leave a couple months earlier so we could take Jean's mother camping in Bavaria but the squadron added the condition that I had to be OR before I could take leave. I fully understood and accepted this. I was way overdue becoming OR and the problem was getting high level attention. But surely, I thought by July I'll be complete!

In that same letter I went on to describe the monumental, almost comical effort that did result in my successfully completing the TAC check.

> "The next attempt was the following Monday. I knew a successful check was impossible even before we took off but at times they expect you to try the impossible regardless. It amounted to this: I started engines on my airplane but Tom Roth (who was now my check pilot for life if need be) had trouble with his jet after engine start and had to shut down, deplane and try a second one. He told me over the radios to shut down engines for fifteen minutes to save gas while he went to his second airplane. After starting the second time we found almost a dozen F-4's in front of us waiting to take off. By the time we took off I had burned so much fuel that I knew I didn't have much chance of completing the low level. But we tried anyway. We flew high altitude to the Munich area, descended to our start route point and I was at Bingo fuel. So, we climbed back up to altitude and came back home. At the squadron, Lt. Col. Watson told us that for the next day we were priority number one and if need be could have every airplane on the flying schedule to get our check out of the way."

Another Failed Attempt

> "Tuesday morning I was up with the sun and at the squadron at 4:30 for another go at it. Where every previous day for over a week had been marginal weather for flying low levels, Tuesday dawned a bright and beautiful day and for the first time I really felt good about the chances of success. We began briefing at 0600 and were out to our airplanes by 0720. We started engines on time and I had the same problem Tom had the previous morning. We both shut down engines and Woody, my back seater, and I raced to another jet. At a pre-briefed time we began again. The engines started OK. Everything checked out OK. We taxied. At the end of the runway maintenance did their quick check and everything was still OK. Tower cleared us for takeoff, we taxied onto the active, checked engines and everything was a go. I gave the final run up signal to Tom, and when I looked at him for acknowledgment he was sadly shaking his head - no! His anti-skid system wouldn't engage. Tower cleared us back to the quick check

area and Tom called for specialists to come out and look at his airplane. While they were looking him over trying to fix it my master caution light came on. I checked my instruments and discovered the hydraulic pressure gage was quickly falling toward zero. We taxied back to the parking area both in absolute amazement - three broken F-4's and it wasn't even 0900 yet.

TAC Check - Yes

Tom and I regrouped after that. I re-briefed the mission for the afternoon, maintenance handpicked two jets that they guaranteed were 'supremo', we took off and flew the low level and I missed my target by only a thousand feet and seven seconds. I don't know who was happier, Lt. Col. Watson, Tom or myself. During the last and final push to get my check finished it had taken four attempts and two fourteen hour days - plus a few airplanes.

The Underrated WSO

In my descriptions of missions I don't give due credit to the Weapons System Officer, WSO, the 'guy in back', the GIB. The pilot is the person in command of the airplane and everything that happens to the airplane is his responsibility even if he is a second lieutenant and his GIB is a full colonel. The pilot is responsible for his aircraft. However, a top notch professional WSO makes the pilot's job immensely easier and can keep his pilot out of trouble or even save his life. A great WSO is always two steps ahead of the airplane anticipating what is coming up and preparing for it. He is also constantly monitoring what the pilot is doing, backing him up so mistakes don't happen.

"Lapse 61, Eiffel Control, climb immediately to eight thousand feet."

"Roger, Eiffel, Lapse 61 is climbing to nine thousand feet."

"Uh, Captain," says my GIB, "I think that was eight thousand feet."

I've flown with many WSOs who were passengers in the rear cockpit and their attitude was that if it didn't involve 'WSO duties' such as navigation and radar work, it was the pilot's job and they wouldn't question what he did. Some of them died a split second after their pilot because of this attitude. Then I've flown with other WSOs that considered themselves a part of their pilot and what a difference they could make in getting the job done. They were eager to get 'stick time' and some pilots even let them do occasional back seat landings although they never talked openly about it because it was against the rules. When I slight the WSO in relating my experiences it is not out of disrespect but because theirs is another story. My first two WSOs at Hahn were both very good and highly experienced. The first was Lee Boughner and the second was Woody Wilson.

An interesting aside concerning Lee, he was an excellent WSO but his fame was even greater as a snorer! In the BOQ at Zaragosa, we had two officers to a room.

When signing in you could choose a roommate and I quickly found out from others that Lee's roommate was invariably the last one to sign in. I went to Zaragosa many times while crewed with Lee but I never had to room with him.

A Night RBS Mission

"No ceiling, visibility 2.5 nautical miles and fog, alternates are Ramstein and Bitburg. Temperature is two degrees centigrade and critical temperature is zero degrees. At about 2300 hours tonight the surface temperature will be the same as critical temperature and fog will form dropping visibility to two tenths of a mile. Your briefing number is 11-175 and briefing time is 1830. Any questions?"

I quickly ask a few questions about our alternate airfields feeling that the chances are good we'll be using them tonight and then hang up the weather hot line so someone else can use it. Night flying looks shaky at best tonight for the squadron.

The previous three evenings had started out the same way but the temperature had dropped sooner than expected, the fog formed in a matter of minutes and flying was canceled. Last night three F-4s were at the end of the runway ready for takeoff but were canceled as the fog rolled in across the field.

Well, hoping for the best my back seater, Lee, and I begin flight planning. The flight calls for a night join-up with a KC-97 refueling tanker and then flying a night low level route terminating with us doing a simulated drop of a nuclear bomb at the Radar Bomb Scoring site (RBS). The simulated bomb drops are scored by the RBS site and scores are called in to the squadron. All of the aircrews also put a dollar in a hat with the money going to the crew with the best bomb score. The real prize, though, is bragging rights because the winning crew is expected to buy the beer after flying is finished.

Planning for the flight begins with filing a flight plan. While Lee does that I begin computing our aircraft gross weight, center of gravity, takeoff distance and speeds and landing distance and speeds. Then we both make up our maps, measuring distances and computing times that it will take between various points throughout the flight. After this is completed we find an empty briefing room and sit down to talk about all aspects of the flight so we will be as prepared as possible for any circumstances. As we finish I glance at my watch - 8 o'clock. Since we had planned for a 9 o'clock takeoff, backing up the standard thirty minutes gives an 8:30 start engine time and 20 more minutes to that means an 8:10 station time. That leaves 10 minutes for a last check with the weatherman, collect our personal equipment and get that last cup of hot coffee.

"Air on number two engine."

"Air on two," replies the crew chief and with the sound of rushing air from the starting unit, the rpm gauge begins rising. At ten percent rpm I move the throttle forward and check for fuel flow. I simultaneously push in the ignition button on the throttle. In a few seconds the temperature of number two begins rising indicating a good light. Within seconds it is accompanied by an ever increasing whine and the rpm steadies at 65 percent. All instruments check good so I start over with the number one engine. Then, run through the checks; radar altimeter, speed brakes, flaps, ailerons, rudder, stabilator, stability augmentators and a couple more magical systems that I'm convinced no-one understands, they're just magic. Meanwhile, Lee is checking out a myriad of black boxes in the back seat that to me are also magic. He checks the radar, bombing computers, navigation computers, a radar warning device and aligns the Inertial Navigation System (INS), probably the most sophisticated piece of equipment in the aircraft. The INS is a system made up of three extremely sensitive gyroscopes that can detect the slightest change in velocity along the three axis. Thus, if you tell it where it is at the beginning of the flight it can tell you quite precisely where you are at any given time during the flight. . The INS also tells us how much wind we have along with drift and ground speed, and by inserting the proper coordinates will give us the direction and distance to any point on the Earth's surface with an accuracy of four miles per hour of flying.

Our jet along with the others is parked in a half round reinforced concrete shelter which is lit up by several rows of fluorescent lights. Looking out into the blackness of the night I can see the evenly spaced blue lights outlining the taxiway as it curves around past several other aircraft shelters and then leads off to the runway. As I wait, another F-4, lit up like a Christmas tree with red and green position lights and bluish-green fluorescent formation strip lights, taxis quickly by on its way to the runway.

"Cleared primary and sink," I hear from Lee. The inertial navigation system is ready to go and so are we. I switch the navigation system to primary and activate another spring-loaded switch to synchronize the other INS dependent systems.

"Ground Control, Lapse 65, taxi one, IFR."

"Roger, 65, taxi runway 22, altimeter 2986."

The crew chief disconnects his mic cord, pulls the chocks from the wheels and guides us out of the tight confines of the shelter. We both leave our canopies open enjoying the crisp night air as we taxi to the runway.

A Night Takeoff

Approaching the runway I hear a roar as the previous plane begins his takeoff roll. What an awesome sight as the afterburners light. Thirty feet of flame suddenly spews from each tailpipe like giant torches, bright white, gradually blending to orange and then blue as it tapers to a fine point. Evenly spaced throughout the flame are the more brightly colored 'shock diamonds', one for each of the four stages of the afterburner. In moments the noise is gone and all that is visible is a small white light climbing into the night sky, and then that disappears also as the pilot comes out of afterburner at 300 knots.

We finish our before takeoff checks and Tower clears us for takeoff. The engines are run up to 85 percent with feet clamped firmly on the brakes. The engine instruments still check OK. Lee's breathing rate noticeably increases over the intercom and I know mine is also. The takeoff is the most exciting as well as most dangerous part of the flight. We are fifteen thousand pounds heavier than we will be when we land and if something serious happens there is little or no margin for error. Engine fire, loss of an engine, blown tire, hard-over rudder, split flaps. These are some of the emergencies that could happen but seldom do. When they do, we sometimes get to read about them in the safety magazines.

Nighttime Fire During Takeoff

On one such night take-off, Dan Dick had the scare of his life. As the main gear struts extended his two external wing tanks began to pressurize just as they are supposed to do. However, unknown to him, the gas cap on one of the tanks fell off and the sudden pressure caused most of the gas to come spewing out. As the gas entered his afterburner plume it all caught on fire. As Dan reported later, everything suddenly lit up and in his rear view mirrors all he could see was fire. From the control tower his jet was trailing a 200 to 300 foot long plume of fire. Dan didn't have any other indications of an aircraft fire and guessed at what had happened and within seconds all of the gas had emptied out and the spectacular light show ended.

That happened to me once in RTU but it was during the daytime and the gas never torched off. I ended up with a very heavy wing and not enough gas to do the mission so I flew instrument approaches until I was light enough to land.

I turn the landing light off for the takeoff. For a second or two everything is dark but as my eyes adjust two rows of parallel blue lights appear as they stretch off into the distance for a mile and a half. For takeoff I focus on the far end of the runway where they seem to converge and steer the plane for that point until airborne.

The throttle levers move full forward and brakes are released. In a second or two the afterburners light and 35,000 pounds of thrust begin moving our 51,000 pound jet down the runway, ever so slowly at first but within 10 seconds we are barreling along at 140 miles per hour. Up to that point we are both closely watching the engine instruments but now we are going too fast to be able to stop on the remaining runway. If anything should happen now we either have to take off or eject. As I move the control stick back the nose begins to get light and at 190 mph it rises off the ground. A second later we are traveling 205 mph and leap into the air. Gear and flaps are quickly retracted and at 300 nautical miles per hour or knots, I come out of afterburner, steady the speed at 350 and establish an easy 10 degree climb. We both begin breathing normally again and finally have enough time to get off the instruments and begin looking outside a little.

The steady low throb of the engines is a reassuring sound interrupted occasionally by the chatter of the radios as air traffic controllers sort out their night traffic and closely follow its progress. Outside the plane the night is quiet and tranquil. The black sky is sparkling with bright stars much brighter than I've ever seen from the ground. Off to the left, probably twenty miles away and fifteen thousand feet high are the lights of an airliner very likely destined for Frankfurt. To the east a half moon is already well above the horizon and by its light we can look down and see white patches of the evening's first fog forming in low spots on the ground. The white streetlights of hundreds of farm towns quietly slide by beneath us, as do the headlights of cars and trucks as they move at seemingly a snail's pace towards their destinations.

Night Air Refueling

Suddenly our quiet thoughts are interrupted by hearing our call sign on the radio.

"Lapse 65, this is Hardtire control. Your tanker bearing 095 degrees, 45 nautical miles." Hardtire is a military radar site whose job includes doing tanker rejoins as well as air intercepts and ground close air support.

Looking in that direction I see the airliner - but maybe it isn't an airliner. Distances are very deceiving at night and what looks to be twenty miles could be ten or even sixty. Lee has already locked on with his radar and confirms it is the tanker at forty-five miles.

"Roger, Hardtire, we have contact with the tanker and a visual and are turning left for a rendezvous and climbing to twenty thousand feet. Say tanker's altitude and heading."

Five minutes pass and we are one mile behind the tanker waiting for the previous plane to finish refueling. He calls off and drops away to continue his mission.

"Lapse 65, this is Burma 17, you are cleared in to the pre-contact position."

I acknowledge and we close up to within one hundred feet and stabilize our position there. Besides the position lights and flashing beacon light I can now make out the dark form of the large four-engine plane. It is a KC-97, an outdated tanker that was built from the airframe of a B-50. The only place I know of where they are still used is in Europe and soon, the last of them will have a final resting-place at Davis-Monthan's 'bone yard.'

"Lapse 65, you are cleared to the contact position."

After opening the refueling door that is on the back of the plane behind Lee's canopy we slowly start closing up on the tanker. When we have only a few feet to go I can finally see the refueling boom, a thirty-foot pipe that has limited movement sideways, up and down as well as in and out. We slow our speed so it just matches the tankers and then carefully inch forward foot by foot until the boom nozzle is just above my canopy. We slide forward a little more and it is now above Lee's canopy.

"65, stabilize."

The boomer lies on his belly in the tail of the tanker looking at us through an observation window. He has all the controls for moving the boom and turning the gas flow on or off. He is in control now and will command whatever is necessary. Move forward, back, up, down, disconnect, emergency breakaway. Usually he doesn't have to say much.

With deft hands he darts the boom nozzle out the remaining two feet and into our open refueling receptacle. "65, contact and you're taking on fuel."

Now, all I have to do is maintain this position for about three minutes however it always seems more like thirty. As fuel is taken on the aircraft weight greatly increases, six and a half pounds for each gallon and power is constantly increased bit by bit to maintain speed. The nose of the aircraft slowly rises bit by bit to maintain altitude and the controls gradually get a sloppy feeling as the airplane gets closer to a stalled condition. Not infrequently, 100 percent military power is insufficient and the pilot must quickly pull one throttle back and push the other into minimum afterburner. With skill this can be done with not much more than a bobble and refueling continues. I only had to do it one time and was pleased with myself at how smoothly it worked.

"Lapse 65, you have 8,000 pounds of fuel, disconnect - now."

I depress my disconnect switch and Lee confirms we are free of the boom so we slowly drop back from the tanker. In three minutes we've taken on eight thousand pounds or eleven hundred and fifty gallons of fuel. We are ready to press on with our planned misson.

The time is 9:25 and our start route time is 9:40, 15 minutes away. Checking his map, Lee determines we are 90 miles from the start route point. Six miles a minute will work out fine. That figures out to 420 knots ground speed. I contact the supervisor of flying (SOF) to see how the fog is doing. So far, everything is still fine but he tells us things will probably begin getting worse in an hour. We just might make it in time.

After reestablishing contact with air traffic control I tell him our intentions and we begin a quick descent from 20,000 feet to 5,000 feet maintaining 420 knots ground speed on a heading that will take us to the start route point.

The Night RBS Low Level

Approaching the start route point we offset ourselves about six miles to allow for a 180-degree turn. Then we smoothly roll into a 60-degree bank turn to fly over the start route point on the proper heading.

"Eiffel Control, Lapse 65 is two minutes from bravo 07 start route point. Am I cleared into the night low level route?"

Eiffel Control clears us in and as I begin to roll out of the turn I can see a distinctive shaped bend in the Mozel river. We are right over the point. Lee calls to hack our clocks and we simultaneously start our clocks. A quick check of the instruments shows we are at 3,800 feet and 410 knots, a little slow. My job now is mainly flying precisely, 3,800 feet, 420 knots and on a heading of 212 degrees. We are on an instrument flight plan and this is instrument flying. If we encounter clouds – no problem.

Now it is up to Lee to do the job he has trained for and he is one of the best. He switches to ground mapping mode on his radar and because it is night the radar is the only means of following the low-level route precisely. Relying on hundreds of hours of training Lee looks at the map of the route and visualizes how it should look on radar. An example of what his thoughts might be are probably something like this: '20 miles ahead, our route passes one mile left of a river bend. The river should appear black. And that high ridgeline should show to the left of the point. Ya, there it is. Now, at fifteen miles are three towns that form a triangle. Our route should take us over the town on the right. If I turn down the intensity just a little, those towns should pop out from the surrounding terrain. Sure enough, there they are...'

"Steer right three degrees and we'll be on course."

So, I turn right three degrees. A three-degree correction doesn't seem like much but this leg of the route is 60 miles long and three degrees of heading error would put us three miles off course.

While Lee is working with his radar he also cross checks his airspeed and, more importantly, altimeter. 3800 feet that we are flying at on this leg guarantees us 1500 feet above the highest obstacle within three miles of our course. That isn't much of a safety margin when flying at night and it isn't all that uncommon for altimeters to stick or begin showing erroneous indications, thus, we rely on two altimeters rather than one. To sum it all up, for the next fifteen minutes or so Lee is going to be as busy as a one armed paperhanger.

We are approaching the last turn point called the IP, initial point, prior to the RBS target and now the pace quickens and we begin the most critical portion of the route. Once again my job is easy. Delivery mode switch to offset bomb. Navigation function switch to navigation computer. Dial in the radio frequency for the radar bomb scoring site.

"Courtroom, Courtroom, Lapse 65 is approaching the IP."

Courtroom is a specialized ground radar site. Using precise pencil width radar they can track us in from the IP to the target. Their computer knows our altitude, heading, speed and direction and although we simulate dropping a bomb it predicts where a real bomb would have hit in relation to the target.

Over the turn point I turn to the final run-in heading. We are about three minutes from the target. Lee is working feverishly now with the radar. The target is one that won't show on radar, however, during the flight-planning phase Lee found a point that would show on radar. He then measured how many feet east or west and the same for north or south from the target this point was. He now has those numbers inserted in the bombing computer and is looking for that point or offset on the radar. When he sees his offset he moves a vertical and horizontal line, the along track and cross track cursors, on his radar so that they cross over the offset. Then, he pushes an insert button and, presto, magic. The crossed lines move the predetermined distance and settle on the non-showing target. Following Lee's directions I turn the aircraft until we are perfectly lined up with the target.

Using another computer, Lee tells it at what distance from the target to simulate releasing a bomb. This is determined from our altitude and ground speed. Once again, magic. The computer says, 'OK, Lee, go ahead and drop that bomb....NOW,' and Lee transmits, "bombs away." In addition, the computer transmits a tone to precisely show when the simulated bomb was released.

In a couple minutes as we are now heading back in the direction of Hahn Courtroom tells us we had a 1,200 foot miss which is a very good score. We all pray we'll never have to use this system in earnest because the bomb to be released would be a thermonuclear hydrogen bomb and there wouldn't be any winners for the best bomb.

Mission complete. Let's head back for home. We contact Ramstein Control for clearance back to Hahn AB.

"Lapse 65, you are cleared to Ramstein, out the 290 degree radial for 15 nautical miles, then direct to Bitburg TACAN at 7,000 feet."

With the work over we both relax a little and enjoy watching the lights of villages speed by beneath us. Soon, we are told to contact Eiffel Control and then our own Ground Control Approach (GCA). GCA has very precise radar with the capability of guiding an aircraft to landing without the pilot ever having to look outside. However, for safety reasons, we require at least a 300-foot ceiling and one mile visibility before attempting to land.

GCA tells me to descend to 1500 feet and directs me to a point 10 miles from the end of the runway. I slow the aircraft to 250 knots and lower gear and flaps. When they are down the aircraft quickly begins slowing down. We have 6,000 pounds of fuel left, add two knots per thousand pounds, and that gives 12 knots. Now add that to a basic speed of 137 knots and that gives a Final Approach speed of 149 knots (about 175 miles per hour).

As the airspeed indicator approaches 149 I smoothly add power to maintain 149 knots. 87 percent on each rpm gauge will get me in the ballpark. Then, fine adjustments from there will give a precise power setting to maintain airspeed.

Now the GCA final controller takes over.

"Lapse 65, this is your final controller. Check wheels down, turn 225 degrees. Do not acknowledge further transmissions."

In this manner we are guided towards the runway and at four miles we intercept the glide path. *"Lapse 65, begin descent."*

Relying on experience I reduce power by two percent on each engine, lower the nose two degrees by using the attitude indicator and check the vertical velocity indicator. It should read about 750 feet per minute rate of descent.

"Lapse 65, on course, on glide path, on course, on glide path, going left of course, turn 229 degrees. Coming back to course, on course, turn 227 degrees, now going above glide path. Above glide path, adjust descent rate, coming back to glide path, on glide path, on course. At decision height, over approach lights, take over visually."

I acknowledge taking over visually and switch to tower frequency. The touchdown point is about 2,000 feet ahead. I visualize where I want to land and keep flying to that point. Two seconds pass and I'm only 50 feet above the runway. The blue runway lights begin rising up to meet me and I shift my focus to the far end of the runway so I can more accurately judge my height above the runway surface. At the last moment the control stick comes smoothly all the way back and the plane has only enough speed to level out as the wheels gently touch the runway. I pull the throttles back *and release the drag chute by pulling back on a lever that is next to the throttles on the left side of the cockpit. As it blossoms the sudden deceleration gently pushes me forward against my shoulder harness. Now, I get on the brakes and start slowing down even more. The thousand foot remaining markers initially zip by quickly. Seven, six, five, four and then more slowly as the speed reduces; three, then two and by 1,000 feet remaining we are at taxi speed.*

After pulling off the runway, "Ground Control, Lapse 65 is clear of the active and taxiing back." We drop the drag chute, complete the after landing checks and follow the blue taxiway lights that lead back to our shelter.

We both raise our canopies. The cold night air feels chilly but good. I glance off to the left and see another F4 rolling out on the runway, his drag chute billowing behind and I also see the landing lights of another on final approach as he slowly descends toward the runway. Above, the stars are shining brightly and the moon is continuing its course through the sky. Looking off to the right the green and white rotating beacon on the tower is illuminating the haze that is forming, the first sign of impending fog. It is 10:30 and I think to myself the weatherman will be right on the money tonight. But, everyone should be safely down soon.

It has been a good night. A cold beer is going to really taste good and who knows, our 1,200 foot score might just win the pot of dollar bets we all made earlier in the evening. What a fantastic feeling of accomplishment I have as I think back through all of the events we successfully accomplished. There can't be another feeling like it in the world. There can't be.

Hahn's Two Missions

There were two squadrons at Hahn when we got there, the 10th and the 496th. The primary mission of the 10th was nuclear strike with a secondary mission of conventional bombing and a tertiary mission of air defense. The 496th was primary for air defense with a secondary role of conventional bombing. About half way through our four year tour at Hahn, a third squadron was formed, the 313th, and its role was the same as the 10th and by my fourth year, the 496th lost its air defense role also in favor of nuclear strike.

Air to Air versus the Air to Mudders

When we got to Hahn, my squadron was sort of looked down upon by the 496th, because we had the inglorious job of attacking the ground as compared to their almost mythical role as fighter pilots pitting their flying skills against another pilot's to see who would win the aerial engagement. We were the ignoble air to mudders. They were the inheritors of the fame and glory of Eddie Rickenbacker and the Red Baron, Baron Manfred Von Richthofen.

Exercises

During exercises the dissimilarity and inequality continued. They sat five minute alert that was called 'Zulu' Alert. They had five minutes to be airborne even from a sound sleep. They would have frequent practice scrambles from which they would fly intercept missions. Ours was called 'Victor Alert' and we had 15 minutes to be airborne. We were never practice scrambled because of the danger involved - our planes had real live nuclear bombs strapped beneath them. If we had been scrambled it would have been the real thing.

At the beginning of an exercise, the first reaction was scrambling Zulu Alert. The second was sounding our klaxon causing us to dash to our planes, get strapped in and then calling the command post to receive an exercise (or real) launch message. We would verify it as being authentic by using our top secret classified authenticators and it was over. That was all. Finished, finito. The 496th was beating back the fictitious enemy at 40 thousand feet and we were back in the lounge beating back boredom.

During an exercise the 496th flew an amazing number of sorties. They flew combat air patrol missions, intercept missions and even air combat tactics missions against aircraft from other bases. They were given daily taskings to protect the base against enemy aircraft.

We prepared for imaginary missions. We were given taskings to fly air-to-ground missions. Usually this meant doing the elaborate mission planning; getting in-depth intelligence briefings on the target area, constructing low level maps to use in flying to the target area and determining what types of bombs to use for the particular target and briefing the mission to the flight members. After the brief the flight would go out to their airplanes and accept the bomb laden aircraft from maintenance and preflight it to make sure everything was correct. Then, that part of the exercise was terminated and we were given new taskings and we would go through the same steps all over again. Wow! What fun!

F-4 Refueling

'Going Nuc' and Certifying

Towards the end of the exercise scenario as the war heated up we would stop the conventional bombing planning and transition to a nuclear scenario. Maintenance had to download all of the conventional bombs and upload real nuclear weapons. Our individual aircrews were assigned actual targets in one of the Warsaw Pact countries - we didn't have enough gas to be able to fly to a target in Russia - and we studied the already constructed packages for our particular targets. After exhaustive target planning and study with our WSO's, three or four aircrews were chosen to 'certify' their targets. The certification crews were like the condemned and the rest of us breathed a huge sigh of relief. The selected crews were tasked to brief a board of 20 or 30 high ranking officers that was headed by the wing commander. A certification briefing lasted from 45 minutes to an hour and most of us dreaded the task. To us the best you could do was break even!

The Elephant Walk

Frequently, the exercise terminated in what was called an elephant walk. An exercise time-out was called while maintenance downloaded the nuclear bombs. When the bombs were all safely back in the nuclear bomb dump (actually, underground bunkers), the exercise was back on just like nothing had happened. We were sequestered in our squadron building during this period waiting for word that nuclear war had been declared by the President. Our first indication of this event was the sounding of a very loud klaxon in our squadron building. When that happened we all piled into trucks and crew vans and sped out to our planes that we had previously 'cocked' to start engines. We each listened to the war message on the command post freq and then authenticated and taxied to the runway. With tower clearance we then took the runway and lit the afterburner as if to take off. At afterburner light the throttle was pulled back to idle and the aircraft was simulated to be airborne on its nuclear strike mission. As we all taxied back to our aircraft shelters one after another we resembled a long row of elephants in a parade - hence the term elephant walk.

The Taxiing Tenth or the Gay Blades

Never to miss an opportunity the 496th came up with another nickname for us, The Taxiing Tenth. Our official nickname, though, was The Fighting Tenth. Our shoulder patch was of a beautiful design. It consisted of a blue and white shield with a target on it that had a sword stuck in the bull's eye. It also had two sets of eighth notes in the background. Based on this patch the 496th coined another nickname for us, The Gay Blades. The patch of the 496th was of a grotesque hooded falcon on a gloved hand holding lightning bolts. Our name for them was The Electric Chickens. The ribbing we gave each other was 95 percent in fun but we all placed a high

10th TFS 'Singing Sword'

value on squadron loyalty. The feeling between squadrons was similar to the feeling between fraternities at college.

We sometimes did fly during an exercise. Occasionally we had real close air support where we supported an army exercise. For the number one exercise every year, the much dreaded Operational Readiness Inspection, ORI, everyone in the squadron had to fly one sortie to the gunnery range and three fourths of all bombs had to be qualifying. To not do so meant failing the ORI and having to repeat the bombing aspect of it.

A Surprise Launch

During one exercise the inspectors surprised all of us by having us really fly after the elephant walk. After taxiing down the runway we were told to hold on the parallel taxiway and when everyone had 'walked' down the runway, we were issued flight clearances and told to fly. I think this was in answer to speculation that perhaps we were trying to cover up airplanes that were really unfit for flight. We launched every plane. Our squadron commander, Lt. Col. Watson, wouldn't stand for 'trying to fake it.' On that launch, though, I was wearing a heavy winter flight parka that had a genuine wolf's hair collar. I quickly discovered I couldn't look to either side because all I could see when turning my head was brown wolf's hair. The parkas weren't designed for fighter type aircraft and if I had known I was going to fly I would have worn my heavy weight flight jacket.

Zulu Alert

As I've already alluded to, the differences in the squadrons extended to their alert commitments. The 496th sat Zulu Alert. Their shift was for one 24-hour period and if scrambled had to be airborne in only five minutes. Their alert facility was a large aircraft shelter that held two aircraft and their crew quarters were in the upper part of the shelter. They had a lounge area, a room where they could watch movies and sleeping quarters. In the center of the facility was a fireman's pole. When the klaxon sounded, the crewmembers had to jump into their flight suits and flying boots, slide down the pole and sprint the few feet to their jets.

496th TFS 'Fightin' Falcons'

Their crew chiefs also lived in the facility but they worked normal eight-hour shifts. Each aircraft's crew chief was always waiting at the plane with starting unit already running when the crew arrived. It took about two minutes to get both engines started and they were taxiing. The alert taxiway had a 45 degree angle to the runway and when the tower air traffic controllers saw the airplanes emerge from the shelter they immediately issued a takeoff clearance and the F-4s wouldn't even slow up taking the active. They did a rolling takeoff and usually were airborne with a few seconds to spare.

Beware the 'Queertrons'

One time, as lead pulled onto the runway, he positioned a switch to its proper position and a wiring short in the F-4 caused two aim-9 missiles to shoot off from under his wings. You can't imagine the surprise of the pilot to see the missiles skipping down the runway leaving vivid white smoke trails in their wake. Both missiles slid under the BAK 9 arresting cable that sits a couple thousand feet down the runway and is used for an F-4 to catch with its hook during a landing emergency. The rear fins caught in the cable and the missile motors continued to burn their propellant for a few more seconds until they were spent. Of course both alert birds aborted their takeoff and when the lead pilot called the command post to report the incident the command post controller made a step into infamy. He told the pilot to sit in his cockpit and to keep his hands raised and in view of the ground. The obvious intent was the controller believing the pilot had botched things up with his switches now wanted to prevent the pilot from covering up the evidence. However, there is no way to purposely fire a missile from the ground and a maintenance investigation revealed the wiring flaw that caused the mishap to happen. As aircrews we got loads of laughs at the command post controller's expense.

Victor Alert – Babysitting a Nuc

Victor Alert was what the 'taxiing tenth' pulled. The most obvious differences were that we had three crews on alert instead of two, we stayed on alert for two days during the week or three for the weekend rather than for 24 hours, and we had 15 minutes to get airborne instead of five. I guess another difference was the 496th was virtually assured of coming back. If we were launched we were quite sure we wouldn't be coming back.

Our Cold War

All nuclear strike squadrons had what were called three primary alert lines, targets that were especially important to the enemy. The targets were usually airfields in East Germany or Czechoslovakia and we were the 3rd delivery system scheduled to strike them, the first two being missiles and long range flying B-52s. To get to our respective targets required flying a specified low level most of the way and our routes were supposedly distance and time de-conflicted from all of the other hundreds of nuclear explosions that were in the big master plan. Deconfliction meant missing a nuclear explosion by 10 miles or two minutes. If you or anyone else was off by a few miles or a minute de-confliction went out the window. Our flight plan allowed for us to have enough gas to make it back to Hahn unless we had to alter our route or had to use afterburner to make up time. Our rules stated we would continue on with our mission as long as we had enough gas not to get back to Hahn but to perform an escape maneuver from our dropped nuclear bomb. When the engines flamed out we would eject and then, as you can imagine, we would really be on our own. As I said earlier, none of us really expected to come back. If nuclear war had ever occurred there probably wouldn't have been much to come back to. Fortunately, the unthinkable never happened. We were bargaining chips in a very big game. This was our war, 'the cold war.'

If war had occurred, the plan for our dependents was for them to drive across France to the coast where hopefully transportation might be found to get across the ocean back to the US. This wasn't talked about very much and we didn't think about it very much either because it all was so unlikely to happen. Yes, we were on 15 minute alert with thermonuclear bombs and there was a lot of hot rhetoric between us and the Soviet Union but both sides also were aware of the acronym, MAD (Mutually Assured Destruction).

An interesting side note is that we had a fail- safe system called the DCU-94 panel in our cockpits that would allow arming of our bombs ONLY if a special code was inserted. That code was directly controlled by the President, no one else. Only the President could authorize the waging of nuclear war and that is why the President always had his 'red telephone' near him wherever he went. The red telephone gave him almost instant contact with the Soviet leaders as well as our military leaders for disseminating the code. The DCU-94 panel worked so well that we gave the entire system to the Soviets so they could also use it with their nuclear delivery vehicles. It was in everyone's best interest that the possibility of accidentally releasing a nuclear weapon be minimized as much as possible.

We had one WSO, Karl Horn, who was a second generation American. He grew up speaking both German and English in his home. Karl had relatives in neutral Austria and he jokingly told people that when he came back after dropping his bomb, if Hahn was no longer there, he and his pilot were continuing on to Austria where they would eject over his relatives' property. Karl also had a very engaging outgoing personality and was used on numerous occasions by the wing commander when German VIPs were being entertained. Karl was a very willing, charming and impressive escort for them.

The Dreaded Certification Board

To become operationally ready in the 10th, we had to certify before the certification board. The board was headed by the wing commander with the director of operations present along with the vice-wing commander, squadron commander, sometimes the base commander and the heads of all of the wing staff agencies. In all, the board consisted of 20 to 30 officers who listened very intently to what you had to say. They all had a hand in determining if you really knew enough to have the responsibility of babysitting a nuclear weapon.

The certification was done as a flight crew; a pilot and his crewed WSO but the vast majority of the cert was the pilot's responsibility. His part of the briefing lasted for over 30 minutes at which time the WSO would brief the WSO duties, how he would use the radar from the IP to target, weapons settings and things like that. The last part of the cert was what we called 'stump the dummy.' In pilot training this was done by a lieutenant or captain evaluator. This was the wing commander. He usually asked two or three questions and then others on the board might each ask a question. If the cert was done in a strong manner, the question session was a mere formality but if the performance hinted of weakness, the crew was in for a tough time of it. I never heard of anyone failing a cert but more than once a crew was told to go back and study some more - really, a polite way of saying 'you didn't hack it, so next time do it right and stop wasting our time.'

During one of my certs after I'd gained the confidence that comes from experience I was fielding questions. By now I thought I had heard all of the standard questions because the squadron maintained a question bank to prepare new aircrews. The chief of stan eval, though, came up with a new one and it wasn't a particularly good question. The question he asked was if you saw a MiG on your tail how would you tell if it was a MiG 21J? My answer that got a few smiles from those on the panel was, 'if it was close enough to tell what model MiG 21 it was I'm definitely having a bad day and it wouldn't make any difference what model it was.'

For my first certification, I probably spent a hundred hours studying Secret and Top Secret war plans that the Soviets would have given a fortune to know. I had to be an expert on them. Then, I studied about the nuclear bombs we had, weapons release tactics, escape and evasion procedures, and probably most important of all, the 'line' (target) that I was assigned to certify on. The package for each line was a thick red plastic folder that contained a tremendous amount of information that had to be learned but most important of all was the five by eight inch plastic covered target book that we would each have in our respective cockpits. This book contained a flip type map of the low-level route to the IP and finally to the target. For the certification I was expected to practically know this route by heart.

For my first certification I was more nervous than I can ever remember being in my life but I had prepared so thoroughly for it that the actual cert was almost anticlimactic, especially, when I realized that I was the expert in the room. I knew more than any of the colonels did about what I was briefing. After that I found certs to be much less stressful. Oh, I did sweat enough to get back into the books to regain my polish but the feeling of dread was gone. Certification was an annual requirement and when Hahn had three squadrons on Victor Alert and three times as many aircrews certifying every year it must have been quite a drain on the wing commander's time.

After returning to the States, at Homestead AFB, someone came up with the idea to require all OR (Operationally Ready) aircrews to do conventional bomb mission certifications for the European Theater. Many of the IPs were really sweating it but with my recent knowledge gained from four years in Germany that certification was an absolute breeze, especially since I was probably the most knowledgeable pilot on the NATO war plans at Homestead. I don't think they even had a copy of the plans at Homestead. This program lasted for only a few months before it was recognized to be a needless waste of time.

Victor Alert - Forced Relaxation

Victor Alert itself was quite pleasant. I didn't enjoy a weekend tour, though. We were offered a compensation day off following a weekend alert but no one ever took it because they had too much work to do at the squadron. Thus, you lost your weekend completely if you were scheduled for alert. On days that we went on victor, we showed up at the squadron with a bag packed. The fenced in and highly secure victor alert area was just a block down the road from our squadron building. Change over time was five pm but we usually showed up at the alert facility at 4:30 so we could do some target study, get a target area weather brief and take a short test.

At 5 o'clock the three off going crews met with the three ongoing crews and we'd climb into the crew van and go out to our respective aircraft shelters for the formal change over. The shelter was a reinforced concrete inverted U shape structure with huge massive steel doors. The back of the shelter had an opening in the roof and a deflector so the exhaust of a running F-4 would be deflected out and up. A red cord was stretched across the front of the shelter and that delineated the 'no-lone' zone. Each alert shelter was guarded 24 hours a day by armed sentries. To enter the shelter you had to show a security badge as well as be on an authorized access list.

The term no lone meant that one person could never be in the shelter by himself except perhaps in an emergency such as a fire. To violate this rule meant being spread eagled on the concrete by the sentry. The no-lone zone concept was taken as dead serious. In addition to that we had two-man control over the top-secret authenticators that were called 'cookies' because they resembled Chinese fortune cookies. The cookie had a brittle plastic case that had to be broken to retrieve the authenticator paper that was inside.

Since the cookies were stored in the aircraft one crewmember could never be in the cockpit alone without violating the two-man control rule. If an alert aircraft had to be worked on by maintenance, the aircrew removed the cookies and until they were placed back into the cockpit, the two crewmembers had to always be together. They were referred to as being married. We groaned when maintenance had to work on our alert birds.

The alert facility was very comfortable. It had a movie room and we were on the regular circuit for 8-mm versions of all of the current running movies. Thus, we had the luxury of running an exciting scene over and over again if we wanted to. During one Western movie that had a civil war era setting, I thought I noticed something unusual as the camera was panning through a scene and I called out to stop the movie and back it up. When we replayed it, sure enough, in the distance you could see several cars parked under a tree with people watching the scene that was being filmed. You sure couldn't do that in a movie theater! We also had a lounge area where you could watch TV or study and everyone had his own private bedroom.

Perhaps the nicest feature of all was that we had a key to the cafeteria and if we got hungry at night we could rummage around for left over desserts. I could always find cake and ice cream and sometimes pie or pudding. The chefs never complained about this and in return we always left the kitchen just as clean as we found it.

One benefit about Victor Alert that made it much more palatable was that we could 'expand', meaning that as long as we had a brick, a hand held radio, we could take an alert vehicle and go to places such as the BX or the officers' club or even the movie theater. Because of the nature of our job we had priority and could go to the head of lines. We also had special seating at the theater that was right next to the side exit door where our alert truck was parked. If we had a recall while expanded, we flipped on the flashing yellow light and got back to the alert facility as fast as was reasonable. The married guys especially valued being able to expand because they could spend time with their families. Dinner at the O' Club and the movie theater were frequent family functions while on victor.

We were notified of an alert exercise by the klaxon, a very loud raucous horn that was activated by the command post. Whenever we heard the klaxon we ran for the alert vehicles and sped to our respective aircraft shelters. The sentry was already notified of the alert and was waiting for us and could use visual recognition to let us into the shelter where we very quickly climbed the ladder to get into the cockpit. While getting strapped in a quick check of the lights above the entrance to the shelter would tell us what the status was. Flashing green meant start engines, steady green was cockpit alert and amber meant standby. A red light meant to forget it, the alert was canceled or a mistake. However, not until we made radio contact with the command post did we know for sure that it was only an exercise.

> "Raymond 15 (command post's call sign), this is Lima Yankee 01."
>
> "Roger Lima Yankee 01, standby for an exercise message." At that point we finally knew that it was indeed another exercise. Then, when all 3 planes were up on radios, the command post continued to read an exercise message to us. We copied it down to include the self-authentication and if it was correct, we shut down and went back to the alert facility.

Forward Air Controller Experiences

For my last two years at Hahn I was a Forward Air Controller (FAC) augmentee. Each of the three squadrons gave up one pilot to be a FAC augmentee. Usually the additional duty was for one year. I guess I did such a good job, the director of operations kept me on an additional year as chief FAC. I was less than thrilled but cheerfully accepted the unasked for honor. When defeat is inevitable, sit down and enjoy it!

A FAC's job is to work closely with the Army providing advice on use of air power to support their ground operations. Many FACs do the job from the air flying a slow moving airplane but other FACs are embedded with their Army unit and some are even jump qualified when assigned to an airborne unit. For these FACs the job was a full time one. In USAFE (mainly Germany) we had part time FACs, called FAC augmentees and we served on an as needed basis.

We were attached to an Army battalion and had a ROMAD to work with. ROMAD stood for 'Radio Operator, Maintenance and Driver.' We worked out of a specially equipped jeep called a MK-107. It was a top heavy vehicle because it was filled with radios with two or three long antennas sticking up. One antenna was so long it had to be dismantled when on commercial roads because it would contact power lines! We pulled a small trailer for our personal gear and a tent.

As the name suggests, the ROMAD was a specialist in driving and radio communications including minor field repair when something went wrong. He was permanently with the FAC augmentee's battalion which was a tremendous benefit for his FAC in getting the job done.

Those selected for FAC duty attended a three week long USAFE Air Ground Operations School, AGOS, at Sembach Air Base. At this very intensive school I learned everything I needed to know to be a forward air controller. I also got much practical experience in the field controlling fighters in simulated Close Air Support (CAS). Then I traveled to Illisheim Army Post near Nuremburg in northern Bavaria to my assigned army battalion to meet the Battalion commander and get an orientation briefing and tour. Then it was on to my brigade headquarters in Nuremburg to meet my respective Air Liaison Officer, ALO. You might think of an ALO as a FAC with a master's degree. After another orientation I went back home to wait for tasking. Usually, that was whenever my battalion deployed to the field for an exercise, called an ARTEP. Taskings occurred three or four times a year.

My battalion was an infantry battalion and was called 'the first of six,' the first Battalion in the 6th Brigade. The people I met were very friendly and I immediately liked them all. From these officers and NCOs I developed the highest respect for what the army was and treasured my experiences with them as a FAC.

I didn't volunteer to be a FAC. I went from being MR or Mission Ready and flying a minimum of 60 sorties per half year to MS, Mission Support, and 48 sorties per half. Following the Army around in the field didn't appeal to me at all. With the Army it was either mud or dust and being a FAC involved a lot of waiting for things to happen. However, after I became a FAC and got to know my Army counterparts I really appreciated the opportunity and the experience. For one thing I had always looked down at the army somewhat as country cousins, the backward branch of the Armed Services. However, that feeling turned to a deep respect after I got to watch them in action.

The US Army – The Best

The Army can be divided into two categories, combat arms and support. I was dealing solely with the combat arms people. They were the combatants, the equivalent of operations in the Air Force. And, they were the most disciplined group of people I've ever dealt with. In the Air Force there isn't a great deal of rank distinction between junior officers. Not so in the Army. Everyone had either higher or lower rank and you'd better not forget it. At times I felt like they might have taken it to extremes such as you never saw an officer drive himself. If he had a jeep assigned to him he also had a private assigned to drive that vehicle and that is all he did; drive and wait. To us in the Air Force it seemed a waste of manpower, not to mention it was fun to drive a jeep!

The Army had its reasons for everything it did and a lot of it boiled down to the fact that they had to work with a lower common denominator in enlisted people, hence, rules had to be simple and interpreting the rules could result in chaos. This was brought home when I saw some army tech manuals written in comic book form.

I was also particularly impressed with the Army sense of unit pride and morale, their map reading abilities and their stamina. Once a field exercise got underway there was no time out to eat or sleep. Everyone took naps if and when they could; otherwise, you didn't get any sleep for the last two or three days of the exercise. Hot meals were a seldom seen luxury. I was also awed by their ability to control their units at all levels from divisions and brigades down to platoons. They could reorganize units by borrowing a couple tank platoons from this battalion and an infantry company from that one and assign them to so and so battalion that was spearheading a push through the enemy's flank. Their situational awareness was astounding as each night they would receive the next day's tasking and in turn task lower units to support that tasking.

While this planning was going on into the wee hours of the morning, my ROMAD and I would find a nearby spot that was surrounded by trees, thus tank proof, pitch our tent and zonk out. I always let the army know where I was, though, in case they needed advice on air support. After one big exercise I received a letter of commendation by way of the Army brigade commander to my wing commander for my faithful 24 hour a day support of my assigned battalion. I was surprised at this because I had only done my job but later, from other FAC's and prior FAC's, I discovered they never lived with the Army. At dark or earlier, they would find out where their units were going to be the next morning and then find a local German gasthaus to settle into for the night.

A Cobra Bite Can Be Deadly

An ARTEP exercise is a field exercise where you have the 'good' blue forces fighting the 'bad' red forces to right some international wrong that was committed. Saddam Hussein's steamrolling over Kuwait could have been a typical scenario but on a much smaller scale. The ARTEPs I participated in all occurred in the vast Hohenfels Army Range complex, an area the size of a county. After two or three exercises my ROMAD and I became quite familiar with the range and could respond with relative ease to support our battalion for calling in close air support. During one ARTEP we even slipped behind enemy lines to collect intel on the enemy location. We were caught but since our modified jeep had USAF markings on it I did some fast talking to avoid being incarcerated. We were 'neutral observers.'

Later during that same exercise we were waiting in our Mk 107 jeep after controlling a mission. Our three radios as usual were whirring away making a lot of noise but we were used to that. We always monitored two Air Force frequencies and one Army freq. There was constant chatter but unless we heard our call sign we weren't concerned. We were parked in a strategic location where we could respond quickly if needed for more air support. There was a perimeter road intersection behind us and a deep ravine in front of us. As we sat there gazing across the ravine enjoying our brief break from the war a cobra helicopter suddenly rose out of the ravine a hundred yards away and hovered pointing its six barreled gatling gun right at us. The pilot and gunner were both wearing helmets so we couldn't make out their expressions but I'm sure they were smiles in reaction to our shocked faces. Bang bang you could almost hear them say. During that experience I realized how aptly named the Cobra was. It resembled a raised up ready to strike Cobra.

Flying in Weather

It wouldn't seem right to not include a page or two on Hahn's weather and instrument flying. Hahn did indeed have the worst flying weather of any Air Force Base. There wasn't even a close contender when looking at the number of days each year the weather was below allowable flying minimums, 300 feet ceiling and one-mile visibility. A typical winter day began with weather reported as 100 total obscuration and RVR 100. Translated that meant a ceiling measuring light beam didn't penetrate beyond 100 feet and the runway visual range (visibility measured at the end of the runway) was 1,000 feet. There frequently weren't any alternate bases available either. An alternate required a minimum of 1,000-foot ceiling and two miles visibility or 500 and one above the lowest compatible instrument approach available. We couldn't fly when the weather was less than 3,000 feet and three miles unless we had an alternate base available.

The KC 10 Tankers Saved the Day

It might seem overly restrictive requiring an alternate base to be available when the ceiling is almost a half mile and visibility of three miles but then consider the consequences of having the weather unexpectedly turning sour and you don't have an alternate! That was the case in a near tragic incident of two flights of five Marine A4's that were flying across the Atlantic on their way to Spain. Each flight was accompanied by a KC-10 air refueling tanker and they had a planned stop in the Azores islands. The nearest land to the Azores is in Spain, over a thousand miles away so there is no alternate. If the weather isn't good you just don't go. On this particular day the weather was forecast to be just fine but while they were enroute a totally unexpected weather system moved in closing the airfield. Without going into detail, heroic actions on the parts of three different KC-10 aircraft, each coming very close to ditching themselves due to giving away most of their own fuel, were able to get all 10 A-4's safely down. The crew of one of the KC-10's received the highest award possible for their actions, the Mackay Trophy. A full accounting of this incredible incident can be found by googling 'Mackay Trophy.'

At Hahn in the winter there were days when, because of our high elevation, we were above the clouds and the rest of Germany was 'socked in.' Our nearest alternate was in England and our divert fuel was 10,000 pounds. We usually took off with 17,000 pounds so a flight under these conditions didn't last very long and terminated with a heavy weight landing. It also didn't help that Hahn had a single runway and if that were closed for any reason, a divert would be required.

A Typical Winter Day

A typical winter day began with the weather below minimums of 300 and one. As the day progressed the ceiling gradually rose until by noon we were above minimums. The Supervisor Of Flying (SOF) would declare weather cat A's only, meaning only the most highly experienced could fly. The squadrons quickly realigned flights and missions and launched as many planes as they could. The ceiling might get up to 400 feet, sometimes even 500 and then as the temperature began to lower so would the ceiling. By mid-afternoon we were once again below minimums and by the end of the day the fog was back on the ground.

When I was a weather cat A (highest experience level) I was scheduled to fly a single ship instrument sortie and when the weather was called to be above mins I was the first in line for takeoff. The more I looked at the ragged gray ceiling the less it looked to be 300 feet high. I called the SOF and he assured me it was 300 feet. So, I took the runway, closed canopies, and began my takeoff. After I broke ground I reached for the gear handle and before the gear was retracted we were in the clouds - no more than a hundred feet. I called the SOF back and suggested he hold the others on the ground. He readily concurred.

I flew my mission and called the SOF again. The field was way below minimums. I diverted to Ramstein AB, 45 miles away, and drove a staff car home that evening. We were the only sortie at Hahn that day.

Early in my tour at Hahn, when I was still a newbie, I was given a jet and told to go out and fly instruments just to get a sortie - the weather had been bad for many days. I entered the weather at about 500 feet and I climbed to 35,000 feet never breaking out of clouds. I continued on to Gutersloh in northern Germany where I did a TACAN penetration and approach. I descended to 700 feet, TACAN minimums, and went missed approach when I never broke out of the clouds. After flying two GCA's (Ground Controlled Approaches) to 500 feet and still not breaking out I finally returned to Hahn. I flew for an hour and a half and never got out of the clouds. I actually felt quite comfortable. It was then that I knew I had become acclimated to Hahn. Sometime later, incidentally, I discovered that what I had done was illegal – a violation of the rules. You can't begin an instrument approach if the weather is below your minimums even to do a low approach. My reasoning was since I had no intentions of landing at Gutersloh it was OK. I was wrong but got away with it.

One year when it was the 27th of December, I still needed a couple sorties to complete my required minimum of 60. To not get minimum sorties raised serious questions and required a request for waiver to headquarters USAFE. Wings didn't like requesting waivers.

I launched on a cross-country to Alconbury AB, in England. The weather was marginal for flying but was supposed to be better the next day. On the next day we got our weather brief and found the entire continent was socked in. After conferring with the Director of Operations (DO) I launched for Germany on the hopes a base might open up long enough to land. We got back to Germany but everything was still closed. Back to Alconbury we went. On the 29th we tried again with the same luck, and again on the 30th. The 31st found such bad weather we didn't even try. I called back to Hahn and told Jean to enjoy herself at the officers' club New Years Eve party that I had already bought tickets for. My WSO and I brought in the new year as guests of Alconbury's O' Club.

Finally, on the 2nd of January, with Hahn still hopelessly socked in, Ramstein thought they might rise above minimums for an hour. The DO said to get home ASAP and we did, flying just below the mach all the way. We caught the very short window at Ramstein breaking out of the weather at 300 feet, landed and drove home in a staff car. The squadron mercifully sent a different crew back to retrieve the airplane when the weather finally broke.

Instrument flying became a matter of pride at Hahn. We sometimes had new lieutenants arrive who had zero weather time. They had gone through UPT at Williams AFB in Phoenix, Arizona and then RTU at Luke AFB, also in Phoenix. They quickly had their eyes opened and learned instrument flying at Hahn. We became absolute experts at flying GCA precision approaches. It became a matter of pride to be able to fly one from start to finish without the controller ever calling us off on glide path. However, to do this we discovered there was what seemed to be a bend in the glide path at three miles. At that point you had to push over a little and increase descent rate by a hundred feet per minute and then take out the correction promptly at two miles.

Four Ship Weather Trail Departure

I was number four of a four-ship airfield attack mission. We were tasked to perform a mock attack on a base in England in support of a local exercise they were having. We were enduring our typical winter weather at Hahn so lead called for a three mile radar trail departure and join-up on top when we were clear of clouds. My back seater did a very good job keeping the three planes in front of us on his radar and we climbed and climbed and climbed. We finally broke out on top at 44,000 feet as we were approaching the English Channel. The air was so thin for our weighted down airplanes that it required the use of afterburner to get up to 45,000 feet and the rejoin was tricky to say the least. I got about 50 knots of overtake to close the distance between us and lead who was initially nine miles ahead. With two miles to go I came to idle to slow up. Nothing happened. I put out the speed brakes but in the thin air at that altitude they had almost no effect. Finally, by yawing the plane with full rudder (basically, turning the airplane sideways) the airspeed began to drop and just in time. I got co-speed with lead with perhaps a thousand feet to spare preventing an embarrassing overshoot. At that altitude we were all barely hanging in the sky because the F-4 isn't made to be way up there. So, in the event of an overshoot I couldn't slow down without falling into the clouds which were barely a thousand feet below us. About all I could have done is a shallow turn away from the flight to get a couple miles of lateral separation and then turn back in for another rejoin attempt. Thank goodness that wasn't necessary.

Fortunately, the weather in England was much better and we had a very successful airfield attack and being ten thousand pounds of jet fuel lighter, the return trip was much easier.

Low Altitude, On the Wing, Weather

Another time I was on the wing of a flight lead that I didn't really trust very much. We were in a loose formation at 4,000 feet looking for the start route point of a low level that would terminate in a close air support mission. The weather was marginal with visibility barely three miles in haze and an obscured ceiling. Finally, lead found the start point and cleared me to take spacing as he swooped down to begin the low level. I was thinking that the weather wasn't good enough to be doing this so instead of taking the usual 1 minute spacing which would have been 7 miles I dropped back a couple thousand feet and informed lead. As we continued the route the weather got worse and worse and I got closer and closer to him until I was only a couple hundred feet back. He finally called for me to join up and I just barely got in before he entered clouds that were quite turbulent. To my surprise I realized lead was continuing the low level in the weather. He was using his inertial navigation system, INS, for headings and position. I asked Lee, my WSO, where we were in relation to Ramstein. He tuned in the TACAN and reported we were 30 miles north. I then asked what the emergency safe altitude for our position was. Emergency safe altitude is 500 feet above the highest obstacle within 25 miles of the TACAN. We were 500 feet below the emergency safe altitude. Without another word I turned away from lead's wing, went to full power and began a climb. Then I informed lead that I was lost wingman and that he was below emergency safe altitude. He just replied with a 'roger.' I then told him I was switching to Ramstein RAPCON for an IFR clearance and I'd see him back home. I didn't break out of the weather until 30,000 feet. That was the first and only time I ever initiated a break off from a flight leader.

During the debrief, lead never once admitted to any mistakes and his only comment to me was that he thought I was a little shaky on the wing! I was thoroughly disgusted. We all could have died that day. Later, after reflecting on what had happened I realized I should have reported the incident to the operations officer.

Cross Country Flying

When the end of the half was quickly approaching and many people still needed a lot of sorties to get their minimum requirements we resorted to cross country flights on weekends. The contract the aircrew made was if at all possible they would leave in the late afternoon on Friday and return in the afternoon on Sunday and get 5 sorties. So, we had the choice of flying three times on Saturday and one on Sunday or two and two. Most opted for the three and one scenario since that allowed for sleeping in on Sunday and a leisurely single sortie to get home.

We were restricted to going into USAFE bases unless special circumstances existed requiring landing at a non-USAFE base. We had a cross-servicing plan with all of the other NATO bases so in times of war if any of our planes had to emergency divert to one of their bases they would be able to service it with oil, fuel, liquid oxygen and the like. The opposite was also true. We had to be able to service NATO's non-US made planes. This plan required occasional sorties to other NATO bases on a cross-country flight to give their maintenance people practice at servicing our planes. These were coveted flights because the host NATO base usually went all out to 'wine and dine' the aircrew. It added some spice to a cross-country.

And Then There Was France

We had a one-time tasking to send a maintenance team to a French base to give them training in servicing an F-4. France was a non-NATO country and had seldom seen an F-4 except for an occasional emergency divert. While our team was there we sent two F-4s to be used for the training. We were a little apprehensive about the tasking because the French had a notorious reputation for being obnoxious and hard to get along with. When our maintenance crews and aircrews returned it became boring listening to them tell of the wonderful treatment they had received at the hands of the French. Their French counterparts, though, had trouble understanding why we couldn't drink wine at the noon meal and then go back to work. The French Air Force people that we had contact with were very apologetic for the reputation of their countrymen and explained repeatedly that the French Air Force wasn't like that. They were displaying the common bond between people who fly.

French Low Levels

We frequently had need to fly over France. I liked flying French low levels for two reasons. One, the countryside was just lovely beyond words. It was mostly agricultural and the rolling countryside was a mass of different shades of green, dissected with narrow winding blacktop roads and punctuated with small farming villages. The second reason was the minimum altitude of 200 feet for flying low level. In Germany it was 300 feet and the difference was spectacular. At 200 feet there was a substantial increase in the thrill of speed, in the rush of flying.

One low level I particularly liked took me all the way across France with a target on the coast near Calais. From there we did some sightseeing by flying at a thousand feet a quarter mile off shore north along the coast to Dunkirk. The German fortifications that the Allied invasion force had to overcome on D-Day were still very much in evidence. As we began our climb north of Dunkirk we could clearly see the white cliffs of Dover just 25 miles off our left wing. After getting clearance from Belga Control in Belgium we would be cleared direct back to Hahn. What a ride. I flew it several times.

To fly into France for a military training flight required prior authorization besides a flight plan. To get the authorization we had to list where we would be entering France and at what time. If we were off by more than five minutes we would frequently be denied entry. On my first aborted TAC check with Tom Roth I chose a French low level. He was really excited about flying it because he was attached to the 496th, the other squadron, for flying and seldom got to fly low level, much less in France.

On a cross-country flight it was much easier. We were on an ICAO (international) flight plan and they had ample knowledge we were coming. Upon being handed off to France Control we'd check in with them but they seldom answered us. We could hear their controllers talking to other aircraft (mostly in French) but they routinely ignored us and would only talk to us if we got significantly off the jet route.

Military aircraft used TACAN for navigation and it operated on a UHF frequency. Civilian aircraft used VOR that operated on a VHF frequency. In the whole world, navigation stations had VORTACs; a TACAN co-located with a VOR; the whole world except for France! To navigate in France was difficult. If we could see the ground from 35,000 feet we might use ground references. If we couldn't we might use contrails left by preceding jet liners allowing for the prevailing winds that of course would be blowing them away from the correct ground path. We also had non-French TACAN stations that we could use when within 150 miles of the border but they were only useful for position checks, not course flying. Many of the French controllers probably just thought Americans were not very good pilots.

Emergency Fuel Over France

I had formed an unpleasant opinion of the French from the way they treated us in the air - until one day when I needed help. I was number two in a two ship returning from Aviano AB in Italy. I had just become Operationally Ready (OR) and my flight commander, Charles Wimberly, was my flight lead. Shortly after takeoff I reported to Chuck that my external centerline fuel tank wouldn't feed. By my calculations we would have to turn back because we wouldn't have enough fuel to get back to Hahn. Chuck responded after a minute of silence that I'd be OK and we continued on our route. My back seater and I continued to calculate our fuel situation and by the time we were half way across France I called Chuck again and told him I didn't have enough gas to get to Hahn. Before he could respond, France Control who seldom talked to USAF airplanes had heard my transmission and called to ask if I had a fuel problem. I told him about my non-feeding centerline. He immediately cleared me to "any altitude you want and you are cleared direct to Hahn." I replied with a warm thanks and we immediately started a climb to a more optimum altitude, inserted the INS coordinates for Hahn and centered the needle. The direct course saved about a hundred miles of flying and another quick calculation showed I'd make it back with 1500 pounds of fuel. We're supposed to be on the ground with 2,000 but that was close enough considering the alternative - an emergency divert in France. My opinion of the French changed quite a lot that day.

Favorite Cross Country Bases

The favorite places to go on cross country were to Aviano AB, Italy where you could easily get into Venice, Torrejon AB in Madrid Spain and any of three bases in England, all with easy access to London. My number one favorite destination was England because as I liked to put it, the British never forgot who won the battle of Britain; the fighter pilots. I never had a request for exception denied when I was flying in England.

Isle of Man

During one cross-country I was nearing my destination of Lakenheath AB and still had loads of gas left. On a whim I keyed the mic and asked Eastern Control if I might change my routing to overfly the Isle of Man. Half of my heritage comes from the Isle of Man and I'd never seen it. His immediate response was a cheerful yes and I was cleared from present position direct to the Isle of Man and then back to Lakenheath. It was a lovely sunny summer day and as we approached the coast I very quickly sighted the island country. The greenness of the island contrasted sharply with the deep blue of the Irish Sea. I offset myself by 20 miles to the south for a good view and then reluctantly turned back for Lakenheath. From my airplane at 35,000 feet the island looked surprisingly small but I felt a strong desire to someday see this quaint island from the ground.

Coastal View of Isle of Man

Stonehenge

The next day as we were taking off I asked my back seater if he knew what Stonehenge was. He did and I suggested we go there on our way home. I keyed the mic and asked tower if I could have my clearance amended to include a low altitude departure and a fly over of Boscom Downs. From talking to a British pilot once I remembered that he said Stonehenge was within the traffic control area of Boscom Downs and since we had a squadron pilot named 'Bosco' the name stuck. The tower operator said he would take care of it and when cleared for takeoff I was given the standard instructions to contact departure control. I decided the tower operator had forgotten my request. On departure I was given a level off at 5,000 feet and some radar vectors. This wasn't the normal way to depart anywhere but perhaps I was being vectored around some other traffic. Usually you are cleared to a departure procedure that includes a course to be flown. Then, with a flicker of excitement I thought maybe my request wasn't forgotten. When I heard the departure controller telling me to contact Boscom Downs I was absolutely elated.

Boscom Downs picked me up and issued vectors for a precision approach. I was a bit heavy for this but I complied not quite knowing what was coming up next. When I was on final the controller cleared me straight through. That's unusual I thought. I asked him if it would be possible to get radar vectors to Stonehenge. In a very crisp British accent, my controller replied that vectors were in progress and that Stonehenge was straight ahead for eight miles. The controller then began issuing a restriction and I thought here goes. We'll be limited to 1500 feet for the overflight and will be lucky to see anything. "Lapse 65, remain at or below 500 feet during overflight." I just couldn't believe it. Gosh how I loved these Brits. Holding back my emotions I answered with a 'roger.' He continued providing direction and range. It became obvious I was going to pass just to the right of the monument. I was level at 500 feet but visibility was limited to about 5 miles on this beautiful sunny Sunday. We got closer and closer and I just couldn't pick it out. Suddenly, there it was. To my left 11:00 for about three or four miles I could plainly see the stately monoliths that I'd read so much about and seen so many pictures of. I totally lost it when I keyed my mic. I replied very unprofessionally, "heh, I see it, I see it." My controller, still using his best stiff British accent, replied, "ah, yes, it is quite the thing. But it will be a lot better when we get a roof on it." I acknowledged his humorous remark by keying the mic and chuckling.

Stonehenge 'from the ground'

When I was just about up to Stonehenge I thought it would be nice to circle it. By now I could see 15 or 20 tour buses parked adjacent to it. I asked if it would be possible to circle the monument. My controller responded that it would but - OK, here goes the restriction. For noise abatement he'll direct me to climb to a couple thousand feet. "Lapse 65, stay at or below 500 feet." I was beside myself with joy.

Knowing it would take a very tight turn to stay within a mile I rolled into about 70 degrees of bank. I was still quite heavy since we'd been airborne less than a half-hour so I pushed the throttles full forward to military power. I completed my turn at 300 feet and saw everything below except the exasperated looks on the faces of the tour guides who I'm sure were totally drowned out by the noise of my F-4 in full power.

Like the Isle of Man I would like to go back some day to see it from the ground. After receiving my departure instructions I warmly thanked my tour guide controller and turned back for Germany.

Monster Hunting at Loch Ness

My favorite of favorites in cross-countries was going up to Scotland and dropping down on Loch Ness to do some 'monster hunting.' Scotland is a long ways from London, almost an hour of flying time. To do the Loch Ness route I had to fly from an English base and land back at an English base. I filed high altitude to Luchers Air Field and then canceled IFR and let down to do some exploring.

Loch Ness, home of 'Nessie'

My first trip to Loch Ness was on late November 1974.

> We took off from Alconbury at 1:45 and began flying up the northern coast of England at 25,000 feet but unfortunately, there were a lot of thin clouds obscuring most of the scenery. I didn't quite appreciate how far away Scotland was and it was 45 minutes after takeoff that we were finally over Luchers. I canceled our IFR flight plan, began a descent down to 8,000 feet - there was a cloud layer just below that with only occasional holes - dug out a map of the area and began flying northwest on a heading of 330 degrees. 60 miles later, with just a little bit of luck, a big hole appeared in the clouds and there it was, Loch Ness. We had some monster hunting in store.
>
> Keeping in mind the 4,000-foot hills my map showed in the area, I rolled into a tight bank and spiraled down over Loch Ness, leveled out 500 feet above the water and then began a gradual descent down to 50 feet on the radar altimeter. We picked up one bank of the lake and flew the entire length of 40 miles at a leisurely 250 knots. Never have I seen anything so

beautiful. As I already mentioned, the lake is very long but I was surprised to discover that it was only a mile or so wide but then again it is a land locked fjord. Along the shore there were beautiful thatched roof houses every couple miles, all seemingly freshly painted and clean. High above us as we looked up at the steep banked hills bordering the western shore of the lake were tumbling waterfalls and where they had cut through the stone hills there were dense stands of fir trees. I didn't see any boats though. As we approached the southwestern end of the lake I regretfully began climbing up to head back to England. Our fuel had reached the quantity I had calculated we needed to get back safely to England with. I found another hole to climb back up through and in so doing got a good look at the more typical Scottish countryside, numerous small lakes with frequent stands of timber, smooth rock hills with snow covering the very tops. It looked wind-swept, rugged and cold. Why, it looked like it was fit for sheep and little else. I think I now know why the Scots are such a rugged lot.

I took several different back seaters along on this trip and they all had a thrill from it as did I and I'm sure that at 50 feet we were leaving a rooster tail from our exhaust behind us in the water. We never did see Nessie!

A Long Day

On another cross country, I needed an hour of night time so we carefully planned on flying to England on Friday, then on to Ramstein AB, Germany the next morning followed by a long flight from there to Torrejon AB, Spain (Madrid). On that leg we'd timed our takeoff to allow one hour of night flying going into Torrejon. All went as planned. In fact, things were going so smoothly that we had time to burn at Ramstein so we made a base exchange run. We took off right at our preplanned time and turned towards Spain. Almost two hours later we were right on schedule and on final at Torrejon. It had been dark for almost an hour and suddenly I felt really tired. After a yawn I said on the intercom to my back seater, "gee, this sure has been a long day." Then there was quiet in the cockpit as we both hit upon the same thought. Crew rest! We both computed our crew duty day and realized that we were thirteen and a half hours into it. We were limited to only twelve hours from beginning of the day until engine shut down at the end. We had planned everything so carefully but for some unexplained reason, neither of us had considered the 12-hour day limitation. We fudged the times on the forms so they conformed to 12 hours and we never heard a word about it. If I had blown a tire on landing or gotten hot brakes or anything else to get into the spotlight, I could have been in serious trouble.

Test Squadron for Pave Spike

The 10th was chosen to do extensive testing of the laser guided bombing system. The project nickname was Pave Spike. A laser guided bomb (LGB) was just a regular bomb that had a guidance kit attached to it. The kit included a laser guidance seeker head on the front and maneuvering fins at the other end. A target was 'designated' by a designator F-4 and when the LGB was dropped 'in the basket' it would precisely guide to within a few feet of that spot. The system got its start in Vietnam but was only reaching maturity a few years later with a high tech system on the F-4 that was operated by the back seater WSO. He had complete control of the laser designator and his radar scope became a TV screen allowing him to zoom in on the target. With a joy stick he kept the cross hairs trained on the target until bomb impact.

Since my squadron, the 10th, was chosen for the testing and lasers were quite new the powers that be decided we all had to have very comprehensive eye exams to document the conditions of our eyes preventing someone years later from making a liability claim due to laser damage. The exam consisted of taking color photos of our retinas. When I had my exam my eyes were dilated and I was told to look through an eye piece and then the technician turned on a bright light so he could precisely focus and adjust the instrument. As the picture was about to be taken I was thinking that light was about the brightest light I'd ever looked at. Then the flash went off. Oh my gosh, was that bright. And I still had one more eye to do.

Because of the intense training involved, only six aircrews were selected to do the flying testing. I wasn't one of them and it didn't bother me in the least. The overall goal of the testing was to see how effective the LGB would be in Europe during winter conditions. The missions required low level flying, finding targets and designating them and simulating bombing them. The targets had detectors for evaluating the accuracy of the simulated bombing. If the ceiling was above 1500 feet the mission was weather cancelled! The crews got a lot of flying but it was very intense flying and done under calculated danger and good fortune was with them. A lot of sorties were flown without incident.

A Deadly Accident and a Passive WSO

My squadron gained an experienced pilot who had been stationed in England when his unit was disbanded. His name was Larry and he applied for and received a COT, Consecutive Overseas Tour. He was assigned to the 10th squadron and we were very happy to get him; wow, a combat ready pilot who can be quickly made mission ready. What we didn't know about Larry was that he had a history of pushing the limits with rules. His assigned WSO was a friend of mine that I had frequently flown with. His nickname was Moon and he was good at working his radar and carrying out his back seat duties. His attitude however, was if it didn't involve the back seat it was the pilot's job and who was he to question the pilot's decisions. Moon was a very passive WSO who put his complete faith and trust in his pilot.

One winter morning Larry and Moon launched as a single ship for a close air support mission. With two wing tanks and a centerline tank they were very heavy and on climb-out as they were passing through 15,000 feet Larry spotted two F-4's about 10,000 feet beneath them on a bisecting heading. Larry decided to launch an unauthorized attack on the F-4s and rolled into a steep dive. Because of his heavy weight he was not able to pull out of the dive and both Larry and Moon died when their F-4 hit the ground. The accident investigation revealed an ejection had been initiated but it was way too late to be successful. Larry was a bachelor. Moon left behind a young wife.

When the accident happened I was working directly for the director of operations at wing headquarters and during the investigation I happened to stop by wing life support and they had a clear plastic bag containing Moon's very soiled flight suit and flying gear, evidence I suppose that had been collected for the investigation. I will never forget the eerie feeling I had looking at that bag knowing it had been worn by a friend when he died. I also realized that with a more forceful WSO the accident very possibly might not have happened. Years later as an F-4 instructor I used the tragic story of Moon as an example to student WSO's of why they had to be an active member of an F-4 crew.

Bombing the Yellow Tank

During my four years at Hahn we had many strange taskings that came to us through USAFE headquarters at Ramstein AB. One such tasking was to give Britain's Prince Charles an orientation flight so he could observe our latest bombing technology, the laser guided bomb. One of the most interesting to me, though, was being tasked to support a live bombing demonstration for a group of VIPs. The mission was to drop 500 pound bombs (MK 82's) on an old dilapidated army tank at the Army's Hohenfels range. The tasking was for a two ship on each of two consecutive days to drop three MK 82s each on the tank.

As mentioned previously, Hohenfels was a very large Army range complex covering a hundred or more square miles in an area that was very close to the East German border. As a FAC augmentee I was very familiar with the range layout where I supported my assigned battalion.

For this particular tasking, the Army had positioned a tank a couple miles from the reviewing stands where the VIPs could watch the Air Force in action. The Army always had real live tanks with real live people all over the range complex so it probably was very prudent when they decided to paint the target tank with yellow paint – no offense, flyboys!

Part of the safety rules for this mission was that we could not turn on the master arm switch until wings level on final for our bomb drop. Then, with 'bombs triple' selected three bombs would be released hopefully bracketing the tank. Also, for safety reasons we were told to drop the bombs in high drag configuration but with a low drag delivery – a bomb delivery that we never ever practiced because it was totally unrealistic but also totally safe. I was selected to be in the two-ship for the second day. Boy, this was going to be fun! Then the results came in for the first flight even before the jets had returned to base. Both planes had forgotten to arm the master arm so no bombs were dropped.

Suddenly, the good deal flight lost much of its luster. Very high attention was now focused on our flight to redeem the Air Force's credibility with our bombs. We briefed the mission very thoroughly with higher ups sitting in. We went out to our F-

4s with their loaded 500 pound bombs and were observed as we preflighted the bombs. We taxied out to the arming area at the end of the runway where the chief of wing weapons, a major, supervised the ground check of the bombs to make sure the required safety pins were pulled. On the half hour flight to Hohenfels very little was said in the cockpits. Then we were each rolling in on the yellow tank. Lead was in first calling 'in with master arm on.' His bombs were considerably short of the tank. When I rolled in I set my aim-off distance well beyond the tank and when my sight reached the target my mind was saying, 'there is no way these bombs will make it to the target' and I delayed two or three more seconds. When it looked about right I mashed the pickle button and began an aggressive pull. With a good climb going I dropped a wing in time to see 3 little dirty puffs of smoke and they bracketed the yellow tank. I was at once elated that I had hit the target but also disappointed. This was my first at dropping live bombs and I guess I had expected to see something much more spectacular than the little puff balls – perhaps a brilliant yellow orange flash like you see in the movies. But, we had achieved our objective; we had hit the ground with six bombs and at least scared that little yellow tank.

In-flight Emergencies

All in all I had a very charmed time when flying and the bad in-flight emergencies never seemed to happen to me. However, there were a couple that really got my attention.

A Tiger by the Tail

When I was still quite inexperienced in the F-4 I came back from a fairly routine mission; a single ship low level. My back-seater at the time was Woody, a highly experienced WSO with a walrus style mustache. Upon landing I deployed the drag chute and everything seemed quite normal until we rolled over the midfield Bak 9 arresting cable. I must have had my feet on the brake pedals anticipating starting to brake when we heard a loud bang and the airplane gently began pulling a little towards the right side of the 150 foot wide runway. Woody said in the interphone that he thought we had blown a tire and to turn off the anti-skid which I did. For the next several seconds I wasn't too concerned because I still had adequate directional control. However, as we slowed more, the pulling to the right became more pronounced and I engaged nose gear steering which helped. Soon, though, I realized that we weren't going to stay on the runway because of the increasing pull to the right. Instinctively I stomped full pressure on the left brake pedal in an effort to blow the left tire and immediately it did blow. The pulling to the right ceased and with steering I was able to come to a stop on the right side of the runway.

I didn't know how bad things were so I added a bunch of power to see if I might be able to limp off the runway; there was a taxiway just a few feet ahead. The plane didn't move so I called Tower and reported what had happened. Tower also asked if I could clear the runway because there were several F-4s that needed to land and they didn't have much gas left. I told them I was unable and the F-4s diverted to Bitburg, 30 miles away.

After deplaning I inspected the damage and found that I had worn the brake stacks very flat to the point that they were now skids. There was no way, short of using afterburner, that I would have been able to move the airplane.

Unintended Landing at Spangdahlem

Another in-flight emergency occurred during a routine low approach I had flown at a neighboring air base, Spangdahlem. After advancing the throttles for the go-around, I retracted the gear and then the flaps. As the flaps were retracting, however, the plane began to roll to the right. It seemed like such a positive cause and effect that without even thinking I put the flap handle back down and the rolling tendency stopped. I pulled the throttles back to slow up so I wouldn't reach flap blow-up speed. My options were to leave the flaps down and go back slow speed to Hahn which was only 30 miles away or to land at Spangdahlem. I chose the latter and contacted tower to declare an IFE. Not knowing exactly what had caused the rolling motion I maneuvered for an opposite direction landing. I shut down the engine as soon as I cleared the runway and after getting out of the airplane discovered that a broken bleed air line (it contains super hot air from the engine that aids in producing lift on the wings) had failed to turn off and my left flap was almost burned off. An immediate return to Hahn would have been very interesting.

All of my other emergencies were minor; single hydraulic failures, losing a generator, anti-skid failure and the like. There was the time, though, when my trim motor burned out and under some circumstances could have led to a difficult landing. The trim motor moves small flight control surfaces that can reduce or eliminate heavy forces on the control stick and is controlled by a four position round button on top of the control switch. During flight trim is constantly being applied without even thinking; up, down, left, right, to keep the stick as light as possible. After takeoff I noticed that the stick got heavier and heavier as I increased speed and I couldn't trim out the heavy forward force. I declared an IFE but had to burn down gas to get light enough to land so I had to fly for about 20 minutes using both hands on the stick to keep the nose from pitching forward. I had no idea how I was going to do a controlled landing in this manner and was just a little bit worried.

Finally, I was light enough to land and on final approach I began to slow up. The heavy stick forces began to lessen. Heh, I thought, this is good. As I slowed up more and more the stick forces diminished more and more until when I was at my landing speed the stick was trimmed hands off. Talk about lucking out – but then again, why not!

A Convenient Spot to Eject

One of my IPs when I first got to Hahn told me of his first flight when he got to Hahn a couple years earlier. He was with an IP and they were flying a mission in support of a nearby Army field exercise. Suddenly, they got a 'fire warning light' and soon after confirmed they were indeed on fire. The bold face procedure is simple – **if fire is confirmed, eject.** They ejected at ten thousand feet and as they were descending in their parachutes they could see an Army field ambulance racing across a field and it was waiting for them when they landed. After being loaded up in the ambulance they discovered that the Army thought it was all part of the exercise!

Director of Operations Training

For my last two years at Hahn I was selected to work at Wing Headquarters. I became a 'wing weenie.' Many people wanted the staff jobs where they could get daily visibility of the wing commander and Director of Operations (DO), but I just wanted to stay in the squadron and fly. But, I was called and I went. DOT was run by Major Hank Belinski but he was due to be reassigned back to the States. I was selected to replace him. I was a senior captain at the time. There also was a younger captain WSO, Herb Brasington, and a cute married Buck Sergeant, Bev Harr. Hank soon left for the states well before I knew what the job was about so I was left in charge with not much confidence. But, we all got along very well in the office that we shared and with Herb's sage advice based on his experience in the office and Bev very efficient in office procedures, things went very smoothly.

Reporting to DOT were two agencies that ran themselves, wing egress, headed by a career senior master sergeant, Sgt. Charlie Wisecarver, and wing records, an office that kept track of flying time for all of the wing's aircrews. It was run by a German woman and she had been doing the job so long she never made a mistake.

Herb learned how to use the computer and in the mid 70's using a computer meant feeding in punch cards when you wanted to enter data. Likewise, to enter a program to retrieve reports you spoke to the computer via punch cards. Herb was the reports guy and that was just fine by me. He also handled many other routine jobs such as overseeing life support and records as well as writing their performance reports. I soon learned that the majority of my time was in putting out brush fires for the DO, Colonel Roy.

Col. Roy was a straight shooter. He was very stable, solid in his decision making and had a good sense of humor. I liked him a lot and I don't think I ever questioned his decisions - except perhaps making me the chief FAC that extended my FAC duties to a second year. I ran the Supervisor Of Flying (SOF) program, was in charge of the Runway Supervisory Unit (RSU) and probably most important for routine duties, I managed the aircrew manning in the wing.

When I came on board there didn't seem to be any system for keeping the squadrons balanced in experience levels. When we got a computer RIP on an incoming aircrew member, Herb would look it over and announce what squadron the fellow would fit in with best. A note would be attached with the recommendation and it would be forwarded to Col. Roy who might or might not go along with it. I quickly recognized that a better system was needed when one of the squadrons lost four pilots to reassignment in one month and suddenly was critically manned requiring the next four pilots who came through the door. I constructed a four-year flow chart that would reflect at any time during the four years what the projection was for experienced pilots, inexperienced pilots and WSOs between the two squadrons. This way I could spot potential manning conflicts as much as two or three years ahead of time. Unaccompanied (usually unmarried) aircrew members usually came with an 18-month assignment while accompanied aircrew members had 36-month assignments. This variability in assignment length allowed me to relatively quickly even up projected squadron strengths. In my recommendations to Col. Roy I always referred to this balance. He never turned down my recommendation.

The 313th Tactical Fighter Squadron

After I had been in DOT for almost a year, the 313th TFS was added to Hahn. The squadron patch was of a mean looking bulldog's face. The squadron manning was filled by transfers from the 10th and 496th and also by Consecutive Overseas Tour (COT) assignments from two squadrons in Europe that were being deactivated. The new squadron commander was Lt. Col. 'Bugs' Bugeda who was being promoted from the Ops Officer position at the 10th.

Lt. Col. Bugeda was a good friend of mine and we had golfed a lot together as well as socialized but more importantly to Bugs was his friendship with Col. Roy. Col. Roy liked Bugs because he was a strong leader and was very mission oriented; the stuff squadron commanders are made of. When the 313th was selected as USAFE squadron of the year Bugs more than proved himself.

In forming the new squadron what Bugs wanted Bugs got to include myself as an attached pilot. I revamped my manning projection book to include the 313th and Col. Roy was quite surprised when I showed him how unbalanced the manning had become in favor of the 313th. From day one Bugs made it a point to see the RIPs of incoming aircrew members and always put in his bid to Col. Roy for people he wanted and when he didn't get many of his requests he would get annoyed with me. He was forever trying to get special treatment from me but I made it a point to work for the best interest of the 50th TFW and not the 313th TFS. I think Bugs realized I was doing the job the way he would have also done it. My fairness between the squadrons wasn't lost on the other squadron commanders.

Bugs did take care of his people and in spite of my not playing favorites and being an attached pilot, he also took care of me. Because of my late start in flying and then two years on mission support status I lacked in flying hours and never got checked out as a flight lead. When I got my reassignment to F-4 RTU at Homestead without any fanfare Bugs saw to it that I was upgraded to flight lead status. I don't think I realized the favor he had done me until I began my IP flight training. A flight lead designation was a prerequisite for IP school.

It was usually during one of these periods of disfavor that Bugs would ask me to do a wood working project for him. Perhaps he felt I was more vulnerable at those times. Since I loved doing such things I never turned him down. One of the projects that comes to mind was making a built in bookcase into the front of the Operations duty counter to hold aircrew publications. Another project was a series of three alert warning boxes that were lit from inside with Christmas tree lights. I had made such a system for the 10th squadron and now Bugs wanted one for the 313th.

We had three different warning systems that were used concurrently during exercises. One was for defense conditions or DEFCONs, another was for attack warnings and the third was for a USAFE warning system. Each system had five or six options so each of the three long boxes had separate compartments for each condition. In addition was a box with 'Exercise' lit up in yellow lights, 'Actual' in red, and 'Fade Out' in white. Fade out meant the end of an exercise and in addition to the words it had the outline of a frosty beer mug with foam dripping down one side. Of course each compartment window had to have its own switch so the wiring of the boxes was a big job in itself so I enlisted the help of civil engineering. The boxes rested above the scheduling board and the control panel with its twenty some labeled toggle switches was mounted on the wall next to the scheduling board.

In making the plexiglass face plates for the boxes I used a technique I developed myself. After cutting out the plexiglass faceplate to fit each box I outlined each compartment. Then, with the sticky protective backing still on the backside of the plexiglass I drew the letters on a piece of paper of the same size. Using carbon paper I transferred a reverse image to the plexiglass backing. After carefully cutting the outlines of the letters with an exacto knife I meticulously peeled off all of the backing material except the letters. I then sprayed the surface with black spray paint and after drying I peeled off the remaining letter shaped backing leaving clear unpainted images of the letters. After lining each compartment with shiny aluminum I attached the faceplate. Each compartment had an appropriately colored Christmas light protruding through its back for illumination.

When viewed from the front, the back painted plexiglass left a perfectly smooth, unblemished, shiny surface. I used this same technique for making plaques for special purposes. First, I cut out the plaque in oak wood, routed the edges and sanded. Then I cut out a piece of plexiglass to fit the front surface of the plaque beveling the edges to fit exactly. After drawing and cutting all of the lines of the reverse image as previously described, I peeled off only one color at a time. After spraying that color and letting it dry, I peeled off the next color and sprayed repeating the process until I had sprayed all of the colors. The process was quite time consuming and I had to turn down many requests for plaques but the result was a very unique gift.

A New DO

Colonel Sams replaced Col. Roy when the latter was reassigned. The wing commander had four deputies under him, the director of operations, director of maintenance, base commander and the comptroller. Only the DO was a flying position. Col. Sams had previously been the comptroller. We were all very puzzled at such a move because usually DO's are chosen from assistant DO's who are chosen from squadron commanders who are chosen from Operations Officers - there is the operations side of things and then there is the support side and there usually isn't much mixing. DO's, by the way, are usually the only deputies to be promoted to wing commander. The current wing commander at that time was an exception who had a non-operations background. That might explain how Col. Sams received his DO position.

Col. Sams first job was to get current in the F-4. He had been out of the cockpit for some time. After that came learning the duties of the DO, which I don't think he ever did. It was almost impossible to get a decision from him. Col. Sams was a wonderful, kind, caring person but a leader he was not. He was three ranks above me but when dealing with him I always felt like I was dealing with someone of lesser rank. I liked Col. Sams but I much preferred working for Col. Roy.

With the end of our four years in sight, Jean and I decided we weren't quite ready to leave this wonderful base or this lovely Europe. I applied for a one-year extension. I talked it over with Col. Sams and asked that if my extension was approved that I be allowed to go back to the squadron and be checked out as a flight lead and flight commander. He approved my request so I put in for the extension. It wasn't approved and I soon got an assignment to become an F-4 IP at Homestead AFB in southern Florida. Since many of my contemporaries had recently gotten assignments as T-38 instructors at fighter lead-in school or as forward air controllers or air liaison officers I was quite happy with my assignment.

Portrait of Captain Olson taken at Homestead AFB

Chapter Eleven

An F-4 Instructor Teaching Others

> *In reference to an overly aggressive student, "his fangs grew so long they punctured his G suit."*

Germany to Florida

We reluctantly left Germany on the 20th of November 1977, just ten days short of four years. There was a saying we first heard in the 10th squadron about three squares that everyone filled in Germany. They were getting a grandfather clock, having a car accident and having a baby. We left Germany having filled all three.

Never have two people been happier to get on a stuffed, cramped cattle-car of a plane than Jean and I at Wiesbaden. It wasn't because we were happy to leave Germany. We would have loved to stay another year. It was because we came within a whisker of missing the plane. I've never heard of anyone missing a port call and I'm sure it wouldn't have stood well if a whole family of five had done so. Let me back up a little.

During our last week at Hahn several of our friends offered to drive us to Wiesbaden for our port call and because of how much luggage we had we took two of them up on their offer. We spent the last few days in the BOQ enjoying the change in routine. The girls continued to go to school and life went on. I even participated in a golf tournament and won a Thanksgiving turkey that I reluctantly had to give away. We could hardly have cooked a turkey in our BOQ room. The BOQ was quite close to the DO complex where I had worked for the last year and that was handy for me because I continued to work right up to the last day. In fact, I even went in a couple hours before we were to leave to take care of some last minute things.

At the appointed hour of 9 am one of our two rides showed up and we loaded half of our things into her car. Then we waited and waited and waited. Finally, our second ride showed up a full hour late. She had misunderstood or misheard the time we told her we had to leave. We were frantic. As we sped out of Hahn I realized it would take a little bit of luck and a whole lot of praying for us to make our flight. We made it to the Wiesbaden terminal without further incident, and our drivers let us off at the entranceway. We got our luggage checked and raced for our departure gate to find our flight was already over half boarded. From that point on everything became quite routine.

Bayonne Where?

Since my assignment was to Florida my port call was for Charleston, the nearest port of entry. I drove my car to Bremerhaven in northern Germany three weeks before our port call and had it shipped to Charleston. It was scheduled to arrive a week before us. A week before our departure Jean was going over the shipping papers for the car and asked me, "why does this say the car is going to Bayonne, New Jersey?" The next day I rushed through a change in our port call so we would land at McGuire AFB, New Jersey. If Jean hadn't caught that we would have been in a real fix with us in South Carolina and our car in New Jersey. She probably saved me from having to take a bus to New Jersey to pick up the car. How the mix up occurred remains a mystery to this day.

Picking Up the Car

After we landed in New Jersey I made inquiries at our motel and found that Bayonne was about 75 miles to the north and that a bus shuttle left very early each morning. Bayonne was one of its stops. I left the next morning while the family was still sleeping and got on the bus and settled back for the two-hour ride. The bus made one stop after another and more and more people got off the bus until I was the only one left. By now I had a very funny feeling not to mention a queasy stomach because I'd just seen a sign indicating we were in Pennsylvania, not New Jersey. When I told the bus driver that I thought we were going to Bayonne he informed me that I had gotten on the wrong bus. The Bayonne bus left about 15 minutes after his did. I thought this was truly the story of my life. It couldn't have happened to anyone else. Jean lets me out of the house by myself to get the car in Bayonne, New Jersey and I end up in Pennsylvania!

The bus driver was a very nice man. He said after some breakfast he'd see about getting me to Bayonne and he did. He managed to link up with another bus that was going there and made the transfer and it didn't cost me a cent. Well, almost!

The bus terminal was on one side of the freeway and the Port of Bayonne was on the other. I'd have to get a taxi to get to the terminal. When I got into the taxi, we set off. The meter was running. The driver made small talk. He asked me if I was just returning from overseas. I replied yes, from four years in Germany. He reached up and turned the meter off and charged me 10 dollars. I'd been watching that meter and it might have reached three dollars. I'd been cheated but I was in no mood to do anything except retrieve my car and get back to my family. I paid the ten dollars and decided the tip was already included. I arrived at the port by noon and with very little hassle or paperwork picked up the car.

Just as it had four years earlier in Wiesbaden the car once again gave me a feeling of safety. We owned this car. It would take us wherever we wanted to go whenever we wanted to. I got back to the motel in time for supper. Jean had been a little worried and when I told her my tale she probably thought, 'why of course.'

A Side Trip to DC

It was the last week of November and we wanted to take leave over Christmas so we reporting in at Homestead and then drove back to Michigan and Wisconsin for a month of leave. We made these plans thinking we would be landing in South Carolina. Now, we were faced with a lot of driving; from New Jersey all the way to the southern tip of Florida and then a round trip of about 3,800 miles to Michigan and Wisconsin. Since we would be passing right through Washington D.C. we decided to stop off and visit some of Jean's relatives. We even took a couple days off to see some of Washington D.C. with Jean's uncle, Dick Shea, acting as our guide and driver. We were driving our Volkswagen and Dick, a speechwriter and longtime resident, chuckled at our green USAREUR (US Army Europe) license plate. He speculated that in this town of bureaucrats and special privilege elite's he could park the car anywhere and it wouldn't be ticketed because the police wouldn't know what kind of license plate that was.

We did a whirlwind tour of the Capitol, the Mellon Art Museum, The Smithsonian Air Museum, the White House and the major monuments and then were once again on our way to south Florida; south to a sub-tropical paradise where engine heaters were unknown and snow was only found on a sno-cone.

Arriving at Homestead

We finally got to Homestead in early December. I found my squadron, the 308th, and met the commander, Lt. Col. Roberts, who was a weapons system officer. He was the only WSO who was commander of a fighter squadron I'd ever heard of before or since, but he was a real nice person. Scuttlebutt was that he had a very high ranking sponsor in the Air Force.

Family photo after getting back to the States. Jean and the girls; Mandy, Becky and Jill

The next thing I did at Homestead was put my name on the housing list. We had never lived in base housing and Jean said she wanted to do so now. So we did. I was told that I was number two and we should have a house waiting for us when we got back from up north. That should coincide with the arrival of our household goods. After arranging for our things in storage at Tampa to be shipped to us, we did some exploring of our new home.

Homestead's 'Beaches'

When we asked for directions to the beach we were disappointed in the answer. There were no beaches. The action of the Gulf Stream prevents sand from washing up and accumulating on that particular part of the coast. If you travel north you will encounter beaches - but not at Homestead. However, we were given directions to a tidal pool. The tidal pool was at Bayfront park and was manmade. It was perfectly circular and looked like someone had bulldozed out a several acre depression right next to the ocean and then cut a connecting canal. Countless truckloads of beach sand later provided a sandy beach and voila! a swimming pool that was cleaned twice a day by the tide.

We didn't know how the girls would take to water after being landlocked in Germany for a good portion of their lives but they adapted in minutes. Our first trip to Bayfront found the girls in the water continuously until we dragged them out to go back to base. Even Amanda loved sitting in the water and playing in the sand even though she wasn't particularly fond of baths.

Jean got Jill and Becky registered in school and by the time we left on our trip to the north, they had two weeks in. Jill and Becky adapted to their new school amazingly well. However, we were disappointed in Florida's lack of emphasis on education. Most schools were short on textbooks. Jill's science book was 11 years old and falling apart. Their math books weren't much better.

Until I attended Instructor Pilot School I was of little use to the 308th squadron but I filled some ground training squares and found other ways to stay somewhat busy until our trip north in mid December. The people were very friendly and although it never quite equaled the 10th in camaraderie, the 308th was to become our second favorite squadron.

The Volare!

During our two weeks at Homestead we also bought a car. We had seen a Plymouth Volare on display at the base exchange in Germany and decided that was what we wanted. Without even considering anything else I bargained the best price I could get and we bought our Volare, a station wagon. It was the worst car we ever had and six years later when I totaled it in Panama City, nary a tear was shed. When we bought the car, Chrysler was attempting to dig itself out from bankruptcy and we sure helped them do it.

A Trip up North

We had lovely family reunions in both Menominee, Michigan and Poplar, Wisconsin but were anxious to get back to warm Florida and continue our lives at a new air base. As we started out we were towing our camper trailer that Jean's brother, Jack, had taken care of for the previous four years. Our trip back south was quite uneventful until we reached northern Florida when the trailer blew a tire and the spare was unusable, obviously a poor preflight on my part. This happened on a Sunday morning and we were unable to replace the tire until the stores opened on Monday. We had planned on getting back to Homestead on Sunday and the squadron was expecting me to be at work on Monday. I called the Homestead command post to let them know I would be getting in a day late. On Monday we replaced the tire and completed our trip back to Homestead.

Hello to the 308th

Tuesday morning, when I went in to the squadron I was told the operations officer wanted to see me. I reported to his office and received a royal chewing out for being a day late. It seems I had been scheduled for a simulator mission the previous morning and for obvious reasons was a no-show. This was the first time I met the operations officer and I wasn't very impressed. Welcome to the squadron! I never heard another word about it.

True to word, we had a house waiting for us upon our return. It was a three bedroom two bath and not far from the flight line. With three children we really hoped for a four bedroom but were told that since all three of our kids were of the same sex we only qualified for a three bedroom. Now go figure!

I had a slot for IP school at Luke AFB, in Phoenix, Arizona at the end of the month. The school was nine weeks long and I was concerned about how I would do. My concern was the school had an air to air phase and I had been only air-to-ground since F-4 RTU. I had never received an air to air checkout. But, I wasn't about to give it undue worry until I could do something about it.

Driving to Phoenix

The Volkswagen 412 station wagon became my car and I drove it out to Phoenix. It was a long way. My first 12-hour day got me as far as Pensacola where I got a room at the BOQ. As I started out the next morning, the car began running so rough, it wouldn't stay running. I'd start, put it in gear and a block away it would conk out. My plan was to keep doing that until I got to the base garage and then decide what to do. I was really worried because I was on a tight schedule with two thousand miles ahead of me. Many starts later I got to the garage and the car began running just fine. I drove it around base for a test and it continued to run just fine. When I pulled out on I-10 heading west I was less than confident about the condition of the VW. I knew deep down that cars don't fix themselves. This time it did! The only thing I can think of is that during a gas-up I'd gotten some water with the gas and it finally managed to work its way through.

The second day got me as far as San Antonio and the day after that I drove another 800 miles to Tucson. I took a planned day off in Tucson to stop by and see our old house on East 42nd Street and then paid a surprise visit to Bob and Traudl Hall whom I hadn't seen for six years.

IP School and the 310th TFS

At Luke AFB I was assigned to the 310th TFS. I knew three instructors there who had been with me at the 10th TFS at Hahn Air Base. My class consisted of about 15 pilots and five WSO's. There were three other pilots that I knew from Homestead. One of them, Mike Lichty, had been in the 496th TFS at Hahn when I was there. I barely knew him then but we became good friends at Luke. He gave me immeasurable help and support during the air to air phase.

The IP School lasted during February, March and one week of April, a fine time of year to fly in Arizona. The best way to describe the school was as a mini RTU except the IPs pretended to be students and we, the students, pretended to be IPs. Almost all of our flying was in the back seat. We also had academics and simulators. All training emphasized how to teach.

Landing From the Back Seat

The first challenge was learning to land the F-4 from the rear cockpit. I soon discovered that it was useless to try to look out the right front. You couldn't see anything because of the placement of equipment. On the left side if you really craned your neck you could see a little. On my first back seat ride I really surprised myself when, on my third attempt, I actually made a landing. The wind was from the right and I quickly learned that was ideal. With a right crosswind, when on final approach, I had to crab or point the airplane a little to the right or into the wind. This kept the plane's ground track on the runway heading. It also allowed me with a lot of neck straining to see out the left side. Then, I just had to monitor glide path to keep flying to my aim point.

I really worried about what I would do when I first encountered a left crosswind where the airplane had to be crabbed to the left. After several flights it finally happened. My instructor told me that I could occasionally take a peek out the left side by just pushing the right rudder pedal. This momentarily swung the nose of the aircraft to the right just long enough to check my runway alignment and then make a correction if required. When down to a hundred feet I was close enough to the runway environment to be able to see it even out the right side. I got fairly good at landing from the back seat once I realized we weren't expected to be smooth about it. Landing the F-4 from the back seat required aggressively maneuvering the airplane to the runway; man-handling it. The landings were seldom graceful. Some described them more like typical Navy carrier landings, controlled crashes!

We were advised to thoroughly brief our students about the difficulty in back seat landings and when demonstrating a landing, they were to sing out if the alignment didn't look right. This came about after a student in the front seat at an RTU Base just sat there and watched as his IP demonstrated a landing - straddling the edge of the runway. The F-4 suffered major damage but there were no injuries except to the IP's pride and to the student's grade.

Air to Ground

In the air-to-ground phase we learned the job that the WSO did as well as instructed the pilot. It was easy to forget that an IP also needed to teach student WSOs. I had to learn how to operate the radar, do the BIT (Built In Test) checks, align the Inertial Navigation System and perform many kinds of radar bomb deliveries. We flew several radar low levels over the Gila Bend range complex where the terrain's most dominant features were of volcanic peaks and ridges. Compared to Europe's flat terrain we got excellent radar returns. The low levels were extremely easy to fly and some turn points could be seen from 20 plus miles away.

The most demanding part of the air-to-ground phase was Ground Attack Tactics or GAT. Some missions required five or more hours to prepare for.

Letter Extract on Ground Attack

> *I spent almost five hours today at the squadron preparing for a flight early Monday morning. That flight comes under the heading of ground attack tactics. Instead of going to a range and dropping practice bombs on a scoreable circle I am going to an uncontrolled range that has many simulated targets such as airfields, AAA sites, command posts and the like. I have to plan and develop tactics to attack designated targets from low-level approaches. This also involves using tactical type deliveries. Instead of rolling in on the target from a preplanned altitude and heading I will choose a visual reference point a certain distance from the target and perform a pop-up attack using this reference point. While flying at 500 feet a climb is begun at this point. When the target is identified, I roll the airplane partially inverted and pull down into a dive that will allow the bomb to be dropped on the target. It sounds a bit complicated but with a lot of pre-mission planning it isn't. The purpose of tactical deliveries is twofold: To surprise the enemy and to be exposed to enemy ground fire for the shortest time possible.*

Tactical Deliveries were considered to be potentially very dangerous. During the pop-up we had a MAP or Minimum Approach Point. If you passed that and you didn't have your target in sight you went through dry. The danger was target fixation. If you acquired the target inside the MAP and pulled down into your planned dive you would be too steep to be able to pull out after bomb release. This was the cause of many accidents.

Rain in the Desert

We had a problem during GAT that was totally unforeseeable. In one week we received over four inches of rain. The problem for us wasn't the rain itself but what the rain did. It turned the desert green. Much of our flying during this phase was low level over the desert and to find our way around or to stay in a designated area we had visual landmarks. Ideally these landmarks were mountains or black volcanic deposits but occasionally they were dry washes or desert trails. Likewise, our targets were SAM sites or AAA sites that had supply roads that formed very distinct and identifiable patterns such as a circle or a Star of David. When the desert grass grew almost overnight, these features vanished from sight - overnight.

Night Flying

We had night transition - or night landings - combined with ground attack night and night air refueling. We completed all of our night requirements on three sorties each with everyone being able to finish in one week. I have yet to find anyone who likes diving at the ground at night. However, due to the excellent instruments in the F-4, it isn't as dangerous as it might seem. Scary? Yes. Dangerous? Not so much.

Air to Air

By far the most demanding phase was the Air Combat Maneuvering, ACM, or perhaps better described as dog fighting. Letter excerpts on air to air:

> *This is the most demanding area of flying fighters and an area I haven't participated in since RTU almost five years ago. Basically, this is maneuvering at speeds from 150 knots to one and a half times the speed of sound, visually finding your opponent and then using one or more of many fundamental maneuvers modifying them as necessary to end up behind him in a position to shoot him down. Once this is mastered another plane is added so it becomes two against one. This adds the requirement of coordinating the attack to put to use the advantage of having another fighter. After the 2 v 1, another opponent is thrown into the fight making it 2 v 2. This combination allows for a much more complex situation where you have sequential attacks, split plane maneuvering, defensive splits and more.*

Problems in ACM

I had my problems in the ACM phase as I expected I would. After RTU at MacDill AFB I never did get a front seat check out in air to air. (At Hahn with our very specialized air-to-ground mission, we always got waivers for the air to air requirements.) Here at IP School I was in the back seat for my air to air checkout. I was required to brief and lead a 2 v 1 ACM mission. The briefing part wasn't that difficult thanks to my friend, Mike Lichty, helping me in putting it together. The flying part was very hard – and stressful.

> *Thursday I had to brief and lead a mission that involved sequential moves. Having never seen it before I naturally ran into problems trying to tell others how to do it and even more problems when we flew. As flight lead, I had to tell everyone where to fly and then when the engagement began there I was, flying at five to six G's, trying to keep two other airplanes in sight.*

> *When I couldn't do that, I had to remember what direction they were last going and then try to get everyone back together again to do another set-up. I busted (failed) that ride. I had the chance to try again on Friday and I'll get another chance tomorrow with a 5:00 am brief. But, I keep smiling and saying I can do it and I will do it. I busted the second ride also but passed the Monday morning ride.*

Due to my lack of air to air training I was given a chance to fly the air-to-air simulator and learn some of the basic principles of ACM. What an experience that was.

The Air to Air Simulator

> *I had the opportunity to fly a simulator last week that was simply magic. I know no better way to describe it. The sim was the closest thing to actual combat flying. I got into the cockpit and strapped in even hooking up my G-suit. When I pushed a button the cockpit moved forward into a darkened area. When the lights came on I could see the floor (ground) which consisted of large checks with a long runway visible in front of me. Looking up in every direction I could see a milky white sky.*
>
> *Another pilot did the same in a cockpit to one side of me. He would be my adversary and we would dog fight to the death!*
>
> *What I was actually seeing were images projected on numerous panes of glass. The images came from another room where VCR cameras recorded a miniature world. The floor was photographed by a camera that moved up and down vertically showing my relative altitude. It moved horizontally reflecting my aircraft's speed. A second camera photographed the other aircraft, a model, and projected its image where it would be flying in relation to me. A third camera was trained on the model that represented my aircraft and projected its image to the other pilot.*
>
> *So, the stage was set. I advanced the throttles and had the sensation of moving down the runway. Faster and faster. At lift-off speed, the nose rose and suddenly, the checkerboard ground began to drop away and the squares grew smaller and smaller. When I reached 10,000 feet on my altimeter, I moved the stick sideways to roll upside down and the visible world smoothly turned upside down. When I applied back pressure on the stick to do a split S maneuver the ground once again began to move to give the sensation I was entering a dive. Approaching straight down all I could see was the checkerboard ground and the squares were getting visibly larger. As I pulled out of my dive I increased the G and my G suit began to inflate contributing to the illusion of flight. Even my seat cushion was an accomplice to the illusion deflating slightly as if my body were being pressed into it. As the G increased to five the lights in my simulated world started to dim giving the sensation of graying out and had I continued to increase the G the lights would have blacked out completely. I leveled out*

at high airspeed and very close to the ground. The large squares were just screaming by and as I began another climb, the ground quickly dropped away beneath me.

Then, I saw a small speck about 30 degrees left of me. I turned my F-4 and pointed at it while simultaneously plugging in the afterburner. That had to be another aircraft - my enemy. "Wolf lead has a bandit left 11:00 slightly high, range four miles. I'm engaged." I push the nose over to more quickly gain airspeed and my airspeed indicator shows I'm supersonic, Mach 1.3. The speck is now big enough to show it is an aircraft and I point the nose slightly behind him and begin a pull-up to his altitude. Range is now two miles and his size is growing rapidly. My nose is quite high now and I'm quickly approaching his altitude so I roll inverted and pull back down to roll out behind him. Oh, oh. He sees me. I know because he suddenly turned hard into me. Knowing I'm going to overshoot I roll back upright and pull the nose almost straight up to reduce my forward motion. Now, my G-suit is fully inflated and the world is growing dim. Looking down beneath me I see the defender turning to get away from me. He is smart. If he had tried to follow me he would have easily run out of airspeed and fallen off first. I pull the nose back down and once again point at him. With the altitude advantage my airspeed quickly increases and I begin once again to close on him. Looking at my sight I can tell his range is 8,000 feet. I want to close to 4,000 feet to shoot my infrared heat seeker missiles. As I put him in my sight I hear a low growl in my headset telling me the missile seeker heads are looking at the heat from his engine. At 4,000 feet I squeeze the trigger and hear a missile slide off the missile rail under my wing. I squeeze again and another missile leaves. He must have seen the missile smoke trail because he has rolled into a hard turn. The missiles missed him so I reach down and turn on the master arm switch that arms my gun. I am now close enough to visually identify my opponent as a MiG-21. Increasing G I put the MiG in my sight and hold him there. At 1,500 feet I'll begin firing. The sight shows the closure. 3,000, 2,500, 2,000, 1,500. I squeeze the trigger and hear the sound of the gun, a low vibrating sound much like a kitchen blender as the gun fires 100 bullets a second. All of a sudden the MiG disappears in a blinding flash and I roll and pull to miss the debris.

The flash disappears as does the ground and sky -- everything is just milky white and I hear the simulator controller say that he will reset us for another fight. For five minutes I had completely forgotten I was in a simulator. I was flying an F-4 fighting a MiG-21. I was soaked in sweat and tingling from excitement. Now, the world reappears and I am the defender. Looking behind me I see a MiG-21 closing quickly. If I don't do something soon I'm going to die. Here we go again.

Dissimilar: Flying Against the F-5's

The most difficult part of air to air was behind me. The phase ended with flying against the Aggressors. The Aggressor squadron was based at Nellis AFB, Nevada and they sent packages (groups of two or four aircraft) of F-5 aircraft all over the country to train other aircrews in Soviet tactics and air to air flying. We had four flights against the aggressors. The first two were 1 v 1 BFM using canned pre-briefed setups. The third flight was ACM, a 2 V 1 and also used canned profiles. The last flight was the graduation of air to air, a 2 v 2 DACT mission. For this mission the F-4's and F-5's briefed their tactics separately. It was no longer a training sortie. Our school IPs were in the front seats and the students did the job of a WSO. We had one primary goal, to survive against the F-5 and if possible get a kill. These pilots were some of the best in air to air and their planes were more maneuverable than our F-4's and much harder to see. They definitely had the advantage.

The F-5s took off early, went out to the flying area to 'hide' and waited for the F-4s to arrive. We picked up the F-5s on radar when we entered the area and turned to meet them head-on. One plane moved out two miles to one side and a mile lower hoping the F-5s would only see the highest F-4. At five miles the offset F-4 began a hard climbing turn towards the higher F-4. At the speeds we were flying at our closure rate was a mile every four seconds and we quickly picked up the F-5s visually. They picked us up as well. One F-5 rolled inverted and quickly entered a dive while the other one began a hard climbing turn. For the next four minutes we fought continuously and remained in full afterburner. We never got below four G's on our aircraft. Much of the time was spent at six to seven Gs. Approaching bingo fuel we managed to disengage ourselves from the enemy and made a successful retreat. We never reached a position where we could have shot them down but they never were able to shoot us down either. It was a complete draw. Considering the circumstances we felt we were successful. During the debrief, the aggressor lead was very generous in his praise for us.

The Long Trip Back to Homestead

My IP School was finished. I was an F-4 IP and I was headed for home and my girls. I couldn't wait. Mike Lichty and I decided to drive part of the way together. He was driving a yellow Jeep and since we both had CB radios we could stay in contact with each other. It would make the time go by faster. However, Mike wanted to stop overnight to see some friends in Dallas so he planned to turn off on I-20 at Fort Stockton, Texas whereas I would continue on I-10. When looking at a map it appeared that the I-20 route wasn't much longer and there was a chance we might meet up again. I told Mike I was planning on spending my second night in Louisiana. Mike said he would be rejoining I-10 in Lafayette early on the third morning.

We hadn't been on the road an hour, however, when my CB broke. The connector where the mic plugs in became loose and I didn't have the tools to repair it. I pulled alongside Mike and using fighter pilot sign language I indicated to him that I couldn't talk but I could still hear. Our communication after that was on the order of, "Heh, Ripsaw, (Ripsaw was my tactical call sign so I used it on the CB. Mike was Cowboy) if you need to stop for gas soon flash your lights." Mike was a very outgoing CB personality and loved to talk. I was more reserved, the type that mostly just listened. So, it was fitting that it be me to lose the talking capability.

Splitting Up is Hard to Do!

Even though we had a very limited means of communicating, it was with sadness that I watched the yellow Jeep peel off for the I-20 exit. We had gotten an early start and were passing through Fort Stockton at 7 pm. My plans were to continue on to San Antonio if I could. West Texas was a desolate place in the daytime. At night it was much worse. The five or six hour drive to San Antonio was a long haul. I slept in the next morning because I had a relatively easy leg to Lafayette where I planned on spending my second night.

I very foolishly left Phoenix with less than ten dollars in my pocket. I had a credit card and decided I would just be careful with my spending and only get gas where I saw the Master Card logo in the window. The late 70's were far from being a cashless society and a lot of business establishments wouldn't take credit cards. If I had to I could have used the card to get a cash loan from a bank. However, when I got to Homestead I still had a dollar or two left.

The Rejoin

I got on the road at 6 am on the third morning because I was driving the rest of the way to Homestead - about 18 hours or more. I pulled out on I-10 and thought, 'wouldn't it really be neat to turn on the CB and hear the Cowboy's voice.' But what would be the chance of that happening.' The range of a CB is at most two miles. He could be 3 miles in front or 3 miles behind me and I would never know it. Well, I turned on the CB and there he was, the Cowboy, and as usual he was talking up a storm. I just couldn't believe it. What an incredible coincidence. Of course I couldn't talk to him with my broken radio but the only logical thing to do was to assume he was in front of me so I sped up. I got my VW up to 85 and began passing cars right and left. Whenever I topped a rise I'd anxiously peer ahead as far as I could see looking for a yellow Jeep. Mike's voice kept getting louder so I was confident he was in front of me and at the next rise, there he was. A half-mile in front of me I spotted a bright yellow Jeep with a black canvas top. I closed the distance rapidly and finally was right behind him. Mike didn't appear to see me until I pulled up next to him and then I wish I'd had a camera to capture the expression on his face when he looked over. It was a mixture of amazement, disbelief and incredulousness with a sprinkling of happiness. We were a two ship again and the miles melted away before us. After that nothing could go wrong and nothing did - almost.

At our last gas stop in the Kissimmee area I pulled out first since I was leading the way. I gunned the car down the on-ramp only to hear something terrible on the radio. "Ripsaw, you're going the wrong way!" It was too late. I couldn't stop or back up. I found myself on I-10 North. I had to continue and hope a service road on the Interstate was near. After two miles I still hadn't come across one so when there was a lull in the traffic, I quickly braked in the left lane, sped across the median and up onto southbound I-10. I caught up to Mike in a few minutes.

Next stop was Homestead and home. It was Sunday, April 9th, 1978. I made it home for Mandy's second birthday.

Learning to be an IP

It didn't take long to fit into the routine of being an instructor pilot. I really loved the job. I began learning the practical ins and outs that went with the job, things I didn't learn at Luke. For one I learned that when writing out a grade sheet after a flight, one of our less cherished jobs, treat it as a legal document because it might become one. If a student washed out of RTU he would go before a Flight Evaluation Board or FEB. The FEB was a legal proceeding and legal counsel represented the student. Based on the findings of the board, the student might be reinstated into RTU training, he might be assigned to a different type aircraft (usually a multiengine transport type) or he might have his wings taken away.

A key part of the evidence at an FEB was the grade book. Each grade sheet was very closely scrutinized. It was expected that grade sheets would be an unbiased and accurate reflection of what the student accomplished on each flight and of how well he did.

Letter Excerpts

In a letter to my folks I wrote of the enjoyment and reward I was getting from teaching others to fly an F-4.

> *For the first time last week I took off in the back seat with a student in the front who had never flown the F-4 before. It was quite an experience from the standpoint that I was completely responsible from the takeoff to the landing - from the back seat! It wasn't unlike the feeling I had when I did my first solo takeoff in the T-41. 'Now you've done it. You have no choice but to land this thing all on your own.' In the above case, my student, Greg, was first rate. With some relief he began doing very nice landings after I did one back seat demonstration.*

I continued about the immediate rewards of seeing your student's performance improve as a direct result of your one on one training.

> *It still is very rewarding to teach him things he has never done before in an airplane and see the progression from a steep learning curve. It is definitely more exciting than teaching a ninth grade class what Shakespeare really meant when he wrote Hamlet. I guess no matter what our job is we all end up as teachers sooner or later. I think I enjoy being a teacher more than most. Perhaps it is inherited.*

As I read those lines twenty some years later, I find them most prophetic.

Four Different Syllabi

We had four types of classes in RTU. The B syllabus was for pilots and WSO's who were fresh out of UPT or UNT (pilot training and navigator training). The class lasted for seven months. The C syllabus was for experienced pilots and WSOs who were going to the F-4 for the first time. It took about four months to run through a C class. Many C syllabus pilots, for instance, were coming from T-37s and T-38s where they had been IPs. The T syllabus was the easiest and shortest and was for prior F-4 experience pilots and WSOs. A T class was with us for about two months. The last type was the I syllabus and was the class I had just completed at Luke. It was the lollypop of classes because the IPs got to do a lot of front seat flying.

An interesting note about the I syllabus. The Air Force sent four of us all the way to Arizona for two and a half months to attend an I syllabus course where we had to fly F-4C aircraft. Luke flew only C models of the F-4. At the same time there were a couple pilots from Luke attending an I syllabus course at Homestead where they had to get checked out in an F-4E because Homestead only flew the E model. Now figure that one out.

During my four years at Homestead I taught more classes than I can remember and we taught all of the four different syllabi. The B syllabus was the most common and the one I liked the best. The typical B course class was about 14 pilots and 14 navigators. They were usually all second lieutenants and very impressionable. They were very motivated, studied hard, and easy to mold. I also found it very rewarding because they had a very steep learning curve. Just a short time before we got them they had been flying trainer aircraft and now we were teaching them to do things in a plane that the average civilian wouldn't be able to comprehend. These young men were quick learners and were the tops in their classes or they wouldn't have gotten Fighter assignments.

Washing Out

Occasionally we would get a pilot in from UPT that shouldn't have made it that far. How this happened I didn't know. Perhaps he had just been lucky and got all lenient check pilots or maybe someone was looking out for him. Whatever the reason, it caused the student and us a lot of grief. It was heart breaking for the instructors because we only had students who wanted to be there and when we found one that didn't have what it took, it was our duty to him and the Air Force to see that he not make it through RTU. A student was allowed three extra rides in a phase and a total of ten extra rides in the course before coming up for elimination. The 'chiefs' at wing headquarters really resisted washing pilots out. It was like they felt the wing wasn't doing its job if we didn't graduate everyone who entered training.

When I returned from Luke, the 308th was in the middle of a B syllabus course. In fact, my very first sortie as an IP was a night ground attack sortie. What a way to cut your baby teeth! But, there was one pilot by the name of Lt. Doug who the squadron had identified as a likely case for washing out. He had failed or pinked many rides already and we hadn't even gotten into the hardest phase, air to air. Doug was the subject of numerous conversations between the squadron commander and the DO. More than once he was up for elimination rides but he always pulled through by a whisker. And then, one day he didn't. He went before an FEB and the recommendation was to put him back in training and complete the course by flying only with an IP. We did as we were told and Doug went on to his gaining unit at Hill AFB, Utah. We later found out that Doug only flew four times at Hill and they were mostly evaluation flights. He was FEB'd and he lost his wings. If we had been allowed to wash him out he most likely would have gone on to a multiengine airplane and continued as a pilot. We did Doug a great disservice by not washing him out.

An Inept Wing Commander

Our wing commander at this time was Col. Jeb who had been a POW in North Vietnam. Col. Jeb was shot down as a major and received two promotions while a POW. He emerged from captivity as a colonel. After a staff job or two he was made recurrent in the F-4 and assigned as the wing commander at Homestead. Col. Jeb was mentally unfit for command. There were horror stories of how, at his staff meetings, he would scream and berate some of his officers for even the slightest provocation. The result was that no one would tell Col. Jeb anything he didn't want to hear.

One of Col. Jeb's more notorious pastimes was driving his blue staff car with its distinctive white top out to the RSU unit by the end of the runway and grading landing patterns. Later he would contact the squadrons with his results and at times suggest corrective action to be taken for what he considered improper patterns and landings. It didn't take long for this to result in pilots doing a 'white top' check first thing when coming back to the pattern. If the white top was at the RSU they full-stopped instead of doing practice approaches. Col. Jeb was also merciless on his Supervisors Of Flying, SOFs. It became a standing joke for the SOFs to go up to the tower and come back at a later time having been fired by Col. Jeb. At first this was a very traumatic experience for a SOF but then it became rather routine and the SOFs were soon reinstated.

Col. Jeb was the reason Lt. Doug wasn't washed out of RTU. He was the reason Doug later lost his wings. When Col. Jeb was promoted to Brigadier General and sent to Hurlburt Field to be in charge of Special Operations we all breathed a sigh of relief. However, he had been there less than a year when we received inquiries about B/G Jeb's involvement in the Lt. Doug affair. There were other inquiries also. Then we found out that B/G 'J' was very quietly being court marshaled and mustered out of the Air Force and into retirement.

A student by the name of 'Jobie' also had troubles in our squadron. His IP was an influential flight commander who refused to accept that 'Jobie' was unfit to fly a fighter. In Jobie's case he would go up and fly two or three really good missions and then almost kill himself by doing something really unpredictable and dangerous. His flight commander nursed Jobie almost all the way through the air to air phase when

Jobie ran out of extra sorties and was eliminated and FEB'd. In Jobie's case he ended up getting a C-130 and he actually seemed happy at the way it turned out.

Washouts at RTU were infrequent. I never heard of one in anything but a B syllabus class. During my four years at Homestead we ran through about six 'B' classes and encountered three real problem students of which two were washed out. One of them was a student of mine, Lt. Ken. Ken started out OK but when we got into the air to air phases he started running into trouble. Ken tried really hard and he so wanted to make it through but he had a real problem with situational awareness, being able to keep up with what was going on around him. At least twice while I was flying with him I think he would have killed himself if I hadn't taken corrective action.

On an ACM sortie we were doing 2 v 1 coordinated attacks where one plane attacks while the other repositions. When ready, the not-engaged fighter calls the engaged fighter off and he takes up the attack. It is similar in ways to two foxes chasing a rabbit. The key is to receive acknowledgment from the engaged fighter that he is coming off and then to visually confirm that he is indeed coming off before you proceed with your attack. During the final phase of an attack, a fighter has to get into the same vertical plane as his target. If two planes are attacking at the same time then they are both in the same plane and in great danger of having a mid-air. Ken had just called the engaged fighter off and called himself engaged. I always was especially alert when with Ken and when he called engaged I immediately asked if he saw the other fighter come off. I had very limited visibility out the front of the aircraft and the last I saw the other fighter was in front of us herding the target around and we were settling right into his vertical plane. Ken responded that he had seen the other fighter come off. I waited several more seconds and then just couldn't stand it anymore. I told Ken I had the aircraft. I unloaded to zero G and quickly rolled inverted to look beneath us. What I saw turned my blood cold. We were seconds away from merging with the other fighter who was still engaged. I quickly rolled and pulled to get out of the other fighter's plane and called a 'knock it off.' We were just about bingo fuel anyway, so we went home and I pinked Ken for a dangerous sortie.

On another occasion we were on a GAT mission doing pop-up deliveries. I previously mentioned the danger of continuing an attack from inside the MAP and that is what happened to Ken. He took too long in finding his target, floated the airplane to well inside the MAP and when he at last located his target I was sure he would call off dry. I could see the target below us and to hit it would have required a 60-degree dive. We were doing 20-degree attacks. I confirmed with Ken that he had the target and then couldn't believe my eyes as he started pulling the nose down into a dive. I let him go as far as I possibly could hoping he would recognize the dangerous situation that was developing. I finally took control and recovered the aircraft. Ken pinked that ride also plus many others with other IPs. He could really fly a good airplane at times and he had a great attitude and desire to fly a fighter but he could not think three dimensionally in a fluid situation and that is a must for a fighter pilot. During stressful tasks he also lost situational awareness – sight of the big picture.

As an instructor I tried to allow my students to learn by doing and thinking. Sometimes you can learn more from one mistake than you can from doing something correctly ten times. I was flying a transition sortie with a major in a T syllabus and the major was having trouble holding it all together - he was way behind the aircraft. He had been off flying status for several years and was getting recurrent and it wasn't coming easily. We were making a level turn to initial from ten miles and my major was totally absorbed in maintaining his altitude and keeping his airspeed at 300 knots during the turn. He just forgot about one thing. We only had 90 degrees of turn to make to be lined up with the runway and he should have been looking outside and only cross-referencing his instruments. Instead, he was 100 percent on instruments. I could hear him talking to himself about airspeed and altitude. We passed the runway heading and continued turning. 360 degrees more and we passed the runway heading again and we were still turning. As we were approaching the runway heading for a third time I told him to roll out. Later, I realized I let him go too far. I allowed him to embarrass himself and there wasn't anything to be gained. Allowing one 360-degree turn would have accomplished the same thing.

On another occasion we were fighting air to air. We had called off our wingman and then we engaged. I watched as the target aircraft very quickly pulled up into a vertical zoom. By his relative motion I knew he had a lot of energy, more than we did, and the prudent thing to do would be to half follow but wait below for him to fall off and come back down. Then we could hammer him because I didn't think he had maintained sight of us. My student, however, had different ideas. He followed but with a hundred less knots of airspeed. As we were passing 70 degrees of climb I glanced at the airspeed indicator and saw it was already down to 350 knots and falling quickly. Rather than call it off or take control of the aircraft I reached down and tightened my lap belt for the wild ride that was sure to come. We were pointed straight up when my student realized the situation we were in. All I heard from him was, "oh, oh." I knew that as long as we kept the stick centered the airplane might do all sorts of crazy things but in the end the pointed end would again be pointed downhill and soon after we would regain flying airspeed. I just reminded my overly aggressive young fighter pilot to keep the stick centered. Two things could have happened. We could have fallen forward and had to deal with a bunch of nasty negative G's during the recovery or we could somewhat comfortably fall off on our backs. The first thing that happened was the F-4 came to a stop in its vertical zoom, then it started to slide backwards still in a vertical attitude. The heat waves from our exhaust engulfed our canopy and then, mercifully, we fell over on our backs and started acting like a normal plane again. The target pilot, a highly experienced IP, gleefully watched this happen, ruddered his nose down and came after us for an easy kill. When it was all over I told my aggressive but now shook-up student to be careful 'to not let his fangs puncture his G-suit.' In debriefings, the maneuver we did was called the falling leaf and almost always results in losing the advantage.

The T Syllabus

T syllabus classes were really fun. The class duration was short so we zoomed through the phases in record fashion. The pilots all had previous F-4 experience and didn't very often scare you with their flying. One such class was really special. It was entirely made up of an Air National Guard unit from Ellington AFB, Texas. This unit was transitioning from A-7s to F-4s. Our students had more F-4 experience on average than we did. In fact, one of them had invented a tactical formation that years later still carried his name, the Jo-Bob Box formation. Most of them were airline pilots during the week and guard fighter pilots during the weekends; weekend warriors. We allowed their experience to determine how to run the course. Often times we allowed our students to even brief and lead although we never allowed them to forget that we were the instructors and were thus responsible. Our 'students' appreciated how we adapted to their experience level and we all had fun doing it. They were aware that we could have done it strictly by the book.

The only difficulty we encountered was with getting our students to conform to AFR35-10 standards - cut their hair. The Air Guard was always more lenient in grooming standards but as long as they were assigned to the 308th as students they were active duty and had to comply with 35-10. The matter came to a head when the Guard commander intervened and suggested that if they wanted to continue flying fighters to get a haircut. They did and the problem vanished.

The only problem with the T Syllabus was that as IPs we didn't get to fly in the front seat at all. Since we were dealing with experienced fighter pilots they were allowed to lead under the supervision of an IP. In all of the other syllabi the lead IP was in the front seat with either a student WSO or an IWSO in his back seat. In the I Syllabus we got to fly just about everything from the front seat.

The C Syllabus

The C Syllabus class was nice in a different way. These students came to us as fully qualified aircrew members from other aircraft, with most of them coming from T-38s where they had been IPs themselves. We also occasionally had students from T-37s, FAC aircraft and even multi-engine planes. I soon discovered that it made a big difference what kind of plane a student was coming from. As a rule, the slower the aircraft the slower the student would think in the F-4 and the harder it would be to get him performing at the speed of an F-4. A good example was students coming from T-37s and T-38s. They were all IPs with the same mission, training student pilots. But, the T-37 only flew at half the speed of the T-38 and it took much patience with these slower thinking students. It was easier to teach a second lieutenant right out of pilot training because his last plane was the faster T-38. Now, I must caution that this was only my observation, not the results of a scientific study.

During my tour at Homestead, the problem was recognized at Air Force level and they began sending everyone through a fighter lead in (FLIT) program where they flew the AT-38 which was a T-38 that had been modified so it could drop bombs. At FLIT they got everyone used to flying and thinking at an F-4's speed. FLIT also served as a filter to catch pilots who lacked the aptitude or desire to go on to a fighter aircraft.

One of our students in a C Syllabus was 'Westy' Westmoreland, a very well-liked T-38 IP from Laredo. Westy was tall, probably right at the max height for fighters, and good-natured. He always had an amused smile on his face and a pleasant word to all. I had flown several times at Laredo with Westy as my IP and the thought of me now flying as his IP made me feel a bit awkward. But not so to Westy. He really showed his character by being the best student he could be. The C Syllabus was nice because we got our front seat lead missions along with experienced students whom you could breathe a little easier with.

The I Syllabus

The I Syllabus was also nice. We got to do all of the flying in the front seat. I should rephrase that to say we got to ride in the front seat. Much of what we did was teaching the student who was in the rear cockpit how to fly the plane. As I think about it, the fear factor was much lower sitting through a back seat landing where I could look out the front 'picture window' and see everything that was happening. When in the back I had to use a combination of looking at instruments and craning my neck trying to see around the student's helmet to evaluate and monitor what the student was doing. While in the 308th we only had one I Syllabus class.

Grade Books - Ugh

I already mentioned grade books and grade sheets. These were so important you could always find the squadron commander and operations officer on Saturday morning going through each student's grade book reviewing the previous week's progress and making notes to IPs should questions come up. As an IP we always reviewed at least the previous sortie and sometimes several before flying with a student. As much as we hated writing grade sheets after a sortie, we all knew how important it was to the student's training to provide a written record of what and how he did on a particular sortie lest he forget mistakes from rides past and repeat them.

When we did air refueling it was always in combination with a syllabus sortie, frequently ground attack and then we had two grade sheets to fill out. If you were number one or three, and you had a crew solo (student pilot and student WSO flying together) on your wing you also had to fill out grade sheets for them. My worst mission for grade sheets was an air refueling to the range where I was the IP in the backseat of number three. In a four ship there is always an IP in the front seat of one but on this particular sortie, lead ground aborted. I ended up leading a 3 ship from the rear cockpit with two crew solos on my wing. I had students everywhere - five of them. And, since this was to the tanker I had ten grade sheets to fill out after the flight! I think the squadron supervisor made a poor decision to allow the flight to continue but staying on 'the sortie line' was very important.

Continuation Training

The Air Force recognized that IPs in an RTU setting needed to get front seat time just to maintain their own proficiency not to mention morale. So, in our sortie budget or PFT (Programmed Flying Table) we were allowed sorties for Continuation Training, CT. At times we were able to get the aggressors to come in for some really fun DACT or we got to go on deployments to exercises such as Red Flag and Maple Flag. In addition, for a while anyway, the wing sponsored a wing turkey shoot on the last Friday of the month. Each squadron put up a four-ship to fly to the range to drop bombs. They flew low levels terminating in a LADD delivery. The smoke from the flight lead's practice bomb was used for determining accuracy for Time On Target (TOT). It wasn't uncommon to have TOTs to within a second or two. The TOT was given so many points as were the bomb and strafing scores with the winning squadron being determined in this fashion. Awards were presented at happy hour at the O' Club.

The best deal I ever had for continuation training was going out west to Nellis to attend Operation Red Flag. Red Flag was set up during the Vietnam War in response to the inordinate number of airplanes we were losing. A study showed that a pilot was most likely to be shot down during his first two weeks of war so Red Flag was set up to give him that two weeks. It worked. Our combat losses dropped dramatically.

We took 12 airplanes to Red Flag, but only ten were to be flown in the Red Flag exercise. The other two were participating in Operation Green Flag which was highly classified at that time. I'll come back to Green Flag later.

Operation Red Flag took place on the sprawling Nellis Range complex. The area took up a good part of the state and included the infamous area 51, or dreamland as we called it. It also included areas where below ground nuclear testing had taken place years earlier. Each test site was readily visible from the air because the nuclear blasts left small craters.

Area 51, Dreamland

When flying to the exercise area of the Nellis range complex our flight path skirted area 51. The actual mystery airfield and accompanying buildings were probably 20 or more miles away but could be seen in the distance. In our aircrew in-brief, we were warned in no uncertain terms that to venture even one mile into area 51 meant an immediate recall to Nellis with an immediate landing, a debrief and being sent home. The repercussions were quite severe and the warning made enough of an impression on us that over flights were virtually unheard of.

At the far northwestern corner of the range complex was Tonapah Air Base, another classified area that now is famous because that is where the Stealth Fighter, the F-117, was based.

Several fighter squadrons were invited for each Red Flag Exercise. In addition, support aircraft also deployed in to play their role in the simulated war. We had C-

141 aircraft that were intelligence gatherers, KC-135 tankers for refueling support, B-52s for high altitude density bombing, AC-130 gunships, OV-10s for Forward Air Controllers, RF-4s for photo reconnaissance and others. Each weekday had morning and afternoon mass attacks on the heavily defended targets on the range complex. Each fighter squadron was assigned a day when they were in charge of planning the attacks, tasking all of the units with a tasking message, doing a mass briefing for all participants and finally conducting a mass debriefing.

The mass briefing took place in an auditorium in the Red Flag operations building. When all of the participants were seated, there were few seats left over. Frequently there were two or three hundred people at the briefings. The mass briefer was usually a Lt. Col. operations officer and planning was a squadron effort taking a good part of the previous day. The mass briefing began three hours before the first take off and lasted 30 to 45 minutes. Overhead slides showed call signs and frequencies, takeoff times, tanker refueling times and most importantly de-conflicted Times On Target (TOTs) plus much other vital information that was needed by everyone for a successful coordinated attack. Following the mass briefing individual units got together to more specifically brief their parts and following that individual flights got together for flight briefings.

Arrayed against us was a well-organized and well practiced permanent enemy force. These guys did this every day of every week all year long. There were aggressor airplanes, surface to air (SAM) sites using authentic Soviet equipment, AAA sites and ground forces that would step out from behind a rock and shoot what was nicknamed a smoky joe, a simulated shoulder launched heat seeking missile that left a short smoke trail in the sky. Most of these threats had their own particular tracking radars that activated our Radar Homing And Warning (RHAW) gear in the cockpit. All of this threat activity was funneled into a central computer. All aircraft carried special transponders that continually fed position, airspeed, altitude, attitude and weapons status into the central computer.

For the end of the mass debrief, Red Flag personnel gave an exercise summation and showed reenactments of particular engagements during the day. You could sit there and watch a three-dimensional replay of your aircraft as it was engaged by F-5 aggressors or as it was targeted and simulated shot down by an SA-6.

During the early part of the week many planes were 'shot down' but as aircrews learned from their mistakes, the losses dropped off quickly.

The classified Green Flag exercise was a mini Red Flag scenario except we didn't have to plan or brief the mission. The Green Flag staff did the briefing. Each fighter unit got two slots for Green Flag and we flew in support of Green Flag for the entire two weeks. My squadron commander at the time, Lt. Col. Tim McConnell, did the choosing for the highly coveted slots - although almost no one knew what it actually involved - and he chose himself and a very experienced IWSO and me with my crewed IWSO, John Lawson, nicknamed 'Lowboy.' I felt honored to be chosen because it turned out to be an experience of a lifetime.

Green Flag - Flying Against MiGs

Before we flew the first time we were given a security briefing where we signed statements saying we would not divulge the classified aspects of Green Flag under great penalty. Then we were briefed on what it was all about. After 20 years surely it is no longer classified but at the time if word had gotten out it would have been very embarrassing to the State Department. The US had gotten very friendly with a third world country that formerly had been friendly with the Soviets. We gave this country a lot of military aid to include F-4s. In fact some of our F-4s at Hahn were refurbished and sent to this country. This country in return, very quietly gave us some of their MiGs and other Soviet equipment that we then could train with. For the first time we could directly compare our equipment against theirs. The MiGs were stationed at the desolate and classified Tonapah Air Base. It wasn't likely anyone on the ground would ever see one and they were always in hangers whenever a Soviet satellite was due to be overhead.

Maj Olson on right with crewed WSO, Capt John Lawson

In Green Flag we got to fly air to air BFM against MiG 17s, MiG 21s and MiG 23s. What an experience that was. Before this I had seen one MiG that was a static display at Luke AFB. I think it had been pieced together from several crashed planes from the Korean War. I had studied pictures of these planes for years so I could visually recognize them from a great distance. I had memorized their capabilities. I had learned how to fight them with an F-4 and how to not fight them.

Suddenly, I had one right on my wing, a MiG 21. The pilots, of course, were USAF on special assignment - I discovered that one of them was a friend of mine from F-4 RTU at MacDill. Now the pilot of this MiG was directing me through maneuvers so I could see firsthand what a 'Fishbed' (NATO designation of a MiG 21) could do. I was extremely impressed. I had always been told about its turning capabilities and to never slow up and turn with one and now I found out why. From a neutral, co-altitude, co-speed position we began maneuvering against each other. In one turn he was at my 6:00 in a position to shoot me down. I was awed by how it could turn. However, the F-4 was much more powerful and could use the vertical to great advantage. Lesson learned was don't slow down when fighting the Fishbed and keep a vertical fight going.

I couldn't wait to fight the MiG 23, Flogger. When we got our first information on this plane when I was in Germany we were told that it could out accelerate and out-turn the F-4. In other words if you met one in the air and he saw you he could chase you down and then shoot you down. Don't mess with the Flogger. Now I had an opportunity to actually see it do this. What I discovered was amazing. The Flogger was much faster at accelerating but it couldn't turn well at all. If you saw the Flogger you could easily defeat it by just turning into it and causing an overshoot. The problem, though, was the size of the MiG 23. It looked like our F-111, a swept wing fighter-bomber, but it was half the size and extremely hard to see in the air. Without GCI radar to warn you, it would be unlikely to pick one up before it was firing at you.

After several BFM type missions against the different MiGs we flew actual air-to-ground missions with the MiGs acting as the aggressor aircraft. Our scenarios were very similar to what the Red Flag folks were flying except our aggressor aircraft were the real thing. Also, our flying was done between the Red Flag morning and afternoon exercises.

Eating an Apple is a Piece of Cake!

A typical mission involved flying north along the eastern edge of the range complex, skirting by the edge of area 51, and hitting a tanker to top off our gas tanks. We refueled at 18,000 feet. I'd never refueled below 26,000 feet before and I made a delightful discovery. I'd heard stories about how in Vietnam pilots became so good at air refueling that one pilot actually ate an apple while refueling. This seemed impossible to me. It took all of my concentration and then some to stay steady on the boom. Now, here I was at 18,000 feet, hooking up for my first time at an altitude that was a mile and a half lower and the air much thicker. It was an absolute piece of cake to refuel. I was amazed and delighted. So that is how they did it in Vietnam. Now, if I only had an apple!

The Air-to-Ground Battle

> *Simulated enemy territory began just to the west of the tanker track. When we left the tanker we pushed over to begin a dive towards the brown desert floor. We assumed the enemy had been watching us on radar and we wanted to get out of radar coverage to preserve some element of surprise. Visibility was a hundred miles or more. Distant mountain peaks 50 miles away seemed close enough to reach out and touch. The terrain was largely volcanic in origin providing the predominant colors; dark brown, burnt sienna, and dirty orange. Ancient lava flows now were ridges that we had to quickly pop over during our low-level ingress to our targets lest we highlight ourselves to the enemy's radar. The desert floor came rushing up*

to us. We went into our ingress formation of two-mile trail. Our thoughts were this formation would be harder for an aggressor to find us both and if he attacked lead, number two might get an easy kill. If he attacked two, lead would make a hard turn back into the aggressor.

We were going as fast as we could go, about 540 knots. At this speed the controls were extremely sensitive. I could feel the stabilator vibrating through the stick to my gloved hand. The terrain was flashing by on either side as we sped up a valley. I reminded myself of the primary task - avoid the rocks. 90 percent of attention is outside clearing the terrain and navigating. 10 percent is scanning the skies looking for bandits. Occasionally I would catch a fleeting glimpse of lead when he would roll into bank for a turn or momentarily plan-form himself as he pulled up to pop over a small ridge.

We were each carrying six live Mk-82 five hundred pound bombs. We had our switches set up to ripple them off over the target with half second spacing between each bomb. I double-checked my switches; bombs ripple, direct, mills set. All I needed was to select master arm and I should get an amber 'arm' light. I didn't want to have to re-attack the target because of a switch screw-up. Up ahead and fast approaching was the IP, the last turn point before the target. 'Lowboy' (John Lawson, my back seater) reviewed our IP to target procedures. John was one of the best. Lead had his own IP to target heading so we would be de-conflicted from each other's bomb fragmentation.

Our route was taking us across a dry dusty, lonely lakebed. I could see lead ahead of me. Suddenly, his flight path was intercepted by white smoke trails, perhaps a dozen of them. At 540 knots there is only one option. Push it up. Go faster and maybe a bit lower. These must be the 'smoky joe's' we had been briefed about. The lonely lakebed wasn't as lonely as it appeared. It concealed trucks covered by desert- camouflaged netting. If our presence wasn't known before it sure was now.

Over the IP I rolled into 80 degrees of bank and pulled into a 5-G turn. I heard one grunt from John in the back seat. I knew he was spending all of his time looking out right now. We hadn't seen any MiGs but they had to be there. I hacked my clock and readjusted the throttle to slow back to 540 knots. Rolling out on the final attack heading I glanced at my IP to target map to double-check my landmarks. Gosh, things were happening fast. I felt like I was hanging on by my fingernails.

Our weapons delivery was going to be from a pop-up and we wouldn't be able to see the target until climbing in the POP. Being off course even a little right now would have a drastic result. I fine tuned our course and then picked up a small landmark that marked the pop-up point. I advised John that we were almost there and then we were. I pulled back on the stick into a 4-G climb. At 20 degrees I eased off and started looking for the *target. It should be left 10:30, a SAM site with a dirt service road leading to it. There it was! I started a left roll when my attention was abruptly derailed. A large silver flash went right by my cockpit. A quick glance showed it was a MiG 21. He must have been in his attack on us when I began my pop-up. Lucky me. I had inadvertently caused the MiG to overshoot. I continued my roll, reverting all concentration back to the target but mumbled to John, "did you see that MiG?" He had. Rolling out, I checked my dive angle. It was right on. I was tracking right to the SAM site. John called out the pickle altitude and I mashed the pickle button and held it for three seconds, more than enough time for all six bombs to be released.*

I pulled out of the dive a ton and a half lighter and began a shallow climb to the right and our egress back home. A glance back at the target area showed small, dirty gray clouds of smoke over the SAM site. We would get feedback later on our bombing accuracy. Now, in order of priority, see if that MiG was still in the area and try to get back with lead for mutual support on the way home.

Dangerous Flying

Red Flag was probably one of the most demanding and dangerous non combat missions in the Air Force. It was accepted that there would be losses from the training and there were, usually two to four crashes a year.

One early afternoon after landing from our mid-day sortie, a large crowd of crew chiefs were waiting for us as we pulled into our parking spot. I was really puzzled by this. After engine shut down, my crew chief climbed the ladder to my cockpit to give me my pins. He announced that he was really glad to see us. I asked why and he told me that it had been announced that an F-4 had crashed on the range and they didn't know who it was. There were only a handful of F-4s airborne and they had thought it might have been me. It turned out to be an F-4 from a Texas guard unit that shared an operations counter with us. That afternoon it was a very strange feeling to look at the scheduling board and see one line with a call sign, two aircrew names, a take-off time and no landing time.

Disaster Again!

The very next afternoon we were again taxiing back to the chocks and again there was a crowd of crew chiefs. I was dumbstruck to discover that we were doing a replay of yesterday. An F-4 was again missing and they again thought it might have been us. It was the same guard unit. With the second loss they packed up and went home - minus two airplanes and four aircrew members. I couldn't imagine what a nightmarish return the unit was facing with four families left without husbands and dads. To this day I can't imagine how the second aircrew could have gone out the very next day after losing two friends in a crash and doing exactly the same thing.

Vertical Jinking

The accident investigations came up with the same findings for both airplanes. Both aircraft were operating normally at ground impact. Both aircraft had impacted the ground shortly after crossing a ridge. Upon interviewing other squadron aircrews investigators learned that both pilots of the accident aircraft had talked about doing vertical jinks to cross ridgelines. The accepted method of crossing a ridgeline while low level was to climb up until over the ridge and then to either roll into bank to pull back down or to push

Getting the flight together

over. Both of these maneuvers resulted in the aircraft being exposed to radar or enemy fire for up to 20 or 30 seconds. In a vertical jink, the pilot rolled completely inverted and then pulled down to achieve a dive followed by another rollout in time to pull up before impacting the ground. Both accident boards concluded that the pilots had performed vertical jinks and hit the ground. Vertical jinks were specifically outlawed after that. What a waste of four lives!

Red Flag was a lot of hard work and involved dangerous flying that we had trained for in preparation. Safety was always emphasized but to provide realistic training accidents were going to happen. Red Flag was also fun. It was always a real thrill when you got a large group of fighter pilots together. Invariably, long lost friends would be found. I came across several from previous assignments.

Big Time Gambler in Vegas

On two occasions I traveled with a group into downtown Las Vegas for a three-dollar steak dinner and some gambling. On both occasions I only carried ten dollars with me for gambling and when that was gone gambling became a spectator sport for me. I did side bets on both the craps table and on black jack. I observed to see how other players were doing and when I found someone who seemed to be on a winning streak I'd bet a dollar on him to win. The best I ever did was to get almost 20 dollars ahead. But, both nights found me broke within two hours.

A Five Hour Flight Home

I was again one of the lucky ones for the return trip to Homestead. We had twice as many aircrews at Nellis as we had airplanes. Since I didn't get to fly a plane to Nellis it was only fitting that I got to fly one back home and I did. We had a mass redeployment briefing for three 4-ships. We were scheduled to meet up with one KC-135 tanker for in-flight refueling that would allow us to make the five-hour flight nonstop. After the briefer finished with all of his standard slides he had one last slide. Every name of the 'gamblers' was listed with their net gains or net losses during the two weeks. There was only one person who was leaving Las Vegas richer; a wife. She had won her money playing the slot machines. Now, that should tell you something. What happens in Vegas stays in Vegas!

We had a lovely sunny day for our redeployment. Everything was happening just as planned until fifty minutes after takeoff on the first fuel check after our tanks had gone dry. We were two thousand pounds short of everyone else. The only explanation was we had been shorted on gas. Aside from that everything was going smoothly and we were enjoying watching the countryside slip by almost seven miles below us and our tanker was right where he was scheduled to be. 'Lowboy' was the first WSO to get a radar contact so he directed the flight for the rendezvous and as expected he did a great job; the 4-ship fell right into position behind the KC-135. I was surprised when lead got on the boom first even though we had been two thousand pounds low on every fuel check. When lead directed someone else to get on next I couldn't believe it. I told John to get his charts out and start figuring emergency divert bases along our route because we were going to need one if for some reason we couldn't take on gas. When the second person finished and lead directed the third flight member to go next, I broke in and announced that we had less than two thousand pounds of fuel remaining and if we couldn't get gas we would be an emergency. Only then did lead allow us to get fuel. I was greatly relieved when, after hooking up to the boom, I saw the fuel indicator begin to rise. I stayed on the boom for 20 minutes and took on twenty-one thousand pounds of fuel. I had never taken more than six thousand during one refueling before this. My only explanation for lead failing to put us on the boom first is that he didn't hear our fuel check correctly. He never mentioned the incident after the flight.

Maple Flag

At a later time my squadron sent a deployment of six airplanes to Cold Lake, Canada to participate in an ongoing exercise called Maple Flag. It was run by the Canadian Armed Forces but the US was frequently invited to send participants. Maple Flag was a scaled down version of Red Flag but instead of a mountainous desert type terrain, you had the flat, indistinguishable terrain of western Canada. Cold Lake was located on the Alberta, Saskatchewan border. It wasn't my turn for a good deal so I missed out on this one and only know what I heard afterwards. The flying it seems wasn't all that great but in the evenings the Canadians taught our aircrews a wicked game involving a pool table, two billiard balls and a lot of very rough shoving. The game was called 'crud' and caught on like wildfire at every fighter base that attended Maple Flag.

"You're On Fire; Eject"

A fellow flight commander, Ed Tinney, went to Maple Flag and his back seater was Rick Sergeant, a highly respected IWSO. On one particular mission they had completed their bomb runs and were egressing the target area while looking out for the bad guys. Suddenly they heard on 'guard', the emergency radio channel, "F-4 heading 150 degrees at five thousand feet, you're on fire. I repeat. You're on fire. Eject." Of course that got everyone's attention and Rick said he told Ed, 'gee, I hope that isn't one of ours.' Then, Rick noticed they were heading 150 degrees and they were at five thousand feet. He turned around in his seat to look back and discovered the entire back part of their jet was in flames. Rick immediately informed Ed of his discovery and in the same breath, knowing that they could explode at any moment, said he was going to do a duel sequenced ejection at the count of three. He started his countdown but Ed told him to wait a second so they could analyze the situation. Rick's reply was there was nothing to analyze. They were on fire. Fires don't go out by themselves. Again he started his countdown and again Ed told him to wait. The third time, Rick told Ed to be in position because he wouldn't be stopped again. He ejected them and probably saved Ed's life. A chopper picked them up in less than 30 minutes.

The accident investigation revealed an afterburner fuel line had broken, fortunately a very unusual occurrence and not something anyone could have spotted. It just happened. This incident illustrated a much too common cause for fatalities during aircraft accidents – the aircrew waited too long to initiate ejection. I was briefed many times during my flying career about this tendency. About five years later an F-100 I was scheduled to fly had the same malfunction resulting in a fire and loss of the aircraft.

Air Defense Alert

In addition to teaching how to fly the F-4, the four squadrons at Homestead rotated the job of Air Defense Alert. Just as the 496th did at Hahn, we kept two airplanes on five minute alert - and we were the most active alert force in the Air Force. Our enemy wasn't the Soviets or the Chinese or the Libyans. It was the drug runners. When we practiced intercepts we frequently would have the target airplane slow up and put gear and flaps down to simulate a slow target such as a drug runner would be. We couldn't stay with a drug runner for too long because they could fly very low and slow and could stay airborne for a long period of time. Usually, our job was to make the intercept out over the water and keep surveillance on the suspect aircraft until a US Customs airplane could take off and make the intercept.

We did have some interesting stories to tell, though, and virtually all of them occurred at night because that is when the drug runners liked to fly, under the cover of darkness. We credited one of our pilots with a kill when the plane he intercepted, an old DC-3, turned back out to water where it eventually ran out of fuel and crashed in the ocean. The pilot died in the crash. Another drug runner who was handed off to customs tried to evade the customs pilot by flying very low. He ran into an antenna guy wire and was killed. Usually the drug runners were followed by customs until they landed in a prearranged spot, frequently a clearing in the Everglades. The customs pilot would alert other agents on the ground to respond and then watch helplessly as the plane was unloaded of its drugs and the bad guys escaped in a waiting vehicle. The money to be gained in running drugs was so great the airplane was considered expendable. Seldom did the agents on the ground get there in time.

Klinker, the Balloon Buster

The strangest of all alert stories, however, involved a 'radar balloon.' The balloon was shaped like a dirigible or blimp and contained a surveillance radar. The balloon was moored on one of the Florida Keys and was used to maintain radar surveillance of Cuba. When unreeled the balloon was at fourteen thousand feet and a real hazard to airplanes if you didn't know it was there. One day, the balloon got away! The cable broke and suddenly, this balloon was a much bigger menace to airplanes. It floated up and down the keys for a day and then started floating north over the Gulf of Mexico. The balloon finally lost enough helium to cause it to descend back to earth or in this case, to water. When it was just about on the water, a fisherman decided he just might earn some reward money if he captured this runaway prize. When he caught up to the floundering balloon, he securely attached the balloon's steel cable to his boat. 'Gotcha,' he thought, and then the balloon regained some of its buoyancy and instead got the fisherman. It pulled the end of the fishing boat up and up until the whole front end was out of the water. About the time the fisherman went over the side, the front of the boat broke off, the balloon continued going back up and the boat went down. All the way down. Four more boats and the balloon would be an 'ace.'

Finally, the Air Force was called in to see if they had a solution. 'Why yes, we'll shoot it down,' was the Air Force's answer and Homestead's Alert Force was scrambled. By now the balloon was back up to ten thousand feet and heading in the direction of Texas becoming more and more of a threat to air navigation. The Alert Force commander on duty was Navy Lieutenant Commander Pat Klinker, an exchange officer to the Air Force, and I was his supervisor in E-flight.

Pat intercepted the balloon and asked if he had permission to shoot it down. 'No, not yet,' he was told. It was being discussed at the highest levels. Finally, after almost an hour, with Pat just about out of fuel, he was told to shoot it down. Pat backed off several miles, got a good radar lock and shot a radar guided missile getting a direct hit on the balloon. The balloon quickly deflated and descended one final time. The fighter terminology for killing your target is 'splash.' Pat truly splashed his target that day. He also earned a lot of good natured ribbing and became known as 'the balloon buster.'

I never had such interesting missions although I was scrambled many times from alert. One scramble was especially notable because it happened at 2 am. I was about as sound asleep as one can get when the loud, nerve jangling klaxon sounded. I fell out of bed, somehow managed to get my flight suit and boots on and went racing for my airplane. When I got to it, John was already in the back seat and the crew chief had ground power on. I jumped into the front cockpit, got strapped in and began starting engines all the time hoping tower would call saying it was all a mistake, scramble cancelled. It didn't happen.

At five minutes my wingman and I were taking the runway with clearance to take off on a standard scramble departure. Acting purely on instinct because I still wasn't fully awake, I plugged in the AB and did one of the hottest takeoffs I'd ever done. With proper aft stick the F-4 will break ground at about 175 knots. By the time I got the stick back enough to take off we were at 200 knots. By level off I thought I was finally in there. However, after we had been airborne for a half hour I spotted lights on the ground, a lot of them. It was a city. Why, we must be over the Bahamas I thought. We had been given a lot of vectors from GCI and they must have... Then, I looked at our position off of Homestead TACAN and realized we were over Key West. That was when I realized that I was still disoriented and not functioning at 100 percent. Looking back on it I've always thought, 'if just one thing had gone wrong...' As it turned out, our target faded from radar before we got to it. It might have been anonymous propagation (a false target caused by certain atmospheric conditions), or it could have been a very low flying drug runner.

Clever Drug-runner

The drug runners were very resourceful and thought nothing of paying hundreds of thousands of dollars for a plane that they knew would only be used once before being discarded in the Everglades. I had heard that a pilot could clear more money in one flight than he could make in a career of flying legitimately - but they took tremendous risks and at stake was their freedom or even their lives.

One very resourceful drug runner became notorious in the Homestead sector because of his novel routine. He made runs from the Bahamas about once a month. He managed somehow to join up with a night airline flight from the Bahamas to Miami. I imagine he flew just a hundred yards behind and a little below the airliner so on radar he was merged with the airliner's radar return. An FAA controller, however, noticed a faint blip separate from the airliner just prior to Miami. The blip continued inland where it disappeared. Now alerted, other controllers began looking for a similar phenomenon and the pattern was revealed. I suspect the drug runner was eventually caught.

Range Control Officer

An additional duty I picked up shortly after getting back from Phoenix was that of Range Control Officer, RCO. There were many IPs that absolutely hated this duty but I discovered it to be quite enjoyable. The RCO duty lasted for one week and rotated among the squadrons whenever the base had one or more of its squadrons in a ground attack phase and that was just about always. The RCO drove the five hours north to Avon Park gunnery range on Sunday evening to be prepared for the first range flight early Monday morning. Avon Park was an Air Force installation that was built specifically to run and maintain two ranges, Bravo Range, used mostly by MacDill AFB, and Charlie Range, that was Homestead's. Co-located at Avon Park was a minimum-security federal prison.

Avon Park Gunnery Range

The Air Force only had one officer permanently at the range, usually an end of career lieutenant colonel, and he was in charge of a hundred enlisted people who were almost all civil engineering types; heavy equipment operators, who maintained the appearance of the ranges to include the targets. He also had some operations people who worked the range scoring systems and who also helped the RCO with his duties in the control tower. Additionally, there were the support facilities; a barracks building, the chow hall, an NCO club annex, small BX, a transportation unit for taking care of range vehicles and an administrative function to handle the routine personnel duties. A rescue helicopter flew over every day from nearby MacDill AFB. The chopper spent the day on the ground hoping it wouldn't be needed, then flew back to MacDill. A 4,500-foot emergency runway with arresting cables strung across was available for 'dire emergency' jet landings. The facility was a very low keyed, quiet place with few visitors other than the RCOs.

The RCO trailer was a 60-foot wide mobile home that had 3 bedrooms, a comfortable living room with TV and a very adequate kitchen. It was there strictly for the RCOs to use. During my many trips to Avon Park I usually had the trailer to myself. MacDill didn't have nearly as many flights to the range as Homestead and was much closer, a couple hours by car at most. Thus, the MacDill RCO frequently drove over for the day to cover his few missions. Or, if Homestead was having a light week, only one range would be open for both bases and Homestead usually got to provide the RCO.

The range tower was a 50-foot structure with an operations cab. The cab with its glass roof provided unobstructed viewing in all directions. The cab contained scoring equipment, range maps mounted on tables, several radios, telephones and a publications library. It was very comfortable and, of course, air-conditioned. Around the outside was a catwalk and protective railing. A low building at the base of the tower contained administrative and maintenance offices. It also had a large ready room with couches for relaxing if there was a long break between missions. A radio monitor receiver allowed the range crew to monitor for incoming flights.

The RCO Made It Happen

A typical range flight was a four ship usually of F-4s but I also controlled guard F-100s, A-7s and even helicopter gunships that hovered on the foul line and practiced shooting the machine guns at our strafe target. Flights were almost always well controlled by the four ship flight leads but a skilled RCO was an absolute necessity for a range mission to go smoothly and safely. For that to happen, the RCO had to set up a cadence to control the approximately 80 weapons deliveries of a four ship during its 25 minutes of active range time. The cadence went like this: 'One cleared, three, your score 65 at six.' A few seconds later: 'Two cleared, four, your score 120 at three.' As long as all four airplanes kept their spacing it went well. If the spacing got off, I'd give lead a chance to correct it and if he didn't then I would. 'Three, you're lagging, take it through high and dry.' If a pattern started getting ragged, that call would motivate everyone to pull it back together.

Range Safety

The RCO's primary job was range safety. He owned the range airspace and was responsible for what went on inside it. The scoring operations technicians who were there every week were all top-notch people and really helped me a lot. They made the job almost easy but if I ever found myself day dreaming I was, as Capt. Rodenhauser so aptly put it during pilot training, 'screwing up.' We had to be eternally scanning the skies for light aircraft that occasionally busted our restricted airspace or for turkey vultures that were a major menace to low flying F-4s. Also, as RCO I had to always know where all of my fighters were in the pattern. For instance I once had two call 'base' and almost immediately three, another student, called 'base' as well. I came back immediately with, 'three, are you base or downwind.' The sheepish response from three was that he was on downwind. I also had to be vigilant for range fouls; the most common fouls were for low pullouts for bombing and late firing or lazy pull-out for strafe. A dropping without clearance was considered dangerous and usually resulted in sending the offender home.

Of course any really gross foul could be deemed dangerous with the offender being sent home. One student did such a lazy pull out from a bombing run that I thought he was having aircraft problems and was going to crash. I actually told him to pull up and then I sent him home. I never heard any follow up on what the problem was but it was probably the classic lack of situational awareness.

Bird Strike!

One of the most dangerous of all events was the run-in at 500 feet and 500 knots following a low level to the range. The danger was in colliding with a 10 or 15 pound turkey vulture. One such incident occurred to my friend from Hahn, Mike Lichty.

He was flying on the bombing range at 500 feet and 500 knots (650 miles per hour) on a bomb delivery when he struck a buzzard. The bird smashed through the windshield, then hit the canopy jettison handle blowing the canopy off. It missed his head by a couple inches and then hit the side of his ejection seat doing extensive damage to it and making ejection impossible. There is no question that if the bird had hit him he would have died instantly and his back seater being a second lieutenant inexperienced navigator probably wouldn't have been able to recover the aircraft.

In Mike's case he got an immediate climb going, slowed down to reduce the effects of wind blast and did an emergency landing with cable engagement at Avon Park. Mike was a real pro and handled the emergency exceptionally well. He even received a 'well done award' from the TAC safety magazine.

Alligators R Us

Avon Park was a wildlife preserve and I saw many kinds of animals during my tours there. On one occasion as I was driving back from Charlie Range I came upon a wild pig with five little pigs (not three!) following in single file behind her. When next to the mother I slowed to match her pace. She obviously wanted to cross the road but my car was in the way. She would stop and I would stop. She would grunt and start trotting again with her piglets in tow and I'd start up again. After going through that routine several times I let her go on her way in peace.

And, yes, there were alligators galore. They were everywhere it seemed. One time I was relaxing in the ready room at the base of the tower when my next flight checked in. I ran for the door and threw it open only to discover I was about to step on a seven foot long gator that was sunning itself on the cement sidewalk. Unable to stop because of forward momentum I gave a firm push off with my trailing foot and leaped over it.

On my first trip to Avon Park as I was moving into the RCO trailer on Sunday afternoon I noticed there were paddle boats pulled up on shore by a lake that was right next to the trailer. That evening it was very hot and I thought it might be nice to take one of the paddle boats out which I did. I paddled around for a while and then swam for a few minutes before going to bed. I happened to mention it to the tower NCO the next day and his comment was, "do you know how many gators are in that lake?" I never did that again.

Orientation Flights

One of my all time favorite flights was giving orientation rides. The wing had an orientation ride program set up where deserving young airmen could have a chance to fly in the back seat of an F-4. We weren't instructed on what to do during an orientation ride so I developed my own scenario based on what many of my passengers wanted to do. During our briefing I always emphasized that this was their ride and if they didn't fully enjoy it I had not done my job. Most wanted to do at least some of the lower G aerobatics and some wanted to see it all.

My standard routine called for a normal takeoff with level off at 16,000 feet, then south along the keys to Key West where I did a TACAN penetration and low approach at Navy Key West. This was all quite benign maneuvering not much different from an airliner except you have a fantastic view. If my orientation rider was holding up well, we did a full afterburner 30 degree climb from Key West with a gentle roll to inverted as we approached 16,000 feet and another smooth roll back to right side up for the level off. If that went well, we entered our assigned area and did aerobatics. We would start with a gentle aileron roll, then I'd let my passenger try an aileron roll and some turns. If that was OK we did more advanced higher G maneuvering such as rudder rolls, loops, Cuban 8's, immelmans and then a split S to get back down to lower altitude. For the return to Homestead I liked to cancel IFR clearance and follow the keys back to base at 500 feet for some sightseeing.

I only had one orientation flight where I couldn't follow that pattern. I was giving a ride to a female first lieutenant who was a GCI Controller. During the briefing she told me that she wanted to see everything that we did when we were dog fighting so she could have a better appreciation of her job when she controlled jets in ACM. Everything went fine until the inverted level off. That was it. She wanted to go home immediately. We did and I did a long gradual descent to a straight-in landing. Worried about her self-esteem I told her that as far as I was concerned no one would ever know that we didn't do the mission as briefed. I also told her I admired her spirit because there were many young airmen who refused orientation rides. She at least tried.

A Four-Bedroom House

After we had been at Homestead AFB for about a year I was promoted to major. My commander at the time, Lt. Col. Mick Cooper, was really happy for me and said that I was immediately eligible for a four bedroom house. I applied and we were given one immediately. It meant a move that we would have to pay for but for such a short distance we didn't mind. Our new house location was much closer to the flight line and my squadron. Our back yard was a huge field which gave us very nice privacy. A bonus for the girls was on the other side of this field was the ceramics shop. Jill and Becky became frequent users. The base chapel, bowling alley and officers' club were at the far end of the field - all within easy walking distance. But, most important of all was that the girls, now 4, 12 and 13, no longer had to share a bedroom.

Filling the Wrong Square

About this same time I began a master's degree program. Jean had gotten her master's degree during the year I was in Korea and now it was my turn to catch up. I would later find out that the lieutenant colonel promotion board cared much more about my getting Air Force Command and Staff than a master's degree. I chose a program given by the University of Northern Colorado out of Greeley, Colorado. We did one course at a time and each course took one month. We bought our books in advance and had very lengthy reading assignments to prepare for the first meeting. Our instructor flew in on Friday afternoon and we met from five until nine pm and again on Saturday and Sunday for eight hours each day. On Sunday afternoon we had our mid-term exam and the next weekend was off to study for the third weekend.

On that Sunday afternoon we had our final exam and the course was finished. I did this twelve times in fourteen months and then had to pass the written comps to complete my degree requirements.

The 'Comps'

I took a week of leave to prepare for the comprehensive written tests. I set up our pop-up camper in the back yard and each day took all of my papers, notes, and books for two classes into the camper thoroughly studying those two subjects. A couple courses were electives and didn't need studying. The comps were given on Saturday and Sunday. Each day we had four questions to answer, two in the morning and two in the afternoon and we could write as much as we liked. I never received a numerical score. I was just notified that I had passed and I was awarded my Masters Degree in Psychology and Counseling.

Later, I was shocked to discover that the pass rate for the comps was only about 30 percent and we were allowed two attempts to pass. Most of the people in my classes were civilians from the local area and I gradually realized that many of them were really in the program to find solutions to their own personal problems. In a way it was a relief to me to know that some of them would never become licensed counselors.

And There Were Hurricanes

Hurricanes were a very real concern to us at Homestead. The base was just a few feet above sea level and the five miles of land that separated us from the ocean consisted of very flat terrain - there was nothing to lessen the fury of a hurricane's wind. To add to the danger, the houses in base housing were very flimsily constructed - far below the local building code standards. For example, our house had 24-inch apart studs in the walls; standard was 18 inches. The Air Force was aware of the flimsiness of this housing and had mandatory evacuation should the predicted winds exceed fifty miles per hour. During our stay at Homestead, Jean and the girls had to evacuate twice to northern Florida while I 'hurevaked' an F-4 to Shaw AFB, North Carolina.

An interesting note about hurricanes is that a few years after we left Homestead, Hurricane Andrew hit the Base and did so much damage, the Air Force decided to just close it. Base housing was literally wiped from the face of the earth. I can't even begin to imagine the personal losses to the thousands of people who lived there. I'm sure that most families lost just about everything they owned.

Our first evacuation was for Hurricane David. David was a minimal hurricane that was coming in from the south and had us very concerned. Maintenance was alerted to begin plans for readying the airplanes for possible evacuation but after David passed over Cuba it died out, degenerating into a slow moving tropical storm. This was on a Saturday. We felt relieved that we wouldn't have to pick up and leave. Very early Sunday morning, however, we had a base wide recall. David had regenerated to a dangerous hurricane and we had very little time to get the airplanes airborne for their evacuation.

Maintenance did a spectacular job and the first four ships began leaving within a couple hours. By noon and before the winds began picking up appreciably, we had everything flyable headed to Shaw AFB, North Carolina and everything else safely hangered.

Jean teamed up with many of the squadron wives and families and they 'convoyed' to the Orlando/Kissimmee area where they found rooms in a Holiday Inn. Of course, the women were completely on their own. We were so busy at the squadron with flight planning, giving or receiving briefings and pre-flighting airplanes that we had to rely totally on our wives to fend for themselves. We weren't worried at all, though. Air Force wives, as a rule, are quite self-sufficient out of necessity. It's a way of life.

As it turned out, David, that had been bearing down on Homestead, veered to the east a little sparing Homestead but made a swing back to the northwest making an almost direct hit on the Orlando area where our families had taken refuge. They managed to cope but had flooding in their motel rooms.

Meanwhile, the husbands (pilots and WSOs) were having a good time at Shaw AFB. The officer's club had been especially opened for us and we had a party that lasted until the wee hours. Since it was before cell phones, we didn't know about our wives enduring the wrath of David and partied with clear consciences. The next day we found that David had already passed by Florida and now was posing a threat to

F-4 IP Major Olson at Homestead AFB

Shaw. We were politely asked to go back home so Shaw could evacuate their RF-4s inland to safety. We did and they did.

Saint Elmo's Fire

It wouldn't be right to conclude this chapter without including a narration about a night flight I led to the range. I say this because the telling of this incident had such an impact on my father that he made a copy of it and read it frequently to classes that he substitute taught.

One thunderstorm I didn't enjoy very much occurred two weeks ago. I was leading a two-ship to the bombing range at night. We first refueled from a tanker and then proceeded to the range. On the way, we had to fly close to thunderstorms and with each flash of lightning the sky lit up quite brilliantly. As we approached the range 150 miles north of Miami the clouds parted and the weather was beautiful. On the way back home at 21,000 feet, I discovered that the storms had intensified. There was no longer a way to avoid them completely. Using the F-4 radar my back seater picked out a course that avoided the worst areas.

The first indication I had that things weren't routine was when I saw for the first (and only) time in my flying career the phenomenon known as Saint Elmo's Fire - drops of brilliant bluish white light streaming slowly over the canopy. They looked like drops of rain but I knew that at our speed rain couldn't adhere to the canopy surface. Shortly thereafter the whole world turned a brilliant white as one lightning bolt after another commanded our attention. We were really in the thick of it. Two thoughts occurred to me, one good and one bad. The bad was the F-4 has a well-established reputation for attracting lightning. The good was that I wasn't the one having to fly formation on the wing!

Then, I noticed that when flying wings level on my attitude indicator my heading was changing - that meant I had to be in a banking attitude and my attitude indicator wasn't right. I switched to my standby attitude indicator and my heading immediately swung 60 degrees. Now, I was starting to think I didn't know which end was up. With the help of ground radar and my primary and secondary systems I got through the thick of the storm and with a deep sigh of relief broke out at three thousand feet with the inviting and reassuring lights of Homestead's runway ten miles in front of me. I cleared my wingman off to take spacing for uneventful landings.

Without a doubt that was one of the more trying experiences I've had flying. Without an attitude indicator you can't fly if you can't see the ground or a horizon. That night I was seriously questioning the information my attitude indicator was telling me. After I landed I discovered it was erroneously showing me to be in twelve degrees of left bank and fifteen degrees nose low. It was a good learning experience and the next time it happens I'll be better prepared.

I arrived at Homestead as a captain with some operational seasoning under my belt. Four years later I departed Homestead as a major. I'd gained valuable experiences and training as an F-4 IP, a flight commander and squadron scheduler. We gained some of our most valued friends at Homestead and have fond memories that will last forever.

Next assignment - Korea, again!

Chapter Twelve

Back to Korea

Never fly with a pilot who is braver than you (WSO advice).

The Long Trip West

The journey began at three pm on the 10th of June. It was heart-wrenching to say goodbye to my girls. After one last hug with each, I turned and walked towards the departure gate. I was proud of the way Jean and the girls faced this required separation. They just accepted it. This was the Air Force. Dad would be back.

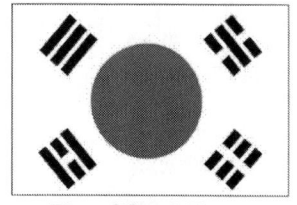

I flew from Miami to St. Louis landing there at 6:30. I collected my duffel bag and suitcase and proceeded to the military terminal where all military personnel were processed for the charter flights to the Orient. It didn't take long to figure out where I needed to go – I just located the longest line and dragged my duffel bag and suitcase in that direction. An hour or so later, after presenting my orders and ID card I had my ticket in hand.

Flag of South Korea

I reflected on my first trip to Korea and how I had changed from that hesitant, nervous second lieutenant radar controller to a much more confident major fighter pilot. I felt like I really knew my way around in the Air Force and was confident I would find old friends in Korea as well as make many new ones. Even though I had to leave my family behind for a year, I was excited about my new assignment and looked forward to new experiences.

Lost Ticket!

I had another hour to kill before our boarding call so I strolled around searching faces hoping to find someone I knew. I didn't find anyone but 'people watching' was still interesting. Since it was early evening I found a bank of pay telephones and gave one last call back to Jean and the girls. By now it was time to get in line for the bus that would take us out to our charter airplane. I noticed everyone up ahead had to show their tickets so I retrieved mine from my bag – they weren't there. I checked a second time and then stepped out of line where I could do a more thorough search of my bag. Nothing! I had lost my ticket. I thought to myself, no one else in the world could manage to lose his tickets so soon after receiving them. I was bordering on panic. I retraced my steps arriving back at the phone booth. That was the only place I might have laid them down. They weren't there. I felt a little better when I realized no one else could use them so whoever found them probably had turned them in to the ticket desk. When I approached the desk my look must have given me away because a young lady airman held up my tickets and asked if I was Major Olson. With a sheepish grin I admitted I was that absent minded officer and my heart resumed a more normal rhythm.

We boarded the most unusual bus I'd ever encountered. It was now night so I couldn't see the exterior very well but it looked like a bus to carry people who had luggage – poles to hold on to were abundant – and we drove out onto the tarmac to our waiting jumbo jet 747. The bus pulled up to the side of this huge airplane and I was thinking how were we to get way up to the entrance on the side of the plane. There were no stairs visible. When the bus pulled in right next to the plane's fuselage I began to understand just how unique this bus really was. The entire passenger compartment began to rise up on stilts until it was level with the plane's entrance – and we boarded.

At 11:30 that night our jet lumbered into the air and turned toward the west and San Francisco, our next stop. Due to the late hour the chattering around me soon dropped off to nothing and the overhead reading lights were winking off as I closed my eyes. Four hours later I awoke to the sound of the landing gear being lowered and we soon touched down in San Francisco. The time was 12:30 am in California.

A Very Long Day

We had little more than an hour at the terminal as many passengers disembarked and others got on. For those of us who were continuing on we dozed the time away. Soon, the doors were closed, engines started and we began taxiing. We took off at 2 am and turned north towards our last stateside destination, Anchorage. Within an hour I noticed the sky begin to lighten and it occurred to me that at this time of year, not too much farther ahead, the sun never set. The flight to Anchorage took five hours and we landed at 7 am under bright sunny skies.

We had one and a half hours of ground time for refueling and many people elected to disembark to see a little of Alaska, myself included. However, we were soon all back aboard and lifted off from America at 8:30 in the morning. Next stop – Yakota AB, Japan. With the plane flying west, the sun was a bright orange orb high in the eastern sky – and there it stayed for the next seven hours. Actually, during that very long morning the sun appeared to reverse its path across the sky and sank a little back towards the eastern horizon. We had taken off at 8:30 local time and landed in Japan at 7:30 local time. We were traveling west slightly faster than the earth's rotation.

After almost two hours on the ground in Japan we once again took off, this time for our final destination, Osan AB, Korea. We landed at Osan at 11 am. Using local times we had departed St. Louis a little before midnight and landed at Osan at 11 am but the trip really took 22 and a half hours.

Osan AB

An officer from my gaining unit met me at the terminal and helped me get to the Bachelor Officer Quarters (BOQ) and then to my assigned room that would be home for the next year. My escort had only been in Korea a couple weeks himself and he understood how I felt at that moment. He gave me a couple phone numbers if I needed anything, pointed out where the Officers' Club was and said he'd stop by the next morning. I immediately crashed onto my bed. Although it was early afternoon in Korea it was very early in the morning in Florida. What a crazy day it had been. Only 364 to go!

The 314th Air Division TACC

My new organization was the operations section of the 314th Air Division. The operations section was the Tactical Air Control Center or TACC. The TACC was in charge of the air defense and air-ground operations of Korea. In addition to two fighter wings, one at Osan and another at Kunsan (Osan also had an air defense alert contingent at Taegu), the 314th air division's TACC owned about eight radar units spread out across the country. The Republic of Korea Air Force (ROKAF) ran them. The TACC also had liaison officers from other commands such as Strategic Air Command (SAC), Military Airlift Command (MAC) and even the Navy. Because of this the task of coordinating all air operations at the TACC was greatly simplified. The TACC easily employed 500 people. Our upward chain of command went to a numbered Air Force in Japan, and then our overseeing command, PACAF, located at Hickam AB in Hawaii.

The TACC was located in a huge reinforced concrete building that was built into a mountain on one side of Osan AB. I had been told that when it was being built, the intention was to have the entire structure underground but when money began to run out, it was decided that if the majority of the structure was underground that would be OK. The exposed part of the building was camouflage painted to blend in with the surrounding rock and then tall pine trees were spray painted on the entire structure. It was appropriately named 'the tree house.'

The Pit

In the very center of the building was what was known as 'the pit' and that is where I worked. The pit was a large two story high room the size of a high school gym. It had large, tall plexiglass plotting boards that covered one whole wall, which showed a map of North and South Korea and even the closest parts of China and Japan. To each side of the main plotting board were the status boards. On these you could find the status of the USAF and ROKAF flying units; how many aircraft on 5 minute, 10 minute, 15 minute and 30 minute alert, or the status of weapons and munitions. There were boards showing the weather at the various bases and much much more.

Behind the plotting boards highly trained ROKAF airmen stood on varying height platforms and with grease pencils they plotted the tracks of all aircraft within our area of operation. This information came from outlying radar sites. Friendly aircraft were plotted in white, unknown aircraft were in yellow and unfriendly aircraft were in red. The plots were updated every two minutes and a six or eight minute history trail was left on the board. For friendly aircraft a two-letter identifier relating to the call sign indicated the identity of the track and unknown or unfriendly tracks had a number identifier that correlated to a target assignment board. The rules were detailed and exact concerning what action needed to be taken for identifying unknowns or in responding to unfriendly North Korean or Chinese tracks. The plotting boards contained a wealth of information, most of it classified secret and it took some time to learn to use them efficiently.

Parallel to and on the bottom floor in front of the plotting boards were two rows of radarscopes and desks, which were manned by personnel who fed information to the plotters behind the plotting boards. Facing the plotting boards beginning about half way across the room were four tiers or daises which contained long counters at which sat people of varied responsibilities and duties all of which contributed to controlling and directing an organized air battle during daily operations, exercises or war. Each tier was four feet higher than the previous so people standing on a lower tier wouldn't obstruct the vision of someone sitting down on the next higher tier. My position as the Senior Operations Duty Officer, SODO, was in the center of the top tier and I was the focal point for all of the other positions.

During routine operations, if the director of operations or his assistant wasn't in the pit, the SODO was in charge and if something of a serious nature came up he had hot lines to higher levels of command.

Because of my distance from the plotting boards I had a small TV screen and joy sticks at my position that controlled two closed circuit TV cameras – really high tech at that time. If I desired to I could zero in on a particular board and then zoom the camera in to enlarge the view to very large size. Of course it could also zoom in on just about any other object (or person) in the room and that ability sometimes did much to relieve late night boredom. Late one night I spotted a small white paper stuck to the far right corner of the plotting board. When I zoomed in on it I read, 'If you can keep a clear head during these times, perhaps you just don't understand the situation!' Clearly, someone was expressing a sense of humor. We had a favorite saying while at work. "Life is a bowl of cherries and this is the pit."

Above and behind my position was a recessed glassed in room which was known as the battle cab. This was where the colonels and generals stayed. From this sound proofed enclosure they were in a position to observe everything that was going on and had phones to everywhere. I found one phone in the battle cab where, late at night, I could quite easily call Homestead's command post and from there get a phone patch to Jean and the girls.

Another glassed in room to the side of the battle cab contained personnel and equipment of an intelligence nature that required a top secret SCI (Specially Compartmentalized Information) to gain entrance. I had possessed a TS clearance for the past dozen years but the SCI aspect of it required an even more thorough investigation of my past. I submitted the forms to get the clearance as soon as I received orders for Korea but my clearance didn't come through until I had only three or four months left in Korea. Obviously, access to this information wasn't necessary to do my job. When I finally did gain access, though, I was amazed to discover the extent of our intelligence capabilities. Even now, almost 20 years later, I am not at liberty to discuss anything specifically about that room.

My position at the TACC was Senior Operations Duty Officer (SODO). The position required a major or lieutenant colonel who was a fighter pilot. However, this requirement could be waived and during my year we had two non-fighter pilots who were SODOs. As time passed, however, I began to realize why the position called for a fighter pilot because both of these people were reluctant to stick their necks out and make decisions on their own. In fact, as I'll talk about later, one of them was fired because of this. A fighter pilot is trained and required to plan ahead, always have back-up plans in mind and to make decisions on his own. A multi-engine pilot is trained quite differently. He is taught to exercise the 'crew concept,' to get input from the other members of his crew and thus will minimize mistakes.

More on the SODO

The SODO position was the highest staff position in operations. We were authorized to have four SODOs. A SODO had to be on duty 24 hours a day every day. During my year we had several different shift schedules but the most common one was a day shift of 10 hours and a night shift of 14 hours. When we only had three SODOs we were forced to run this schedule which allowed one SODO to be on break while the other two ran the TACC. When we had four SODOs we had the luxury of shorter hours.

During peace time flying operations the Air Force person in charge of the daily flying including exercises was a major general (two stars). Should there be an outbreak of hostilities his boss in Seoul who was a three star would take over and the two star would advise him. During the normal eight to five work day, there were two people between the SODO and the two star. They were the TACC commander, a lieutenant colonel, and the Director of Operations (DO), a full colonel. During the day they were in their offices or on the dais with the SODO. During exercises they frequently could be found in the battle cab. During the duty day or during exercises the SODO frequently had plenty of help.

The two star general lived 500 yards from the TACC building, the tree house. If something really important came up the SODO's job required that he immediately contact the general and when time was available to notify the TACC commander and DO. Usually, however, during the day, time would be available to pick up the hotline and notify the DO that things were 'heating up' and he might want to come down to the pit. Then, if a situation continued to progress it would be the DO calling the general. That was the common sense way to do things because it not only relieved the SODO of the responsibility but it made the DO look good.

Calling the General

If an incident happened in the middle of the night, the procedure was different. An incident might be an unfriendly aircraft track popping up in North Korea heading south at a high rate of speed or maybe a fire fight in the demilitarized zone or an unintentional over-flight of one of our aircraft into North Korea. A very common incident at night was the detection of North Korean gunboats in South Korean waters attempting to drop off infiltrators. In this case the SODO was expected to take the first step to counter the incident such as scramble fighters and then call the general.

I knew the procedures when I began working on my own as a SODO but at night I dreaded the thought of an incident occurring that might require my having to call General Hefner. At 3 am during one night shift it finally happened. A high-speed aircraft track popped up heading south. Without hesitation I initiated a scramble of our alert aircraft and instructed my technician assistant to call the general and the deed was done. The general had been awakened out of a sound sleep at three o'clock in the morning and he was rushing in to the battle cab. Now, there wasn't a whole lot to do but monitor the situation. I watched the next two minute track go up on the board. It was still heading south. Two minutes after that, the next track showed the unfriendly was half way through a 180-degree turn. It was turning back to the north. Oh, no. My thoughts were I had called the general in for nothing.

Just about that time, General Hefner came rushing in. He hadn't gone to his battle cab but came directly to my duty station on the upper dais. After a quick glance at the plotting board he smiled and said, "good job, Ole, you scared them away." He then sat down and was chatting with me when the TACC commander and DO came rushing in. He thanked me for calling him and then went back home. General Hefner encouraged all of his SODOs to not hesitate in calling him at night and when the situation finally presented itself I didn't.

The SODO was the eyes and ears of two colonels and a general. This demanded his being abreast of everything that was going on during his tour of duty. Got a problem? Call the SODO. Either he knew it or could find out and his reputation grew. When in doubt, no matter who or where you were, call the

Land of the Morning Calm

SODO. He'll know. We got used to getting the most unusual of calls any time of

the day or night and if we had the time we tried to help even when it didn't fall under our job description. So, one evening I wasn't even a little fazed when a young woman called to ask for an appointment for a gynecological examination. She had dialed a wrong number. My number was one different from Ob/Gyn. Oh, but we laughed over that one.

Passed Over for Lieutenant Colonel

Toward the end of September another major and I were anxiously awaiting the results of the recent lieutenant colonel promotion board. When word came down lieutenant colonel Jim Sackett, my squadron commander, summoned me to his office. I knew immediately that I hadn't been selected. Squadron commanders were given the more distasteful job of giving out the bad news. DOs or even wing commanders called in the new selectees. I found out from Jim that the selection rate for that year was very low. The previous year's selection rate had been over sixty percent but for my selection year it was only thirty three percent. For Homestead, the base I was at when the board met, the rate was even lower, twenty three percent. The facts and figures only softened the blow. I was quite disappointed and had expected to make it.

In spite of knowing that after one pass over the selection rate drops off drastically – to ten or twelve percent - I wanted to find out why I hadn't been selected and what I could do to give myself the best chance possible for the next year. I discovered that when at Homestead instead of getting my masters degree I should have done the Air Force Command and Staff school by correspondence. It was considered much more important to the Air Force and considerably easier to get. Also, I found that in my official photo I was wearing a uniform made of an older fabric. The new uniforms were made of double knit. In response, I went to a local Korean tailor and had a new uniform made followed by having a new official photo taken. That was the easy part. I then registered for the command and staff course and spent my remaining night shifts working on the four-part program of study. I completed the course just prior to leaving Korea. During the following year as I expected I was once again passed over. But, on the bright side, as a major I was able to continue to fly until I retired and that probably wouldn't have happened as a lieutenant colonel.

I often wondered afterward, though, about why commanders didn't provide career counseling to their people. If you smoked there was mandatory counseling by the wing commander. Undeniably, it was my responsibility to direct my destiny but if my commander at Homestead had looked over my records and said, 'Jim, I see you don't have command and staff done. Do it if you want to be promoted.' By golly, I would have done it immediately. It took me almost a year and a half to get my masters degree but only three months to complete command and staff in Korea.

Experiences as a SODO

After in-processing I went to the SODO's dais every day to soak up the job through observing what went on. If nothing was happening I went through a very extensive quick reference library located right behind the SODO position. In a letter I described my ideas on my checkout.

> *29 June, 1982. Today I completed my seventh day of reading and studying the countless regulations, manuals and operations plans, of which most are highly classified, and in a little more than a week I'll be checked out in my new job. I must say it is getting harder and harder to find enthusiasm for my study. The total study would be equivalent to seven or eight credits at a university. If someone previously had invested some time and effort to make a prioritized training guide of what to study the checkout time could easily be halved. The existing program is showing the trainee the equivalent of two sets of encyclopedias worth of information and saying, 'study that.' Much of the material isn't necessary to study, just know where it is for quick reference, but the trainee is the least qualified to know what is necessary and deserving of study and what is not. So, I study it all. During my night shifts I think I will tackle that problem and publish a training guide.*

Ten days later I received my checkout evaluation from a senior SODO and I became a qualified SODO. The evaluation consisted of the evaluator watching me perform the job for one shift and during that time he asked me numerous questions from the manuals, regulations, plans as well as many 'what ifs.' 'What would you do if an F-16 pitched out to land and crashed on the infield?' 'What would you do if a Chinese MiG called in and said he was defecting to South Korea?' It was a good feeling to no longer be in training status and to be pulling my own weight.

Ulchi Focus Lens - Taegu

Six weeks after getting checked out another SODO and I were chosen to go to the Alternate TACC (ATACC) in Taegu to participate in a two week exercise. During the exercise I worked 12 hours on and 12 hours off but I didn't mind. I was excited to have the opportunity to see another part of Korea. The other SODO was Jerry Fowler whom I'd become good friends with making the TDY even better. Then, Jerry, who had bought a used car, asked if I'd like to ride with him. I didn't have to give that much thought. The alternative would have been riding in a military convoy.

The exercise was nicknamed Ulchi Focus Lens and was an annual exercise; a command post exercise that didn't involve real airplanes flying real missions. It was a test of communications and if personnel knew and could follow the procedures contained in the war plans. The ATACC was located in Taegu because Taegu was far enough to the south that it was relatively safe from being overrun in the event of war. Osan, in contrast, was only 60 miles from the border.

I found Taegu to be located in the center of a valley where every available piece of land was used for farming. The city was South Korea's third largest with over a million in population. It boasted many sky-scraper type buildings and wide streets. It was a very modern looking city and buzzing with activity.

On the 23rd of August, Jerry and I drove to Taegu and without trouble located the air base. I couldn't help but think about the thousands of farmers who must have been displaced from their prized farmland in order to make this sprawling base. After in-processing we inspected our living quarters which, we discovered, were open bay barracks with 30 bunks to a room. Then we found the Air Force was going to charge us four dollars a day for such accommodations. Jerry suggested we go downtown and see about getting a hotel room and that sounded great to me. My imagination was already echoing with the sound of a roomful of 30 snoring men.

Hanil Hotel or Open Bay Barracks

I suspect Jerry had already done some asking around because we went directly to the tallest building in Taegu, the Hanil hotel. To our delight we found it would only cost us ten dollars apiece and we immediately moved in. Our room had all the comforts of home; twin beds, armed forces television, a private shower and bath and excellent room service – and unlimited hot water. Since I would be working the day shift and Jerry the night shift we essentially had private rooms.

The ATACC was of very simple construction compared to the 'tree house.' It was a two story wooden building and quite crowded when fully manned. In an air raid it wouldn't have lasted more than a few minutes. The first day of the exercise consisted of learning what communications capabilities we had and then getting proficient with the exercise rules. By the second day a routine had been established along with boredom as we watched the predetermined progress of the simulated war on paper.

Every day during the exercise we had VIPs touring the facility while getting briefed on the exercise. On the third or fourth day the Korean Defense Minister came through. General Hefner was escorting him and they stopped at my position and he introduced me to the defense minister. General Hefner remarked that my last name was the same as the Osan wing commander. Expecting the Defense Minister to know only halting English, I was very surprised when he said to me in perfect English, "oh, Olson. Are you Norwegian?" I would guess the Defense Minister had spent many of his early years in the US, perhaps as a dependent child of an ambassador. I'm also sure he really enjoyed my surprised reaction to his question.

The days flowed by at a steady pace with me relieving Jerry in the morning, handing him his car keys and he relieving me 12 hours later and handing them back to me. I would stop at the officers' club for supper and then make the 25-minute drive back to the Hanil hotel. At the first opportunity I went exploring and found a luxurious roof top lounge with prices much more than I was willing to pay. I also found a sauna and weight/exercise room in the basement and many delightful gift shops spread throughout. After a 12 hour shift, though, my usual routine was to go to my room, take a hot shower, watch a little of the armed forces TV and then go to bed. It was an exhausting schedule with no break until it was all over.

Car Electrical Fire

One evening after an uneventful day I was returning to the Hanil in Jerry's car. It was just getting dark and I was anxious to get back to my hotel room. About five blocks from the hotel I smelled smoke and moments later flames appeared from under the dash to the left of the steering column. Fortunately, traffic was light and I was able to quickly maneuver to the right curb and stop the car. After shutting off the engine I jumped out not knowing quite what to do. A cab driver who must have been following me recognized I was in trouble and pulled over to the curb in front of me and jumped out of his car offering to help.

Jerry didn't have a fire extinguisher so I looked around and spotted a sliding type door to an apartment building just a few feet away. Guessing it was a private residence and might have water inside I slid it open. Inside was a Korean family sitting on the floor at a very low table in traditional Korean fashion eating their evening meal. Naturally, they looked up in great surprise. I'm sure it was most unusual to have an American barge into your home uninvited. I told them in English that my car was on fire although I didn't think they couldn't understand me. I frantically looked around and spied a large urn sitting on the floor. It appeared to be filled with water. I mumbled something about needing to borrow it and hurried back out the door.

When I got back to Jerry's car a Korean had the hood up and he was doing something. Other Koreans had gathered around and were watching. I thought he must be up to no good and attempted to get him to leave the car alone until he motioned toward what he was doing. He had found the fuse box and was removing all of the fuses – a great move. I told him with a thankful smile, 'kom ap sumnida', thank you, and applied my attention to the flames under the dash. With three or four upward thrusts with the urn I was able to splash enough water to put out the flames. I returned the urn to the stunned Korean family, thanked them and again returned to my car. It was then that I realized the Korean under the hood was the cab driver who had pulled over to help me. He now had a towrope out and was attaching it to my front bumper. That solved my most immediate problem of what to do with the car and how to get to the Hanil.

The cab driver asked me in broken English where I was staying and I told

Seoul, Capitol of Korea

pointed to it. He told me he would tow me there. With gratefulness I agreed and we were soon on our way. He pulled me right up to the covered entranceway of the hotel and disappeared inside returning two minutes later with a Korean I recognized as a hotel manager. The manager told me the cab driver's brother owned a parts store and could fix the car for me. Suspecting a rip-off in progress I told him that it wasn't my car but I'd tell the owner of the offer. I thought I'd lay that problem on Jerry but I was very concerned because it would be a big job and probably quite expensive to rewire all of the burned wiring. With that I went inside to make a call to Jerry. I called him from my room and Jerry was devastated but he told me it could have happened to him as well and he was happy the car was at least at the hotel. I said I'd grab a cab in the morning and hold it for him.

The next morning I went downstairs early wondering how best to get a cab and how much that was going to cost when the manager came out from behind his desk with a big smile on his face. He handed me my car keys and said the car was all fixed and ready to go. I must have had an incredulous look on my face because he began to laugh. He explained that the cab driver's brother had worked all night to fix the car and it would cost 60 dollars if that was OK. I just couldn't believe it. Our car was fixed during the night while I was sleeping – and for only 60 dollars. I was expecting to pay that much during the next few days just for cab fares to and from the base. Of course it was OK I told the manager. Thank you, thank you, thank you, kom-ap sumnida a thousand times. I also felt ashamed about suspecting a rip-off.

When I walked up to Jerry back at the ATACC and handed him his car keys as per normal, he had a very quizzical look on his face. "What is this," he asked referring to the keys. "Those are your car keys. The car is outside – fixed." Now Jerry had the incredulous look on his face and it was my turn to laugh. His expression turned into a smile and finally happy laughter as I told him the entire story. He just continued to shake his head in wonder and amazement. I gladly split the 60 dollar repair cost and felt greatly indebted to an unknown Korean who stayed up all night to splice dozens of burned wires to fix the car. We never did find out why it had caught on fire.

A Good Deal Trip and Getting Fired

In November I heard about a plan to test the feasibility of operating the Alternate TACC (ATACC) from the Airborne Command and Control Center (ABCCC), a modified Boeing 707 that had a large disk shaped radar antenna mounted on its back. The test was to be conducted in Okinawa, several hundred miles to the south of Korea. The delegation was being led by the DO, Col. Boles, whom I really liked. When I learned they needed a SODO I quickly volunteered and was immediately accepted since I was the only SODO to apply. The daily test flights were to be 12 hours long but for the opportunity to see a little of another place I was willing to endure the unpleasantness that would come with the TDY. Due to limited flights between Korea and Okinawa, we had to depart on a Friday and that was just great by me. I would have the whole weekend to shop and look around.

We landed on Friday afternoon and after checking in at the BOQ I found my way down to the shopping district to take advantage of the low prices on all Japanese goods. Interestingly enough, I just happened to be in Okinawa for a very historic occasion. At the stroke of midnight on Saturday night, Okinawa reverted back to Japanese rule – it had been occupied by the US since the end of the Second World War. As a US protectorate, Okinawa had existed under US rules to include our traffic system. At midnight, Saturday, it reverted to Japanese rules and laws to include their traffic system. Every traffic signal had another signal next to it that was draped with cloth as were many traffic signs along all of the streets. Beginning at midnight the draped signs were undraped and the undraped signs were draped and voila, Okinawa was now driving on the left side of the road. I don't know how well the drivers adjusted to the transformation but I'm sure there were accidents.

Recalled to Osan

I essentially had all of my shopping done by Sunday when I was summoned to Colonel Boles' room in the BOQ. I was very puzzled wondering what was going on when he said there had been an incident back at Osan and I was needed back there immediately. I had an hour to pack, pay my BOQ fees and get on a plane.

To Scramble or Not To Scramble

Back at Osan I learned that on Saturday, a Chinese MiG had defected to South Korea and the SODO had really messed it up. Basically, he had done nothing – he relied on the ROKAF to take care of it rather than to scramble USAF fighters to make the intercept. The ROKAF SODO elected to divert fighters who were already airborne but in the southern part of the country – a procedure that took 10 minutes longer than a simple scramble would have taken. The end result was that the MiG landed at Seoul AB having never been intercepted. He later told reporters that he fully expected to be intercepted at least 50 miles from the coast and was dumbfounded when he reached the coast and still hadn't been intercepted. He meandered around looking for someplace to land and 10 minutes later saw Seoul AB, did a split S to a lower altitude and landed. He had planned on being escorted to a base to land and never thought he'd have to find one for himself.

While this was happening we had a very sensitive RC-135 intelligence gathering plane airborne and the MiG at one point came within 20 miles of the KC-135. To add to the embarrassment, 10 miles away from Seoul AB is Kimpo International Airport and while the MiG was landing at Seoul AB, the President of Korea was standing on the tarmac waiting for the President of Indonesia to land. It would have been entirely possible for the MiG pilot to have assassinated the President of Korea with one well-placed bomb or by strafing and then he could have shot down the President of Indonesia. Another more realistic scenario and forever embarrassing would have been the MiG landing unescorted at Kimpo and rolling out right in front of the noses of the two Presidents. As it turned out the USAF SODO was fired and I had to come back to take over his duties. The fired SODO flew back to Okinawa to do the job I was slated to do. The SODO, by the way, was one of the two SODO's who didn't have a fighter background. He had also been selected for lieutenant colonel on the recent promotion board. I knew without any doubt that I would have scrambled the fighters had I been on duty. I had already done it under similar circumstances. For one thing I wouldn't have denied the alert pilots the fun of an active air scramble or the joy and honor of being able to make an intercept of a defecting MiG. That is the stuff fighter pilots dream of.

The ROKAF SODO was also fired as were about 10 ROKAF generals. Basically, every ROKAF officer who was on duty that day got the ax and I suspect being fired in the ROKAF was much more serious than being fired in the Air Force. Our SODO was given retraining for a week or so, then another qual check and reinstated although it probably reflected negatively on his next performance report. For the ROKAF officers their careers were definitely over and it probably resulted in some being court martialed.

Another Defection?

A month or so later I was given the opportunity to prove I could do better. An unknown radar return popped up in the southern part of North Korea and it was headed south at a moderate rate of speed. Since there was only one radar return a good assumption was that it was a defector who was flying very low to avoid detection by his own country. Defectors became very wealthy and were given celebrity status because South Korea paid them handsomely for defecting. A defection was a huge propaganda event for South Korea.

Because they are afraid of defections North Korea doesn't normally allow its pilots to fly in the southern part of its country but, in this instance, the pilot somehow managed to get off by himself and flew low level to avoid detection until he knew he could make it across the border. I scrambled our alert F-15s, which made the intercept before the ROKAF interceptors.

I imagine that some high ranking ROKAF officers had their careers damaged as a result but all in all, South Korea was very pleased with the defection and ensuing propaganda. All of the key players were given awards by the Korean Defense Minister, the one I met in Taegu. The award was a lovely, sculpted wooden plaque with a brief description of the occasion. Unfortunately the ceremony was held during the week I was back in the states at the School of Aerospace Medicine (another story). As I will explain in greater detail later, I had a stand-in receive the decoration for me.

During the week of the previous incident I had three more occasions where I had to call the general to the 'tree house.' One was a North Korean high-speed gunboat that tried to sneak into South Korea's coastal waters, probably to drop off infiltrators. After a running gun battle, the South Koreans succeeded in blowing it out of the water with no survivors.

The second incident required my scrambling the alert F-15s again. At 1:30 in the morning an unknown target turned up a bit north of Seoul heading south at a high rate of speed. I immediately called General Hefner. This time I was considerably more nervous than the previous scramble. The first incident had all of the ear markings of a defection and it happened in the middle of the day. This radar plot looked much more sinister, like the pilot might be planning a suicide crash into the Blue House – the President's home, or an attack on an unarmed intelligence aircraft that was airborne. The whole incident turned out to be very anticlimactic when the track suddenly disappeared and a few minutes later was blamed on Anomalous Propagation (AP). AP essentially is a false radar return. General Hefner and I both shook our heads in puzzlement about how that could happen. I suspect he stopped by the super-secret room next to the battle cab to find out what the real story was. I never heard another word on it.

The very next day, just a few minutes after coming on duty we had yet another incident that required my calling in General Hefner. Two unknown tracks appeared off the coast of Korea and penetrated an imaginary line, the Korean Air Defense Identification Zone, KADIZ, and even though we knew they weren't unfriendly because they were coming in from the south, rules said we had to scramble fighters and go out to identify them. They turned out to be two navy aircraft that had filed an incorrect flight plan.

Flight Physical -Diagnosis WPW

I took my annual flight physical during my birth month, October – I'd been told once to never take your physical early because if you failed it you might be cutting yourself out of that number of months of flight pay. When the airman medical technician was taking my EKG he looked at the long roll of paper that was coming out and hastily left the room. In a minute he was back with the flight surgeon. The flight surgeon muttered something about having the leads on wrong and he checked them – they were on correctly. Then he left in a hurry and soon returned with the chief flight surgeon who also examined the print out. When he was through he told me to put my shirt back on and he'd be back. Then he left again. You can imagine what was going through my thoughts about then.

Five minutes later the chief flight surgeon returned and informed me that I had a congenital condition known as Wolfe-Parkinson-White syndrome, more commonly known as WPW. He explained that the condition resulted when the heart develops an alternate electrical route between its first and second nodes. When the brain signals the heart to beat it sends an electrical signal to the first node. From there the signal travels to the second node and finally to the rest of the heart for a coordinated beat. With WPW on every tenth beat or so, the signal traveled along the alternate route. As it continued on to the rest of the heart, it was possible for it to backtrack along the primary pathway at the same time setting up a circuit that could result in rapid heartbeat, tachycardia. My WPW was only found with the aid of the EKG. There weren't any physical symptoms.

Naturally, I had many questions of great concern. Was this or could it become life threatening? Could it be cured or treated and if so, how? How would it affect my flying career? The flight surgeon had no answers at all for me and as it turned out, never attempted to find any answers. I left the flight surgeon's office and went directly to the base library where I found some medical books that talked about WPW and soon I knew more than the flight surgeon about the condition. I also went back to the flight surgeon and discovered there was a heart specialist at the Yong San Army hospital in Seoul and I managed to get an appointment there for the following week.

At Yong San I was given a stress test, an EKG and finally a device strapped to my waist called a Holter monitor with electrical leads attached to my chest. The Holter would provide a 24 hour EKG. I returned to Osan and then came back the next day to talk with the cardiologist about his findings. He confirmed I had WPW and was able to explain the condition a little better but I really felt like I was not much farther along than a week earlier.

I soon received notification from the flight surgeon that I had an appointment at the School of Aerospace Medicine at Brooks AFB in San Antonio, Texas, better known as SAM Brooks. The appointment was for five months hence, in March. Now, another concern was the realization that I would lose my flight pay in April if I didn't get a waiver. The Air Force grants a six-month grace period before cutting off flight pay. It was going to be close. Yet another concern was having to wait all that time to find out if I would be able to continue flying as a fighter pilot.

An Uneasy Truce

I was now well entrenched in my job and very used to living in a country that was technically still at war. South and North Korea had been living under a volatile state of truce for 30 years with incidents happening on a weekly basis that were seldom reported in newspapers.

Someone at work once tallied the number of military exercises that occurred each year in Korea and the number exceeded 150. Many were on a small scale but the major exercises involved the whole country to include the civilian populace. During an exercise if a black-out was called for, the power to the whole country was shut off and there was a true black-out. Cars were expected to pull over and shut off headlights and even during non-exercise conditions during darkness, at traffic lights, all vehicles switched from headlights to parking lights until the light turned green again. It was their custom. In Seoul the enemy was only 25 miles away.

Mid-tour Leave

Half way through my one-year tour in Korea was Christmas so I applied for and received a mid-tour leave that allowed me to spend Christmas in southern Florida with Jean and the girls. When my leave was about to begin I went to base operations to register for standby status on a military flight. The picture they painted wasn't very encouraging. There were practically no remaining flights going back to the States and there was a long list of names ahead of me with the same intentions. At some point in the States I'd still have to purchase an over-the-counter ticket to complete my journey to Miami so I rationalized that it wouldn't cost that much more just to get a ticket from Seoul, which I did. That decision also gave me several more days of worry free leave. On military standby I would have had to begin my return journey a couple days earlier allowing for a probable wait somewhere to get on a military flight again.

Flying Back Home

My flight to the States was quite uneventful until arriving at destination, St. Louis, at a very late hour. During the flight I inquired from a flight attendant about flights from St. Louis to Miami and found the last one left at 11 pm, our scheduled landing time. I resigned myself to a night in the St. Louis airport. We landed a few minutes early and for the first time ever in my life I was one of the first off the plane. I thought with a glimmer of hope that if my luggage was the first off as well I might just catch the last flight to Miami. I couldn't believe my eyes when my luggage actually was one of the very first to appear. Someone was looking out for me I decided.

I saw a porter standing by and told him that if he could get me on flight so and so to Miami I'd give him ten dollars. He put my luggage on a cart and we were off at a run. The flight was already boarded by the time we got there but they held the plane a couple minutes for me as I got my boarding pass. I still hadn't caught my breath when I plopped down in my seat and made ready for an imminent departure. It didn't happen. We waited and a couple more passengers got on. We waited longer and a few more boarded. The airline realized that the flight I had gotten off probably had many more fares bound for Miami and they held the plane for almost an hour! It was after midnight when we finally took off landing in Miami at 2 am. I hired a taxi at the airport and finally got home after three but I was home. What a feeling and what a surprise for my family. They didn't expect me until noon the next day.

The time passed all too quickly but we did go camping at Disney World for two or three days and I stopped by my old squadron to see how things were. I was amazed at how much it had changed in only six months. I felt completely out of place because I was. The 308th was no longer my squadron. The Air Force didn't allow for nostalgia.

We did a lot of things together as a family and soon I was back in the air once again chasing the sun across the Pacific. This time, however, the 747 I was on was only partially full and I had a full aisle to myself to stretch out on. What luxury. I slept quite well and was very surprised when I realized we were descending for a landing at Kimpo Airport in Seoul. My comrades were very happy to see me back because they could go back to a normal, more relaxed shift schedule. And life in the 'land of the morning calm' resumed.

SAM Brooks

SAM Brooks was a facility that had many functions, all of which centered on flight medicine. It was where flight surgeons and flight nurses received their training. Additionally, all results of flight physicals were sent there to be screened. As in my case, if there was a question about a failed physical, the aircrew member went to

SAM Brooks. It was a name I'd been taught to fear because the best thing that could happen to you was 'nothing,' you continued on flying status. The worst thing was being taken off flying status and we all knew of pilots that suffered that fate.

When I received my TDY orders to go to SAM Brooks they included travel by government plane meaning the med-evac. I definitely didn't want that and I spent a week trying one way after another to get it changed. I was to leave on a Thursday for a Monday appointment. I explained that I was in the middle of an exercise and if I went by commercial airplane I could stay until the end of the exercise. I also pointed out that my organization was paying as much for the seat on the med-evac as it would for a commercial ticket. Nothing worked and I soon found myself in line at the terminal to board the med-evac C-141 airplane.

We left at mid-day and a few hours later landed at Clark Air Base in the Philippines. We were transported by bus to the base hospital where we spent the night. I remember how warm and muggy it was as I stepped off the plane – it was the end of March and I had just left a cold wintery Korea.

The next day we resumed our travel. Our destination was Hickam AFB in Hawaii. When we leveled off a new flight nurse, a very solidly built blond major, who had joined us in the Philippines, began making her rounds of the 'patients' taking their vitals. When she got to me I began to explain that I really wasn't a patient like the others because I was just… The look she gave me said, 'are you going to give me trouble?' I decided I would be a patient and let her take my vitals.

We landed in Hawaii and were on the tarmac just long enough to exchange a few passengers and refuel. Hawaii? Ya, I've been there! We soon were continuing our eastward journey landing a few hours later at Travis AFB, California. The time was early evening in California and we were once again transported to the base hospital for the night. Although it was just a little against policy, I convinced the hospital staff to let me out for a while. It was so wonderful to suddenly have the freedom to walk where I wanted and gaze leisurely at the stars. I even found a fast food restaurant within walking distance for some heavenly junk food.

The next day found me on a smaller med-evac airplane, a C-9 Nightingale, a plane made specifically for med-evac purposes. We even had a passenger who appeared to be gravely ill. He was on a special cot in the isle and had a clear plastic tent over him and was being 'dripped' continuously. We made several stops at various bases as we got closer and closer to San Antonio and finally we were landing at Kelly AFB just a few miles from SAM Brooks (Brooks didn't have a runway). I caught a shuttle bus ride to Brooks and checked in.

I was extremely impressed with Brooks right from the start. At the BOQ office upon checking in I was given my medical schedule for the following week with a complete list of instructions. I learned for instance that I wouldn't have to wear a uniform at all, an exercise warm-up suit would be just fine. My first task, though, was to look up the number for a nearby rent-a-junk car. It was called 'The Ugly Duckling' and I soon had a rusty ancient car delivered to the BOQ but the price was right.

The next day was Saturday and I went to the San Antonio airport to meet Jean and she spent the week with me. On the following Friday we got two of the last three tickets on a flight to Miami and we flew home where I got to spend the weekend with all of my girls. Then on Sunday I caught a flight that took me back again to the land of the morning calm and the daily routine of the 'tree house.'

At SAM Brooks I was told that I got a check-up as good as any I could have gotten at the Mayo Clinic and its value was right at twenty thousand dollars. Among the tests I received were an echocardiogram, a treadmill stress test, a 24-hour Holter EKG, and two nuclear tests involving radioisotopes. The only test I didn't get I think was a heart catheterization, which was recommended but not required. I declined it but three years later on a required follow-up visit it wasn't optional. I also got the usual eye, ear, nose and throat tests done with SAM Brooks thoroughness.

During my out brief with my assigned flight surgeon he gave me a very good report saying I was being given wavers for my WPW as well as a condition of hypoglycemia they found. I was cleared to go back to flying. Hoorah!

Cloned at Osan

When I got back to Osan I found I had missed a big ceremony partly in my honor. As mentioned previously the ROKAF held a presentation ceremony to give medals to all of the key players in the successful North Korean MiG defection. There was very little notice given and when my DO, Col. Boles, tried to explain that I couldn't attend because I was in the United States. They said, "no, he must be there. Medal being presented. Must be there." So, Col. Boles did the only logical thing. He created an impostor Major Olson. He found another officer who was about my size and this fellow talked my housekeeper into letting him into my room where he found my Class A uniform. He encountered one problem, though. The jacket had all of my medals and decorations on it but no nametag. Col. Boles solved that problem. The wing commander's name was also Olson, so Col. Boles borrowed a nametag from Col. Olson and the impostor was ready to go. The ceremony I'm told was long and my impostor didn't much enjoy standing at attention for most of it but he did enjoy the reception afterwards and promised me he didn't tarnish Major Olson's fine image.

Going Away Party

My going away party in May was a reminder of how quickly my year-long tour was coming to a close. The party was to say goodbye to myself and two other SODOs who arrived in Korea with me and a squadron commander. Ironically, I had to attend wearing a flight suit because I was scheduled to work that night. Another SODO filled in for me at work for two hours so I could at least attend the dinner portion. To my surprise, General Hefner also attended. His social calendar was usually quite full, especially with ROKAF functions and he seldom made it to our going away shindigs. There also were many ROKAF dignitaries present. They seldom missed an opportunity for American food. Koreans always placed a high premium on protocol and politeness and expected it returned in kind.

General Hefner

General Hefner seemed to take an instant liking to me when I first met him in Korea and he called me Ole from that moment onward. That night I think I found out why. When he introduced me to his wife I discovered that her maiden name was Olson. I also found out that she really was Norwegian and that her grandfather had changed their name from 'en' to 'on' as mine had and for the same reason. Over the years I've decided this was commonly done.

The next morning I was very happy that I had only been spelled for two hours when the very same SODO showed up two hours late and looking like hell. He had gone back to the party. It was a Saturday morning and for his sake I was hoping it would be a quiet day.

A New Assignment

By now I had my new assignment, to the 82nd Tactical Aerial Targets squadron at Tyndall AFB. Because I began flying relatively late in my career (four years after joining the Air Force) I was still a few months short of my 'gate' for flying service which required that I be assigned to a flying position. Otherwise I suspect I might have been sent to a non-flying air liaison officer job. The bright lining of my dark 'pass over cloud' was I got to continue flying until I retired seven years later.

One of the SODOs who arrived in Korea with me, Ken Miller, had come from Tyndall and received a follow-on assignment back to Tyndall and he told me all about the drone aircraft business I was going to. He said I'd probably be dual qualified and be flying both the F-102 and the F-100. Sounded great to me but Ken turned out to be wrong.

The reaction to my family of our new assignment was mixed. Jean was very excited about the move and of the prospects of buying a house. Jill was indifferent. Mandy was very excited and wanted to know if we were getting a house with a pool. Becky didn't initially appear to be looking forward to it because of her friends and involvement in music at her high school.

Jean Goes House Shopping

In discussing the new assignment over the telephone, Jean and I decided we would buy a house this time, especially since this would probably be my end of career assignment. Through a friend she got the name of a good realtor whose husband was retired Air Force and went to Panama City and bought a house. The lady realtor met Jean at the airport and spent the entire weekend with her. She even put Jean up in her own home. Now that was real service.

The New Boss – Is the Pits

In May we got a new boss to replace Col. Boles. I was glad it happened after my going away party. I really liked Col. Boles a lot and the new guy I thought was a real loser. Where Col. Boles reflected the Air Force policy of taking care of its people, the new guy was just about totally mission oriented and to hell with people.

This became apparent the very first day he was on the job and I was happy I'd only have to endure his heavy and unjust hand for another four or five weeks. It is usually the case in the Air Force that an incoming commander will get the 'lay of the land' before starting to make changes and only then with great care. The new boss began making immediate and drastic changes as if we were an organization in trouble and that was not the case at all.

The Day Worker

Our organization, the TACC, was divided into two types of workers; those who worked Monday through Friday, the day worker, and those that worked shifts. The day worker had the envy of the shift worker because his duty hours were 7 until 4:30. He also could leave for lunch and even take time off during lull periods of the day to do all of his personal business on company time. He could even get away to the BX or restock his kitchen during the duty day. The day worker was also known to frequently knock off early on Friday afternoons to go to happy hour and was allowed time off during the day to pursue a physical fitness program. He also got holidays off.

In contrast, the shift worker had to do all of those activities during his break time. He had to work on weekends and holidays unless they coincided with a break. When an exercise ended and the organization got to stand down for a day of rest and reward; the shift worker continued working.

Since my arrival at the TACC that was the way it was. The day workers seemed to have ample time to chat and joke around and frequently didn't seem to be gainfully employed. I also noticed many things that they should have been doing that they weren't such as rewriting outdated regulations. The new boss noticed that many things needed work and his answer was to take away one of our four crews and put them to work to help the day worker get caught up on these projects that had been neglected for so long. That left only three shifts, which required us to go from a 42 hour to a 60-hour workweek. This also left the shift workers with very bad feelings; morale was really low and it was totally unnecessary. That was the only person I worked for in my Air Force career who wasn't people oriented.

My year in Korea was almost over. What a change I found Korea had gone through since my first tour in 1968. They had gone from a backward emerging nation to a modern industrial might. You no longer saw people wearing the traditional Korean dress or encountered the sharp smell of Kimche (a spicy, garlicky, fermented food made from cabbage and other vegetables) that seemed to emanate from the pores of most Koreans' skin. Streets in cities were now paved and children frequently boarded buses to go to large centralized schools. Doors swung open on hinges where they used to slide in grooves and the larger cities were marked by tall apartment buildings. In a nostalgic way I missed the Land of the Morning Calm that now only existed in my memories.

Moving to Panama City

I finally got my port call so Jean and I could finalize plans for our move to Panama City. The move fell almost completely on Jean's shoulders and she did a wonderful job. There was a lot that had to be done and various tasks had to fall in sequence and timed such that we could do the final packing up as soon as I got back home. The day after I got back, we had the cars and camper packed and we were on the road to Panama City.

The only hitch we encountered was the alternator on the VW 412 quit working before we got halfway up the State. That meant every 80 or 100 miles we had to pull over so I could hook up the jumper cables from the Volare to replenish the VW's battery.

We spent one night in a campground and finally got to Tyndall's FAMCAMP camping grounds the next afternoon. As luck would have it the last time the VW ran out of electrical charge was within a half mile of the FAMCAMP! Argggh.

After getting the camper set up I felt the usual excitement and anticipation about going in and meeting my new assignment. Two new aircraft to learn: Wow!

Chapter Thirteen

Fighters As Drones at Tyndall AFB

It's better to die than to look bad (in the traffic pattern).

Tyndall – Stability at Last.

Our assignment to Tyndall was the last of my career. That was my hope when I learned of the assignment because Jill was entering the 11th grade, Becky was a year behind her and Mandy was going into second grade. They had received the benefits the Air Force had to offer - learning there was a whole wide world out there, and developing self-confidence and independence – but now they needed some stability and a place to be able to call their own.

When I learned about the assignment I was told that I would be working with drones. What in the world are drones I thought? I very quickly found that the Air Force had a program where they flew full size and sub-scale targets; drones, out over the Gulf of Mexico and fighter pilots got to shoot missiles at them. I was told I would get checked out in an F-102 or an F-100 – maybe both – but most importantly, I would be flying again.

QF 100 'manned' drone over Tyndall AFB

Why Drones at Tyndall?

Tyndall was originally an Air Defense Command (ADC) base and interceptor jets at one time carried some rockets that had small nuclear warheads. The jets had to be 'nuclear certified' once per year and to do that they were required to successfully fire a practice rocket at a drone. Because Tyndall was right on the Gulf of Mexico with large over water ranges it was the natural location to establish that program which was called 'Combat Pike' and was part of ADC's Weapons System Evaluation Program (WSEP). Once a year all ADC pilots would rotate through Tyndall for this certification and Tyndall became a sort of homecoming base.

As time passed, the air threat to the US began changing from Soviet bombers to missiles and ADC started losing its prominence. As ADC faded so did Combat Pike.

With fewer drones being shot at by ADC, Tactical Air Command (TAC) saw an opportunity to train its fighter pilots and also test its missiles which did not fare well in the war in Vietnam. Combat Echo was established at Eglin AFB, just 60 miles up the coast to serve this need. This is about where things were when I arrived at Tyndall.

As Combat Pike was dismantled, Tyndall became a TAC base and Combat Echo relocated from Eglin. Combat Echo also grew greatly in scope with an increased emphasis on testing the capabilities of our air to air missiles, namely the radar guided AIM 7 Sparrow and the heat seeking AIM 9 sidewinder. With an expanded mission came a name change, the Weapons System Evaluation Program or WSEP. As WSEP was being formed a headquarters was created, the Weapons Evaluation Group, WEG, and eventually three squadrons, the 82nd Tactical Aerial Targets Squadron, the 83rd Weapons squadron and the 84th Test Squadron.

The 82nd TATS

Arriving at Tyndall I found my squadron, the 82nd Tactical Aerial Targets Squadron (TATS) was quite new having been formed only a year earlier and it was very small. The commander, Lt. Col. Bert Strock, was running the entire squadron until his operations officer, Lt. Col. Lionel Boudreaux, arrived from Iceland. We also had two other fighter pilots and a 'pocket rocket' missile guy assigned and two other group headquarters pilots who were attached for flying purposes. These people worked closely with RCA contract personnel, civilians who were all retired Air Force, to run both the sub-scale and full-scale drone programs.

I mentioned that the squadron was small. That wasn't exactly correct. The flying operation was small. The squadron also had the Deployed Liaison Office, DLO, and a watercraft branch, each with 20 or more people. Perhaps when the squadron was formed they threw these two functions in to give it respectability in size.

The 82nd's NCOs, the Best of the Best.

The Deployed Liaison Office was a group of carefully chosen sergeants who represented all of the maintenance specialties such as AGE (flight line generators and jet engine starting units), Weapons, Avionics, Fuels etc., and they were mostly senior ranking.

82 TATS Squadron Patch

Assignment to the DLO was considered a plum assignment and all of its people were carefully chosen for the job. They were extremely capable NCOs who had already demonstrated an ability to work independently.

The DLO took care of units that deployed to Tyndall. These TDY (temporary duty) units were coming to shoot missiles at our drones. Several months prior to a deployment someone from the DLO would go out to the unit and brief them on the maintenance and personnel support they could expect at Tyndall. The representative would spend several days with the unit to get to know them and to be available for any help they might need from that point forward. When the unit deployed to Tyndall, the same representative was on call day and night for the duration of their stay.

The DLO did their job so well they were used as a model for other bases that had a similar function of receiving deployed units. The DLO received the highest rating, outstanding, on every inspection they ever had and they didn't have an officer to lead them! The person in charge was a senior master sergeant, an E-7. The E-7 reported directly to the 82nd TATS commander.

The Air Force's Navy

The Watercraft Branch, sometimes called the Air Force's Navy, was another unit that wasn't run by an officer. The top ranking person was a chief master sergeant, an E-8. The 25 or so men and women in watercraft included boat mechanics, operators and divers. The primary job of watercraft was the recovery of sub-scale drones but they also were called on for other water-related tasks, even search and rescue. After the over water crash of an F-15, the watercraft branch spent several days searching for the pilot's body and aircraft debris. They did find the body.

Another water related task was replacing zinc packs to the underwater bases of antenna towers situated in the gulf. Zinc, when attached to ferrous metal, prevents salt water corrosion so it was essential in preserving the underwater structures. The divers prided themselves in being very macho and stories abounded about hair-raising stunts carried out by the watercraft men. In one such story a diver was at the base of a tower leg at 110 feet quite occupied with his task when he was startled by a tapping on his shoulder. He spun around to see a fellow diver grinning at him through his mask. He had free dived – without scuba gear – and was immensely rewarded for his daredevil stunt.

Operations Section

The operations section of the squadron was responsible for providing sub-scale and full-scale drones to be shot at. Operations was headed up by a lieutenant colonel operations officer and usually four or five fighter pilots who were checked out in flying the current full scale drone aircraft. When I got to Tyndall, the QF-102 full-scale drone was being phased out and its replacement was the QF-100. Seven years later when I retired, the QF-100 was being replaced by the QF-106. Now, a few years after that, the QF-4 is on hand with the retired F-16s scheduled to be next.

The 83rd Weapons Squadron

The 83rd was known as our sister squadron and our squadron buildings were on opposite sides of a parking lot. We even shared the same life support facility for looking after our flying gear. All of their flying members were graduates of the fighter weapons school at Nellis AFB. The units they served flew F-106, F-4 and F-15 aircraft so the 83rd was required to have pilots who also flew those aircraft. They also had one F-4 WSO.

The 83rd mission was similar in many ways to the DLO. They also sent out a designated host pilot to brief the incoming TDY unit. That host pilot helped the unit plan what profiles they would fly when shooting the missiles they were allocated. During his weeklong visit he would also do a lot of flying with the unit's pilots getting to know them better and also to get his required flying hours in. When the unit actually deployed to Tyndall, this same person was primary in briefing and leading the live fire missions and would chase each individual shooter acting as the range safety officer. The 83rd pilots all loved their mission and they were very good at it.

The 84th Test Squadron

This was the last squadron to be formed and their primary job was to do the so called book keeping on missile shots and to look after the missile test parameters. Through their efforts the Air Force learned what the realistic capabilities were of the new variants of the AIM 7s and AIM 9s as well as the latest missile, the AMRAAM. The 84th didn't have any rated (flying) personnel.

Civilian Drone Contractor

The daily performance of the drone program was carried out by a civilian contractor with oversight provided by the 82nd. The contractor provided the maintenance organization to do all maintenance support for the subscale and full scale drones. He also ran a small operations section which consisted of the drone remote controllers. Four or five controllers operated the subscale drone, the BQM 34a, and another six or seven ran the full scale QF-100 operation. All of the full scale operators were retired fighter pilots and four of them flew the QF-100 along with us Air Force 'blue suiters.' Also, the contractor had a detachment at Holloman AFB, New Mexico whose job it was to provide full scale drones to the Army which were flown over the White Sands Missile Range (WSMR). Of all the civilians I worked with both at Tyndall and at Holloman, they were all top notch professionals and just plain fun to be around. They were major players in making the drone program run like a clock.

A Select Group of Officers

When I got to the 82nd TATS I found an outfit unlike any I had ever been associated with before. As mentioned previously, the commander was Lt. Col. Bert Strock and the operations officer was Lionel (Boo) Boudreaux. They were both very capable leaders and well liked. The squadron's other officers were all passed over majors and this was considered a terminal assignment for us as we came up on retirement. Because of this, we felt no competition for recognition or advancement. We simply did the job of operating drones as best we could and we had fun doing it. We also worked very well with the contractor personnel because we liked each other. Discord was nonexistent.

The safety pilots at the 82nd were Denny Hladd, Fred Whitten, Tim Killeen, Sal Bonacasa and myself. In addition to us there was a crusty TSgt, Jerry Kirby who endured our antics and tried hard not to show how much he enjoyed his position among all these officers. We called him Jerry and treated him like an equal but Jerry was too professional to ever forget the separation between NCO and Officer; he always called us 'sir.' There was one non-flying officer position for running the subscale program. The position was filled by Capt Carl Hamlin who was tireless, enthusiastic and had a great sense of humor. Because of Carl's passion for everything sub-scale the rest of us became quite spoiled and seldom had to run sub-scale missions. Carl did it all.

Office Pranks Happened

When it was time to work we were all professionals and did the best job possible; but, at other times we also joked around a lot and occasionally even pulled pranks on each other. There was the time when Sgt Kirby came to work in the morning and soon realized all of his on-top-of-desk items such as pencil sharpener, stapler, telephone, had been super glued to his plexiglass desk top. He found out who the culprit was, Tim Killeen, and unscrewed the mouth piece of Tim's phone handset and reversed the microphone disk. When Tim next answered the phone he could hear perfectly but it wouldn't transmit. "Hello, hello, hello! What's wrong with this - - - phone anyway." When he spotted the look on Kirby's face he knew instantly he had been one-upped.

A more elaborate prank evolved between Sal and me with Tim again the target. For some forgotten reason we had been talking about the German hydrogen filled airship, Hindenburg. It had caught fire while trying to dock in New Jersey during a thunderstorm. The entire disaster had been captured on camera because it was the Hindenburg's maiden voyage. We concocted a scheme where we would strike up a conversation about the Hindenburg after Tim returned to the office – and then pretend to call the German embassy to find an answer to a trivia question. When Tim got back we cleverly maneuvered the office talk to the Hindenburg at which point I led the prank. "Yes, that was quite a disaster when it caught fire. Does anyone remember how many lives were lost?" After no answers were forthcoming, "Sal, why don't you call the German Embassy. They should know." At that point as per the script, Sal pulled out a phone book and pretended to look up the number and made the call. "Yes, is this the German Embassy? Ya, I'm calling from Panama City and some of us in the office were wondering how many people died in the Hindenburg accident. OK, I'll wait." Tim is taking all of this in with wide eyes and an open mouth – disbelief all over his face. "Yes, I'm still here. OK, 33 people. Thanks for the help." Sal turned to me and with a very straight face told me the answer was 33 people. At that point, Tim couldn't hold it in any longer. With an incredulous sound to his voice, "I can't believe you just called the German Embassy. I can't believe it. That didn't happen." And then Tim noticed the smiles creeping across our faces and knew he once again had been had. He might have retaliated by putting petroleum jelly on our phone ear pieces, I'm not sure – but he did retaliate.

Drone Remote Controllers

The contractor, RCA, usually had four full-scale controllers and an equal number of sub-scale controllers. The full-scale controllers were all retired Air Force fighter pilots and like the 82nd pilots, flew the current droned aircraft. This wasn't so for the sub-scale controllers. The small quarter scale sub-scale drone flew more like a radio-controlled model airplane – it was limited to 60 degrees of bank and was flown very much 'by the book.' If problems occurred a fall back solution was to throw a switch that caused the drone to slow by pitching up and then a parachute deployed. Recovery of the drone was then up to the boats.

As a mission commander for sub-scale missions I had a hard time getting used to the fact that the little drones didn't fly like a real jet. I would make suggestions to the experienced controllers on how a maneuver might be more easily done and they would just smile and say, "it don't work that way with this drone, Major." I quickly learned to leave the flying to them.

Shooting Missiles at Drones

The primary mission of the squadron was to provide both sub-scale and full-scale drones to fighter pilots to shoot missiles at. As described at the beginning of this chapter the Air Force's Weapons Systems Evaluation Program (WSEP) goals very simply were to give fighter pilots experience in shooting live missiles at live targets and to very accurately determine just what the capabilities of our missiles were under a wide variety of conditions. However, the cost would have been enormous if even half of the missiles that were fired shot down a drone. The solution was to replace the missile warhead with scoring kits

BQM 34F Supersonic Drone on display

that showed how close they came to the drone. Even this wasn't good enough because our missiles were so accurate they still frequently had direct hits. So, the drones were given a means of defending themselves. No, they couldn't shoot back but they did have heat producing decoy IR pods attached to the wingtips to protect against IR missiles. The pods were propane gas burners and when lit caused the back part of the pod to glow red and produce a hotter IR source than the drone's engine. The pod frequently was stripped off the wing tip by our super accurate IR missiles. Since each wingtip had a pod, that could happen twice before having to terminate the mission. The full scale drones also had radar jamming pods for defending against radar missiles and prior to the missile reaching the drone, the drone was required to do an evasive maneuver such as a high G turn or a barrel roll to throw the missile accuracy off just enough to hopefully cause a near miss.

Drone survivability was a constantly looked at item because drones cost a lot of money – they were a valuable commodity. Occasionally, someone would screw up and the result would be a destroyed drone. Common screw ups were the shooter 'sweetening the shot' by shooting too close to the drone or not calling his missile firing which was the key for the drone controller to begin an evasive maneuver. Sometimes the IR pod would blow out before missile passage and that was usually fatal. On rare occasions the controller might even make an error in the way he flew the drone such as turning the wrong way or delaying an action or responding incorrectly to a drone emergency. Overall survivability was about 5 or 6 missiles per drone kill. As one crusty Major, Fred Whitten, said to the commanding general during a drone accident investigation briefing, "General, flying drones is dangerous business."

Tyndall AFB was chosen for drone operations because it was located right along the Gulf of Mexico. A drone could be launched to the south and immediately was 'feet wet' (over water) with the live-fire over-water range airspace less than 50 miles away. A special runway, the 'droneway' was even constructed south of the main base that allowed drone operations that didn't interfere with main-base flight activities. Other supporting facilities included a precision radar facility for controlling the drones, a scoring facility that could determine how close the missile came to its target and an analysis branch.

Sub-scale Drone AKA 'Baby Drone'

The sub-scale drone carried the designation, BQM-34a, and was made by Teledyne Ryan. For a supersonic target we had the BQM-34f which was a very sleek version of the 34a and had a top speed of Mach 1.5. Both of these targets were designed for parachute recoveries. The 34a was recovered on land but the 34f was too fragile and could only be parachuted into the water where it was immediately plucked out by our watercraft branch. For either subscale target, if it was clipped by a missile but not too badly damaged, it could be put into the chutes and the water recovery boat would try to get it before it sank. If it did sink the drone had a salt-water activated locator beacon to aid in finding it. Then it was up to the divers.

Launching Subscales – Wow!

The sub-scale drones were launched off a launch rail. A rocket bottle attached to the bottom of the drone accelerated the drone to over 150 miles per hour in three seconds. Then, the drone's jet engine powered it for the rest of the mission. The launch crew hunkered down in a reinforced concrete pillbox type structure for their own protection from errant launches. The sub-scale drones were quirky and although most missions were boringly predictable, just about anything could and did happen at one time or another. More than once at launch the attached rocket bottle fizzled causing the drone to crash even before getting the hundred feet to the water's edge. During one spectacular launch, an attachment bolt broke causing the bottle to swing from only one attachment with devastating results. The drone swung around and flew inland a mile or so before crashing in the woods. The most hair-raising incident, though, was when the bottle broke loose completely. A drone with a rocket bottle attached has a significant thrust to weight ratio. On this occasion the bottle probably had a 100 to 1 thrust to weight ratio. Until the bottle spent its fuel in a few seconds it bounced, cavorted and ricocheted all over the launch pad and finally ended up in the woods a mile away. This incident vividly showed the need for the blockhouse and the safety it provided.

Controlling Subscale Drones

Immediately after launch, precision tracking radar picked up the drone and its position was displayed by a pen-plot on a large wall mounted translucent map overlay. The overlay was removed after each mission and could be used in debriefing the mission if necessary. When the fighters came up another precision radar picked them up and plotted them on the same map. The drone controllers flew the drone from consoles that had the same controls, dials, gauges and switches as a real aircraft. Of course they had to fly completely on instruments and used the pen plots to see where they were in relation to the fighters.

Full-Scale Drones

In 1984 when I began at Tyndall the full-scale drone was the QF-102 but it was in its final few months of operational use. Most of the QF-102s had been shot down and were at the bottom of the Gulf of Mexico. The QF-100 was just finishing up its acceptance testing. In 1991 when I retired, the QF-100s were almost all gone and the QF-106 was ready and waiting to take over and that in turn would be replaced by the QF-4 four years later.

To make a full-scale drone was a very lengthy and costly process involving years of development and testing. The process began at Davis-Monthan AFB in Tucson Arizona at the MASDC, Military Aircraft Storage and Disposition Center (pictures on pgs 34 and 38). The MASDC was better known as 'the Boneyard.' Aircraft that were to be droned had to be 'de-mothballed' which was by itself an expensive process. Then they were given a functional check flight and after passing they were flown to the drone factory where unnecessary equipment was stripped out, a new auto-pilot installed, servos and actuators were fitted in and the plane was essentially rewired. When finished, the new drone had a couple hundred up-link channels and an equal number of down-link channels. By contrast a radio controlled model airplane might have four. When flying the drone, the remote controller had more information available to him than an on-board pilot. The full-scale drone business produced some of the best documented accidents in the Air Force.

A Typical Full-Scale Live-Fire Mission

The missile shooters always had an experienced pilot from our sister squadron, the 83rd Fighter Weapons Squadron, leading them and was the shooter chase for missile firings (a prerequisite for the 83rd pilots was to be a graduate of the prestigious fighter weapons school). He was responsible for making sure that the missiles were indeed fired at the drone and all safety rules followed. The shooter chase was also the flight leader and very efficiently directed all aspects of the mission.

A missile firing mission formally began with the mass briefing two and a half hours prior to takeoff. The first part of the briefing was geared for the drone controllers, GCI weapons controller, weapons scoring people and range safety. The flight lead did the planning and briefing. The mass briefing gave an overview of the mission and a quick run-through of each missile firing set-up. On our overprinted briefing cards we copied down each shooter's call-sign, what kind of missile he would shoot, what kind of pass it was to be and instructions for drone defensive maneuvering.

'Mike'

The person attending from the 82nd was the Drone Mission commander (MC), call-sign 'Mike.' A prerequisite for the MC was that he be at least a major and a fighter pilot. Knowledge of how fighters work was essential to managing a live missile firing mission and the MC's responsibilities were considerable.

Following the main or fighter briefing the MC would hurry over to the contractor's briefing room and brief all of the drone control players; remote controllers, range safety people, scoring folks and drone chase pilot. The choreography of a live fire mission involved a whole lot of people and it invariably came off very smoothly.

BQM 34A at launch with a boost from a 'RATO' bottle

The Shoot Box

At the appointed time all mission participants went to their respective duty positions and waited for the shooters to take off. The shooters were directed to the assigned live fire area off the coast and flew about five miles line abreast looking for boats. Range safety who resided at the GCI radar facility plotted all boats on his radar scope and used a template to choose a 'shoot box.' The size and shape of the shoot box depended on the type missile being shot as well as the shooting altitude and provided for the safety of surface vessels. We didn't want flaming drone debris or spent missiles falling on boats. On occasion, especially on nice sunny days, we cancelled a live fire mission because we couldn't find a shoot box.

When the mission commander received word that we had a shoot box, he gave the go-ahead to proceed with the drone mission.

Drone Chase

The drone chase aircraft, a QF-100, usually took off about the same time as the fighters and did his own boat check of the drone launch corridor. If boats were spotted the mission would go on hold until the boats cleared the corridor. On rare occasions a mission was scrubbed because of a boat in the corridor that couldn't be contacted.

On one of those occasions, all efforts at raising the boat operator on marine band frequencies failed. The drone chase made several low passes over the boat and reported no sign of life. Finally, one of our watercraft boats arrived on scene and pulled up next to the boat. The boat owner finally emerged from below deck rubbing his eyes and wondering what all the commotion was about. He had been asleep inside. It was possible he might have also been a bit drunk. By now all airborne participants were too low on fuel and the mission was scrubbed. The boat owner was warned of being in restricted waters and told his actions just cost the Air Force over a hundred thousand dollars.

As drone chase we loved this part of the mission because it was an opportunity to fly low. There was a barrier reef island just a few miles southeast of the launch corridor that had a state park and several miles of lovely beaches very popular with tourists. On nice sunny summer days when the fighter boat patrol was taking a while I liked to drop down to a hundred feet and cruise the length of the beach a quarter mile off shore wagging my wings to the beach goers. At the end of the beach I would plug in the afterburner and perform an abrupt and somewhat spectacular pull up. Was that showing off? Ya, I guess it was, but I never carried it too far. My thoughts were you never knew who might be on that beach watching the show.

Drone Take-off

I really liked flying drone chase. On takeoff from the main base I always requested a visual departure with a right turn out to stay below 1,000 feet. I found this was an opportunity to do some mild but legal hot dogging so to speak. With a flat takeoff I could accelerate to 300 knots quite quickly and at two or three hundred feet I would roll into 75 or 80 degrees of bank with a hard turn to the south and the droneway. It was a most unusual departure and I'm sure it commanded the interest of any observers not familiar with drone operations.

While waiting for a shoot box, the drone chase held in a designated area close to the drone-way where he could expeditiously call for the drone to begin takeoff. The drone needed a one minute countdown for takeoff and we all had our own land markings to use in determining where we could give the one minute call. When the drone chase heard the launch controller say, "chase, standing by your one minute call," it was a matter of pride for chase pilots to come back immediately and say, "on my mark – one minute." Then, if as usually happened, the chase was greatly out of position, he had to modify his ground track to make it all work out. The next call was "30 seconds" and then "roll the drone." At the roll the drone call the chase had to be turning unto runway heading a mile and a half behind the drone as it sat on the end of the droneway. Now, the objective was to catch up to the drone during its takeoff without overrunning it. The chase needed to be close to the drone as it retracted gear and flaps so he could do a 'clean and dry' check; that was to confirm the gear and flaps retracted properly and there were no hydraulic or fuel leaks. The chase was the eyes for the remote controllers in case something went wrong.

While on the Mobile Control once, I watched a very spectacular take-off. The pitch attitude gyro froze as the drone began rotating for take-off. The computer thought the drone wasn't rotating and continued to command the nose farther and farther up. There was an overcast cloud layer at 3,000 feet and when the drone disappeared into the clouds it was in a 70 degree climb. An F-16 can do a 70 degree climb but not an F-100. Basic aerodynamics won out and when it reappeared from the clouds it was now 70 degrees nose low, screaming at the ground in full afterburner. The resulting fireball didn't leave very much drone wreckage behind.

Echo and Romeo

Two pilots flew the full-scale drone by remote control for the takeoff and handed it off to the 'fixed site' before losing sight of it. One was called 'Romeo' and he controlled the plane's rudder or direction left and right. The other was 'Echo' which stood for elevator. He controlled the airplane's elevator or pitch. The Echo and Romeo also did the landing after the mission. The controllers operated from the top of a specially equipped radar van that had two control consoles. The 'mobile' was positioned a thousand feet behind the drone at the end of the runway for takeoff and during the mission was relocated to the approach end of the runway for landing.

Of all the tasks for drone operations, these two controllers had the most demanding because a mistake could easily result in a drone crash. Takeoffs were usually routine and boring unless the drone malfunctioned. If a malfunction was caught early enough the takeoff could be aborted. With its arresting hook lowered the drone stopped Navy style by catching an arresting cable at the far end of the runway. If it happened too late to abort the drone could crash.

The landing was never boring. The mobile was positioned just a few feet off the edge of the runway next to the planned touchdown point. Even if the drone was flying normally it was always an exhilarating experience to watch an F100 flying at more than 200 mph do a controlled crash onto the runway a hundred feet in front of you. If something happened to directional control and it veered toward the control unit there wouldn't be time to do anything except maybe mutter OMG.

For landing, the Romeo had the tough job of aligning the drone with the runway. Since he was offset to one side of the approach course, parallax was a big problem that he countered by using landmarks to guide him. Range was called out to him from a technician monitoring a short range radar scope in the van. At four miles the drone should appear to be over 'four mile tree', a distinctive tree growing off the end of the runway. At three miles, two miles and one mile other landmarks were used. At each mile depending on where the drone was in relation to the landmark a left or right correction was made until approaching the overrun of the runway. Then, it was strictly TLAR – That Looks About Right – until touchdown. Almost always the drone touched down straddling the centerline. Maximum concentration was required; Echo and Romeo didn't do any idle chatting during the landing phase.

During one drone recovery following an uneventful mission the drone just rolled out on final approach when Romeo shouted, "where's four mile tree? It's gone!" The four mile tree had been cut down or fell down. It just wasn't there. The anxiety level rose noticeably for the landing and a special manned mission was scheduled the next day so Romeo could pick out another four mile landmark. It was that important!

The Echo was the controller in charge and controlling pitch required the greatest degree of finesse and experience. When comparing the two positions a sudden change in direction was unlikely and if runway alignment wasn't satisfactory the option was always there to go around and try again although I never heard of that happening. A sudden change in pitch when close to the ground could be immediately disastrous.

During the hot summer months heating of the air on final approach was uneven resulting in invisible large bubbles of air that had different densities. While over the water everything was quite smooth but beginning at the coast, two miles out, Echo had his hands full. This was especially true over the dark overrun. For the last mile on final the Echo was constantly making pitch adjustments as the drone suddenly rose or dropped along its flight path. When it reached the overrun the Echo even anticipated a ballooning of the drone and countered it with forward stick and at the last moment countered again with aft stick. If not done exactly right the drone could touch down in the over-run which wasn't good. If the left tire blew in that situation the drone could veer directly into the mobile unit. The other extreme was landing two or even three thousand feet long making it really hard on Romeo to keep the drone on the centerline as it settled to the runway.

The Drone Will Self-Destruct In ...

The drone had a bomb package located in front of its wing, really the warhead from an AIM 9 missile. After an arming signal and then an activation signal from the ground the bomb would blow causing the drone to be literally cut in half terminating flight instantly. This was a safety precaution to prevent a drone from 'escaping' from the controllers and flying off somewhere on its own. There was also a fail-safe timer where, if radar contact was lost, after a prescribed period of time the bomb would blow.

In spite of these precautions there was one incident before I arrived at Tyndall where a QF-102 drone escaped and orbited overhead Panama City for over an hour. The alert force was launched and when the drone finally strayed out over water it was shot down. The reason the drone wasn't blown up was it had been a manned mission and of course we never flew manned missions with a self-destruct package. A collapsed landing gear during a practice landing dictated a controlled ejection out over the water but the pilot forgot to pull his throttle to idle. The jet continued to fly, and fly, and then fly some more. Imagine the pilot who has climbed into his inflatable raft waiting to be rescued as he watches his 'crippled' plane continue to orbit overhead. Talk about embarrassing!

Now, getting back to the mission in progress, the drone chase did his 'clean and dry' check on the drone; gear and flaps were retracted with no obvious leaking of liquids. Within a couple minutes of takeoff, the mobile unit controllers checked with the fixed site controllers to see if they had a good radar track on the drone. Control was transferred and it was now fixed site's job to control the drone until it was back on final approach for landing. The chase pilot flew a loose formation on the drone until the drone entered the live fire airspace. GCI control then gave the chase a position to orbit that kept him nearby but out of harm's way while the shooters were doing their thing.

Live Fire Profiles

The limiting factor on drone missions was usually the drone's fuel that was normally enough to allow four or five presentations to the shooters for firing their missiles. However, much of that was determined by the setups requested by the shooters. One of our favorites was the two versus one or 2v1. Two shooters would be paired on the drone per presentation. The first shooter shot an AIM 7 radar guided missile from 10 to 20 miles out and the drone did a barrel roll type evasive maneuver until missile passage. The second shooter then took the lead and maneuvered to a position behind the drone. When the second shooter shot his missile, a heat seeker AIM 9, the drone began a high G descending turn. With good luck we could get eight missiles out of the way on one drone mission. With bad luck we might get smacked by the very first missile.

Scoring Without a Kill

The full scale drone had the same evasion capabilities as a real fighter aircraft. It could deploy chaff, use ECM, do evasive turns and drop flares. The 'baby drone' could only turn or use a decoy IR pod for evasion. Our bottom line as keeper of the drones was the drone had to be allowed to do some sort of evasive maneuver at missile firing or it most assuredly would be 'splashed', shot down.

As mentioned previously, the missiles that were fired at the drone had their explosive warheads replaced with a scoring package that sent signals back to a ground station. This device told technicians exactly where in relation to the drone the missile passed allowing them to judge whether the shot would have resulted in a 'kill' if the missile really had a warhead. Occasionally, warhead missiles were shot at drones for various reasons and they almost always resulted in a drone kill.

At times when the drone had structural damage from a previous mission it was given clearance for a one way flight. On these 'no return' missions, the shooter chase was given a warhead missile for the coup de grace if the drone survived the other missiles. The ultimate opportunity for shooter chase, though, was when the drone was crippled preventing recovery and the shooters were out of missiles. He then armed up his 20 mm gun and shot the drone down. There was the time, though, when the drone even survived the gunning and had to be terminated by its destruct package. Shooter chase was on the receiving end of a lot of good natured ribbing and probably even bought a round at the bar that night.

Drone Recovery

Drones usually survived several missions although sometimes we ran into a string of bad luck and lost two or three drones in succession. When the drone survived, GCI control ran the drone chase on an intercept of the drone. We tried to make the intercept as expeditious as possible because by now the drone was usually at minimum fuel and a thorough battle damage check was required before bringing the drone in for a landing. Occasionally, this check resulted in a surprise. 'Uh, Oscar, (call sign of the fixed site drone controller) the drone is missing half of its right wing?' Other examples I saw were bites taken out of the tail or part of the engine nozzles shot away or holes in the fuselage. If the drone was flying OK a quick landing speed controllability check was done and the drone was landed if possible.

Now and then a drone was found to be too unstable at landing speed and if the shooters were still airborne and had missiles left we took the drone back out and continued to present it until it was either shot down or ran out of fuel. If there weren't any shooters available, we flew it back out to a clear area and blew it up.

Good Chute, Good Hook

The drone chase's final job was flying a loose formation on the drone until it landed. Usually he was just there but at times having a drone chase near the drone greatly aided in a safe recovery, especially if things weren't normal; bad crosswinds, a battle damaged drone, civilian air traffic straying into the drone's path to name a few. If everything went as planned, the chase's last comment would be "good chute, good hook."

Safety Pilot – Test Pilot

The pilots who flew the QF-100 were referred to as safety pilots but often times test pilot would have been a more accurate designation. We weren't test pilots, however. That designation was reserved for graduates of the test pilot school at Edwards AFB. In addition to flying drone chase missions we flew missions for controller proficiency, controller checkout, profile proofing and as a test bed for various experimental projects. I always reminded myself that if I ever got bored I needed an attitude adjustment because this was the most dangerous flying I ever did in the Air Force.

The Air Force's typical fighter accident rate was about five accidents per hundred thousand flying hours. I once calculated our accident rate to be somewhere between 100 and 250 accidents per hundred thousand hours.

Accidents Happened

Over the years there were many accidents during manned flying. A flare ignited in an experimental flare dispenser and caused a fire and an ejection for a friend, Fred Whitten. Twice, a collapsed main gear on a touch and go landing caused the loss of the jet and an ejection. An unintentional radar disengagement of the remote control system caused the loss of the jet and an ejection. Twice nose gears collapsed after hard landings and resulted in damage to the jet. A tank cap came off during takeoff causing a catastrophic engine fire and loss of the plane and pilot ejection. A pilot encountered nitrogen narcosis (the bends) during a cross country flight resulting in his death.

A Personal Experience

I am occasionally asked if I ever came close to ejecting. There was only one time that I did and it was during a mobile control site mission involving practice landings. Half way through the mission I rode through a particularly hard landing and, suspecting the landing gear might even be damaged, I didn't retract the gear during the go-around. I would leave the gear down and do a full stop. The auto takeoff mode was engaged from the ground control site but the computer thought that the gear was retracted so it didn't command full power. In fact, I was at 200 feet limping along just above the stall speed unable to gain altitude or increase airspeed. My left hand was holding the throttle full forward overriding the computer that wanted to pull it back. My right hand was holding the control stick and unable to reach the paddle switch located at the base of the stick. I could physically override the throttle position but the computer wouldn't let me select afterburner. So there I was, flying so close to the razor's edge that if I let go of either the throttle or stick I might not recover before hitting the ground. I finally decided that if I was going to gain airspeed I had to raise the landing gear to reduce my drag. I momentarily released the throttle and slapped the gear handle up. The effect was immediate –

airspeed began to gradually increase and I was able to fly out of ground effect. After landing I wrote up the gear for a hard landing inspection but the gear turned out to be OK. I was glad it was our maintenance people and not an accident board that ended up doing the inspection.

Schedule Change or Ejection

One lovely summer day when I went into the squadron I saw a change on the daily flying schedule. On Mondays we flew two flights to support drone controller training, one in the morning and one in the afternoon. I had been scheduled to fly the afternoon flight but now I was flying the morning flight instead. Paul Grignot had swapped flights with me because of a scheduling conflict with him. I flew a routine flight that morning. Paul's flight wasn't routine. On takeoff his F-100 caught on fire. The entire aft end was in flames as his gear retracted and he knew he had only moments to eject. He was taking off to the north. If he could delay ejecting about 10 seconds he could clear the base housing area and be able to aim the crippled jet into the water next to the DuPont Bridge. Approaching the water he rolled into right bank and at the last second ejected. He had one swing in his chute and was in the water. The flaming F-100 crashed a couple hundred yards away. Paul was in the water for about two minutes before a nearby boat pulled up alongside and invited him on board. He wisely turned down the can of beer he was offered. The accident investigation found a catastrophic failure in the afterburner. It had been an accident waiting to happen. I had missed an ejection by a schedule change. I've often wondered how the outcome would have been without the schedule change. I'll never know. Paul received an Air Force safety award for his actions.

Controller Proficiency Training

One of the many exciting missions we had was providing proficiency training for the fixed site controllers. After taking off and flying to the area, we'd give them remote control of the jet. The remote controller then practiced his evasive maneuvers such as four G back and forth weaves, a four G barrel roll or a four G constant airspeed descending turn. These were all aggressive, abrupt maneuvers and uncomfortable to ride through. I always kept my left hand braced against the canopy bow so I wouldn't be thrown around in the cockpit. My right hand lightly held the control stick which had an instant disconnect switch, a paddle switch, which allowed us to 'paddle off' and retake aircraft control if the maneuver didn't work out like it was supposed to. Frequently this was the case and you might hear from the remote controller, "sorry about that" meaning he had screwed up.

My first 'coupled up' (remotely controlled) flight was a real eye opener to me. From the first day of pilot training, smoothness in flying was valued and greatly admired. Beginning with formation flying it was called 'wingman consideration' and a smooth pilot was said to have good hands. So, it was a shock to experience flight done by the computer. The computer had never gone to pilot training. The computer didn't have wingman consideration or good hands. The computer, however, was precise. Tell the computer to turn left 60 degrees and the control stick would slam full left with the airplane rapidly rolling into exactly 30 degrees of bank. Then, the stick would abruptly center until the heading had changed exactly 60 degrees. Now, the process was reversed to roll back to wings level. Wham, bam, what next, you could almost hear the computer say.

Remote Control Touch & Go's

The other controllers, Echo and Romeo, also required proficiency practice - in landings. These were called 'mobile control missions.' A mobile mission was really adrenalin producing. After living through 45 minutes of remote controlled 'crashes' (Echo and Rzomeo called them touch and go's) at the droneway, a fixed site mission was almost boring. For a mobile mission I would make a wide turn out of traffic after takeoff and level at a thousand feet proceeding to a downwind position of the droneway. When the controllers got sight of me I transferred control to them and they did touch and go landings at the droneway until the drone reached bingo fuel. As just mentioned, the landings were usually more like controlled crashes. When the runway came rushing up and not feeling the stick coming back to round out required great resolve to not paddle off. There was a fine line the safety pilot had to identify – if he clicked off prematurely training would suffer, however, safety and possible aircraft damage were always considerations to be weighed. The landings were always firm and we just got used to it. That was the way you had to land a remotely controlled drone. I'm sure maintenance was very good at doing tire changes!

New Controller Checkouts

The worst job of all was when a new echo or romeo was being checked out. On those missions it was common to have to paddle off to prevent a catastrophe. Another attention getter was after the touchdown. The controllers always waited several seconds before bringing the power back in for the 'go' part of the touch and go. Almost always, the jet by now would be angling towards the edge of the runway. It was my job to decide whether we would get airborne again before leaving the edge of the runway. Sometimes it was uncomfortably close. One controller trainee, after countless hair raising, nerve racking missions still couldn't consistently land the jet. He was finally removed from training and we all breathed a sigh of relief.

Test Missions

Test missions were usually monotonous consisting of an hour or more of making straight and level runs while people on the ground collected various types of data from their equipment but some were very exciting or even dangerous.

One such mission was a test of a new drone control system. Test engineers wanted a low altitude over the horizon test of the drone doing four G weaves. I was the pilot unlucky enough to be chosen. When we were 75 miles out over the Gulf of Mexico the computer control system descended me to a thousand feet. I had a tremendous feeling of loneliness as I leveled out over the water. My entire visual world was water and sky. The water was rough that far out and the whitecaps seemed awfully close. Then, 'on my mark' we began maneuvering. At 400 knots the waves were flying by beneath me at a breathtaking speed and suddenly the F-100 rolled into 90 degrees of bank and I felt my G-suit inflate as the stick came back. Knowing that instant death was but two seconds below I guarded the paddle switch and my alertness to aircraft performance soared. After a few seconds of left turn the stick violently jerked to the right and the jet rolled into right bank, however, the maneuver caused the airplane to climb about 300 feet. The computer's answer was to continue rolling to 120 degrees until I was back at a thousand feet. It was extremely unnerving to be partially inverted that close to the water but little did I know that worse was yet to come.

After the next cycle the jet was still above a thousand feet when it was time to reverse turn so the computer followed its software instructions and rolled underneath for the turn reversal. I found myself completely inverted looking at nothing but water through the windscreen. I understood the dynamics of the maneuvering and the computer's reasoning and as I expected the roll continued until we were in only 70 degrees of bank. The altimeter bottomed out at 800 feet before we climbed back to one thousand.

I completed that mission but decided I would never agree to fly such a dangerous mission again. If I had been flying our two-seater model and the test engineer had been in my back seat I think he would have been very agreeable to flying the mission a thousand feet higher. We could have achieved the same results. Perhaps in designing their test profiles, the engineers needed some pilot oversight!

Auto-Landing Malfunction

Computers, though, didn't malfunction. They did exactly as they were programmed to do by their software designers. During another test flight for the new drone control system, this time to test a recent rewrite of the software for auto-landing, I encountered Murphy's Law in action. The engineers had to come up with a way to tell the jet when it was on the runway during the landing sequence. It could then commence the landing routine; command the stick to push full forward, the throttle to drive to idle and the brakes to come on.

Their solution was wheel spin-up. Whenever a jet landed the wheels went from almost zero rotation to a very fast rotation, spin-up. Sounded logical to them. I got to test it. At the end of the test mission during the landing phase and on short final I was high on glide path. Since we were close to the runway my piloting instinct called for a momentary nudge forward on the stick. The computer, though, made a decidedly more pronounced push over and two seconds later I felt the main gear crunch onto the runway. Due to the hard landing I was bounced 25 feet back into the air but I had ridden through worse. Or so I thought.

In previous hard landings the stick would freeze and hold the aircraft attitude as it settled back to the runway. A long landing would result but that wasn't a particular problem. However, the computer with its new software felt the wheels spin-up and decided we were on the ground. Immediately, the stick drove full forward and the nose of the aircraft plunged downward. A second later, as I was paddling off to take control, the nose gear made contact with the runway followed by the main gear. This time it was bone jarring and we again bounced into the air. I froze the stick in a slightly aft position and added a little power that softened the final runway contact – but the damage was already done.

The nose gear was unable to support the weight and folded back smoothly lowering the nose to the runway. Knowing a go-around was out of the question I deployed the drag chute and found I had good directional control with differential braking. I also shut down the engine to prevent doing further damage to it. With the F-100 skidding down the runway on its chin I had an unsurpassed view of the runway out the front during the rollout and soon brought the jet to a stop. My main concern was what the arresting cable would do. The pitot tube that normally protruded out from under the F-100's nose was laying flat on the runway. There was no doubt that it would slide under the cable but then what? Would the pitot tube just snap off (my guess) and the cable slide beneath the jet or would the cable ride up the nose and into the cockpit (my fear)? I attempted to lean forward to get some protection from the instrument panel and windscreen but my harness wouldn't allow it. I was quite confident the cable would slide beneath the jet but I still breathed a bit easier when it actually happened. It would have really hurt if the cable had come into the cockpit.

The emergency fire truck that is always positioned at the droneway during manned flying came racing up as I rolled to a stop. I raised my canopy and began to unstrap as the fireman ran up. In an attempt to inject a bit of humor into the situation, as I took off my helmet I said to him, "boy, that

F-100 scramble from the Vietnam era.

sure was a shitty landing." The guy didn't even crack a smile! I think he was probably disappointed that he didn't have a fire to put out.

Det 1, Holloman AFB

Tyndall was one of two bases that flew full scale drones. The other base was Holloman AFB in New Mexico. The unit at Holloman was called Det 1 as in Detachment 1. They had a much smaller operation and their mission was to fly drones for the Army. Holloman was ideally located on the edge of the Army's White Sands Missile Evaluation Range or WSMER. Whenever the Army had a requirement to shoot at a full sized target, Det 1 was ready. Two projects they got extensively involved in was the development of the Patriot missile system and the Chaparral fully automatic antiaircraft gun.

Ferrying F-100s

All drones delivered to the Air Force had to be modified at Tyndall and those that were needed at Holloman were ferried. That was one of my favorite missions. Fortunately for me, none of the other pilots cared very much to fly airplanes to Holloman so I got to do more than my fair share. Holloman was about 400 miles beyond the F-100's unrefueled range so we routinely stopped at Sheppard AFB north of Wichita Falls, Texas. Flying time to Sheppard was two hours. Holloman was another 45 minutes west.

The reason I enjoyed this mission was it afforded me the opportunity to just get away by myself for two or three days. Before the F-100 I had never been in an airplane by myself – other than the solo sorties in pilot training – and I liked the peace and solitude very much. In the F-100 I depended on no one else. I was it. Free. And, the feeling was most intense at 37,000 feet racing the westward sun as the farms and rivers and cities of the south slipped by beneath me. The only interruptions were occasional calls from ATC as they handed me off from sector to sector. There was very little radio chatter because all military fighter aircraft operated on UHF frequencies. Civilian air traffic was on VHF. The controllers simulcasted on both UHF and VHF but we never heard responses from anyone other than other fighters that might be in that sector.

A Viking Funeral

Occasionally I'd hear a controller answering a question from an airliner that had just passed by going the opposite direction. The question asked was obvious. It would go something like this: "Northwest 349, that is an F-100." Pause as the airline pilot

F-100C Super Saber

asked another question. "He's from Tyndall AFB going to Holloman AFB, New Mexico." Another pause. "Just a second, Northwest 349. Saber 03, Northwest 349 says he used to fly F-100's in Vietnam and he wants to know what the Air Force is still using them for now?" I would give the controller a brief explanation of how they were drone capable and used as targets for live missile testing over the Gulf of Mexico.

Then I'd tell the controller to tell the pilot of 349 to look at it as a Viking funeral for an old warrior. The response was always positive and the controller would dutifully repeat my message to the airline pilot.

Transient Alert

I would have chocks in and the engine shut down at Sheppard AFB two hours and ten minutes after takeoff from Tyndall. Their transient alert, a civilian work crew who were retired military aircraft mechanics, knew the F-100 well and did an excellent job in servicing the jet and stuffing a new drag chute in. They also kept spare F-100 parts such as tires, radios and navigation equipment and could swap out a malfunctioned piece of equipment in record time. I could usually be back in the air 45 minutes later for the final leg to Holloman.

The approach to Holloman provided a scenic tour of the White Sands that from ten thousand feet looked quite a bit like the white whipped topping of a meringue pie. The White Sands is most famous as the site of the world's first atomic bomb, Trinity. It also has a very long runway that serves as one of the space shuttle's alternate landing sites.

A Stone's Throw ...

Occasionally, approaching Holloman I would cancel my IFR clearance and come into the base from the north. Although Holloman lies in a desert, the elevation just a few miles to the north rises rapidly to over a mile high. Where Holloman is marked by gravel and stone, yellow or orange colored dirt and desert type scrub plants, a half hour drive by car will reward you with the beauty of forests and mountain meadows and meandering cool streams. Flying at 500 feet I often treated myself to this panorama of green splendor that seemed only a stone's throw from the dry brown desert. I wanted to drink in as much as I could before turning south to my desert destination.

Ferry Flight Malfunctions

I loved flying the F-100 cross-country to Holloman but was constantly reminded that it was an old war bird and in almost constant need of attention and care. An uneventful ferry flight was rare. I frequently had some type of aircraft malfunction that although usually minor still needed fixing at Sheppard during my servicing stop. A frequent malfunctioning item was the TACAN navigation instrument – in which case I would have to get radar vectors. The IFF or some other flight instrument could also be easily worked around but one particular flight turned out to be considerably more awkward.

A Memorable Flight

At the beginning of this ferry mission, I was just about ready for takeoff at Tyndall when a very nasty thunderstorm opened up on the base. I was kept at the end of the runway for over 15 minutes waiting for the field to reopen. At times the rain was so hard I couldn't even see the control tower. Finally the storm tapered off and I called the weather shop to find out what they could see on their weather radar. They assured me that there were no more thunder cells along my departure route so I called the tower and said I was ready to takeoff.

Looking back on it later I realized how bold of a decision that was considering I was taking off into IFR conditions in an aircraft that didn't have an onboard radar. Also, the clouds extended well above 40,000 feet – and there were unseen embedded thunderstorms in the area. But, I could be vectored around them as long as I had a radio.

My radio quit when I was passing 25,000 feet on my climb-out. Oh well, I was in the weather and it was dark but I decided I just had to play it a bit by ear and hope for the best. When losing your radio, FAA expects you to follow your flight plan to destination. Fortunately, because of my TACAN I knew exactly where I was, 30 miles north of Tyndall and at 62 miles I would turn to a 280 heading that would take me over New Orleans. Then, my TACAN quit. The navigation needle was rotating and the numbers in the distance window just kept rolling. My radio was just static. This was not good. I quickly noted the time so I could dead-reckon my position and then changed my transponder code to 7700, the emergency squawk. I decided I was traveling at approximately seven miles a minute so I should begin my left turn to 280 degrees in another three minutes and I was cleared to 37,000 feet so I continued my climb.

The clouds kept getting darker and darker. I kept reviewing my options and concluded that I was following the best one. I definitely couldn't turn around and go back and being blind without radar that could see through the clouds, my flight plan course was at least as good as any other. I finally leveled at 37,000 feet and made my left turn. Five minutes later the clouds parted and I was in sunshine. Oh, what a feeling of relief. Looking ahead I could see the coastline of Florida's panhandle and Pensacola. I changed my plan. I would maintain VFR, descend and land visually at Pensacola NAS. And then, the static on my radio stopped. I immediately heard my call sign and I answered Center. Yes, I was OK now. I told them I had lost both radio and TACAN but now it seemed my radio was OK. Again I changed my plan. I informed center I'd need radar vectors but I would like to stay with my flight plan and proceed on to Sheppard AFB. Center could have terminated my clearance but they didn't.

An uneventful hour later I was overhead Dallas and turned outbound on a northwesterly heading that would take me to Sheppard's initial approach fix. My radio quit again! I changed my squawk back to 7700 and then to 7600 to indicate my only problem now was loss of radio since they already knew I didn't have a TACAN. It was very hazy but I could see the ground. I thought that perhaps I could locate Sheppard visually. Then I heard my call sign on the emergency radio receiver. "Saber, if you hear Sheppard Approach squawk flash." I turned my transponder momentarily to the flash function. "Saber, I observe your flash. If you have no other problems squawk flash." I repeated the flash. For the remaining 15 minutes every military plane within 200 miles had to listen to Approach giving me instructions. I followed the radio instructions on my emergency receiver and soon picked up the runway and landed uneventfully. An hour later, my trusty transient alert crew had a spare radio and TACAN in the jet and I was off for a totally uneventful flight to Holloman.

Hot Brakes

On another trip I couldn't use Sheppard for a servicing base because they were socked in by weather. I called Kelley Field in San Antonio and their transient alert said they could give me gas but I'd have to repack my own chute. I checked the length of their runway, 11,000 feet long. The weather forecast indicated there was a good headwind. Although I had never done one before in an F-100 I decided that I would just do a no chute landing. Then I wouldn't have to worry about repacking my chute and off I went.

After an uneventful flight on a lovely day I was on short final at Kelley. I quickly reviewed my plan. Land on the 'first brick' with a firm landing and hold the nose up to aero-brake and above all remember to not deploy the chute. I did everything exactly right and when I put the nose down after aero-braking I began monitoring my slowly decreasing speed and the thousand foot runway remaining markers as they whizzed by. I was absolutely amazed at how reluctant the F-100 was to slow down without a chute. Finally at 100 knots I got on the brakes and began to apply steadily increasing pressure. For the last thousand feet I was really standing on them. I finally got down to a safe turn-off speed and followed Tower's directions for transient aircraft parking.

After climbing down from the cockpit I glanced at the wheels and noticed with concern that the brakes were smoking a little. I walked over to one of the wheels and at three feet could feel the heat from the by now cherry red brake stacks. I got no comfort from thinking of the fact that overheated brakes don't hit their peak temperature until 30 minutes later. As I walked the short distance to base operations to file my next flight plan and check weather I glanced back at the smoking brakes and was amazed and relieved that transient alert or tower hadn't called the fire department, a common procedure for hot brakes.

My main concern now was that the heat plugs would melt. In cases like this a safety device on the wheels of fighter aircraft, a wax plug, can melt and deflate the tire. The tire is of course ruined but it doesn't explode. Over the next 45 minutes the brakes cooled off and the smoking subsided. I realized how lucky I was. I came very close to gaining much unwanted publicity. That was my first and last no-chute landing in the F-100.

Accident Investigation

On another trip to Holloman I didn't fly an F-100. I was sent out to be the pilot member for an accident investigation board. On a routine fixed site, remote control mission the manned drone was at 2,000 feet doing a practice run for an upcoming live fire mission. When the drone responded incorrectly, the remote controller, a highly experienced former fighter pilot, told the safety pilot, "you've got it" meaning that he should take over the flying. The safety pilot in the cockpit didn't hear this and coupled with a passive personality became an observer as his aircraft crashed. With no one flying the airplane, the accident was a certainty. As the pilot's jet rolled past 90 degrees with the nose falling through 40 degrees low at 1,500 feet he finally decided he needed to eject. By the time his seat left the aircraft he was in 120 degrees of bank – partially inverted – and 70 degrees nose low. The pilot was way out of the envelope for a survivable ejection but everything worked exactly right and a quarter of a second after his chute blossomed he hit the ground suffering only minor injuries. If the pilot had not landed between the closely interspersed 50 foot sand dunes he would have died. Even though they are only 50 feet tall we determined his parachute opened when he was only 20 or 30 feet from the ground. His guardian angel was on duty that day!

A coupled up drone, as this one was, is constantly transmitting information through over 200 channels to the ground control site. This accident was probably one of the best ever documented. The accident board had two updates each second on the airplane's pitch, roll, airspeed, altitude, heading, engine settings and much more. On a long piece of graph paper I graphed six essential things; pitch, roll, G, heading, airspeed and altitude and it was all correlated with time. From this graph it was very easy to visualize the entire accident sequence.

As the pilot member of the accident board I was asked to re-fly the accident profile. I agreed to do it but suggested that we add 2,000 feet for a safety cushion. I flew the profile with the same controller doing the same actions as during the accident sortie. After flying the profile several times we repeatedly duplicated the conditions that led to the accident – with the exception of course that I paddled off in time to recover the aircraft.

This was my first accident investigation and I found it very interesting. The board president was a full colonel whom I knew previously. As do all accident boards we had a blank check to look at anything we wanted to – and absolutely top priority with every agency we dealt with. For example, the safety pilot's parachute had four out of its twenty four shroud lines broken. We wondered if these old chutes in the F-100 were safe to use. Our life support officer collected those four lines plus the other 20 and sent them off to a research lab in San Antonio to have them stress tested. They all passed the minimum strength specifications and we had the results in a couple days. We had some questions that could only be answered by people back at Tyndall AFB. We got airline tickets and flew to Tyndall to get our answers.

Virtually all interviews we did were recorded on tape and ten hours worth were transcribed by clerk typists. Every morning we began by proof reading and correcting the transcribed pages from the previous day. Because the typists knew nothing of flying, many terms were totally unfamiliar to them and errors were rampant. They would retype the corrected copies and then those would have to be proof read again. After only one day of proof reading I started turning off the tape

QF-100 is escorted by 2 F-15s

whenever the interview began wandering off because the clerks transcribed everything that was on the tape. We didn't need to proof read a conversation about yesterday's Braves baseball game.

When our investigation was completed we wrote up the accident report following strict guidelines set forth in an Air Force manual. The report was several hundred pages long and was sent to Headquarters Tactical Air Command to be reviewed by their safety office and the TAC commander, a four star general. When the report was found acceptable the main members of the board, including myself, traveled to Langley AFB, Headquarters of TAC, and the board president got to brief the accident investigation to the commander. As you might guess the briefing was spit and polish and practiced many times at lower levels – and it wasn't unheard of for the general to reject a board's findings. When that happened you basically went through everything all over again – reinvestigated.

Before I was appointed to the accident board, I had just torn off the roof of our patio because the wood had rotted out and I desperately wanted to finish it before the next rain. When told of my appointment I went to the group commander to plead my case in an effort to get out of the appointment but he said I was the best qualified for the job and he wanted me to do it. Wanting to walk away with something I then asked

Fighters As Drones

if I could at least be approved for a car rental during the investigation. As the saying goes, timing is everything and he readily agreed. When we all assembled at Holloman I found out that even the board president didn't have a car rental – he was given a blue Air Force staff car that didn't even have air conditioning. We used my rental car a lot. The investigation lasted six weeks and we worked six and a half days a week. Although I initially resisted the appointment, I fell back on the axiom, 'when defeat is inevitable sit back and enjoy it.' I truly valued the experience. I eventually got my roof finished but not before it rained – many times.

F-100 Instructor Pilot

When a friend, Fred Whitten, retired I replaced him as the squadron's only IP. The contractors also were allowed one IP. With my lengthy experience as an F-4 IP I was the most qualified for the job although I wasn't crazy about taking it. I felt I had spent more than my share of time in the back seat. Fred was given the job of

QF-100s parked at Tyndall

training his own replacement and seven sorties later I was an IP. Following some ground training at wing stan eval I also was the Stan Eval Flight Examiner (SEFE). For the next couple years, until I retired, I had the dubious distinction of being the only F-100 IP or SEFE in the Air Force – active duty or reserve.

Back Seat Landings

The most demanding aspect of the IP check out was landing from the back seat of the F-model (we called it the family model). We only had one two seater F-100 and it was only for training purposes and had never been made into a drone. Fred, who had never been an F-4 IP, gave me a thorough briefing on flying from the back seat and especially doing landings. I can still visualize the sly grin on Fred's face as he said, "You see, Jimmy, it's about the same as flying from the front seat except you can't see anything."

When Fred thought he had me sufficiently alarmed he took me out to the plane for our first flight. When I climbed into the rear cockpit I couldn't get over how much I could see compared to the F-4. A lot of equipment had been added to the rear cockpit of the F-4 over the years and with each addition forward visibility became poorer and poorer. So, I was pleased with what I found.

Landing from the back I found to be a piece of cake and Fred taught me a lot of things about the F-100 that no one else in the Air Force knew. He especially taught me things about adverse yaw that would have been nice to know when I was flying the hard wing F-4, another adverse yaw airplane.

Fred Whitten

Fred was flippant and cynical with the Air Force. Some thought him to be arrogant. I found him to be one of the most capable people I'd ever known. He didn't rise high in rank because he didn't put a lot of stock in following protocol. After a drone crash he briefed the base's commanding general. "Well, general, you should be happy we haven't crashed more. Flying drones is dangerous business." That wasn't what the general wanted to hear but it was what Fred believed and it was the truth.

In an airplane there were few better than Fred. As we said in the business, he had good hands. He was given an orientation ride in an F-15 and when the F-15 pilot asked him if he wanted to do the takeoff Fred said in his usual nonchalant manner, "sure." The F-15 pilot never asked for the stick back so Fred flew the entire mission– from the rear cockpit, including the landing. Now, I'm sure the F-15 pilot was telling him what and how to do certain things but–Fred did have good hands.

The Deadly Saber Dance

As the F-100 IP I checked out more than a half dozen pilots in the airplane. Most had never flown even the F-4 before so I passed on everything Fred showed me about adverse yaw because it was an unusual phenomenon not encountered in more modern aircraft. In fact it was first discovered in the F-100 and became known as the 'saber dance' because of how the aircraft reacted to it. During uncoordinated flight while landing the airplane looked like it was dancing as it responded to the pilot's incorrect and desperate aileron inputs. It would roll back and forth in ever increasing bank angles and frequently crashed during the landing attempt.

Adverse Yaw – What is it?

A brief explanation of adverse yaw: At high angles of attack (close to a stall) if aileron is used to roll the airplane a difference in drag between the wings causes yaw (skid) opposite the intended direction of roll. This causes the up wing to be more exposed to the relative wind causing more lift resulting in a roll in the opposite direction. The more an inexperienced pilot tries to counter the opposite roll with aileron the more the airplane rolls in that direction. The cure is to use rudder along with aileron to prevent the plane from yawing resulting in what is referred to as a coordinated turn. With modern fighters the computer makes precise control inputs based on what the pilot does with his stick. With computers, all turns are coordinated.

The F-100 pilots were taught in initial training to use rudder for coordinated flight and this prevented adverse yaw. The F-4C, D and early E models were called hard wings, and also had adverse yaw. We were trained to fly with our feet on the rudder pedals. When slats were added to the front of the E model wings adverse yaw was finally and forever eliminated and pilots began to once again fly with their feet flat on the floor. And, when they came to me to learn to fly the F-100 I had to train them to fly using rudder.

At Hahn AB, the 496th air to air squadron had an operations officer who was extremely skilled in flying the F-4 and he purposely used adverse yaw in 'dog fighting' to snap roll, a maneuver his adversaries could never follow. When it came to dog fighting he was legendary.

Max Performing the F-100

I discovered that these pilots who came to the F-100 from the newer fighters remained very timid to max performing the jet even after they finished their check out. One of our pilots, Billy, was highly experienced in air to air fighting. He had previously been in the elite aggressor squadron

F-100D Super Saber

where he flew the F-5 and he talked extensively about his air to air experiences. One day at the end of a two ship mission, Billy and I had some extra gas and I suggested we do a line abreast dog fighting set-up. Both airplanes start out, usually a mile apart, but line abreast and at 'go' they are free to maneuver to get behind the other airplane where, presumably, you could shoot him down.

At 'go' I plugged in the afterburner and snapped into a nose high climbing turn towards his 6 o'clock expecting Billy to do the same. Then we'd end up in a rolling scissors maneuver. However, I was dumbfounded at how timidly he maneuvered and in two turns I was in for a kill. Afterwards, Billy offered a lame excuse and I never brought it up again.

On two occasions I flew with students from the test pilot school. They were sent to us all the way from Edwards AFB just to be able to experience adverse yaw first hand. Those were the only orientation flights I'd ever flown where I was in the back seat but it was very rewarding because of their keen interest in the F-100's flying characteristics. They also weren't in the least bit timid in exploring the airplane's flying envelope to include adverse yaw.

Kick the Tires and Light the Fires

What appealed to me very much about flying the F-100 was it was all so uncomplicated. Before the F-100, a mission took from five to seven hours to include mission prep, briefing, flight, debrief and sometimes filling out grade books. With the F-100 we had a much more informal (and shorter) briefing and debriefs were rare.

Our F-100's were parked 'in the swamp' and that is not a reference to the University of Florida's football stadium. The swamp was an area on the far side of Tyndall's runway and at one time it used to be a short runway. When the drones began operating at Tyndall the area wasn't being used so it went to drone storage.

When I got checked out in the F-100 for each flight you had to find someone to drive you out to the swamp to your airplane and after the flight we could usually catch a ride back in the maintenance van. It was a hassle. I made some inquires in the appropriate offices and found a way for us to get 'flight line' decals for our personal cars and with that we started driving ourselves around the end of the runway to the swamp. No more being dependent on the crew van – everyone was happy. In fact I got an indescribable deep down joy by driving my VW to the swamp and parking it under the wing of my airplane, hopping into the jet and going off to fly. I couldn't help but think that this must have been the way it 'used to be' back in the open cockpit WW I days.

My new found liberties can best be illustrated by one flight in particular. I came racing up in my VW, five minutes late as usual, parked under the plane's left wing, started my engine, did my after start checks, had the wheel chocks pulled and taxied out. During the right turn onto the taxiway (I was later told by maintenance) I was a little late in coming back to idle and my exhaust blew the side chrome off my car. I wonder if that would qualify for the Guinness Book of Records. How many fighter types are there out there who have blown the side trim off their own cars!

Tally Ho the Space Shuttle

A standard profile for instrument proficiency was flying a Standard Instrument Departure (SID) to the east followed by a point to point to the Tallahassee IAF at 20,000 feet. When cleared for the procedure I did a TACAN penetration and low approach to the Tallahassee airport. With tower's approval I would do an afterburner acceleration and a max performance climb to 16,000 feet and then return to Tyndall. The Tallahassee tower didn't get to see many fighters, especially a vintage one like the F-100, so I imagine they enjoyed the modest show.

Although this was a very canned, routine profile, one day it wasn't quite so routine. During my penetration at Tallahassee, the radar controller called out traffic to me; "Saber, you have traffic 2 o'clock, 5 miles and level traveling east." When I looked in that direction I was quite startled to see a 747 with the space shuttle riding on its back. Then, I recalled that a recent shuttle mission had landed at Edwards Test Center in California and when that happens it gets a slow speed piggy back ride back to Kennedy Space Center on a specially modified 747. "Roger, tally ho on the space shuttle," I replied. My thought at the time was that considering the shuttle was an irreplaceable aircraft worth almost three billion dollars it should be given better protection from other aircraft.

Wow! That's Loud!

Our neighborhood in Panama City was beneath the Tyndall AFB outside downwind pattern. For practicing visual overhead patterns you would normally be in the 'inside pattern' and at the proper point on downwind you lowered gear and flaps and began a descending 180 degree turn resulting in a low approach or touchdown. At times for various reasons you might want to break out of the inside pattern and reenter. There was a prescribed ground path for the outside pattern which took you four or five miles away from the runway but still visible from the control tower. When I began flying at Tyndall I realized this ground track went almost directly over our house. To the delight of my daughters I would stroke the afterburner when over our house and the girls knew that Daddy was going by.

One day I was at home when another pilot did the same thing. Over our neighborhood he stroked the AB for a few seconds. I was amazed. No, I was horrified. The house shook. The noticeable jet engine noise that we were quite accustomed to suddenly became an extremely loud roar that preempted all other noises. For a few moments I even thought that a plane crash was imminent. It was actually quite annoying! I decided then and there not to light the AB anymore and was thankful I'd not had any noise complaints called in on me. Well, I almost stopped. When my mother and Aunt Betty were visiting I spotted them in the backyard and couldn't resist doing one more burner light. -

The T-33 T-Bird

The 82nd only had four slots for F-100 drone safety pilots and I was number five when I arrived in 1983. I didn't get to fly the F-100 until a slot opened up. As a consolation prize I was sent over to the 95th TFS, the Boneheads as they were called, to learn to fly the T-33. I was less than thrilled. I had my heart set on flying the F-

T-33 Shooting Star

100 Super Saber, the first century series fighter.

The 95th TFS

The 95th was a squadron composed of one lieutenant colonel, the commander, one major, the operations officer, a couple captains and 30 or more first assignment second and first lieutenants. The mission of the 95th was to provide targets for units all over the United States. If Duluth AB needed four target airplanes for a local exercise the 95th would send four lieutenants in their T-birds to do the job. They also had their own mini RTU. Since they flew the only T-33s in the Air Force they checked out their own pilots, most of whom came directly from pilot training.

When the next class started I became one of five or six students to begin ground training. A couple weeks after that I began flight training. The check-out program was about 20 sorties long and began with transition flying which was basic flying, stalls, aerobatics and landings. Then came instrument flying and an instrument flight check and finally formation flying.

During the middle of the check-out I got a cold that settled in my sinuses and after a very severe sinus block I was grounded for almost three months. When I got back on flying status I repeated a couple transition flights and then completed the rest of the check-out.

Flying the T-33

The T-33 was a very old airplane, considerably older than most of the lieutenant pilots who were flying it. The T-bird was the primary jet trainer in the 50's and 60's and was replaced by the T-38. The prototype made in 1944 became the F-80 Shooting Star, the mainstay of the USAF's fighters at the beginning of the Korean War and was replaced with the legendary swept wing F-86 Saber Jet.

Test Pilot Dick Bong

Famed WWII fighter ace Dick Bong was killed as a test pilot when his F-80 exploded shortly after takeoff. An investigation showed a 'plenum chamber' behind the cockpit had collected gas fumes causing the explosion. The T-33 was developed from the F-80 and had the same type plenum chamber which we always checked during our exterior inspection prior to flight.

Small in scale to what I was used to, the T-33 was a fun airplane to fly and we usually flew with the rear cockpit empty. It was a basic air machine that was exceedingly strong. Even at 40 years old the plane was still certified up to seven and a third G's. It didn't have nose gear steering – you had to use differential braking – and it didn't have an anti-G system either so we didn't have to bother with putting on G-suits.

Although the T-33 was pressurized I soon learned the canopy seals leaked notoriously. There was, however, a trick used at altitude to maintain an acceptable cabin pressure. We located where the air leaks were around the cabin bow and stuffed pages from our in-flight publications into

T-33A on downwind at Tyndall AFB

them. In this manner we could usually maintain a cabin pressure of below 25,000 feet. By Air Force regulation above 25,000 feet of cabin pressure required oxygen under pressure because even with 100 percent oxygen the body couldn't absorb enough into the blood!

The canopy was so strong on the T-33 that an acceptable practice to aid in stopping on the runway was to raise the canopy which then became a huge air scoop. With all other trainer/fighter type airplanes that would be a sure way to lose a canopy. The F-4 for instance was limited to 60 knots with the canopy open.

The Cocked Nose Gear

Another idiosyncrasy was the infamous 'cocked nose gear.' Any of the old heads who have ever flown the T-bird will vividly remember this embarrassing situation. The T-33 without nose gear steering had to be turned by differential braking. That's the same way you turn a tank. You want to go right you brake on the right side. The problem with the cocked nose gear usually appeared when heavy-weight, like before every takeoff. The typical scenario: The inexperienced T-bird pilot just pulled up to the number one position for takeoff and unwittingly stopped with his nose gear turned or cocked. When tower gives clearance onto the runway, our intrepid pilot applies power but the airplane doesn't move because the nose gear is turned perpendicular to straight ahead. Next, is the embarassed call to tower (and the world), "uh, tower, could you send the maintenance truck over to me. My nose gear is a little cocked." When it happened to me, I had an IP in the back seat and he had the technique. He was able to rock the plane by alternating power and brakes until the wheel turned just enough to un-cock.

Our typical mission at Tyndall was to provide intercept support for the weapons controller school. 16 years previously I was a student at that school, terrified of 'live missions' where I actually talked to real pilots. Now, I was on the other end flying the airplanes that long ago appeared so intimidating to me.

We always padded our bingo fuel so we would have a little gas left over to practice formation flying or sometimes fly 'extended trail' formation – thinly disguised dog fighting. The leader would tell his wingman to go extended trail and then tried to flush him out in front. The lieutenants who were inexperienced and untrained in BFM were very easy to outmaneuver but I admired their always 'gung ho' attitude.

Cross Country to LA

During my year flying the T-33 I had an opportunity to go on a four-ship cross country to Los Angeles. On Friday two hops (flights) got us to a base just outside Los Angeles where we checked into the BOQ and then rented a car. On Saturday we drove into Hollywood where we toured Universal Studios. The highlight of the day was sitting in the audience for three episodes of Wheel of Fortune. When Vanna White spent 20 minutes talking with the audience answering questions she came off as being a lovely and very authentic person. I had the feeling she did that just to be nice to us and we all loved her for it. I believe that is why she remains so successful so many years later.

On Sunday we flew two very long hops terminating that evening in Atlanta and on Monday we flew back to Tyndall. On the second flight on Sunday I experienced the most spectacular visual experience of my flying career. We were leveled off at 31,000 feet and between two very distinct thin layers of clouds. The setting sun suddenly illuminated the clouds above us and below us equally causing the entire world to turn scarlet red accented with brilliant streaks of orange. It was a sight I'll never forget.

The Lieutenants

I never met a more admirable bunch of young men then in the 95th. They were clean cut; I never saw one who smoked and they had an unsurpassed enthusiasm for their job and a true love for flying. After being operationally ready for a year most were 4 ship flight leads and deployment commanders responsible for taking several jets to strange bases and carrying on autonomous operations. Such responsibility was unheard of in a front line fighter squadron where detachment commanders were always majors or lieutenant colonels.

While I was flying with the 95th I was selected to be part of a review board to select young officers to attend the Air Force's Squadron Officer's School, SOS. While reviewing records of pilots and non-pilots from Tyndall for possible selection I was amazed at the differences I found. Consistently, the records of the pilots showed supervisors who took great care of them, wrote impeccable effectiveness reports and had them reviewed by colonels. The records of the non-rated officers were generally lackluster. The selection rates reflected this and were 90 percent for pilots and perhaps 20 percent for non-pilots.

Get Home-itis Proves Fatal

During the year I flew with the lieutenants they were always on the go and seldom was the entire squadron at home at the same time. On one deployment two aircraft were out supporting a local flying exercise and when it was time to go home one of the T-33s developed a maintenance problem. The fix required some serious repairs and a functional check flight by an FCF certified pilot. The flight leader was FCF certified so he opted to stay with the sick airplane. Maintenance worked on the jet during the night and into the next day and finally that afternoon it was ready to go. The flight lead did the FCF and it passed but now it was late in the day. Prudence would have led to the decision to call it a day and fly a one hop back to Tyndall the next morning but the flight lead was anxious to get back home. Too anxious.

The pilot took off after sundown and began his climb out in the fading light. He reached his cruising altitude of 31,000 feet and then things went terribly wrong. He experienced electrical problems losing cockpit lighting and many flight instruments to include the attitude indicator (ADI). The T-33 at that time had never been equipped with an emergency ADI and without attitude information the pilot lost aircraft control. He made an emergency radio transmission and then in the darkness fought to regain aircraft control until he impacted the ground somewhere in east Texas. He was one of the most professional and gifted young pilots I've known – but he never attempted ejection. He left a young wife behind and the T-33 was finally retrofitted with an emergency attitude indicator.

Retirement

After five years of flying the F-100 the time came for me to hang up my hat and retire from the Air Force. I had attended enough retirement ceremonies at the group's auditorium with all of the bells and whistles and Class A uniforms that I knew I didn't want anything to do with that. I wanted to just slip away and when I told my squadron commander, Chuck Hood, that I didn't want a retirement ceremony he said uh, uh, no way Jose. I would have a ceremony. It was only fitting that I have one to commemorate my years of service. I said OK, then I want to have it on the tarmac next to my airplane after my last landing. I was surprised when Chuck smiled and said it sounded good to him.

Champagne Flight

My last flight occurred on August third, 1991 on a day when the wing was standing down from flying. I was the only local flight at Tyndall that day so I could have any airspace I wanted and I could take off any time I wanted to. I chose a 1 pm takeoff time and flew to a nearby aerobatic flying area. For the next half-hour I flew every aerobatic maneuver the F-100 was approved to fly and then I came back to an empty traffic pattern and flew about 10 low approaches. I really wanted to do an afterburner closed pattern but my aircrew discipline won out, especially when I realized it might affect others coming after me on their champagne flights. When I was finally low on gas I full stopped and taxied back to a spot right next to my squadron building.

I was very surprised to see a large crowd of people waiting for me. By tradition I knew that I was about to get wet as soon as I climbed down the ladder. That is what happened during one's 'champagne flight', the last flight at an assignment. Tradition!

I unstrapped in the cockpit and an occasional glance at the ground confirmed my expectations. A friend, Steve Boe, was waiting with a wash-down hose. Knowing I was going to get wet I took off my helmet and g-suit and poised myself at the top of the ladder waiting for the right moment. Then, in a flash I was down the ladder and charging Steve and the hose. He got me for only a second or two and then we were each struggling for control of the hose. The crowd was delighted. As the contest continued Steve was losing out. In spite of receiving help from a lieutenant colonel, I was getting the best of them and soon they both ran and they both were wetter than I was.

A bottle of champagne was handed to me and I dutifully opened it and with a vigorous shake of the bottle sprayed everyone within 10 feet. I took a swig and passed the bottle on to others to share. A podium stand had been set up by now and after the group commander said some kind words and read my retirement order he presented me with the MSM, Meritorious Service Medal. I said a few appropriate words and at that moment spotted Jean and daughters Mandy and Becky in the front row of the crowd. I had not expected them. Jean and Mandy had taken off from school and Becky had driven in from Atlanta where she was a graduate student at Emory University. What a wonderful surprise. At that moment I realized their presence meant more to me than I had thought it would.

At the squadron we had a reception with cake and a vegetable tray. The ceremony was exactly what I had wanted – to retire in a soaking wet flight suit immediately following my last flight. Still visibly damp, Major Jim Olson retired and left the Air Force never to look back.

Small Steps Glossary

Terms and Acronyms Appearing In This Book

Glossary

2 ship Formation of two airplanes.

2V2 An aerial engagement of two airplanes fighting two others.

7600 IFF transponder code indicating loss of radio (NORDO).

7700 IFF transponder code indicating an emergency.

AAA (Anti-Aircraft Artillery). Guns of varying sizes for shooting down aircraft.

ABCCC (Airborne Command and Control Center). A modified 707 with a large radar antenna attached to its top, it provides radar coverage of the battle area.

Abort To discontinue the takeoff.

Abort Speed Maximum speed where you could discontinue the takeoff and still stop on the remaining runway.

ACM (Air Combat Maneuvers). Advanced air combat where basic fighter maneuvers (BFM) are used against one or more adversary aircraft in a pre-briefed controlled setting (setup).

ACT (Air Combat Tactics). Using ACM where tactics are used in a completely uncontrolled aerial engagement against 'similar' or 'dissimilar' adversarial aircraft it was frequently flown against 'the aggressors'.

ADC (Air Defense Command). ADC's mission was defense of the homeland and was in its glory during the cold war, the enemy being the USSR. It was deactivated in the 1980's.

ADI (Attitude Direction Indicator). The primary instrument to give both aircraft attitude as well as heading direction it is a gyroscopic ball with an artificial horizon and heading markers on it.

Adverse yaw First experienced in the F-100 it resulted in many crashes until it was understood aerodynamically. It was caused by uncoordinated flight at slow airspeed or high AOA and was prevented by use of rudder during turns. See pg 294 for an aerodynamic explanation.

Aero-braking A technique used for slowing an aircraft after landing.

AFMPC (Air Force Manpower Center). Where air force personnel assignments came from located at Kelly AFB in San Antonio.

AFOQT (Air Force Officer Qualification Test). A pre-entry test for determining eligibility for officer training.

AFSC (Air Force specialty code). Similar to the Army MOS it was a numeric code that designated a person's particular job in the Air Force. For a qualified pilot it was 1115. Letters were added to designate the type of aircraft. 1115F was an F-4 pilot. Prefix letters provided further information. An S prefix was for fighter weapons school graduates. K was for an instructor pilot.

Afterburner When selected on a fighter aircraft, it significantly increases thrust by dumping fuel behind the compressor stages of a jet engine where it is ignited. It also significantly decreases gas mileage. In an F-4 fuel consumption increased by a factor of four.

Aggressors Specially trained pilots who flew F-5 aircraft that were painted to represent soviet camouflage designs. The pilots were experts in soviet tactics and flew their F-5s accordingly.

AGOS (Air Ground Operations School). A school that trained FACs, ALOs and ROMADS. Tactical Air Command's school was at Hurlburt Air Field near Eglin AFB and USAFE's school was at Sembach Air Base near Ramstein Air Base, Germany.

Aileron roll A roll around the longitudinal axis using ailerons to initiate.

Aim 7 Sparrow Semi-active radar controlled air to air missile which guides on continuous wave (CW) radar energy provided by the launching aircraft.

Aim 9 Sidewinder Heat seeking (IR) air to air missile.

Air Force Reserve A major command in the Air Force that shares most of the duties of the regular air force to include flying all of the same airplanes but many of its members are part time having regular jobs in civilian life.

AKA Acronym that stands for 'also known as'.

Alconbury AB Known as RAF Alconbury, it was one of several English bases USAFE had fighters at.

ALO (Air Liaison Officer). The boss of the forward air controllers and assigned to a brigade or higher. He also was the air expert to the brigade commander and staff. His army counterpart assigned to a wing was the GLO, ground liaison officer.

Altitude chamber Capable of holding a dozen people it is a large metal chamber that can be depressurized to a simulated altitude of 45,000 feet. It is used to demonstrate the personal symptoms of hypoxia to aircrew members. See page 52 for a detailed explanation.

AMRAAM (Advanced Medium Range Air to Air Missile). A fully active radar missile, you can shoot it and leave as compared to the Aim 7 where the target has to be kept illuminated with CW energy until it hits its target.

Anti-G suit AKA G suit and humorously as 'go fast pants', it has five air bladders sewn into the garment, covering the calves, thighs and abdomen. As aircraft G increases the anti-G system correspondingly inflates the bladders compressing the lower portion of the body which reduces blood pooling below the waist. The device can increase G tolerance by at least two G's. Also see M-1 maneuver.

AOA (Angle Of Attack). The angle of the wing in relation to the airstream and indicates the amount of lift produced by a wing. The AOA and induced drag are used to compute a C of L, coefficient of lift.

AP (Anomalous Propagation). Radar returns from beyond normal detection ranges of a radar usually caused by radar energy bouncing off a temperature inversion giving what might appear to be a false return.

Approach Control Also known as Radar Approach Control or RAPCON, it provides radar control services to nearby airplanes.

Area 51 A large piece of land near Las Vegas where top secret projects are thought to be developed. Overflight is strictly prohibited.

Arming area Specified area near the end of the runway where live ordinance is armed before takeoff.

Arrival Control See 'approach control'.

ARTEP An army field exercise that lasted 3 or 4 days. It usually pitted 'red' forces against 'blue' forces in an imaginary conflict.

ATACC (Alternate tactical air control center). In Korea it was located in Taegu and in the event of war the command center could relocate there and be relatively safe from being overrun.

AWACS (Airborne Warning And Control System). A modified 707 with a big radar antenna mounted on its back it can provide detailed radar coverage well behind enemy lines.

B Syllabus A 7 month long F-4 training course for pilots right out of pilot training, Also, navigators were trained to become WSO's.

B-4 Bag A multipurpose large zippered canvas bag.

B-52 Stratofortress Eight engine bomber that was the mainstay of Strategic Air Command for decades, it is still in use.

Bandit A Code word for an enemy aircraft.

Barrel roll   Aerobatic maneuver using rudder and ailerons where the aircraft, using varying G, rolls around a distant imaginary point.

Basic survival   A survival course located at Fairchild AFB in Washington State. Training was given in surviving in the wilderness and on how to conduct oneself in a POW situation.

Battalion   An army organizational designation for a unit consisting of several hundred people commanded by a lieutenant colonel. Made up of several companies its Air Force equivalent is the Squadron.

Belga Control   Air traffic control for the country of Belgium.

Below mins   When the weather is less than what is required to be able to land on instruments. For a weather category A it was 300 feet ceiling and 1 mile visibility.

Bergstrom AFB, Texas   Located near Austin, it hosted recce F-4's until its closure in the 90's.

BFM   (Basic fighter maneuvers). Defensive and offensive maneuvers flown by a single aircraft to be able to shoot his opponent down or prevent himself from getting shot down.

Bingo   A pre-computed fuel level where you have to terminate the mission in order to have enough gas to get home.

BIT check   (Built In Test) It enables the operator to check out the functioning of his (radar) equipment.

Bold face procedure   Emergency procedures that are so important they must be performed immediately before referring to a checklist. For abort it was **throttles idle, chute deploy, hook down.**

Bombs triple/ripple   A switch selection that causes bombs to be released three at a time or all in quick succession. Timing between bombs is also selectable.

Bone yard   Located at Davis-Monthan AFB in Tucson, Arizona, it is where all military aircraft are retired for parts supply, resale to other countries or recycling.

Boneheads   Nickname for 95th squadron at Tyndall AFB that flew T-33's. They later converted to F-15's.

Boomer   The aircrew member on a KC-135 air refueling tanker who operated the boom to 'plug in' receiving aircraft.

BOQ   (Bachelor Officer Quarters). Temporary or permanent quarters for single or unaccompanied officers, especially when on TDY.

BQM 34a   Subsonic drone target AKA as the 'baby drone' because it was only about 10 or 12 feet long. It was made by Raytheon and used extensively by the Air Force and Navy. See subscale.

BQM 34f   Supersonic version of the BQM 34a it was capable of speeds of Mach 1.5.

Small Steps Glossary

Brigade Army organizational unit consisting of several battalions usually commanded by a colonel. The Air Force equivalent is the Wing.

Bubble check Very close in fly-by of a radar site's radar antennas. See page 27 for more.

BX (Base Exchange). The retail outlet on Army and Air Force bases. The Navy call them PX's for port exchange.

C ration Food pack meals developed during WWII consisting of individual meals contained in vacuum sealed cans.

C Syllabus F-4 training course designed for pilots with experience in another fighter aircraft. Course duration was about 3 months.

C-130 Hercules A cargo aircraft with 4 turboprop engines. It was the workhorse airplane for short haul missions and could land on unprepared surfaces. It is considered to be the most successful cargo aircraft ever.

C-141 Starlifter The mainstay for long haul cargo aircraft. It was partially replaced by the C-5 Galaxy that could also carry oversized cargo (tanks).

C-47 Sky Train Also known as the Goony Bird, it achieved fame by 'flying the hump' in Burma during WWII. It is the military version of the DC-3, a tail dragging airplane and is still being flown today in 3rd world countries.

C-9 Nightingale A med-evac aircraft, the Air Force flies it all over the world for medical evacuations.

Cable engagement An arrested landing using a tail hook to snag a cable stretched across the approach end, mid field or departure end of military runways. The cable is attached to B-52 brake drums on each side of the runway. Upon engagement, the jet will come to a stop very quickly. Catching a cable is very useful for planes with directional control problems.

Cantonment area The living quarters area of an installation. At Mangil San, Korea it was where the chow hall, barracks and other support facilities were located at the base of the hill.

CAP (Combat air patrol). A defensive action designed to deny the enemy the use of surprise attack. In Korea there was a dawn CAP and a dusk CAP which were considered primary times for an air assault if it were to happen.

CBPO (Consolidated Base Personnel Office). Where all of the base's administrative functions occurred.

Cement bomb A MK-82 five hundred pound bomb casing that was filled with cement to allow realistic bombing training without the 'bang' or explosive danger.

Certification Board A reviewing board made up of the various wing staff agencies and headed up by the wing commander.

Certifying An annual requirement for all aircrews that 'sat' nuclear alert (victor alert). It consisted of a very detailed briefing about an alert line to show the board that the aircrew could credibly attack the target and maybe even return home.

Chain of command An inviolate rule was to follow the chain of command with complaints or in reporting anomalies and began with the flight commander, squadron commander, director of operations and finally wing commander.

Chandelle A graceful, climbing 180 degree turn with the nose climbing ever higher until the completion of the turn which then required a close to zero G pushover to level flight.

Clark Air Base Located in the Philippines it was the primary staging area in the Pacific for Japan, Korea or SEA. Clark AB was sufficiently damaged by the eruption of Mount Pinatubo in 1991 that all base personnel were evacuated and the base was closed.

Climb schedule With the T-37 the optimum climb airspeed decreased with altitude requiring constantly adjusting airspeed during the climb.

Close trail A formation where wingmen fly up to 2 ship-lengths behind and below the plane in front of them – a very fun formation to fly because the lead is free to do mild aerobatic maneuvers.

Cocked An aircraft on alert status that was completely prepped and ready for a quick response takeoff.

Cocked nose gear A condition that happened to the T-33 aircraft because it had a free- wheeling nose-gear (no nose gear steering). See page 297.

Cold War A period in our recent history when the US and USSR nuclear arsenals had proliferated and the danger of a nuclear war was very great.

Collateral board Can be convened following an aircraft accident and its purpose is to find fault for the cause of the accident. This contrasts with the accident board whose only goal is to find the cause in an effort to prevent future accidents.

Combat Echo TAC's program for testing air to air missiles and providing firing experience to aircrews. See page 269 for more.

Combat Pike ADC's program for certifying its interceptor aircraft for using nuclear missiles. See page 269.

Comps Comprehensive exams that are the culmination of a masters' degree program. They can be either written or oral.

Comptroller An officer who was responsible for finance and accounting, usually an O-6.

Contact check A check ride early in the training in a new aircraft that focused on contact flying activities such as aerobatics, stalls, slow flight and landing patterns.

Contact flying The initial flying when checking out in a new aircraft. See contact check.

Continuation training Referred to as CT it was Training done by instructors to maintain their own flying proficiency and was usually air to air or air to ground training. Turkey shoots on the gunnery range were a common means.

Crew rest A requirement for all aircrews before they flew was for 12 hours of uninterrupted rest from the end of the last official duty on one day until showing up for work the next day.

Crew solo A student pilot and a student WSO flying together.

Cross country Consisted of flying an aircraft away from the home base, usually during a weekend and was planned for 5 'hops' or sorties.

Cross-under A three step maneuver where a wingman moves from one of his leader's wings to the other.

Cuban 8 An aerobatic maneuver consisting of three fourths of a loop, a roll to upright and three fourths of another loop with another roll to upright. At completion the aircraft has described a figure 8 lying on its side.

Curvilinear A method of delivering a bomb on a target where the fighter is constantly changing heading and altitude. Accuracy is usually diminished but survivability from AAA is greatly increased.

Dart Deployed aerial recoverable target . See page 137 for a complete description.

Davis-Monthan AFB Located in Tucson Arizona it is the home of MASDC (boneyard) where retired aircraft are stored for later use as parts or metal recycling. Some even get to fly again.

Day shift Hours varied but usually from 7 am until 4 pm and was part of the three shift rotation.

Departure Control Provides radar guidance to aircraft as they depart the base and frequently makes hand-offs to an FAA regional facility.

Det 1 (Detachment 1). Located at Holloman AFB, NM, its mission is providing drone support over the White Sands Missile Range (WSMR) for Army projects such as the patriot missile.

DH (Decision Height). An altitude during a precision approach where the pilot has to make the decision to land or go around. It frequently was 300 feet for the F-4.

DLO (Deployed Liaison Office). A part of the 82 TATS that received deployed units that came to Tyndall for TDY. See Page 269.

DME Distance Measuring Equipment. A partner instrument with the TACAN that shows the distance to the station.

DNIF (Duty Not Including Flying). This is a frequent result when reporting to the flight surgeon when sick.

DOT (Director of Operations Training). A staff member (or his/her office) that does much of the DO's staff work.

DR (Dead Recon). The basis of all navigation, it consists of using time, distance and heading. If all else fails there is DR (if you know where you are to begin with!).

Drag When airplanes need to take spacing from each other, they 'drag' by slowing up a specified number of knots for an amount of time. Also, one of the four components of aerodynamics; lift, weight, thrust, drag.

Dreamland A prohibited highly classified area located near Las Vegas where top secret projects are thought to be worked on. AKA area 51.

Drone chase A jet usually of the same type as the full scale drone that chased the drone for takeoff through departure and again for the approach and landing – the eyes and ears for the ground controllers.

Droneway A specially constructed 8000 foot long runway south of Tyndall's main runways, it is positioned so that drones taking off and landing spend a minimum amount of time over land.

Eastern Control An air traffic control facility that controlled civil and military aircraft over England .

Echelon A formation where all wingmen are on the same side of the leader and in numerical order. Turns are always made away from the formation and all aircraft stack level. This is the usual formation that leads to flight split-up such as in the overhead traffic pattern or upon range entry.

Echo Stands for 'elevator' and is the call sign for the remote controller at the droneway who visually controls the up and down movement (pitch) of the drone.

Edwards AFB Located by the Mohave Desert it is the home to most of the Air Force's flight testing and the test pilot school.

Eject Emergency escape from a fighter aircraft or the command to do so.

EKG Echocardiogram (EKG comes from the German spelling of the term). A simple test of the heart that can pinpoint many irregularities. The School of Aerospace Medicine has the most extensive collection of EKG's in the world.

Elephant Walk The simulation of nuclear bomb laden aircraft taking off where they take the runway and briefly light the AB and then taxi back to parking.

Evasive maneuver An escape maneuver for the drone to avoid harm from the terminal phase of an air to air missile, It provides a score for the missile and an opportunity to fly again.

Extended trail Similar to close trail formation except each aircraft flies up to a thousand feet behind the leader following his flight path.

F-100 Super Saber The Air Force's first supersonic fighter and the first of the 'century series' fighters.

F-102 Delta Dagger The first workhorse interceptor for ADC it was later modified to become the F-106. Both were delta wing supersonic aircraft.

Small Steps Glossary

F-105 Thunder Chief or 'Thud' Originally intended to be a nuclear bomber it did a great job during Viet Nam but suffered tremendous losses to missiles.

F-106 Delta Dart A follow-on to the F-102 it was a very popular interceptor for a long time.

F-117 Nighthawk The first stealth aircraft, it was limited to night time bombing. It was a very closely guarded secret making its debut during the Panama Canal invasion and led the way during Desert Storm in Iraq.

F-4 Phantom II In its hay day in Viet Nam it was produced by the thousands in C, D, and E models for the Air Force and many other variants for the Navy and other countries. It was known for being able to do just about anything but nothing really well.

F4 RTU (Replacement Training Unit). During the war in SEA a lot of pilots were trained to fly the F-4 and then fed into the pipeline for SEA to 'replace' other pilots who had completed their combat tours. Now it applies to units that give check-out training to pilots and WSO's.

F-5 Tiger II Was similar in size to most MiG aircraft and made an excellent aggressor MiG simulator when flying DACT. First version was called the Freedom Fighter and that evolved into the T-38 Talon.

FAA (Federal Aviation Administration). A federal agency that is in charge of all matters concerning aviation. Military aviation also had to comply with FAA requirements.

FAC (Forward Air Controller). An Air Force pilot who worked with the Army in receiving air support requests and planning and controlling air support. In Viet Nam the FAC flew O-1, OV-10 and A-1E aircraft and thus were airborne FACs. Later, they were mostly ground FACs and traveled with their assigned army battalions.

FACP (Forward Air Control Post) A small radar unit (sometimes mobile) that was a gap filler.

FAF (Final Approach Fix). The fix (point) from which the IFR final approach to an airport is executed, and which identifies the beginning of the final approach.

Fairchild AFB Located in Washington State it was the home for basic survival school to include the Trek and the POW camp.

FAMCAMP (Family Camp). Most bases have camp grounds for military families that want an inexpensive place to set up their campers for a few days.

FCF (Functional Check Flight). A flight profile to check how well an airplane performed in relation to certain minimum specifications. An F-4 required an FCF following a double engine change or if it hadn't flown for three weeks or longer (hanger queen status).

FEB (Flight Evaluation Board). A legal reviewing board that is sometimes convened to determine if a pilot should continue in a course of training, be reassigned to a multi-place aircraft or even have his pilot wings taken.

Ferrying A non-operational flight where an aircraft is moved to a different operating location.

Fighter Lead-in Training (FLIT) Established for the purpose of giving RTU destined pilots a less expensive exposure to the different areas of flying a fighter aircraft. The aircraft flown was a modified T-38 that could carry bombing dispensers and captive missiles.

Fighter Weapons School Located at Nellis AFB, Nevada (Home of red flag) it trains the Air Force's weapons and tactics experts in the various fighter aircraft.

Fingertip Also known as close formation it is flown with 3 to 5 feet lateral clearance between aircraft wingtips.

Flight Surgeon A doctor who is trained at the school of aerospace medicine at Brooks AFB in San Antonio (known as SAM Brooks), they are required to regularly participate in flying activities. In the F-4 they could carry out some of the duties of a WSO.

FLIT See Fighter lead-in training.

Formation check One of the many flight checks in UPT it evaluated formation flying and various formation maneuvers.

Formation landing Done once in UPT for those pilots who were going on to fighter aircraft. A formation landing was done by flying fingertip but stacked level with lead until touchdown and was done regularly after UPT.

Foul A call made by the RCO on an air/ground gunnery range or by dart chase for committing an unsafe act.

France Control Air Traffic Control in French airspace.

FTO (Flight Training Officer) At OTS, he or she was responsible for all aspects of training for a flight of approximately 18 OT's.

Full scale drone A real fighter aircraft that had been retrieved from the MASDC (bone yard), de-moth balled and modified for remote control operation.

Full Stop A landing that results in a full stop as opposed to a touch and go or a low approach.

G (Gravity). An increase in weight that results from a change in acceleration most frequently due to turning. At 5 G's, a 200 pound person would effectively weigh 1000 pounds.

G suit See 'anti-G suit'.

GAR (Ground Attack Radar). A phase in RTU that was oriented to simulated nuclear deliveries using the F-4 radar to find the target.

GAT (Ground Attack Tactics). After learning the basics of dropping bombs, this phase taught the use of tactics in delivering the bombs to the target.

Gate An old term used in ADC for going maximum speed using afterburner.

Gatling gun The F-4 internal gun in the e model and gun pod in the c and d models. It had 6 barrels that rotated, hence the name, Gatling gun.

GCI (Ground Controlled Intercept). GCI controllers had the job of vectoring pilots on 'bandit' aircraft using precise parameters to make an intercept. 90 degree beam and 135 degree front were examples of typical intercepts.

GIB (Guy In Back). The WSO in the F-4 back seat who among other duties ran the radar and monitored his pilot as time and duties allowed.

GLO (Ground Liaison Officer). An army officer, usually a captain or major, assigned to a wing to advise in Army matters.

Grade book Grade books for students were in alphabetical order in holders lining the squadron hallway and were checked diligently before flying with a student and a grade sheet was done after a flight. Squadron commanders and operations officers often spent Saturday mornings checking all grade books.

Green Flag An offshoot from Red Flag with a different focus and objectives.

Ground effect A cushion of air close to the ground that causes aircraft to tend to float down the runway when landing.

Ground speed True airspeed when adjusted for wind is ground speed, the speed an aircraft is traveling over the ground.

Gunnery camp A base with an air/ground range nearby that fighter squadrons deploy to for the purposes of filling their semi-annual bombing squares.

Gunnery qualification Each gunnery event such as strafe, rockets or low angle bombing, had qualification criteria and to qualify in the event a pilot had to have at least three in a string of six scores within those parameters.

Gunnery range A scoreable range controlled by an RCO. See page 119 for a description and photo.

Headquarters USAFE US Air Forces Europe is a major command and is located at Ramstein AB, Germany and has five operating bases. It was 90 minutes by land and 15 minutes by air from Hahn AB.

Hickam AFB, Hawaii Headquarters for Pacific Air Forces on the island of Honolulu, Hawaii.

High yoyo A BFM maneuver that can prevent overshooting your opponent by momentarily flying above his flight path to lose overtake and then sliding back to the inside of the turn. If botched it invites the opponent to attempt a reversal and a change in roles.

Holloman AFB, New Mexico Home for Det 1 where they operated drones over WSMR for the Army.

Hot pit refueling To help in quick turning an aircraft to a second sortie the aircrew, after landing, would be directed to taxi to the hot pit refueling area where hoses from underground fuel storage would be hooked up to the airplane while it was still running. This saved waiting for a fuel truck after engine shut down. Maintenance loved it; pilots hated it.

Houston Center A regional FAA facility that controlled all aviation for the south central part of the country.

Hurevac (Hurricane Evacuation) An evacuation of aircraft that are in the path of a hurricane. All bases in the south and east have evacuation plans and agreements to go to other bases for a temporary 'bed down' until safe to return to home base.

I Syllabus A course of flying and academic training to train instructors in a certain aircraft.

IAF (Initial Approach Fix). A point identified by a TACAN radial and DME (distance)for the purpose of initiating an instrument descent for a non-precision approach or a radar pick-up for a precision approach.

ICAO International Civil Aviation Organization, a UN organization that standardizes aviation rules for the entire world.

IFE (In-flight Emergency). When declared it commands traffic priority.

IFF (Identification Friend from Foe). A transponder carried by all military and commercial and most private aircraft that sends a special identification signal to control radars. It also provides other information about the aircraft.

IFR (Instrument Flight Rules). Special rules that must be followed when flying in weather conditions or in certain designated airspace.

IFR Clearance A specific clearance required by all aircraft when in IFR conditions. Typically, it is required when destination weather is less than a 3000 foot ceiling and/or 3 miles visibility. It can be given by any FAA facility to an aircraft once identification is made.

IFR Downwind A specified path parallel with the runway that is offset by about 10 miles and is flown by aircraft to position themselves for an instrument approach to that runway.

ILS (Instrument Landing System). A self contained precision approach landing system that can be flown without the use of a radio (NORDO). Course and flight path guidance are provided by pitch and bank steering bars on the ADI.

IMC (Instrument Meteorological Conditions). Weather conditions that require the use of IFR rules.

Immelman An altitude gaining aerobatic maneuver that consists of half of a loop. When inverted at the top, a roll to wings level is done. An immelman is also a BFM maneuver where a pilot is attacking another aircraft using a climbing turn.

Indicated Airspeed (IAS). A measure of the amount of air molecules passing by the airplane. This is useful in seeing how close you are to the airplane's stall speed. With a constant ground speed, as altitude is increased air density and indicated airspeed will decrease.

INS (Inertial Navigation System). A system of three gyros, one for each of the three axis, once it is aligned any movement of the aircraft is recorded as resistance by the appropriate gyro(s) and a corresponding change in motion

Instrument check An annual requirement for all pilots that measures instrument flying skills.

IP (Instructor Pilot). A graduate of the I syllabus and qualified to perform certain duties not allowed to other pilots. For instance a touch and go landing couldn't be done without an IP on board.

IR Missile (Infrared Missile). A missile such as the AIM 9 sidewinder that guides on IR (heat) energy.

KADIZ (Korean Air Defense Identification Zone). Most countries have identification zones surrounding them where aircraft must be identified before entering. This is usually done by a properly filed flight plan. If identification isn't made an air intercept is sometimes required.

KC-10 A modified DC-10, it is an in-flight refueling tanker that is replacing the KC-135 tanker.

Kelly AFB, Texas Located in San Antonio it is the Air Force's manpower center – AFMPC.

Kimpo Airport, Korea An international airport just outside of Korea's capitol, Seoul. When assigned to Korea most US military personnel flew into Kimpo.

Knock it off An order that could be given by anybody in an aerial engagement to terminate the 'fight'. Sometimes given due to an observed unsafe condition or bingo fuel it most often is because training objectives have been met.

Knot ICAO unit of measure for speed based on nautical miles per hour. A nautical mile is 6080 feet whereas a statute mile is 5280 feet. 100 knots is about 115 mph. Also see Author's Note on page 2.

Lackland AFB, Texas Located in San Antonio it is the recruiter training headquarters for the Air Force.

LADD Low Altitude Drogue Delivery. A method of delivering a nuclear bomb that will result in an air burst of the weapon.

Locked up A radar return locked up by a radar would automatically track it and compute required turns to achieve aircraft or missile intercept.

Loop An aerobatic maneuver where the aircraft flight path describes a circle when viewed from the side. In an F-4 it required at least 500 knots and 10,000 feet of altitude.

Low yoyo An offensive BFM maneuver to gain closure on the bandit by trading altitude for airspeed while staying inside his turn.

Luchers Air Field, Scotland A royal air force base in northern Scotland.

M-1 maneuver A technique that a pilot learns that allows an increase in G tolerance. It requires tightening of muscles below the lungs and forcibly expelling air in bursts when breathing to avoid relaxing the diaphragm muscles. It is essential to withstanding high G forces. See G Suit.

MacDill AFB, Florida An Air Force Base near Tampa that has been in the F-4 and F-16 RTU business because of the proximity of Avon Park gunnery range and over-water air to air ranges.

Mackay Trophy An award given by the USAF for the most meritorious flight during the year.

Mangil San A radar site situated on the west coast of South Korea 30 miles due west of Osan AB.

Maple Flag A Red Flag type exercise held at CFB Cold Lake, Alberta Canada.

MASDC (Military Aircraft Storage and Disposition Center). Known as the bone yard the dry climate of Tucson, Arizona makes this an ideal site for storing retired aircraft.

Mass briefing A briefing held for all participants of an exercise or air operation where the common elements are given to everyone and timing deconfliction times are provided. This is followed by unit and flight briefings further delineating roles and responsibilities.

Max power Known also as VMax it means using full afterburner to get maximum thrust and airspeed.

MDA (Minimum Descent Altitude). An altitude an aircraft descends to during the terminal phase of a non-precision approach until the runway is sighted.

Med-evac An air evacuation for medical reasons, frequently on the C-9 Nightengale, a specially equipped DC-9.

Medina AFB, Texas An annex of Lackland AFB, located in San Antonio, it was home to the Officers' Training School.

Mexico Beach A small community 15 miles south of Panama City, Florida, it was a favorite place where people TDY to Tyndall AFB could rent half of a duplex for a few weeks.

Mid-shift The shift that connected day shift and night shift (midnight shift).

Small Steps Glossary

MiG – A name applied to many of the Soviet fighters that were designed by the famous Russian aircraft designer, Mikoyan.

MiG 23 Flogger A small swing wing fighter that was extremely fast but not much at turning. To see it was to defeat it.

Mike Call sign of the drone mission commander, usually an Air Force major or lieutenant colonel.

Mil power (Military power). Maximum power available without using the afterburner.

Mill An angular unit of measurement for determining the depression of the gun sight. Bomb release parameters determine how many mills the sight should be depressed from level flight.

MK 107 A practice bomb with high drag metal fins giving it the flight characteristics of a nuclear bomb attached to a parachute.

MND-S (Maintenance Non Delivery – Supply). A designation for maintenance when they can't deliver an airplane that is on the flying schedule because supply, for various reasons, hasn't provided a needed part.

Mobile Control AKA RSU. An air conditioned portable unit that is positioned by the end of each runway. The unit has windows on all sides, telephone hotlines to key agencies and UHF radios. An aircrew monitor is assigned to the appropriate RSU as a safety observer.

MR (Mission Ready). A designation for a pilot or WSO who is qualified to perform his squadron's assigned mission having completed required training and passed a qualification check.

MRE (Meals Ready to Eat). The follow on to the canned 'c-ratuions' these are freeze dried and only need water and heat to produce a very palatable meal.

MS - (Mission Support). A designation like MR but reflects a pilot or WSO who is less than fully qualified. The designation is used for support people whose primary job is not in the squadron but at a support agency or a higher headquarters. Mission support only required 48 sorties per 6 months instead of 60.

MSM (Meritorious Service Medal). An award for outstanding meritorious achievement.

NATO (North Atlantic Treaty Organization). An alliance of countries from North America and Europe committed to fulfilling the goals of the North Atlantic Treaty signed on 4 April 1949. It was a counter to the Warsaw Pact.

Navigation check One of numerous proficiency check rides in pilot training that were graded and had a great impact in class ranking, hence aircraft assignment.

NCO Non-commissioned Officer). A military officer who has not been given a commission, non-commissioned officers (usually) obtain their position of authority by promotion through the enlisted ranks.

Night shift On a 3 rotating shift system, the shift that usually begins around midnight until the day shift takes over in the morning.

No flap An approach or landing without the use of flaps possibly due to aircraft control problems. They were required to be periodically practiced and used a significantly higher airspeed due to the decrease in lift.

Non-rated Positions in the Air Force that didn't require flying in an airplane.

NORDO (No Radio). A condition where a pilot has lost his receiver and/or transmitter. The situation is communicated to control agencies by squawking code 7600 on the transponder.

Nuclear strike A military conflict or political strategy in which nuclear weapons are used as contrasted by conventional warfare.

O-2 Skymaster A forward air control airplane it was a military version of the Cesna 337 and replaced the O-1 Bird Dog.

OAP (Offset Air Point). A point that would provide a radar return and used for identifying a target that didn't have a radar return.

Option approach When requested from tower the pilot has the option of landing, tough and go or low approach.

OR Operationally Ready). Used to mean the same thing as MR (mission ready).

Order of rank Enlisted rank is indicated by chevrons with a star. Beginning with airman basic with no chevrons it continues with airman, airman first class and senior airman. Above this are the NCOs, beginning with 4 chevrons as staff sergeant, then technical sergeant, master sergeant, senior master sergeant and finally chief master sergeant. Officer rank begins with 2nd lieutenant, 1st lieutenant, captain, major, lieutenant colonel, colonel and then on to the general officers, brigadier general, major general, lieutenant general and general . Pay grades consist simply of E-1 through E-8 and O-1 through 0-10.

ORI (Operational Readiness Inspection). The big inspection in the Air Force that can make or break a wing commander, it tests a wing's ability to wage war.

Orientation flight An incentive flight given to specially chosen younger non-rated officers and enlisted as recognition of outstanding performance.

OT (Officer Trainee). A designation and title of address that is given to people going through officers' training school.

OTS (Officer Training School). A facility for training young people to become 2nd lieutenants in the Air Force, it was located at Medina annex in San Antonio but now is at Maxwell AFB, Alabama.

OV-10 Bronco Made by North American Rockwell, it is an armored aircraft designed for light attack and forward air control. It allows FACs to 'shoot back'.

Overhead A type of traffic pattern where the pilot approaches at 300 knots and 1500 feet and 'over the numbers' rolls into 60 degrees of bank for a 180 degree level turn to downwind. After lowering gear and flaps he begins a 180 degree descending turn to the runway for landing.

Overshoot Completing a turn beyond the intended or desired point; in the traffic pattern it might result in 'going around' for another try and in a dog fight it might mean becoming the target.

Paddle off A 'paddle switch' located below the stick grip allowes the safety pilot in a droned aircraft to instantly take back control of the aircraft.

PAR (Precision Approach Radar). An approach where the pilot is guided to the runway for landing by a radar final controller.

Passed Over Not being selected for promotion by a promotion board.

Pave Spike Nickname given for the laser guided bomb program.

Pickle A verb meaning to push the pickle button on the control stick to release a bomb.

Pickle Button A red button switch on the upper left of the pilot's stick grip that is operated with his thumb.

Pinked A failed student ride (sortie). The grade sheet was outlined with a red marker to call attention to it in the student's grade folder.

Pitchout A rapid roll into 60 degrees of bank for a turn of 180 degrees.

Pitchout and rejoin A maneuver done to break up a flight for the purpose of practicing rejoins. After lead pitches, the wingman waits for 10 seconds before also pitching, Upon rollout he will be about 2 miles behind lead. Lead will then use an exaggerated wing rock followed by a 30 degree bank turn and the wingman will start a rejoin using cutoff and airspeed to do so.

PJ (Para-rescue Jumper). A highly trained enlisted aircrew member on a rescue helicopter.

PK (Probability of Kill). A way of assigning value to the lethality of a missile or other weapon.

PLF (Parachute Landing Fall). A method for safely absorbing energy with thighs and side when hitting the ground after parachuting. In training the method was practiced again and again by jumping off a platform into sand.

Point to point Before the age of satellite navigation pilots had to be able to mentally determine a heading from their present position off a TACAN to another point from that TACAN. 'Old heads' will remember two memory aids; Charlie brown plus 30 and brown Charlie plus 45.

Poncho shelter In a survival situation a shelter that could be made from two poncho halves.

Pop up delivery A tactical delivery that minimizes a pilot's exposure to enemy fire while delivering a bomb on target. It also results in aircrew fatalities when the MAP is violated.

Port call A date and time to be transported back home following an overseas assignment.

POW (Prisoner Of War). Military or civilians who are captured and held by an enemy.

POW camp A facility for holding POWs prisoner so they can't escape.

QF-100 A modified F-100D that had up-link and down-link radio channels allowing it to be controlled remotely.

QF-102 The predecessor drone to the QF-100. Used by the USAF at Tyndall for missile testing and at WSMR by the Army for patriot missile testing.

QF-106 The drone that followed the QF-100.

QF-4 The latest aircraft to be made into a drone, it followed in the footsteps of the QF-106.

Qualification Achieving minimum parameters for at least three times in a string of six attempts. Qualification in all weapons events was a requirement to becoming mission ready.

Queertrons A humorous way to describe to the aircraft maintenance folks that something inexplicably happened to an electronic system. 'The radar stopped working because of suspected queertrons' and this comment hopefully was accompanied with a smile to show you weren't serious about 'Queertrons'.

Quick check inspection Sometimes referred to as 'last chance' it is a quick inspection given to aircraft just before they take the runway for takeoff. Frequently found discrepancies are hydraulic or fuel leaks or cut tires that happened during taxi out.

Quick turn An abbreviated procedure that allows an aircraft to fly two or more sorties on the same day. Sometimes this required hot pit refueling which the aircrews detested.

Radar lock An automatic feature available in the F-4 radar that when chosen would automatically track a target and compute firing solutions for the AIM 7 missile. The WSO's response would be 'I'm locked'.

Radome A plexiglass dome covering the nose of the aircraft and the enclosed radar dish. The plexiglass is invisible to radar energy.

Ramstein AB Germany Headquarters for USAFE and home for a fighter wing it was an airbase located a few miles from Hahn AB.

Rated Refers to officer and enlisted positions that required flying in performance of assigned duties.

RBS (Radar Bomb Scoring). A system that had very precise radar that when locked on to a fighter could score a simulated bomb release. The aircraft provided a signal to the site for the bomb release.

RCO (Range Control Officer). A pilot who was assigned the job of controlling aircraft on a gunnery range, usually for a week at a time. His primary duty was for safe operation of the range.

Red Flag An advanced aerial combat training exercise hosted at Nellis AFB, Nevada. The purpose is to train pilots from the U.S. and other allied countries for real combat situations.

Refusal Speed The speed a plane can accelerate to and still be able to stop on the remaining runway if something goes wrong. Similar to 'abort speed'. After refusal speed aborting the takeoff isn't a good plan.

RHAW (Radar Homing And Warning). A device developed during Viet Nam to warn pilots whenever enemy radar was looking at them. It would provide an azimuth for the threat and a warning when a missile was launched.

Rip A computer printout of a person who was assigned to an organization by the AFMPC.

RLADD (Radar Low Altitude Drogue Delivery). A method of delivering a nuclear weapon from low altitude that will result in an air burst.

RLD (Radar Lay Down). A method of delivering a nuclear weapon that will result in a ground burst. The bomb's parachute insures a soft landing and adjustable timers are activated for detonation allowing safe escape for the airplane.

ROKAF (Republic Of Korea Air Force).

ROMAD (Radio Operator Maintenance And Driver). The specially trained NCO that was the right hand man of the ground FAC.

Romeo The drone controller who controlled the rudder (direction) during takeoff and landing at the droneway.

Round robin A navigation sortie where an airplane flies to several defined points in succession.

Route formation A very loose fingertip formation that is flown up to two ship widths out from the leader. Route formation is especially used when visual lookout is desired but a tactical formation is impractical.

RSU (Runway Supervisory Unit). See mobile control.

RTU (Replacement Training Unit). A training wing that specializes in training 'replacement pilots' for fighter aircraft.

RVR (Runway Visual Range). A visibility reading by an instrument situated at the approach end of the runway and is used when the weather is very poor.

Saber Dance Out of control wing rocking of an F-100 that was experiencing adverse yaw. See adverse yaw.

Saint Elmo's Fire An electrical weather phenomenon where luminous plasma is created on a grounded object in an atmospheric electric field (thunderstorm). See page 245.

SAM Brooks (School Of Aerospace Medicine) at Brooks AFB in San Antonio, Texas. All flight surgeons and flight nurses are trained at SAM Brooks and many aircrew members are sent there to resolve medical issues that might be jeopardizing their flying status.

SAM site (Surface to Air Missile) site that typically described a very recognizable pattern on the ground. In SEA the most common SAM was the SA-2 and the site was the 6 pointed Star of David.

Scramble The act of launching air defense aircraft on an unknown or hostile aircraft. They were required to be airborne in no more than 5 minutes – even when aircrews were sound sleep.

SEA (South East Asia). Referred specifically to the geographical area that was involved in the Vietnam war.

Sea Tac Seattle Tacoma airport located between Seattle and Tacoma. Go figure!

SEA Volunteer Fighter pilots usually volunteered for duty in SEA by entering a volunteer statement in their personnel records.

SEFE (Stan Eval Flight Examiner). A pilot who works in the Stan Eval office and among other things administer annual instrument and mission qualification flight evaluations to the wing's pilots.

Seoul Korea Capital of South Korea it is located a scant 30 miles from North Korea, within artillery range.

Shack A term meaning a direct hit on the target with a bomb.

Sheppard AFB, Texas Located near Wichita Falls, it was the primary refueling base when ferrying F-100s from Tyndall to Holloman AFB, New Mexico.

Shoot box An area that is free of boats thus allowing shooting at drones without endangering anyone on the water from falling debris.

SIE (Self Initiated Elimination). The most common reason for OT's to wash out in OTS, they just told their training officer they were quitting.

SIF/IFF (Selective Identification Feature/Identification Friend from Foe). See IFF.

Sight reticle A lighted sight that could be seen in the plexiglass combining glass when looking through the front windscreen. In the basic bombing mode the sight could be depressed a computed number of mills to provide a reference for when to pickle the bomb.

SMALL STEPS GLOSSARY

Simulated single engine Loosing an engine in the F-4 could be simulated by pulling the throttle of one engine to idle. Simulated single engine landings were a required proficiency but could be practiced only with an IP on board.

Sinus block When flying with a head cold a possible danger was a blocked sinus. The frontal sinuses were the most common to block and are located just above the eyes. A blocked sinus was very painful and frequently only relieved by using Afrin and the passage of time.

Sinuses Empty cavities within facial bones that if blocked can cause severe pain. The maxillary sinuses are above the teeth and the frontal sinuses are in the bone of the forehead.

Situational awareness Sometimes referred to simply as SA it refers to a pilot's ability to be aware of what is happening around him and to predict what can happen in the next few seconds. SA is probably the most often reason for pilots to 'pink' rides or wash out of RTU.

Slow flight Flying an aircraft just slightly above the stall speed taught flying skills during the most critical phases of flight, takeoff and landing.

SODO (Senior Operations Duty Officer). During non-duty hours the SODO, usually a lieutenant colonel, was the person who oversaw the operation of the TACC. He had a hotline to the commanding general and didn't hesitate to use it.

SOF (Supervisor Of Flying). A highly experienced pilot whose duty station is in the control tower, his job is to oversee the daily flying and coordinate and provide aid during in-flight emergencies.

Solo A flight by a student without his instructor pilot.

Sortie A single flight by one aircraft. Launching four aircraft to bomb a bridge would be four sorties.

SOS (Squadron Officer's School). A formal school at Maxwell AFB, Alabama tailored for junior officers. To attend the school in residence requires selection by a board. Anyone can take the course by correspondence.

Soviet Union Formally known as the Union of Soviet Socialistic Republics or USSR it was a collection of republics held under the iron fist rule of Russia. Warsaw Pact countries of Eastern Europe were puppets under the Soviet Union's control.

Spangdahlem Air Base, Germany A USAF air base located 30 miles from Hahn AB and next door to Bitburg AB. All three bases plus Ramstein had squadrons of f-4's.

Spin An out of control airplane that lacks forward motion will usually go into autorotation as it falls.

Splash A code word for an air to air kill.

Split S An aerobatic or BFM maneuver where the pilot rolls inverted and completes the last half of a loop; trading altitude for airspeed.

Squawk To activate your transponder.

Squawk flash When directed by ATC the pilot activates the 'ident' feature of his IFF which for a few seconds causes a double return on ATC's radar scope.

SRO (Senior Ranking Officer). In a POW situation, the highest ranking 'line' officer is the commander of the POWs regardless of what the enemy might want or dictate.

Stall At high angles of attack (high lift, nose high situations) the air flow over the top of the wing begins to separate from the wing's shape causing turbulence and reduced lift and greatly increased drag.

Standby Inspection A high stress Saturday morning inspection at OTS.

Stealth Technology that greatly reduces the radar return of an airplane (or ship).

Steep bank turn A turn usually using 60 degrees of bank which requies maintaining constant airspeed and altitude, it quickly discloses a slow instrument cross check.

Subscale drone AKA the baby drone, it is about a quarter the size of a full size fighter and is parachute recovered if not catastrophically damaged by a missile.

Supersonic flight Flying at speeds greater than mach 1. Speed of sound is mostly dependent on air temperature so going supersonic is easier at higher altitudes where the temperature is colder.

SUU 21 gun pod A pod containing a 6 barreled 20 mm Gatling gun and carried on the centerline of an F-4 C or F-4 D. When the E model was developed it included an internal gun.

T Syllabus A short F-4 course for pilots and WSO's who had previously flown the F-4.

T-33 Shooting Star A trainer version of the F-80 it was a two seat jet airplane that was the most widely used jet trainer in the world.

T-37 Tweet The primary jet trainer for decades, it had two side by side seats and was very forgiving to student pilots.

T-38 Talon A supersonic very sleek advanced jet trainer made by Northrup.

T-41 Mescalero A Cesna 172 used in UPT for a first exposure to flight and the first eliminator for students lacking 'the right stuff'.

TAC (Tactical Air Command). An Air Force major command responsible for training and preparedness for tactical forces. TAC has since been deactivated and its mission absorbed by Air Combat Command under a major Air Force reorganization.

TAC Check Tactical Check. A flight evaluation to determine if a pilot could perform his squadron's assigned mission. It was required to attain MR status.

SMALL STEPS GLOSSARY

TACAN (Tactical Air Navigation). An air navigation system using UHF provides azimuth (direction) and distance to the station.

TACAN Penetration and Approach A non-precision approach using published procedures for each particular runway will allow an aircraft to descend from 20,000 feet and make an approach to the vicinity of the runway. Weather ceiling minimums are frequently about 700 feet ceiling in lieu of 300 feet for a precision approach.

TACC (Tactical Air Control Center). The primary command structure for Air Force tactical warfare as it supports the Army, it interfaces with Navy and Army forces.

Tactical formation A formation designed to enhance a tactical advantage both offensively and defensively. Loose deuce, fluid four, two ship line abreast and Jo Bob Box are some of them.

Tally ho Code word for 'I see you/it'. Sometimes it is abbreviated to 'tally'. 'I have a tally on the target.

Tarmac Short for tar macadam, a tar and gravel surface. Any large paved area at an airport is now commonly referred to as the tarmac,

TDY (Temporary Duty). Anytime someone is assigned to travel away from his/her assigned duty station.

The trek A portion of basic survival training that involved several days of living and navigating in the woods.

Three hop An easy way of saying a flight to another destination will involve three sorties.

TLAR (That Looks About Right). A common reference to an unscientific method of determine when bomb dropping parameters are right, usually a result of a whole lot of experience in dropping bombs. It has now been replaced by smart bomb technology.

TOT (Time On/Over Target). A specified time for the first bomb to hit and is used for weapons deconfliction or timing accuracy determination.

Touch and Go Landing practice where after landing power is added to take off again for more landing practice. In TAC they could only be done with an IP on board.

Trail Departure Aircraft take 30 seconds spacing during takeoff which will result in three miles separation. Distances are maintained by use of aircraft radar.

Transponder A device required by all aircraft that provides a non-radar return to appear on ATC radar scopes. See IFF.

Travis AFB, California Operated by Air Mobility Command.

Trim Small opposite direction control surfaces that reduce stick control force by allowing airflow to keep the major control surface positioned.

True Airspeed (TAS) an aircraft's speed through the air after adjusting for air density. When adjusted for wind, ground speed is obtained. Most airliners fly at about 480 KTAS. With a 100 knot tailwind their ground speed would be 580 knots.

TSQ 61 van In a mobile FACP it was the radar control van that housed two control scopes.

Tweet Nickname for the T-37.

Two hop See three hop.

Tyndall AFB, Florida Located in Panama City it is home to the Air Force targets drone program.

UHF Ultra High Frequency. A radio frequency spectrum that is used primarily by the Air Force.

Unconventional A reference to nuclear weapons.

Unloaded Without any G on the aircraft. An aileron roll is done 'unloaded'.

Unusual attitude recovery A required maneuver on an instrument check it taught the proper sequence in recovering when the aircraft is doing something that wasn't intended perhaps through distraction within the cockpit or spatial disorientation.

Up slope fog A weather condition that occurs when the air temperature approaches the dew point. As saturated air moves up a slope it can cool causing fog to form from condensation.

UPT Undergraduate Pilot Training. A year long course that required flying three different aircraft with the end result being awarded the Air Force's silver wings.

USAFE United States Air Forces Europe. An Air Force major command it is responsible for all air activities in Europe and England.

USAREUR United States Army Europe. The Army's counterpart to USAFE.

Valsalva procedure A technique where you pinched your nose and then created pressure by trying to expel air through the nose. This was highly effective in clearing ear blocks but had almost no effect on sinus blocks.

Vertical S's Maneuvers performed on instruments that taught how to use an instrument cross check. There were four versions of increasing difficulty. See page 75.

VFR letdown Descending in visual conditions.

VHF (Very High Frequency). A radio frequency spectrum used almost exclusively by civil and private air traffic.

Victor Alert Nuclear alert that required aircraft to be airborne within 15 minutes. See page 187.

Visual A radio call meaning you have a friendly aircraft in sight as contrasted with 'tally'. A wingman saying to lead, 'I'm visual, tally' means I see both you and the bogey.

VOQ (Visiting Officer Quarters). Temporary billeting for people who are TDY.

VOR penetration A difficult instrument procedure using a VOR beacon that required overflying the beacon and descending going outbound and timing for the turn back inbound. TACAN has largely replaced this procedure.

VORTAC A co-located VOR and TACAN giving navigation guidance to both VOR and TACAN equipped aircraft.

Warsaw Pact A coalition of Eastern European countries heavily dominated by the USSR that faced off with NATO.

Washing out A term used in referring to a student who was eliminated from a training program for whatever reason.

Water survival Located at Homestead AFB, Florida it was a requirement for all aircrew members.

Weapons Controller Also known as a Weapons Director they were officers who controlled aircraft using a radar scope. Students who washed out of UPT frequently found themselves in this career field.

WEG (Weapons Evaluation Group). The headquarters at Tyndall AFB that was responsible for the drone program and the WSEP program.

Wiesbaden Air Base The point of entry for most service personnel entering Germany, it was located near Frankfurt.

Wifferdill A slow, lazy type low G maneuver that began by raising the nose 30 degrees or more and then rolling into a lot of bank and turning back the way you came from. The purpose was to clear for other aircraft (and it was fun).

Wing Commander Usually, he was the highest ranking officer at a base and had two or three squadrons under his command. The base commander, maintenance commander and resource manager also reported to him.

WSEP Weapons System Evaluation Program. See page 269.

WSMR White Sands Missile Range. The site for 'Trinity', the first nuclear test, it was also the location for most of the Army's missile testing.

WSO Weapons Systems Officer. The F-4 back seater or GIB and perhaps the bravest person in the world, he worked the radar and other weapons systems and totally relied on his front seater to not blow it. See page 171.

Zulu Alert Air to air alert, they were required to be airborne in no more than 5 minutes when scrambled. See page 183.

Retirement Photo

Major Olson says good bye to the Air Force